Water Resources Practice Problems

First Edition

Timothy J. Nelson, PE

Water Resources Practice Problems
Timothy J. Nelson

To report errors in this text, contact: tim@engineeringvideos.net

13-Digit ISBN: 9780615755632
10-Digit ISBN: 0615755631

EngineeringVideos.Net
Copyright © 2013

Table of Contents

Introduction

Water Resources Practice Problems provides 111 multiple-choice water resource engineering problems to assist civil engineers in preparation for their professional licensing examination. This book is ideal for those who are already familiar with the subject of water resources engineering and could benefit from more example problems.

Content

This book covers the fundamental topics of water resources engineering, including Open Channel Flow, Pressure Flow, and Hydrology (see Table of Contents for full list). The problems found in this text are similar in content and scope as the water resources problems found on the NCEES Civil Engineering Professional Licensing Examination.

Each problem is a separate and complete problem; the solution to one problem does not depend on the solution to a different problem. Problems can be solved in any order. All problems are quantitative, there are no 'word problems'.

There may be more than one method to determine the correct answer. The method used to solve each problem in this text is not necessarily the only way to determine the solution.

How this Book is Organized

This book is divided into three sections: Problems, Detailed Solutions and Quick Solutions. Page numbers are assigned to each section and subsection in the Table of Contents.

Problems: The Problems Section lists all 111 problems, three problems on every page. All problems are multiple choice. The problems are ordered by topic.

Detailed Solutions: The Detailed Solutions Section includes a restatement of the problem, followed by an analysis showing one way to determine the correct answer.

Quick Solutions: The Quick Solutions Section only includes the letter corresponding to the correct answer (A, B, C or D).

Problem Layout

Each problem is divided into 4 parts: Find, Given, Analysis, and Answer.

Find: The parameter to be determined / calculated is identified and labeled.

Given: The variables are identified and labeled; usually a figure is provided. Four possible answers are given.

Analysis: The problem is solved. Equations, figures and tables are positioned on the left side of the page, while notes and commentary are positioned on the right side of the page. The analysis concludes by identifying the value of the parameter to be determined/calculated.

Answer: The letter (A, B, C or D) corresponding to the correct answer is indicated in a box.

Additional Notes

Equations, inequalities and approximations are labeled and numbered using the notation shown below. Relationships involving 'at least' (≥) and 'at most' (≤) are considered inequalities. Not all equations are labeled.

$$equation = eq.\#$$
$$inequality = ieq.\#$$
$$approximation = approx.\#$$

Unless otherwise stated, the fluid in the problem is water, at standard temperature and pressure. Water is assumed to be incompressible.

Figures are not necessarily drawn to scale.

For Open Channel Flow problems:
• Unless otherwise stated, assume all flow is normal flow (not accelerating flow or decelerating flow).
• The normal depth of flow is simply referred to as the 'depth', and specific energy is simply referred to as 'energy.'

For Pressure Flow problems:
• Where pipes are drawn horizontally and no elevation change is mentioned, assume there is no elevation change in the pipe.
• Unless otherwise stated, assume pipe properties remain constant along the entire length of the pipe.
• If a pipe diameter is provided, assume the diameter is the interior diameter of the pipe, unless the problem specifically states it is the 'outside diameter' or the 'nominal diameter.'

Water Resources Practice Problems

For <u>Pump</u> problems:
- Lower case 'p' represents pressure, and upper case 'P' represents power.
- If pump efficiency is not provided, then assume 100% efficiency.
- Unless otherwise stated, assume all pumps are single stage.

For <u>Hydrology</u> problems:
- The rational formula for solving peak runoff from a watershed, $Q_p = C * i * A$, approximates the units of acre-inch per hour equals cubic feet per second, even though these units differ by a factor of 1.0083.

For <u>Groundwater</u> problems:
- Unless otherwise stated, assume pumping has been in operation for a long time and that equilibrium/steady-state conditions exist.
- Unless otherwise stated, assume the hydraulic conductivity of the soil is equal in all directions.

Section 1: Questions

(page intentionally left blank)

Open Channel Flow #1

Find: R ←the hydraulic radius

Given:

d=14[ft] ←the total depth of the water

r=8[ft] ←the radius of the semicircle

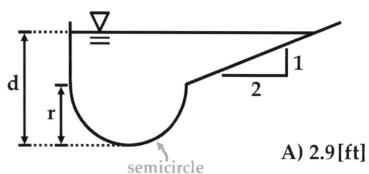

semicircle

A) 2.9[ft]
B) 3.7[ft]
C) 4.5[ft]
D) 5.2[ft]

Open Channel Flow #2

Find: R ←the hydraulic radius

Given:

D=8.00[in] ←pipe diameter

d=5.87[in] ←water depth

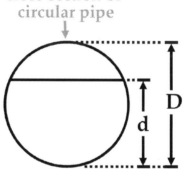

cross section of circular pipe

Section A-A′

circular pipe

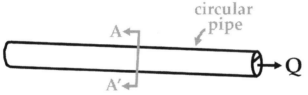

A) 1.2[in]
B) 1.6[in]
C) 2.0[in]
D) 2.4[in]

Open Channel Flow #3

Find: d ←the depth of flow in order to maximize the hydraulic radius

Given:

cross section A-A′ of circular pipe

D=1.00[m] ←pipe diameter

maximum R ←the hydraulic radius is maximized

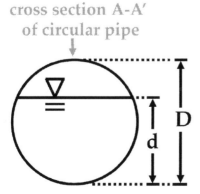

circular pipe

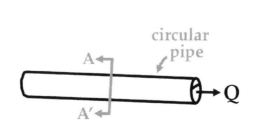

A) 0.811[m]
B) 0.823[m]
C) 0.835[m]
D) 0.847[m]

Water Resources Practice Problems

Open Channel Flow #4

Find: n_2 ← roughness coefficient 2

Given:

$n_1 = 0.0293$ ← roughness coefficient 1

$n_c = 0.0318$ ← composite roughness coefficient

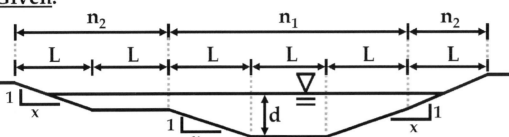

L=15 [ft] ← constant length across the channel

$x = 2$ ← side slope

$d = 11.4$ [ft] ← water depth

A) 0.0277

B) 0.0334

C) 0.0354

D) 0.0383

Open Channel Flow #5

Find: S ← the channel slope

Given:

$d = 5$ [ft] ← water depth

$b = 8$ [ft] ← base width

$Q = 2,312$ [ft³/s] ← flow rate

$n = 0.013$ ← roughness coefficient

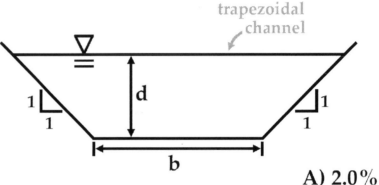

trapezoidal channel

the channel side slopes are 1:1

A) 2.0%

B) 2.3%

C) 2.6%

D) 2.9%

Open Channel Flow #6

Find: d ← the normal depth of flow

Given:

$n = 0.015$ ← roughness coefficient

$v = 3.92$ [ft/s] ← velocity of water in the channel

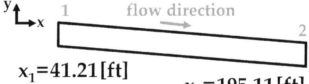

flow direction

$x_1 = 41.21$ [ft]

$y_1 = 88.02$ [ft]

$x_2 = 195.11$ [ft]

$y_2 = 87.84$ [ft]

side view of the channel

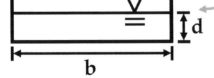

cross-section of the channel

$b = 6.5$ [ft] ← the base width of the channel

A) 0.5 [ft]

B) 1.0 [ft]

C) 1.5 [ft]

D) 2.0 [ft]

Open Channel Flow #7

Find: h_f ← the headloss in the channel

Given:

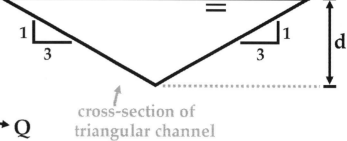

cross-section of triangular channel

L=350 [m] ← channel length

Q=120.4 [m³/s] ← flow rate

n=0.015 ← roughness coefficient

d=2.31 [m]

water depth

A) 0.6 [m]
B) 1.8 [m]
C) 3.9 [m]
D) 7.4 [m]

Open Channel Flow #8

Find: d_c ← critical depth

Given:

Q=10 [m³/s] ← flow rate

r=0.85 [m] ← radius of the channel bottom

d_c

r

semi-circular channel bottom

A) 1.28 [m]
B) 1.70 [m]
C) 2.40 [m]
D) 3.40 [m]

Open Channel Flow #9

Find: b ← the base width of the rectangular channel

Given:

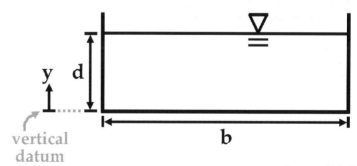

d=2.5 [ft] ← normal depth

y   d

vertical datum

b

Q=80 [ft³/s] ← flow rate

E=3.026 [ft] ← total energy of the channel flow (expressed as total head)

A) 4.5 [ft]
B) 5.5 [ft]
C) 6.5 [ft]
D) 7.5 [ft]

Water Resources Practice Problems

Open Channel Flow #10

<u>Find:</u> n ← the roughness coefficient

<u>Given:</u>

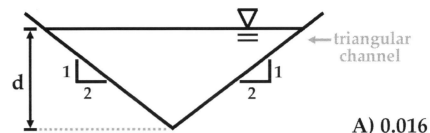

← triangular channel

$F_r = 0.903$

↑ Froude number

$d = 1.45\,[m]$ ← water depth

$S = 0.005$ ← channel slope

A) 0.016
B) 0.018
C) 0.020
D) 0.022

Open Channel Flow #11

<u>Find:</u> ΔE ← the change in energy across the hydraulic jump

<u>Given:</u>

$Q = 150\,[ft^3/s]$ ← flow rate

$b = 6\,[ft]$ ← channel width

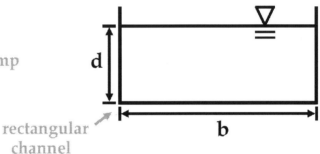

rectangular channel

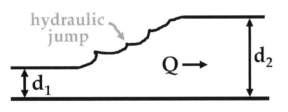

hydraulic jump

$d_1 = 1.1\,[ft]$

↑ water depth before the hydraulic jump

A) -1.84 [ft]
B) -3.37 [ft]
C) -5.75 [ft]
D) -9.12 [ft]

Open Channel Flow #12

<u>Find:</u> d_2 ← the water depth at section 2

<u>Given:</u> $b = 1.7\,[m]$ ← channel width

total energy is conserved between section 1 and section 2 in the channel

$d_1 = 1.21\,[m]$ ← water depth at section 1

$Q = 1.55\,[m^3/s]$ ← flow rate

$w_p = 0.4\,[m]$

↑ pier width

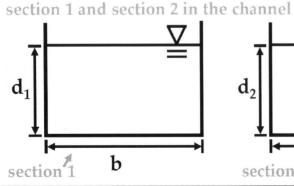

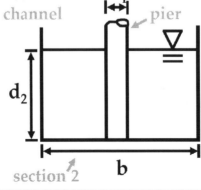

A) 1.15 [m]
B) 1.19 [m]
C) 1.23 [m]
D) 1.26 [m]

Open Channel Flow #13

Find: Flow Type
Given:

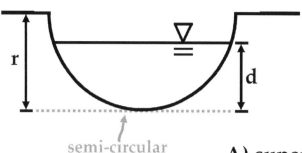

r=0.79 [m] ← channel radius

d=0.56 [m] ← depth of flow

S=1.00% ← channel slope

n=0.013 ← roughness coefficient

semi-circular channel

A) supercritical
B) subcritical
C) critical
D) not enough information

Open Channel Flow #14

Find: d_c ← the critical depth
Given:

$Q_c = 2.367 \times 10^{-4}$ [m³/s]
the critical flow rate

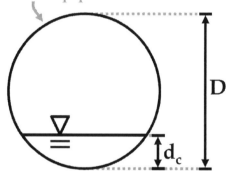

circular pipe

$v_c = 0.3163$ [m/s]
the critical velocity

D=0.078 [m]
the diameter of the pipe

A) 13 [mm]
B) 20 [mm]
C) 26 [mm]
D) 38 [mm]

Open Channel Flow #15

Find: E_{min} ← the minimum energy of the channel flow
Given:

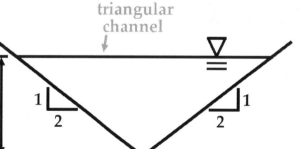

triangular channel

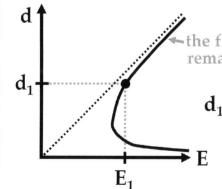

the flow rate remains constant

$d_1 = 10$ [in] ← depth at point 1

$E_1 = 10.3321$ [in]
energy at point 1

A) 6.68 [in]
B) 7.52 [in]
C) 8.35 [in]
D) 9.19 [in]

Water Resources Practice Problems

Open Channel Flow #16

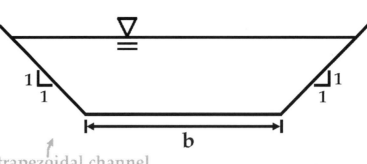

Find: Q ← the flow rate

Given:

$F_r = 1.00$ ← the Froude number

$b = 12 \,[\text{ft}]$ ← base width

trapezoidal channel
with 1:1 side slope

$A = 55.7 \,[\text{ft}^2]$ ← the cross-sectional area
of the water in the channel

A) 380 [ft³/s]

B) 425 [ft³/s]

C) 540 [ft³/s]

D) 625 [ft³/s]

Open Channel Flow #17

Find: $L_{1,2}$ ← the length between
sections 1 and 2

Given: $Q = 93.4 \,[\text{ft}^3/\text{s}]$ ← flow rate

$d_1 = 2.8 \,[\text{ft}]$ ← water depth at section 1

$d_2 = 3.0 \,[\text{ft}]$ ← water depth at section 2

cross-section of
triangular channel

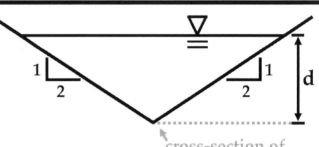

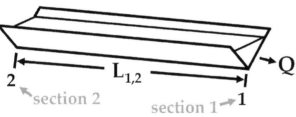

section 2

$L_{1,2}$

section 1

$n = 0.013$

roughness coefficient

$S_o = 0.002$

channel bottom slope

A) 200 [ft]

B) 300 [ft]

C) 400 [ft]

D) 500 [ft]

Open Channel Flow #18

Find: d_2 ← the depth downstream
of the hydraulic jump

Given:

$Q = 28.4 \,[\text{m}^3/\text{s}]$ ← flow rate

$b = 2.1 \,[\text{m}]$ ← channel width

$d_1 = 1.13 \,[\text{m}]$

water depth before
the hydraulic jump

trapezoidal
channel

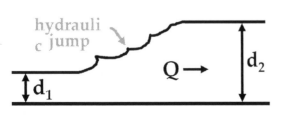

hydraulic jump

$\Delta E = 2.49 \,[\text{m}]$

energy loss
across the jump

A) 3.31 [m]

B) 4.43 [m]

C) 5.85 [m]

D) 6.67 [m]

Open Channel Flow #19

<u>Find:</u> Q ← the flow rate

<u>Given:</u> N=2 ← number of contractions

b=1.50[m] ← actual width of the weir

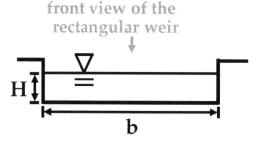

front view of the rectangular weir

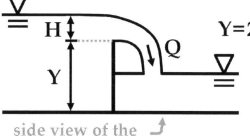

Y=2.81[m] ← height of the weir invert

H=0.15[m]

height of the water above the weir invert

side view of the rectangular weir

A) 0.04[m³/s]

B) 0.15[m³/s]

C) 0.34[m³/s]

D) 0.83[m³/s]

Open Channel Flow #20

<u>Find:</u> N ← number of contractions

<u>Given:</u>

b=3.10[ft] ← actual width of the weir

H=0.77[ft]

height of the water above the weir invert

Q=6.9197[ft³/s] ← flow rate across the weir

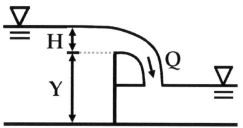

Y=6.50[ft]

height of the weir invert

side view of the rectangular weir

A) 0

B) 1

C) 2

D) not enough information

Open Channel Flow #21

<u>Find:</u> H_{DS} ← the height of the water surface above the weir invert, downstream of the weir

<u>Given:</u>

b=250[mm] ← actual width of the weir

N=1 ← number of contractions

C=0.61 ← weir coefficient

Q_{sub}=0.0192[m³/s] ← submerged flow rate

Q_{free}=0.0227[m³/s] ← "free flow" flow rate

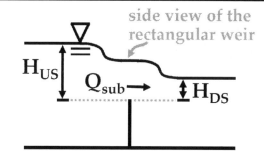

side view of the rectangular weir

front view of the rectangular weir

A) 49[mm]

B) 71[mm]

C) 142[mm]

D) 314[mm]

Water Resources Practice Problems

Pressure Flow #1

<u>Find:</u> h_f ← the headloss through the pipe

<u>Given:</u>

D=100[mm] ← pipe diameter

smooth pipe

T=20°C ← water temperature

v=1.6[m/s] ← fluid velocity

L=40[m]

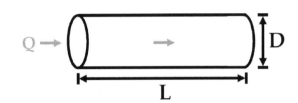

pipe length

pipe is flowing
full of water

A) 0.51[m]
B) 0.85[m]
C) 1.72[m]
D) 2.87[m]

Pressure Flow #2

<u>Find:</u> h_f ← the headloss through the pipe

<u>Given:</u>

d_n=6[in] ← nominal pipe diameter

$D_0 \, \cancel{} D \, \& \, D_e$

Q=1.2[ft³/s] ← flow rate

schedule 40
steel pipe

pipe is flowing
full of water

L=600[ft] ← pipe length

T=45°F

↑
water
temperature

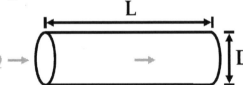

A) 2.0[ft]
B) 3.6[ft]
C) 5.7[ft]
D) 11.9[ft]

Pressure Flow #3

<u>Find:</u> T ← the water temperature

<u>Given:</u>

D=1.0[ft] ← pipe diameter

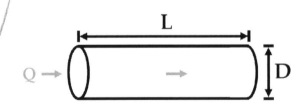

Q=2000[gal/min] ← flow rate

steel pipe

L=600[ft] ← pipe length

f=0.017 ← friction factor

pipe is flowing
full of water

Re=466,400 ← Reynolds Number

A) 40°F
B) 50°F
C) 60°F
D) 70°F

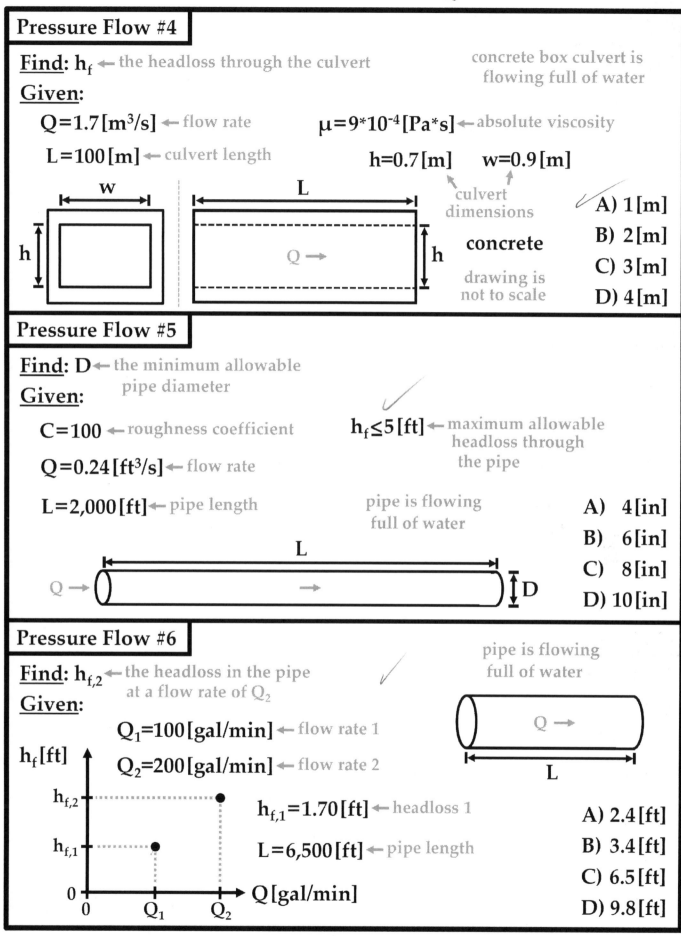

Pressure Flow #4

Find: h_f ← the headloss through the culvert

concrete box culvert is flowing full of water

Given:

$Q=1.7[m^3/s]$ ← flow rate

$\mu=9*10^{-4}[Pa*s]$ ← absolute viscosity

$L=100[m]$ ← culvert length

$h=0.7[m]$ $w=0.9[m]$

culvert dimensions

concrete

drawing is not to scale

w

L

h

Q →

h

A) 1[m]

B) 2[m]

C) 3[m]

D) 4[m]

Pressure Flow #5

Find: D ← the minimum allowable pipe diameter

Given:

$C=100$ ← roughness coefficient

$Q=0.24[ft^3/s]$ ← flow rate

$L=2,000[ft]$ ← pipe length

$h_f\leq5[ft]$ ← maximum allowable headloss through the pipe

pipe is flowing full of water

L

Q →

→

D

A) 4[in]

B) 6[in]

C) 8[in]

D) 10[in]

Pressure Flow #6

Find: $h_{f,2}$ ← the headloss in the pipe at a flow rate of Q_2

Given:

$Q_1=100[gal/min]$ ← flow rate 1

$Q_2=200[gal/min]$ ← flow rate 2

$h_{f,1}=1.70[ft]$ ← headloss 1

$L=6,500[ft]$ ← pipe length

pipe is flowing full of water

Q →

L

$h_f[ft]$

$h_{f,2}$

$h_{f,1}$

0

0   Q_1 Q_2

Q[gal/min]

A) 2.4[ft]

B) 3.4[ft]

C) 6.5[ft]

D) 9.8[ft]

Water Resources Practice Problems

Pressure Flow #7

<u>Find</u>: **C** ← the roughness coefficient

<u>Given</u>: use the equivalent length method

$D = 4\,[\text{in}]$ ← pipe diameter

$h_f = 1.66\,[\text{ft}]$ ← total headloss

$Q = 100\,[\text{gal/min}]$ ← flow rate

$L_1 + L_2 + L_3 + L_4 = 48\,[\text{ft}]$ ← total length of piping

Schedule 40
Steel Screw Fittings

regular 90° elbow ← plan view

swing check valve

A) 90

B) 100

C) 110

D) 120

Pressure Flow #8

<u>Find</u>: **D** ← the diameter of the pipe and fittings

<u>Given</u>:

$Q = 0.14\,[\text{ft}^3/\text{s}]$ ← flow rate

$f = 0.014$ ← friction factor

$h_{L,m} = 0.5584\,[\text{in}]$ ← minor headloss

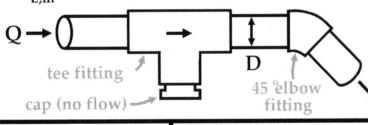

tee fitting

cap (no flow)

45° elbow fitting

D	$L_{e,tee}$	$L_{e,45°elbow}$
1 [in]	3.2 [ft]	1.3 [ft]
2 [in]	7.7 [ft]	2.7 [ft]
3 [in]	11.9 [ft]	4.1 [ft]
4 [in]	17.0 [ft]	5.5 [ft]

table showing equivalent lengths for both fittings

A) 1 [in]

B) 2 [in]

C) 3 [in]

D) 4 [in]

Pressure Flow #9

<u>Find</u>: K_M ← the minor headloss coefficient of the meter

<u>Given</u>:

$Q = 313\,[\text{gal/min}]$ ← the flow rate

$D = 4\,[\text{in}]$ ← the diameter of the pipe and meter

$h_{L,meter} = 4.31\,[\text{lb}_m/\text{in}^2]$

the minor headloss caused by the meter

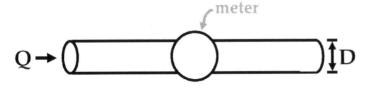

meter

A) 4.3 [ft]

B) 6.2 [ft]

C) 8.1 [ft]

D) 10.0 [ft]

Pressure Flow #10

Find: D_2 ← the diameter of the smaller pipe

Given:

$Q = 0.041\,[m^3/s]$ ← the flow rate

$D_1 = 315\,[mm]$ ← the diameter of the larger pipe

$h_{L,m} = 0.252\,[m]$ ← the minor headloss

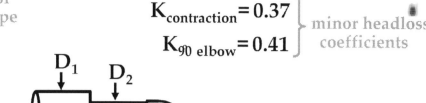

$K_{contraction} = 0.37$ ⎫ minor headloss
$K_{90\ elbow} = 0.41$ ⎭ coefficients

sudden contraction

90° elbow

A) 110 [mm]
B) 140 [mm]
C) 160 [mm]
D) 190 [mm]

Pressure Flow #11

Find: n ← the number of pipes

Given:

$L = 20,000\,[ft]$ ← pipe length

$D = 1.5\,[ft]$ ← pipe diameter

$A = 1.767\,[ft^2]$ ← flow area

$Q_T = 12\,[ft^3/s]$ ← total flow rate (through all n pipes)

$C = 100$ ← roughness coefficient

$h_{f,max} = 25\,[ft]$ ← max allowable headloss

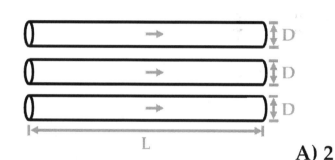

minimize the number of pipes without exceeding the maximum allowable headloss

A) 2
B) 3
C) 4
D) 5

Pressure Flow #12

Find: Q_2 ← the flow rate at time 2

Given:

$D_1 = 4\,[in]$ ← pipe diameter at time 1

$D_2 = 3\,[in]$ ← pipe diameter at time 2

the pipe diameter decreases over time

$L = 6,000\,[ft]$ ← length

$\nu = 1*10^{-6}\,[m^2/s]$ ← kinematic viscosity

$Q_1 = 0.20\,[ft^3/s]$ ← flow rate at time 1

water flows from tank 1 to tank 2

tank 1

smooth pipe

Q →

tank 2

$h_{f,1} = h_{f,2}$ ← headloss and
$f_1 = f_2$ ← friction factor remain constant

A) 0.100 [ft³/s]
B) 0.125 [ft³/s]
C) 0.133 [ft³/s]
D) 0.150 [ft³/s]

Water Resources Practice Problems

Pressure Flow #13

Find: L ← the pipe length

Given:

D=6[in] ← the pipe diameter

C=110 ← the roughness coefficient

$Elev_A$=45.5[ft] ← the water surface elevation at the tank

$Elev_B$=38.6[ft] ← the elevation at the end of the pipe

Q=0.358[ft³/s]
the flow rate through the pipe

neglect minor losses

A) 1,000[ft]
B) 2,000[ft]
C) 3,000[ft]
D) 4,000[ft]

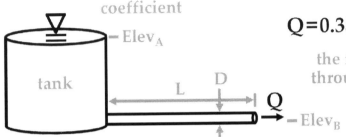

Pressure Flow #14

Find: $Elev_C$ ← the water surface elevation at point C

Given:

D_B=D_C=250[mm] ← diameter at B and C

D_A=450[mm] ← diameter at A

$P_{g,C}$=0[Pa] ← gauge pressure at points B and C

$P_{g,B}$=1.962*10⁵[Pa]

v_A=1.00[m/s] ← velocity at point A

$Elev_A$=$Elev_B$=44.5[m] ← invert elevation at points A and B

constant water surface elevation at top of pipe, as water barely spills over

assume headloss is negligible

pressure gauge

A) 59[m]
B) 60[m]
C) 61[m]
D) 65[m]

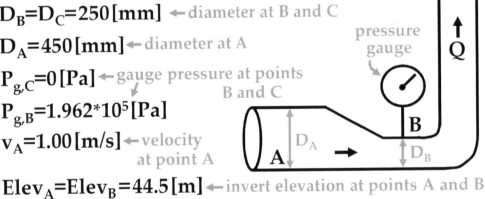

Pressure Flow #15

Find: $h_{f,AB}$ ← the headloss between points A and B

Given:

$P_{g,A}$=3.096*10⁵[Pa]

$P_{g,B}$=3.057*10⁵[Pa]
the gauge pressure at points A and B

Δv_{AB}=0[m/s]

Δz_{AB}=0[m]

constant velocity and elevation at points A and B

pressure gauges

A) 0.1[m]
B) 0.2[m]
C) 0.3[m]
D) 0.4[m]

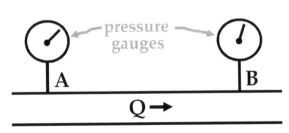

Network Flows #1

Find: Q ← the flow rate

Given:

$L_1 = 350\,[ft]$
$L_2 = 550\,[ft]$ ← pipe lengths

$Elev_1 = 247.8\,[ft]$
$Elev_2 = 181.9\,[ft]$ ← water surface elevations

$D_1 = 4\,[in]$
$D_2 = 12\,[in]$ ← pipe diameters

$f_1 = 0.016$
$f_2 = 0.020$ ← friction factors

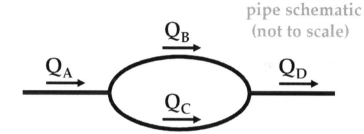

water flows from tank 1 to tank 2

Elev 1 — tank 1 — pipe 1 — Elev 2 — tank 2 — Q — pipe 2

A) $0.08\,[ft^3/s]$

B) $0.22\,[ft^3/s]$

C) $0.64\,[ft^3/s]$

D) $1.38\,[ft^3/s]$

Network Flows #2

Find: Q_c ← the flow rate through pipe C

Given:

$Q_A = 20\,[ft^3/s]$ ← the flow rate through pipe A

$L_B = 1,200\,[ft]$
$L_C = 2,000\,[ft]$ ← pipe lengths

$C_B = 100$
$C_C = 105$ ← roughness coefficient

$D_B = 1.5\,[ft]$
$D_C = 2.5\,[ft]$ ← pipe diameters

pipe schematic (not to scale)

Q_B — Q_A — Q_D — Q_C

ignore minor losses

A) $5\,[ft^3/s]$

B) $8\,[ft^3/s]$

C) $12\,[ft^3/s]$

D) $15\,[ft^3/s]$

Network Flows #3

Find: Q_F ← the flow rate through pipe F

Given:

$Q_A = 800\,[L/s]$
$Q_C = 1,200\,[L/s]$
$Q_H = 1,000\,[L/s]$ ← flow rates
$Q_K = 1,400\,[L/s]$
$Q_L = 1,800\,[L/s]$

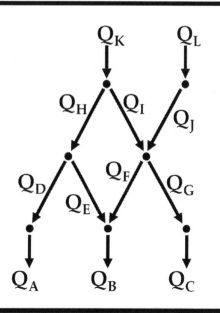

Q_K Q_L — Q_H Q_I Q_J — Q_D Q_F Q_G — Q_E — Q_A Q_B Q_C

A) $400\,[L/s]$

B) $600\,[L/s]$

C) $800\,[L/s]$

D) $1,000\,[L/s]$

Water Resources Practice Problems

Network Flows #4

Find: C_A ← the roughness coefficient through pipe A

Given:

pipes A, B and C are connected in series

$Q \rightarrow$ pipe A   pipe B   pipe C

$Q=2,000\,[\text{gal/min}]$ ← flow rate

$h_f=10.5\,[\text{ft}]$

$\left.\begin{array}{l} C_B=100 \\ C_C=105 \end{array}\right\}$ ← the roughness coefficient through pipes B and C

headloss through pipes A, B and C

$\left.\begin{array}{l} L_A=500\,[\text{ft}] \\ L_B=500\,[\text{ft}] \\ L_C=800\,[\text{ft}] \end{array}\right\}$ ← pipe lengths

$\left.\begin{array}{l} D_A=12\,[\text{in}] \\ D_B=18\,[\text{in}] \\ D_C=24\,[\text{in}] \end{array}\right\}$ ← pipe diameters

A) 90
B) 95
C) 100
D) 105

Network Flows #5

Find: Q_C ← the flow rate through pipe C

Given:

$D_A=6\,[\text{in}]$

$D_D=12\,[\text{in}]$ ← pipe diameters

$D_B, D_C, D_E=8\,[\text{in}]$

$L=250\,[\text{ft}]$ ← the length of each pipe

$f=0.018$ ← the friction factor of each pipe

$Q=1,600\,[\text{gal/min}]$ ← the flow rate through the pipe network

A) $0.88\,[\text{ft}^3/\text{s}]$
B) $0.94\,[\text{ft}^3/\text{s}]$
C) $1.02\,[\text{ft}^3/\text{s}]$
D) $1.10\,[\text{ft}^3/\text{s}]$

Network Flows #6

$Q_{A,in} \rightarrow$ A   B $\rightarrow Q_{B,out}$

C   D $\rightarrow Q_{D,out}$

Find: Q_{AB} ← the flow rate through pipe AB

Given:

$\left.\begin{array}{l} C_{AB}=C_{AC}=90 \\ C_{DB}=C_{CD}=110 \end{array}\right\}$ ← roughness coefficient

$L=200\,[\text{ft}]$ ← length of each pipe

$D_{AB}=4\,[\text{in}]$ ← pipe

$D_{CD}=8\,[\text{in}]$ ← diameter

$D_{DB}=D_{AC}=6\,[\text{in}]$

$Q_{A,in}=500\,[\text{gal/min}]$

$Q_{B,out}=200\,[\text{gal/min}]$

$Q_{D,out}=300\,[\text{gal/min}]$

A) $124\,[\text{gal/min}]$
B) $137\,[\text{gal/min}]$
C) $150\,[\text{gal/min}]$
D) $163\,[\text{gal/min}]$

Network Flows #7

Find: $h_{T,J}$ ← total head at junction

Given:
WSEL$_A$=200[ft]
WSEL$_B$=180[ft] water surface elevations
WSEL$_C$=140[ft]

Pipe	L	f	D
AJ	400[ft]	0.015	6[in]
BJ	400[ft]	0.015	6[in]
CJ	800[ft]	0.020	12[in]

the length, friction factor and diameter of each pipe

A) 152[ft]
B) 156[ft]
C) 160[ft]
D) 164[ft]

Network Flows #8

$h_f = 0.0827 \frac{fL}{D^5} Q^2$

Find: D_{AJ} ← the diameter of pipe AJ

Given: L=500[m] ← length of all pipes

$h_{T,J}$=62[m] ← total head at the junction

WSEL$_A$=88[m]
WSEL$_B$=38[m] water surface elevations
WSEL$_C$=18[m]

D_{BJ}=180[mm]
D_{CJ}=180[mm] the diameter of pipes BJ and CJ

f=0.018 ← the friction factor of all pipes

A) 200[mm]
B) 250[mm]
C) 300[mm]
D) 350[mm]

Network Flows #9

Find: WSEL$_C$ ← the water surface elevation of reservoir C

Given:

Q_{AJ}=414[gal/min] ← the flow rate through pipe AJ

C=100 ← all roughness coefficient

L=120[ft] ← all pipe length

D_{AJ}=4[in]
D_{BJ}=12[in] pipe diameters
D_{CJ}=8[in]

WSEL$_A$=150[ft]
WSEL$_B$=135[ft] water surface elevations

A) 81[ft]
B) 94[ft]
C) 98[ft]
D) 102[ft]

Water Resources Practice Problems

Pumps #1

Find: h_T ← the total head lift provided by the pump

Given:

$Q = 6.613 \, [\text{ft}^3/\text{s}]$ ← flow rate

$p_s = 42.1 \, [\text{lb}_f/\text{in}^2]$ ← suction pressure

$p_d = 118.4 \, [\text{lb}_f/\text{in}^2]$ ← discharge pressure

$d_s = 12 \, [\text{in}]$ ← diameter of the suction pipe

$d_d = 6 \, [\text{in}]$ ← diameter of the discharge pipe

A) 16 [ft]

B) 92 [ft]

C) 176 [ft]

D) 193 [ft]

Pumps #2

Find: Q ← the flow rate

Given:

$p_s = 100 \, [\text{kPa}]$ ← suction pressure

$p_d = 250 \, [\text{kPa}]$ ← discharge pressure

$d_s = 300 \, [\text{mm}]$
diameter of the suction pipe

$d_d = 165 \, [\text{mm}]$
diameter of the discharge pipe

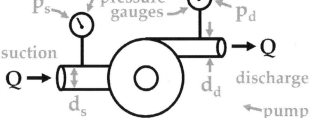

$h_T = 18.20 \, [\text{m}]$
the total head lift provided by the pump

A) 0.100 [m³/s]

B) 0.135 [m³/s]

C) 0.170 [m³/s]

D) 0.250 [m³/s]

Pumps #3

Find: Q ← flow rate

Given:

SG = 1.00 ← specific gravity

P = 25.0 [hp] ← motor power

$\text{Elev}_A = 145.8 \, [\text{ft}]$ ← water surface elevation in reservoirs A and B

$\text{Elev}_B = 260.1 \, [\text{ft}]$

$\text{Elev}_P = 85.4 \, [\text{ft}]$
pump elevation

$\eta_P = 0.75$
pump efficiency

neglect headloss in the pipe

A) 650 [gal/min]

B) 720 [gal/min]

C) 780 [gal/min]

D) 865 [gal/min]

Pumps #4

<u>Find</u>: d ← the pipe diameter

<u>Given</u>: (all pipe has the same diameter)

Q=1,253 [gal/min] ← flow rate

C=100 ← roughness coefficient

L=500 [ft] ← total length of pipe

P=50 [hp] ← motor power

$Elev_A$=52.11 [ft] ← water surface elevation in reservoirs A and B

$Elev_B$=145.97 [ft]

η_p=0.737 ← pump efficiency

water

neglect minor headloss

A) 6 [in]
B) 8 [in]
C) 12 [in]
D) 18 [in]

Pumps #5

<u>Find</u>: t ← the total time the pump can run

<u>Given</u>:

Q=0.0147 [m³/s] ← flow rate

Δh=45 [m] ← elevation change

η_m=0.80 ← motor efficiency

η_p=0.65 ← pump efficiency

c=$0.12/[kW*hr] ← unit cost of electricity

C=$3.00 ← total funds to be spent on pumping

neglect headloss in the pipe

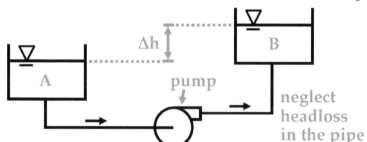

A) 1 [hr]
B) 2 [hr]
C) 3 [hr]
D) 4 [hr]

Pumps #6

<u>Find</u>: Δz_{PB} ← the vertical rise between the pump and the water surface in reservoir B

<u>Given</u>:

$h_{T,s}$=130 [ft] ← total suction head

SG=0.9 ← specific gravity

L=100 [ft] ← pipe length

f=0.018 ← friction factor

η_p=0.70 ← pump efficiency

Q=8.54 [ft³/s] ← flow rate

P=50 [hp] ← pump power

D=12 [in] ← pipe diameter

Δz_{PB}

pump
suction   discharge

A) 163 [ft]
B) 167 [ft]
C) 170 [ft]
D) 184 [ft]

Water Resources Practice Problems

Pumps #7

<u>Find:</u> η_p ← the pump efficiency

<u>Given:</u>

$Q=5.75\,[\text{ft}^3/\text{s}]$ ← flow rate

$\Delta h_{AB}=463.5\,[\text{ft}]$ ← change in total head between reservoir A and reservoir B

3 stage pump

$n=3{,}000\,[\text{rev/min}]$ ← the rotational speed of the pump

neglect headloss in the pipe

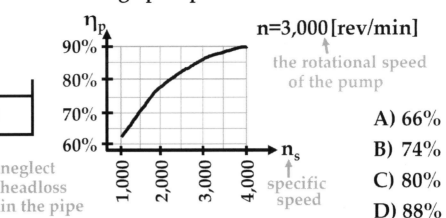

A) 66%
B) 74%
C) 80%
D) 88%

Pumps #8

<u>Find:</u> C ← the pumping cost

<u>Given:</u> $n_s=47.33$ ← specific speed

$t=18\,[\text{hr}]$ ← pumping duration

$c=\$0.13/[\text{kW*hr}]$ ← cost of energy

$\eta_m=0.74$ ← motor efficiency

$\eta_p=0.82$ ← pump efficiency

$SG=1.05$ ← specific gravity

$\Delta h_{AB}=15.7\,[\text{m}]$ ← difference in total head between reservoir A and reservoir B

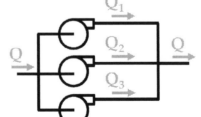

neglect headloss in the pipe

$n=2500\,[\text{rev/min}]$ ← rotational speed of the pump

A) \$10.30
B) \$11.40
C) \$13.90
D) \$15.70

Pumps #9

<u>Find:</u> P ← the power of each pump

<u>Given:</u>

$h_d=58.3\,[\text{m}]$ ← discharge head just downstream of each pump

$h_s=14.8\,[\text{m}]$ ← suction head just upstream of each pump

$\eta_p=0.82$ ← pump efficiency

$SG=1.05$ ← specific gravity

all three pumps have the same pump curve

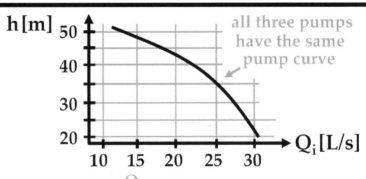

A) 3 [kW]
B) 10 [kW]
C) 20 [kW]
D) 30 [kW]

Pumps #10

Find: v ← the fluid velocity

Given:

$$h = 40\,[ft] + 0.08 * Q^2 \left[\frac{ft * min^2}{gal^2}\right]$$

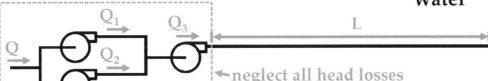

system curve

pump curve

h

Q

$d = 6\,[in]$ ← pipe diameter

(assume only one pipe in the system)

$P = 5\,[hp]$ ← pump power

$\eta_p = 0.73$ ← pump efficiency (assume constant)

A) 0.61 [ft/s]

B) 2.21 [ft/s]

C) 4.09 [ft/s]

D) 7.32 [ft/s]

Pumps #11

Find: Q_1 ← the flow rate through pump 1 (at the operating point)

assume all pumps are running

Given:

$P_1 = 10\,[kW]$ ← the power of

$P_2 = 20\,[kW]$ ← pumps 1, 2 and 3

$P_3 = 5\,[kW]$

$\eta_p = 0.82$ ← efficiency of all pumps

$f = 0.015$ ← friction factor

$L = 200\,[m]$ ← pipe length

$D = 0.1\,[m]$ ← pipe diameter

water

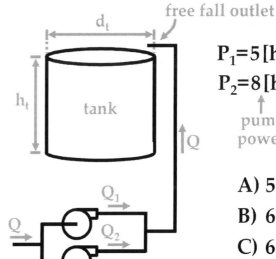

neglect all head losses through the pump station

A) 16 [L/s]

B) 24 [L/s]

C) 49 [L/s]

D) 73 [L/s]

Pumps #12

Find: h ← the head lift provided by the pumps

Given:

$\eta_{p,1} = 60\%$ ← efficiency of pump 1

$\eta_{p,2} = 85\%$ ← efficiency of pump 2

$d_t = 120\,[ft]$ ← tank diameter

$h_t = 30\,[ft]$ ← tank height

$t = 3\,[days]$ ← time required to fill the tank completely (starting empty)

water

free fall outlet

d_t

h_t

tank

Q

$P_1 = 5\,[hp]$

$P_2 = 8\,[hp]$

pump power

Q_1

Q

Q_2

A) 53 [ft]

B) 60 [ft]

C) 66 [ft]

D) 75 [ft]

Water Resources Practice Problems

Hydrology #1

Find: $P_{3[hr]}$ ← total rainfall after 3 hours

Given:

C=0.65 ← runoff coefficient

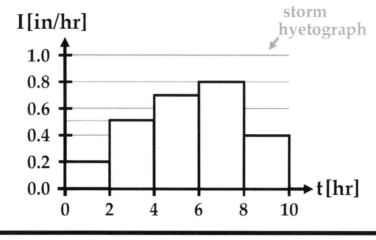

storm hyetograph

A) 0.5 [in]
B) 0.6 [in]
C) 0.7 [in]
D) 0.9 [in]

Hydrology #2

Find: $i_{2[hr]-5[hr]}$ ← average hourly rainfall rate (between hour 2 and hour 5)

Given:

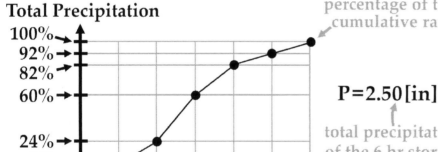

Total Precipitation

percentage of the cumulative rainfall

P=2.50 [in] ← total precipitation of the 6 hr storm

A) 0.43 [in/hr]
B) 0.57 [in/hr]
C) 0.83 [in/hr]
D) 0.90 [in/hr]

Hydrology #3

Find: $Q_{O,2}$ ← average outflow for month 2

Given: $E_A=0.12$ [in/day] ← evaporation rate

$Q_{I,1}=230$ [ft³/s] ← average inflow for month 1

$Q_{I,2}=275$ [ft³/s] ← average inflow for month 2

$Q_{O,1}=215$ [ft³/s] ← average outflow for month 1

A [ft²]$=12,150*V$ [acre*ft]$^{0.37}$ ← reservoir geometry

$E_{F,2}=4,383$ [ft³/day] ← evaporation rate at the end of the second month

$V_{I,1}=12,000$ [acre*ft] ← initial reservoir volume

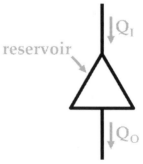

reservoir

A) 220 [ft³/s]
B) 235 [ft³/s]
C) 255 [ft³/s]
D) 270 [ft³/s]

Hydrology #4

Find: Q_{3-4} ← the average runoff flow rate between hours 3 and 4 of the storm

Given:

$P_{ave,excess} = 0.893\,[cm]$

average excess rainfall over the watershed (for the entire storm)

$A = 25\,[km^2]$ ← area of the watershed

t[hr]	Q[m³/s]
0-1	7
1-2	18
2-3	20
3-4	Q_{3-4}
4-5	5

runoff hydrograph

A) 10 [m³/s]
B) 11 [m³/s]
C) 12 [m³/s]
D) 13 [m³/s]

Hydrology #5

Find: A ← the area of the watershed

Given:

$P_{ave,excess} = 1.5\,[in]$

average excess rainfall depth of the storm contributing to runoff (for the entire storm)

$P = 2.0\,[in]$

total rainfall depth

unit hydrograph of the watershed

t[hr]	Q[ft³/(s*in)]
0-1	150
1-2	620
2-3	700
3-4	400
4-5	80

A) 2 [mi²]
B) 3 [mi²]
C) 4 [mi²]
D) 5 [mi²]

Hydrology #6

Find: $Q_{p,u}$ ← the peak runoff of the NRCS synthetic unit hydrograph

Given:

$t_R = 5\,[hr]$ ← storm duration

the watershed has a uniform ground slope

$Elev_A = Elev_D = 271.41\,[ft]$

$Elev_B = 337.67\,[ft]$ ← ground elevations of the watershed

$Elev_C = 111.41\,[ft]$

$L_{AC} = 8,000\,[ft]$ ← the length between points A and C

$CN = 60$ ← curve number

square watershed

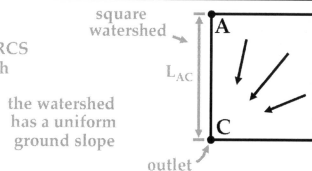

outlet

A) 68 [ft³/(s*in)]
B) 121 [ft³/(s*in)]
C) 213 [ft³/(s*in)]
D) 576 [ft³/(s*in)]

Water Resources Practice Problems

Hydrology #7

Find: $Q_{10[hr]}$ ← the runoff 10 hours into the storm

Given:

$A_d = 2.225\,[mi^2]$ ← drainage area

$t_R = 8\,[hr]$ ← storm duration

use the NRCS synthetic unit triangular hydrograph

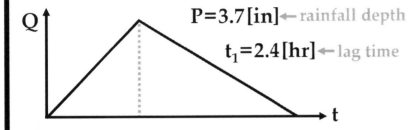

$P = 3.7\,[in]$ ← rainfall depth

$t_1 = 2.4\,[hr]$ ← lag time

A) 70 [ft³/s]

B) 110 [ft³/s]

C) 170 [ft³/s]

D) 410 [ft³/s]

Hydrology #8

Find: V_E ← the volume of water that evaporates from the reservoir

$t = 7\,[days]$ ← duration of evaporation

Given:

$T = 24.5\,^\circ C$ ← air temperature

$u_2 = 3.5\,[m/s]$ ← wind velocity

$z_2 = 2\,[m]$ ← height of wind measurement

$z_0 = 0.03\,[cm]$ ← roughness height of the water surface

$V = 12,000\,[m^3]$ ← reservoir volume

$V = 3.7 * A^{1.47}$ ← reservoir geometry relationship (where V in [m³] and A in [m²])

$R_h = 45\%$ ← relative humidity

reservoir

A) 2 [m³]

B) 13 [m³]

C) 25 [m³]

D) 97 [m³]

Hydrology #9

Find: $f_{(t)}$ ← the infiltration rate

negligible ponding depth

Given:

$K = 0.15\,[cm/hr]$ ← hydraulic conductivity

$\Psi = 21.85\,[cm]$ ← suction head

$\theta_e = 0.330$ ← effective porosity

$\eta = 0.398$ ← porosity

$\theta_i = 0.180$ ← initial saturation

$t = 2\,[hr]$ ← elapsed time

soil profile

continuous ponding

use Green-Ampt infiltration method

A) 0.15 [cm/hr]

B) 0.57 [cm/hr]

C) 1.05 [cm/hr]

D) 3.28 [cm/hr]

Hydrology #10

Find: t_p ← the time it takes for ponding to begin

Given:

$i = 0.60 \,[\text{in/hr}]$ ← rainfall intensity for the entire storm

$f_o = 1.5 \,[\text{in/hr}]$ ← initial infiltration rate

$f_c = 0.2 \,[\text{in/hr}]$ ← final infiltration rate

$k = 0.5 \,[\text{hr}^{-1}]$ ← decay constant

use the Horton infiltration method   the storm lasts long enough for the ponding to begin

precipitation → ↓ ↓ ↓ ↓

ponding →

infiltration →

soil profile →

A) 1.85 [hr]

B) 2.35 [hr]

C) 3.00 [hr]

D) 3.55 [hr]

Hydrology #11

Find: $Q_{5[\text{hr}]\text{-}6[\text{hr}]}$ ← total direct runoff from the storm, between hours 5 and 6

Given:

t [hr]	$Q_u\,[\text{m}^3/(\text{s} \cdot \text{in})]$
0-1	50
1-2	200
2-3	250
3-4	70
4-5	20

← unit hydrograph

$i = 1.00 \,[\text{in/hr}]$ ← rainfall intensity, and

$f = 0.20 \,[\text{in/hr}]$ ← infiltration rate for the entire storm

$d = 4 \,[\text{hr}]$
↑
storm duration

A)   0 [ft³/s]

B) 118 [ft³/s]

C) 272 [ft³/s]

D) 472 [ft³/s]

Hydrology #12

Find: $Q_{u,2[\text{hr}]\text{-}3[\text{hr}]}$ ← the unit hydrograph value during the third hour of the storm

Given: $f = 0.31 \,[\text{cm/hr}]$ ← infiltration rate for the entire storm

t [hr]	$Q\,[\text{m}^3/\text{s}]$
0-1	8.46
1-2	58.09
2-3	132.32
3-4	120.15

← direct hydrograph runoff flow rates

t [hr]	$Q\,[\text{m}^3/\text{s}]$
4-5	37.7
5-6	0

t [hr]	i [cm/hr]
0-1	0.78
1-2	2.31
2-3	1.76

rainfall intensities

A) 18 [m³/(s·cm)]

B) 26 [m³/(s·cm)]

C) 47 [m³/(s·cm)]

D) 75 [m³/(s·cm)]

Water Resources Practice Problems

Hydrology #13

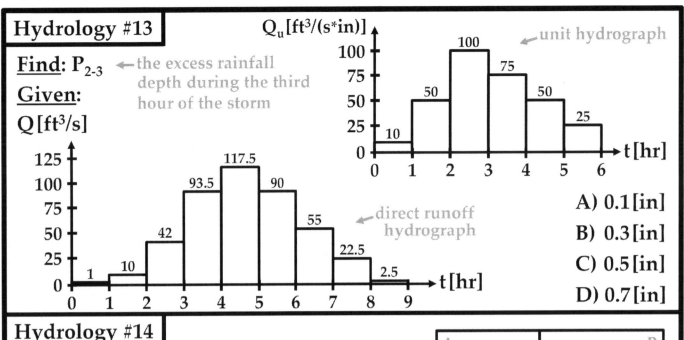

Q_u [ft³/(s*in)] ← unit hydrograph

Find: P_{2-3} ← the excess rainfall depth during the third hour of the storm

Given:

Q [ft³/s]

← direct runoff hydrograph

A) 0.1 [in]

B) 0.3 [in]

C) 0.5 [in]

D) 0.7 [in]

Hydrology #14

Find: Q_p ← peak runoff from the watersheds (measured at the outlet)

Given:

$A_A = 6$ [acre] ← area of watershed A

$A_B = 10$ [acre] ← area of watershed B

$t_{c,A} = 40$ [min] ← time of concentration of watersheds A and B

$t_{c,B} = 60$ [min]

storm intensity relationship

$C_A = 0.45$ ← runoff coefficient of watershed A

$C_B = 0.70$ ← and watershed B

$$i = \frac{120\,[in*min/hr]}{t_c + 20\,[min]}$$

A) 9.7 [ft³/s]

B) 10.5 [ft³/s]

C) 14.5 [ft³/s]

D) 16.8 [ft³/s]

Hydrology #15

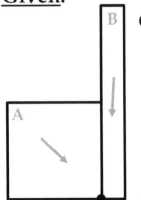

i [in/hr] ← storm intensity curve

Find: Q_p ← peak runoff (at the outlet)

Given:

$C_A = 0.80$ $C_B = 0.50$

runoff coefficients of watersheds A and B

$A_A = 4.0$ [acre] ← area of watershed A

$A_B = 1.5$ [acre] ← area of watershed B

$t_{c,A} = 20$ [min] ← time of concentrations

$t_{c,B} = 40$ [min]

outlet

A) 2.0 [ft³/s]

B) 3.2 [ft³/s]

C) 4.0 [ft³/s]

D) 6.4 [ft³/s]

Hydrology #16

Find: Q_p ← peak hourly runoff flow rate

Given:

$Q_u [m^3/(s*cm)]$

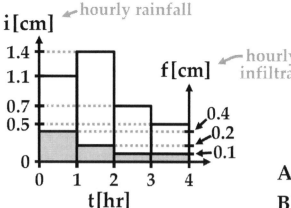

hourly rainfall

hourly infiltration

unit hydrograph

A) 9 [m³/s]
B) 16 [m³/s]
C) 23 [m³/s]
D) 57 [m³/s]

Hydrology #17

Find: P_e ← the excess rainfall depth (which contributes to runoff)

Given:

$P_g = 2.50 [in]$ ← gross rainfall depth

ARC = I ← antecedent runoff condition

soil group = B

¼ acre residential lots ← land use

use NRCS method

A) 0.09 [in]
B) 0.65 [in]
C) 0.91 [in]
D) 1.34 [in]

Hydrology #18

Find: T ← the recurrence interval of the storm

Given:

C = 0.78 ← runoff coefficient

A = 0.05 [km²] ← watershed area

$Q_p = 0.22 [m^3/s]$ ← peak runoff rate

$t_c = 60 [min]$ ← time of concentration

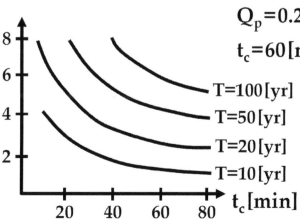

intensity duration frequency plot

A) T < 10 [yr]
B) 10 [yr] < T < 20 [yr]
C) 20 [yr] < T < 50 [yr]
D) 50 [yr] < T < 100 [yr]

Water Resources Practice Problems

Groundwater #1

Find: Q ← the flow rate

Given: $y_1=y_2=239.75$ [m] ← aquifer thickness

$\Delta y_{1,2}=-4.61$ [m] ← headloss between wells

$L_{1,2}=98.1$ [m] ← horizontal length between observation wells 1 and 2.

b=200 [m] ← aquifer width (into and out of the page)

T=20° C ← water temperature

$k=1*10^{-8}$ [cm²] ← intrinsic permeability

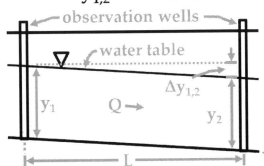

A) 0.02 [m³/s]

B) 0.07 [m³/s]

C) 0.18 [m³/s]

D) 0.47 [m³/s]

Groundwater #2

Find: v_{pore} ← the pore velocity

Given: $y_1=y_2=250$ [ft] ← aquifer thickness

e=0.42 ← void ratio

$L_{1,2}=3.0$ [mi] ← horizontal length between observation wells 1 and 2.

$\Delta y_{1,2}=-317$ [ft] ← headloss between wells

b=1.2 [mi] ← aquifer width

$\eta_e=0.9*\eta$ ← effective porosity (porosity)

K=10 [ft/day] ← hydraulic conductivity

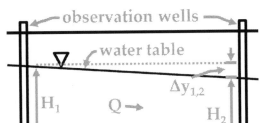

A) 0.20 [ft/day]

B) 0.40 [ft/day]

C) 0.55 [ft/day]

D) 0.75 [ft/day]

Groundwater #3

Find: θ_Q ← the direction of the flow rate

Given:

$L_{AB}=L_{AC}=L_{BC}=500$ [ft] ← the distance between wells

$h_A=243.5$ [ft]

$h_B=232.1$ [ft] ← total head at all the wells

$h_C=236.7$ [ft]

K=8 [ft/day] ← hydraulic conductivity

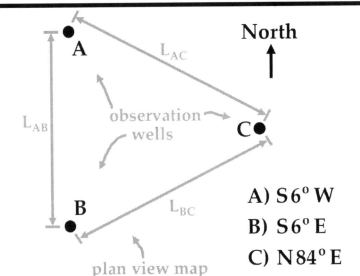

plan view map of well locations

A) S 6° W

B) S 6° E

C) N 84° E

D) N 6° E

Groundwater #4

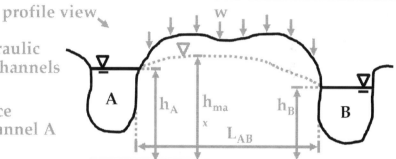

profile view of the 3 observation wells

hypothetical water table

Find: h_B ← the head at well B

Given:

$L_{AB}=L_{BC}=300\,[m]$

$L_{AC}=600\,[m]$ ← horizontal length between the wells

$h_A=41.5\,[m]$ ← total head at well A

$h_C=34.5\,[m]$ ← total head at well C

$K_{AB}=5\,[m/day]$ ← permeability between wells A and B

$K_{BC}=20\,[m/day]$ ← permeability between wells B and C

A) 36 [m]

B) 38 [m]

C) 39 [m]

D) 40 [m]

Groundwater #5

profile view

Find: h_{max} ← the maximum hydraulic head between the channels

Given:

$h_A=17.4\,[m]$ ← the water surface elevation in channel A

$h_B=15.4\,[m]$ ← the water surface elevation in channel B

$w=0.011\,[m/day]$ ← recharge rate

$L_{AB}=750\,[m]$ ← horizontal distance between the channels

$K=32\,[m/day]$

hydraulic conductivity

A) 17.4 [m]

B) 17.7 [m]

C) 18.0 [m]

D) 19.0 [m]

Groundwater #6

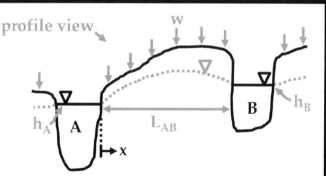

profile view

Find: x where $h_x=159.0\,[ft]$

the distance from channel A where the water table is at a height of 159.0 feet.

Given:

$h_A=153.8\,[ft]$ ← the water surface elevation in channel A

$h_B=157.4\,[ft]$ ← the water surface elevation in channel B

$w=0.25\,[ft/day]$ ← recharge rate

$L_{AB}=1,200\,[ft]$ ← distance between channels

$K=50\,[ft/day]$

hydraulic conductivity

A) 100 [ft]

B) 200 [ft]

C) 300 [ft]

D) 400 [ft]

Water Resources Practice Problems

Groundwater #7

constant head permeameter

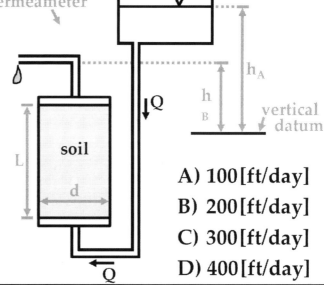

Find: K ← the hydraulic conductivity

Given:

h_A=34 [in] ← upstream head

h_B=20 [in] ← downstream head

L=18 [in] ← length of soil sample

d=2.111 [in] ← diameter of the soil sample

t=3 [min] ← time it takes to fill a known volume

V=13.41 [in³]

A) 100 [ft/day]
B) 200 [ft/day]
C) 300 [ft/day]
D) 400 [ft/day]

Groundwater #8

falling-head permeameter

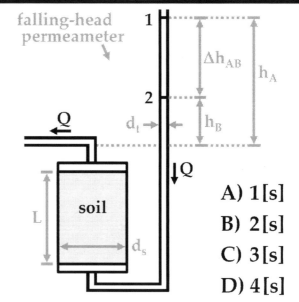

Find: t ← the time it takes the water level to drop from h_1 to h_2.

Given:

h_A=78 [cm] ← initial headloss

Δh_{AB}=47 [cm] ← change in headloss

L=14 [cm] ← length of soil sample

d_s=8.5 [cm] ← diameter of the soil sample

d_t=1.2 [cm] ← diameter of the tube

K=0.13 [cm/s] ← hydraulic conductivity

A) 1 [s]
B) 2 [s]
C) 3 [s]
D) 4 [s]

Groundwater #9

Find: V ← the volume of water flowing beneath the embankment

Given:

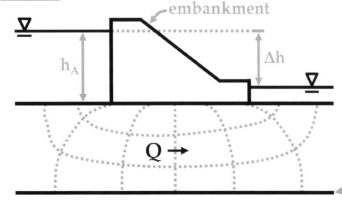

h_A=9.5 [m] ← upstream depth

Δh=8 [m] ← headloss across the embankment

K=0.001 [cm/s] ← hydraulic conductivity

t=1 [week] ← duration

b=20 [m] ← width of the embankment

A)   7 [m³]
B)   28 [m³]
C)   480 [m³]
D) 1,940 [m³]

Groundwater #10

Find: r_2 ← the radius from the well where the aquifer thickness equals y_2

Given:

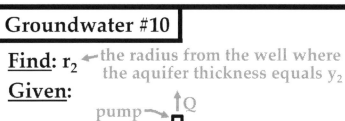

$y_1 = 408\,[ft]$ } aquifer thicknesses (phreatic zone)
$y_2 = 412\,[ft]$

$Q = 120\,[gal/min]$ ← pumping rate

$K = 144\,[in/day]$ ← hydraulic conductivity

$r_1 = 4\,[ft]$ ← radius for y_1

A) 575 [ft]
B) 665 [ft]
C) 755 [ft]
D) 845 [ft]

Groundwater #11

Find: s ← the aquifer drawdown

Given:

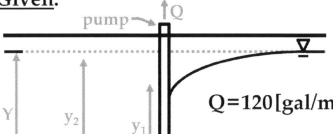

$Q = 2{,}725\,[m^3/day]$ ← pumping rate

$K = 1\,[cm/min]$ ← hydraulic conductivity

$r = 7\,[m]$ ← radius from the well

$t = 1\,[day]$ ← duration of pumping

$Y = 20.1\,[m]$ ← aquifer thickness

$S = 0.0051\,[m]$ ← aquifer storativity

non-steady state conditions

A) 0.34 [m]
B) 0.72 [m]
C) 1.72 [m]
D) 5.90 [m]

Groundwater #12

no cone of depression exists at the time pumping begins

non-steady state conditions

Find: t ← the duration of pumping

Given:

pumping is continuous

unconfined aquifer

$Q = 100\,[gal/min]$ ← pumping rate

$s = 10.7\,[ft]$ ← drawdown

$r = 19\,[ft]$ ← radius

$S = 0.002$ ← storativity

$T = 1{,}400\,[ft^2/day]$ ← transmissivity

A) 1 [day]
B) 2 [days]
C) 3 [days]
D) 4 [days]

Water Resources Practice Problems

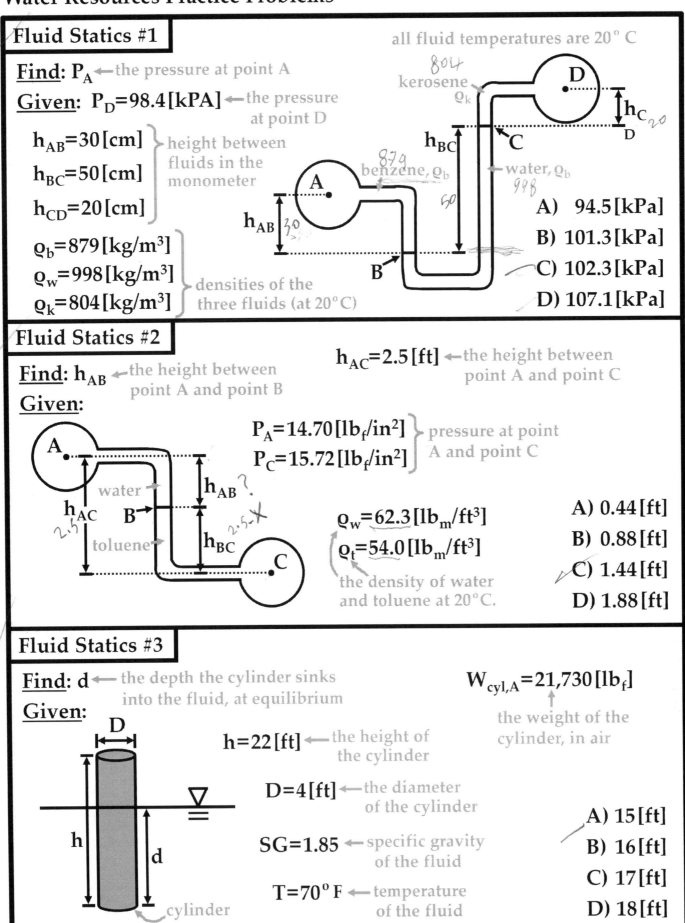

Fluid Statics #1

Find: P_A ← the pressure at point A

Given: P_D=98.4 [kPA] ← the pressure at point D

h_{AB}=30 [cm]
h_{BC}=50 [cm] } height between fluids in the monometer
h_{CD}=20 [cm]

ϱ_b=879 [kg/m³]
ϱ_w=998 [kg/m³] } densities of the three fluids (at 20°C)
ϱ_k=804 [kg/m³]

all fluid temperatures are 20° C

804
kerosene, ϱ_k

D

h_C 20

h_{BC} C

879
benzene, ϱ_b

A

50

water, ϱ_b
998

h_{AB} 30

B

A) 94.5 [kPa]
B) 101.3 [kPa]
C) 102.3 [kPa]
D) 107.1 [kPa]

Fluid Statics #2

Find: h_{AB} ← the height between point A and point B

Given:

h_{AC}=2.5 [ft] ← the height between point A and point C

P_A=14.70 [lb_f/in²] } pressure at point A and point C
P_C=15.72 [lb_f/in²]

A

water

h_{AC}
2.5

B

h_{AB}?
2.5-x

toluene

h_{BC}

C

ϱ_w=62.3 [lb_m/ft³]
ϱ_t=54.0 [lb_m/ft³]

the density of water and toluene at 20°C.

A) 0.44 [ft]
B) 0.88 [ft]
C) 1.44 [ft]
D) 1.88 [ft]

Fluid Statics #3

Find: d ← the depth the cylinder sinks into the fluid, at equilibrium

Given:

D

h

d

cylinder

h=22 [ft] ← the height of the cylinder

D=4 [ft] ← the diameter of the cylinder

SG=1.85 ← specific gravity of the fluid

T=70° F ← temperature of the fluid

$W_{cyl,A}$=21,730 [lb_f]
↑
the weight of the cylinder, in air

A) 15 [ft]
B) 16 [ft]
C) 17 [ft]
D) 18 [ft]

32

Fluid Statics #4

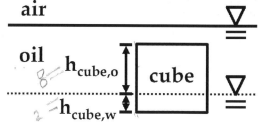

Find: ϱ_{cube} ← the density of the cube

Given:

$\varrho_o = 56.2\,[lb_m/ft^3]$ ← density of the oil

$\varrho_w = 62.4\,[lb_m/ft^3]$ ← density of the water

$h_{cube,o} = 8\,[in]$ ← height of the cube in the oil

$h_{cube,w} = 2\,[in]$ ← height of the cube in the water

$V_{cube} = 1,000\,[in]$ ← volume of the cube

equilibrium condition →

A) $57.4\,[lb_f/ft^3]$

B) $58.7\,[lb_f/ft^3]$

C) $60.0\,[lb_f/ft^3]$

D) $61.2\,[lb_f/ft^3]$

Fluid Statics #5

Find: $W_{sphere,A}$ ← weight of the entire sphere, in air

Given: $r = 1.75\,[ft]$ ← sphere radius

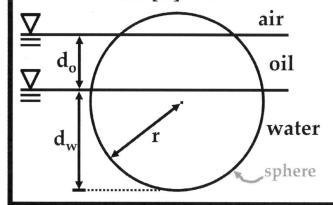

$SG_o = 0.89$
$SG_w = 1.00$ } the specific gravity of each fluid

$d_o = 1.00\,[ft]$
$d_w = 2.00\,[ft]$ } the depth of the sphere in each fluid

$T = 70\,^\circ F$

temperature of both fluids

A) $1,271\,[lb_f]$

B) $1,399\,[lb_f]$

C) $1,525\,[lb_f]$

D) $1,652\,[lb_f]$

Fluid Statics #6

Find: ϱ_{cube} ← the density of the cube

Given:

$s = 0.31\,[m]$ ← the side length of the cube

$m_{mass} = 15\,[kg]$ ← the mass, m

$V_m = 0.0070\,[m^3]$
volume of the mass, m

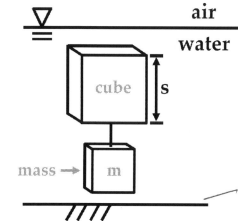

this system is in static equilibrium

temperature of the water
$T_w = 25\,^\circ C$

A) $490\,[kg/m^3]$

B) $610\,[kg/m^3]$

C) $730\,[kg/m^3]$

D) $999\,[kg/m^3]$

33

Water Resources Practice Problems

Fluid Statics #7

Find: SG ← the specific gravity of the fluid

Given:

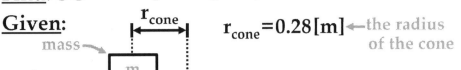

$r_{cone} = 0.28\,[m]$ ← the radius of the cone

$\varrho_{cone} = 850\,[kg/m^3]$ ← the density of the cone

$h_{cone} = 1.12\,[m]$ ← the height of the cone

$m_{mass} = 20\,[kg]$

$d_{cone} = 0.93\,[m]$ ← the depth of the cone submerged in the fluid

A) 1.05

B) 1.31

C) 1.58

D) 1.86

Fluid Statics #8

Find: F_R ← the hydrostatic force acting on the gate

Given:

$d_{top} = 1\,[ft]$ ← vertical distance from the water surface to the top of the gate.

$w_{gate} = 5\,[ft]$ ← width of the gate

$h_{gate} = 4\,[ft]$ ← height of the gate

$T = 50\,°F$ ← water temperature

cross section of the gate

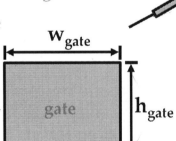

$\theta = 30°$ ← angle

A)   125 $[lb_f]$

B) 2,500 $[lb_f]$

C) 3,750 $[lb_f]$

D) 5,000 $[lb_f]$

Fluid Statics #9

Find: F ← the force required to hold the gate shut

Given:

the gate is in the shape of an equilateral triangle

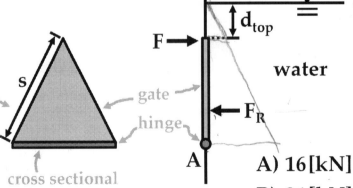

cross sectional view of the gate

$s = 3\,[m]$ ← the length of one side of the gate

$d_{top} = 1\,[m]$ ← the depth to the top of the gate

A) 16 [kN]

B) 21 [kN]

C) 26 [kN]

D) 31 [kN]

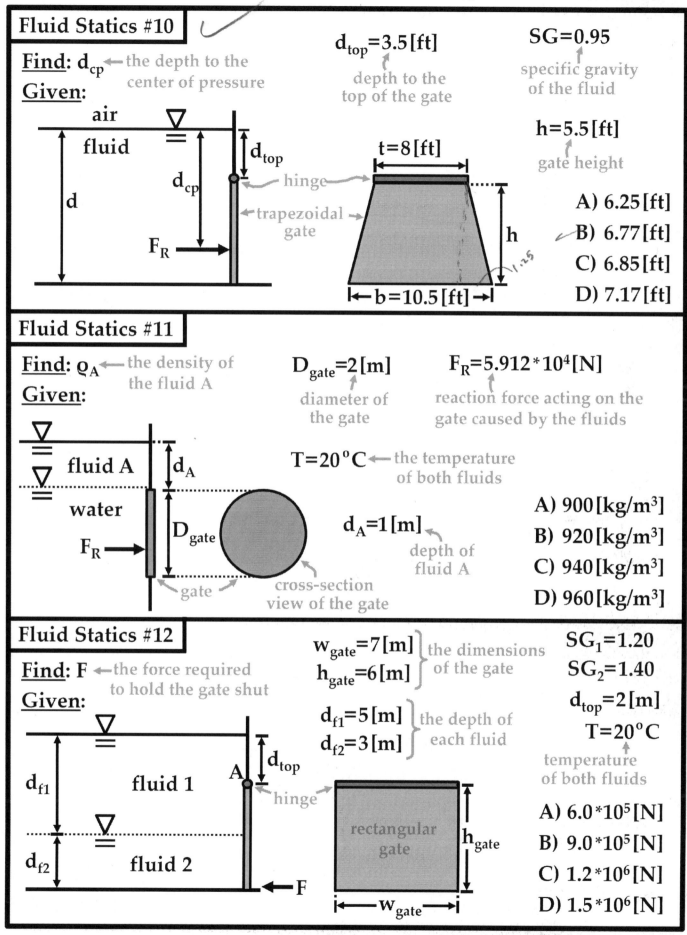

Fluid Statics #10

<u>Find:</u> d_{cp} ← the depth to the center of pressure

<u>Given:</u>

air

fluid

d

d_{cp}

d_{top}

hinge

trapezoidal gate

F_R

$d_{top}=3.5$ [ft]
depth to the top of the gate

SG=0.95
specific gravity of the fluid

$t=8$ [ft]

$h=5.5$ [ft]
gate height

h

1.25

$b=10.5$ [ft]

A) 6.25 [ft]
B) 6.77 [ft]
C) 6.85 [ft]
D) 7.17 [ft]

Fluid Statics #11

<u>Find:</u> ϱ_A ← the density of the fluid A

<u>Given:</u>

fluid A

d_A

water

D_{gate}

F_R

gate

cross-section view of the gate

$D_{gate}=2$ [m]
diameter of the gate

$F_R=5.912*10^4$ [N]
reaction force acting on the gate caused by the fluids

$T=20\,^{\circ}C$ ← the temperature of both fluids

$d_A=1$ [m]
depth of fluid A

A) 900 [kg/m³]
B) 920 [kg/m³]
C) 940 [kg/m³]
D) 960 [kg/m³]

Fluid Statics #12

<u>Find:</u> F ← the force required to hold the gate shut

<u>Given:</u>

d_{f1}

fluid 1

A

d_{top}

hinge

d_{f2}

fluid 2

F

rectangular gate

h_{gate}

w_{gate}

$w_{gate}=7$ [m]
$h_{gate}=6$ [m]
the dimensions of the gate

$d_{f1}=5$ [m]
$d_{f2}=3$ [m]
the depth of each fluid

$SG_1=1.20$
$SG_2=1.40$

$d_{top}=2$ [m]

$T=20\,^{\circ}C$
temperature of both fluids

A) $6.0*10^5$ [N]
B) $9.0*10^5$ [N]
C) $1.2*10^6$ [N]
D) $1.5*10^6$ [N]

Water Resources Practice Problems

Fluid Dynamics #1

Find: F_R ← the reaction force required to hold the vane stationary

Given:

$Q = 0.10 \, [m^3/s]$
flow rate

$v_o = 28 \, [m/s]$ ← velocity of flow

$\varrho = 900 \, [kg/m^3]$ ← density of the fluid

neglect forces due to gravity and pressure

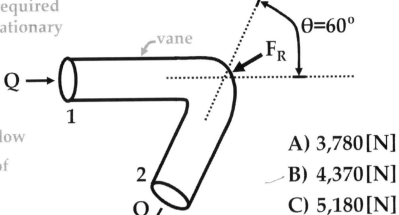

$\theta = 60°$

vane

F_R

Q →

1

2

Q

A) 3,780 [N]
B) 4,370 [N]
C) 5,180 [N]
D) 5,960 [N]

Fluid Dynamics #2

Find: $F_{R,x}$ ← the reaction force in the x-direction to hold the nozzle stationary

Given:

$\varrho = 62.3 \, [lb_m/ft^3]$ ← the density of the fluid

$d_1 = 2 \, [in]$
$d_2 = 1 \, [in]$ the diameter at the two ends of the nozzle

$P_1 = 45 \, [lb_f/in^2]$ ← the pressure at end 1

$v_1 = 7 \, [ft/s]$ ← the velocity at end 1

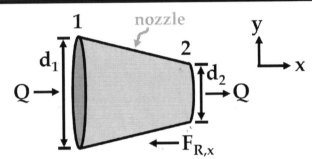

1   nozzle

y

d_1

Q →

2

d_2

→ Q

x

$\leftarrow F_{R,x}$

assume there is no headloss in the nozzle

A) -6 [lb_f]
B)   6 [lb_f]
C) 99 [lb_f]
D) 104 [lb_f]

Fluid Dynamics #3

Find: m_{block} ← the mass of the block

Given:

$h = 3 \, [m]$ ← the height difference between the tip of the nozzle and the block

$\varrho = 998 \, [kg/m^3]$ ← fluid density

$A_1 = 4.42*10^{-3} \, [m^2]$ ← flow area at the nozzle

$v_1 = 13.2 \, [m/s]$ ← flow velocity at the nozzle

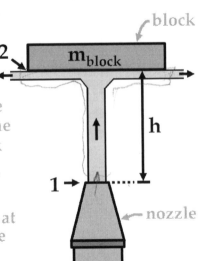

block

2

m_{block}

h

1 →

nozzle

the block deflects all flow horizontally

the nozzle and block remain stationary

A) 63.7 [kg]
B) 78.3 [kg]
C) 127.4 [kg]
D) 156.6 [kg]

Fluid Dynamics #4

Find: d ← the diameter of the vane

Given:

v=22 [ft/s] ← velocity of the fluid

ϱ=75 [lb$_m$/ft^3] ← density of the fluid

θ=65°

the vane has a circular cross-section and is held motionless by forces F$_{R,x}$ and F$_{R,y}$.

F$_{R,x}$=50 [lb$_f$]

reaction force in the x-direction

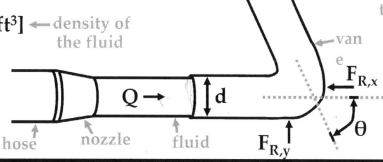

A) 2.4 [in]

B) 2.5 [in]

C) 2.6 [in]

D) 2.7 [in]

hose   nozzle   fluid   F$_{R,y}$

Fluid Dynamics #5

Find: F$_{R,y}$ ← the vertical reaction force, on the cart

Given:

ϱ=999 [kg/m^3] ← fluid density

v$_o$=30 [m/s] ← fluid velocity

v$_{cart}$=15 [m/s] ← cart velocity

A=600 [mm^3] ← cross-sectional area of the fluid

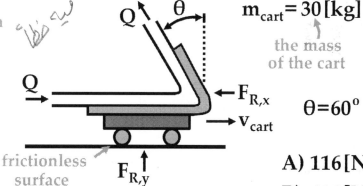

m$_{cart}$=30 [kg] ← the mass of the cart

θ=60°

frictionless surface

the cart maintains a constant velocity

A) 116 [N]

B) 411 [N]

C) 527 [N]

D) 741 [N]

Fluid Dynamics #6

Find: P$_2$ ← the pressure at end 2

Given: ϱ=62.4 [lb$_m$/in^3] ← fluid density

F$_{R,x}$=1,022 [lb$_f$] ← horizontal reaction force

P$_2$=P$_3$

P$_1$=22 [lb$_f$/in^2] ← pressure at end 1

d$_1$=6 [in] ← diameter at end 1

d$_2$=d$_3$=4 [in] ← diameter at ends 2 and 3

Q$_1$=2*Q$_2$=2*Q$_3$=0.64 [ft^3/s] ← flow rates

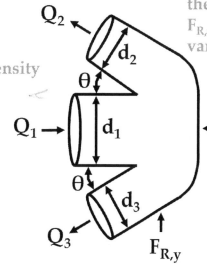

the reaction forces F$_{R,x}$ and F$_{R,y}$ hold the vane stationary

θ=30°

A) 18 [lb$_f$/in^2]

B) 19 [lb$_f$/in^2]

C) 21 [lb$_f$/in^2]

D) 22 [lb$_f$/in^2]

Water Resources Practice Problems

Fluid Dynamics #7

Find: SG ←the specific gravity of the fluid

Given:

$m_{cart}=20\,[kg]$ ←cart mass

$\theta=28°$ ←deflection angle

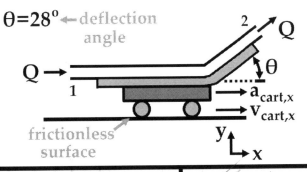

frictionless surface

$v_{cart,x}=0\,[m/s]$ ←the cart velocity in the x-direction

$v_1=v_2=30\,[m/s]$ ←the fluid velocity

$T=30°C$ ←the fluid temperature

$a_{cart,x}=4.62\,[m/s^2]$

the cart acceleration in the x-direction

$A_1=A_2=8\,[cm^2]$

the area of the fluid at ends 1 and 2

A) 1.0
B) 1.1
C) 1.2
D) 1.3

Fluid Dynamics #8

Find: x ← the horizontal distance the fluid travels in the air

Given:

$C_v=0.82$ ← coefficient of velocity

$C_c=1.00$ ← coefficient of contraction

$z_1=15\,[ft]$ ←the elevation of the water level

$z_2=5\,[ft]$ ←the elevation of the outlet pipe

$z_0=0\,[ft]$ ←the ground elevation

$T=70°F$

water temperature

A) 9.6 [ft]
B) 11.1 [ft]
C) 12.6 [ft]
D) 14.1 [ft]

water tank

Fluid Dynamics #9

Find: t ←the time it takes the tank to drain from level h_1 to level h_2.

Given:

$h_1=30\,[ft]$ ←initial water height

$h_2=10\,[ft]$ ←final water height

$h_3=3\,[ft]$ ←orifice height

$d_t=100\,[ft]$

tank diameter

$d_0=8\,[in]$ ←orifice diameter

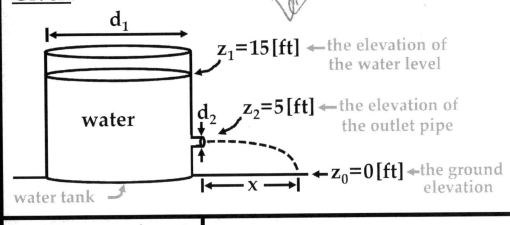

orifice detail

tank wall

flow

"sharp edged" orifice

water tank

A) 1.4 [hr]
B) 4.0 [hr]
C) 6.4 [hr]
D) 10.3 [hr]

Fluid Dynamics #10

Find: P ← the power generated by the dynamic fluid force

Given:

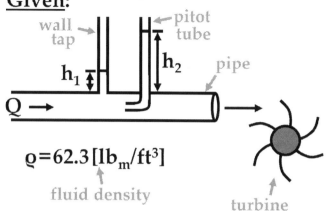

h_1=2.4[in] ← height of the fluid in the wall tap

h_2=13.7[in] ← height of the fluid in the pitot tube

A=5[in²]
↑
area of the pipe

ϱ=62.3[lb$_m$/ft³]
↑
fluid density

turbine

A)   2[lb$_f$*ft/s]

B)   16[lb$_f$*ft/s]

C) 510[lb$_f$*ft/s]

D) 960[lb$_f$*ft/s]

Fluid Dynamics #11

Find: μ ← the absolute viscosity of the fluid

Given:

h=150[mm] ← viscometer height

D=75[mm] ← viscometer diameter

$\dot{\theta}$=100[rev/min] ← angular velocity

T=0.021[N*m] ← torque

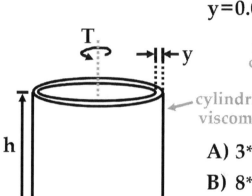

y=0.02[mm]
↑
plate clearance

cylindrical viscometer

A) 3*10⁻³[N*s/m²]

B) 8*10⁻³[N*s/m²]

C) 3*10⁻⁴[N*s/m²]

D) 8*10⁻⁴[N*s/m²]

Fluid Dynamics #12

Find: l ← the length of the plates

Given:

v_{top}=8[ft/s] ← plate velocities

v_{bottom}=0[ft/s]

w=6[in] ← width of the plates

y=1*10⁻³[in] ← plate clearance

F=0.875[lb$_f$] ← shear force on the plates

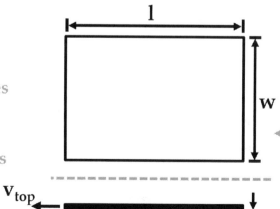

T=50° F
↑
water temperature

← plan view

A) 5[in]

B) 6[in]

C) 7[in]

D) 8[in]

(page intentionally left blank)

Section 2: Detailed Solutions

(page intentionally left blank)

Open Channel Flow #1

Find: R ←the hydraulic radius

Given:

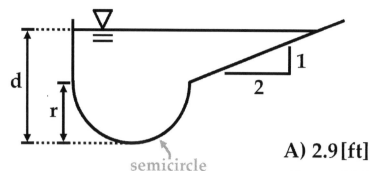

$d=14\,[ft]$ ←the total depth of the water

$r=8\,[ft]$ ←the radius of the semicircle

A) $2.9\,[ft]$

B) $3.7\,[ft]$

C) $4.5\,[ft]$

D) $5.2\,[ft]$

Analysis:

area of flow

$$R=\frac{\Sigma A}{\Sigma P} \leftarrow eq.1$$

wetted perimeter

Eq. 1 computes the hydraulic radius, as the total area of flow divided by the total wetted perimeter.

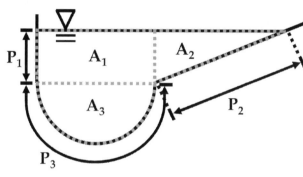

Figure 1

Figure 1 shows how we can divide the channel into 3 parts.

In Figure 1, Part 1 refers to the rectangular, Part 2 refers to the triangular, and Part 3 refers to the semicircle.

$$R=\frac{A_1+A_2+A_3}{P_1+P_2+P_3} \leftarrow eq.2$$

Expand Eq. 1 by writing out the summation terms ΣA and ΣP.

$$A_1=(d-r)*(2*r) \leftarrow eq.3$$

$d=14\,[ft]$ $r=8\,[ft]$

Plug in d and r into eq.3, then solve for area A_1.

Water Resources Practice Problems

$$A_1 = (14[ft] - 8[ft]) * (2 * 8[ft])$$

$$A_1 = 96[ft^2]$$

Plug in d and r into eq.4, then solve for area A_2.

$$A_2 = 0.5 * (d-r) * (2 * (d-r)) \leftarrow eq.4$$

$$d = 14[ft] \quad r = 8[ft]$$

$$A_2 = 0.5 * (14[ft] - 8[ft]) * (2 * (14[ft] - 8[ft]))$$

$$A_2 = 36[ft^2]$$

Plug in variable r into eq.5, then solve for area A_3.

$$A_3 = 0.5 * \pi * r^2 \leftarrow eq.5$$

$$r = 8[ft]$$

$$A_3 = 0.5 * \pi * (8[ft])^2$$

$$A_3 = 100.5[ft^2]$$

Plug in variables d and r into eq.6, then solve for P_1.

$$P_1 = d - r \leftarrow eq.6$$

$$d = 14[ft] \quad r = 8[ft]$$

$$P_1 = 14[ft] - 8[ft]$$

$$P_1 = 6[ft]$$

Plug in variables d and r into eq.7, then solve for P_2.

$$P_2 = \sqrt{(d-r)^2 + (2 * (d-r))^2} \leftarrow eq.7$$

$$d = 14[ft] \quad r = 8[ft]$$

Open Channel Flow #1 (cont.)

$$P_2 = \sqrt{(14\,[ft] - 8\,[ft])^2 + (2*(14\,[ft] - 8\,[ft]))^2}$$

$$P_2 = 13.42\,[ft]$$

$$P_3 = 0.5 * \pi * (2*r) \leftarrow eq.\,8$$

$$r = 8\,[ft]$$

Plug in variable r into Eq. 8, then solve for area P_3.

$$P_3 = 0.5 * \pi * (2*8\,[ft])$$

$$P_3 = 25.13\,[ft]$$

$$A_2 = 36\,[ft^2]$$

$$A_1 = 96\,[ft^2] \qquad A_3 = 100.5\,[ft^2]$$

$$R = \frac{A_1 + A_2 + A_3}{P_1 + P_2 + P_3} \leftarrow eq.\,2$$

$$P_1 = 6\,[ft] \qquad P_3 = 25.13\,[ft]$$

$$P_2 = 13.42\,[ft]$$

Return to Eq. 2, substitute in the areas and wetted perimeters, then solve for the hydraulic radius, R.

$$R = \frac{96\,[ft^2] + 36\,[ft^2] + 100.5\,[ft^2]}{6\,[ft] + 13.42\,[ft] + 25.13\,[ft]}$$

$$R = 5.22\,[ft]$$

Answer: $\boxed{D}$

Water Resources Practice Problems

Open Channel Flow #2

Find: R ← the hydraulic radius

Given:

D=8.00 [in] ← pipe diameter

d=5.87 [in] ← water depth

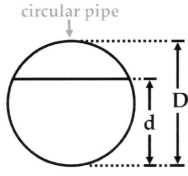

cross section of circular pipe

Section A-A'

A← circular pipe

A'← → Q

A) 1.2 [in]
B) 1.6 [in]
C) 2.0 [in]
D) 2.4 [in]

Analysis:

$$R=0.25 * \left(1 - \frac{\sin(\theta)}{\theta}\right) * D \leftarrow eq.1$$

pipe diameter

angle theta (in radians)

Eq.1 computes the hydraulic radius of a circular pipe based on the pipe diameter and an angle theta, θ.

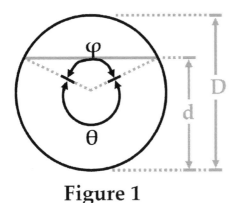

Figure 1

Figure 1 shows angle theta, θ, which depends on the pipe diameter, and the water depth.

Define angle phi, φ, as shown in Figure 1.

Figure 1 shows a cross section of the circular pipe.

$$2 * \pi [rad] = \theta + \varphi \leftarrow eq.2$$

From Figure 1, we know the interior angles of the circular pipe sum to 2*π radians.

$$\theta = 2 * \pi [rad] - \varphi \leftarrow eq.3$$

Solve eq.2 for θ.

Open Channel Flow #2 (cont.)

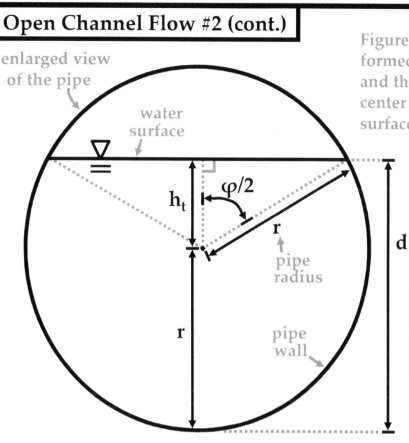

Figure 2 identifies a right triangle formed by the radius of the pipe, R, and the vertical distance between the center of the pipe and the water surface elevation, h_t.

In this problem, lower-case "r" refers to the pipe radius, and upper-case "R" refers to the hydraulic radius.

Figure 2

$$\varphi/2 = \cos^{-1}(h_t/r) \leftarrow eq.\,4$$

Eq. 4 computes $\varphi/2$ by using right triangle trigonometry and Figure 2.

$$\varphi = 2 * \cos^{-1}(h_t/r) \leftarrow eq.\,5$$

Solve eq. 4 for phi, φ.

$$h_t = d - r \leftarrow eq.\,6$$
water   pipe
depth radius

Eq. 6 computes the vertical distance between the center of the pipe and the water surface elevation.

$$r = D/2 \leftarrow eq.\,7$$
D=8 [in]

Eq. 7 computes the pipe radius.

Plug in the pipe diameter into eq. 7 and compute the pipe radius.

$$r = 8\,[in]/2$$

$$r = 4\,[in]$$

Water Resources Practice Problems

Open Channel Flow #2 (cont.)

$$h_t = d - r \leftarrow eq.6$$

$d = 5.87\,[in]$ $r = 4\,[in]$

Plug in variables d and r into eq. 6, then solve for h_t.

$$h_t = 5.87\,[in] - 4\,[in]$$

$$h_t = 1.87\,[in]$$

$h_t = 1.87\,[in]$

$$\varphi = 2 * \cos^{-1}(h_t / r) \leftarrow eq.5$$

$r = 4\,[in]$

Plug in variables h_t and r into eq. 5, then solve for angle phi, φ.

$$\varphi = 2 * \cos^{-1}(1.87\,[in] / 4\,[in])$$

$$\varphi = 2.169\,[rad]$$

$\varphi = 2.169\,[rad]$

$$\theta = 2 * \pi\,[rad] - \varphi \leftarrow eq.3$$

Plug in the angle phi, into eq. 3, then solve for angle θ.

$$\theta = 2 * \pi\,[rad] - 2.169\,[rad]$$

$$\theta = 4.114\,[rad]$$

$D = 8\,[in]$

$$R = 0.25 * \left(1 - \frac{\sin(\theta)}{\theta}\right) * D \leftarrow eq.1$$

$\theta = 4.114\,[rad]$

Plug in variables θ and D into eq. 1, then solve for R.

$$R = 0.25 * \left(1 - \frac{\sin(4.114\,[rad])}{4.114}\right) * 8\,[in]$$

$$R = 2.401\,[in] \qquad \underline{Answer:}\; \boxed{D}$$

Open Channel Flow #3

Find: d ← the depth of flow in order to maximize the hydraulic radius

Given:

cross section A-A' of circular pipe

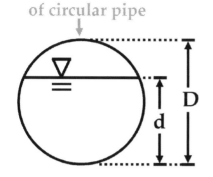

$D=1.00\,[m]$ ← pipe diameter

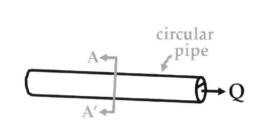

circular pipe

maximum R ↑ the hydraulic radius is maximized

A) 0.811 [m]

B) 0.823 [m]

C) 0.835 [m]

D) 0.847 [m]

Analysis:

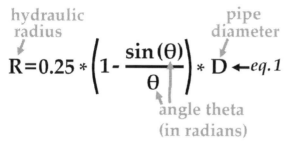

hydraulic radius

pipe diameter

$$R=0.25*\left(1-\frac{\sin(\theta)}{\theta}\right)*D \leftarrow eq.1$$

angle theta (in radians)

Eq. 1 computes the hydraulic radius of a circular pipe based on the pipe diameter and an angle theta, θ.

enlarged view of the pipe

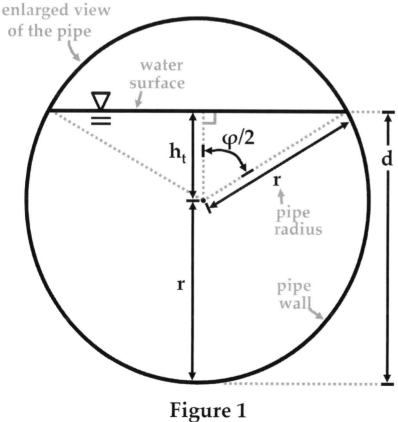

water surface

pipe radius

pipe wall

Figure 1 identifies a right triangle, based on the height, h_t, and the radius, r.

Figure 1

Water Resources Practice Problems

$$\cos(\varphi/2) = h_t/r \leftarrow eq.2$$

Eq.2 can be derived from the right triangle in Figure 1, using trigonometry.

$$\varphi = 2 * \cos^{-1}(h_t/r) \leftarrow eq.3$$
$$h_t = d - r$$

Solve eq.2 for φ, then substitute in d - r for the height h_t.

$$\varphi = 2 * \cos^{-1}((d-r)/r) \leftarrow eq.4$$

$$r = D/2 \leftarrow eq.5$$
$$D = 1 \, [m]$$

Eq.5 computes the radius of the pipe.

$$r = 1 \, [m]/2$$

Plug in variable D into eq.5, then solve for r.

$$r = 0.5 \, [m]$$

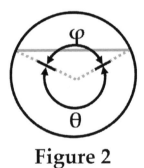

Figure 2

Figure 2 and eq.6 show angle theta and angle phi make up the entire $2 * \pi$ radians of the pipe interior.

$$2 * \pi \, [rad] = \theta + \varphi \leftarrow eq.6$$

Solve eq.6 for angle phi, φ.

$$\varphi = 2 * \pi \, [rad] - \theta \leftarrow eq.7$$

$$r = 0.5 \, [m]$$
$$\varphi = 2 * \cos^{-1}((d-r)/r) \leftarrow eq.4$$
$$\varphi = 2 * \pi \, [rad] - \theta$$

Plug in variables φ and r into eq.4, then solve for angle theta, θ.

Open Channel Flow #3 (cont.)

$2*\pi[rad]-\theta=2*\cos^{-1}((d-0.5[m])/0.5[m])$

Determine which of the four given depth values results in the largest hydraulic radius.

$\theta=2*\pi[rad]-2*\cos^{-1}((d-0.5[m])/0.5[m]) \leftarrow eq.8$

$\theta_A=4.484[rad] \leftarrow$ A) $0.811[m]$
$\theta_B=4.546[rad] \leftarrow$ B) $0.823[m]$
$\theta_C=4.610[rad] \leftarrow$ C) $0.835[m]$
$\theta_D=4.676[rad] \leftarrow$ D) $0.847[m]$

Use eq.8 to convert the four possible solutions for the depth, to a corresponding angle phi, φ.

calculated angles, θ possible solutions for the depth, d.

$R=0.25*\left(1-\dfrac{\sin(\theta)}{\theta}\right)*D \leftarrow eq.1$

Plug in the four values θ_A, θ_B, θ_C, and θ_D, into eq.1 to compute R_A, R_B, R_C, R_D

$R_A=0.3043 \leftarrow$ maximum hydraulic radius
$R_B=0.3042$
$R_C=0.3039$ $d=0.811[m]$
$R_D=0.3034$ water depth of solution A

Use eq.1 and the four values of angle theta (θ_A, θ_B, θ_C, θ_D) to compute the four corresponding hydraulic radii (R_A, R_B, R_C, R_D)

<u>Answer:</u> $\boxed{A}$

Water Resources Practice Problems

Open Channel Flow #4

Find: n_2 ←roughness coefficient 2

Given:

$n_1 = 0.0293$ ←roughness coefficient 1

$n_c = 0.0318$ ← composite roughness coefficient

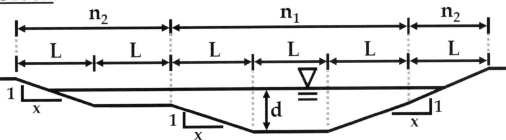

$L = 15\,[\text{ft}]$ ← constant length across the channel

$x = 2$ ← side slope

$d = 11.4\,[\text{ft}]$ ← water depth

A) 0.0277

B) 0.0334

C) 0.0354

D) 0.0383

Analysis:

$$n_c = \left(\frac{\sum P_i * (n_i)^{3/2}}{\sum P_i} \right)^{2/3} \leftarrow eq.1$$

wetted perimeter

Eq. 1 computes the composite roughness coefficient.

Figure 1 identifies the wetted perimeters P_1 through P_6, and the associated roughness coefficients.

In figure 1, notice the lengths P_1 and P_6 only include the length of the slope beneath the water surface.

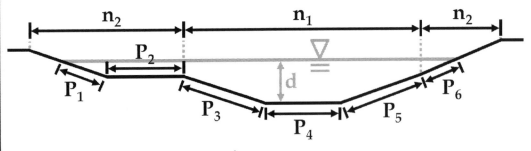

Figure 1

Write out the summations in eq. 1, then solve for n_2.

$$n_c = \left(\frac{\begin{array}{c} P_1 * (n_2)^{3/2} + P_2 * (n_2)^{3/2} + P_3 * (n_1)^{3/2} \\ + P_4 * (n_1)^{3/2} + P_5 * (n_1)^{3/2} + P_6 * (n_2)^{3/2} \end{array}}{P_1 + P_2 + P_3 + P_4 + P_5 + P_6} \right)^{2/3} \leftarrow eq.2$$

Open Channel Flow #4 (cont.)

$$n_2 = \left(\frac{(n_c)^{3/2} * (P_1 + P_2 + P_3 + P_4 + P_5 + P_6) - (n_1)^{3/2} * (P_3 + P_4 + P_5)}{P_1 + P_2 + P_6} \right)^{2/3} \leftarrow eq.\,3$$

Figure 2 shows the perimeter lengths P_1, P_2 and P_3.

To solve eq.3 for n_2, first compute the length of each perimeter value.

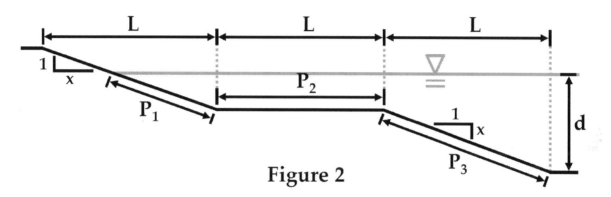

Figure 2

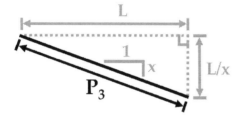

Figure 3

Figure 3 shows a right triangle which identifies the variables used to compute the length P_3, in eq.4.

$$P_3 = \sqrt{L^2 + (L/x)^2} \leftarrow eq.\,4$$

with $L = 15\,[\text{ft}]$ and $x = 2$

Plug in variables L and x into eq.4, then solve for length P_3.

$$P_3 = \sqrt{(15\,[\text{ft}])^2 + (15\,[\text{ft}]/2)^2}$$

$$P_3 = 16.77\,[\text{ft}]$$

$$P_5 = 16.77\,[\text{ft}]$$

From observation, length P_5 equals length P_3. Therefore, both P_3 and P_5 equal 16.77 feet.

Water Resources Practice Problems

Open Channel Flow #4 (cont.)

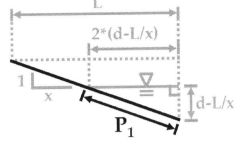

Figure 4

From observation, lengths P_2 and P_4 equal L, which equals 15 feet.

$$P_2 = 15\,[ft]$$
$$P_4 = 15\,[ft]$$

Figure 4 shows a right triangle which identifies the variables used to compute the length P_1, in eq.5.

Plug in variables d, L and x into eq.5, then solve for length P_1.

$$P_1 = \sqrt{(2*(d-L/x))^2 + (d-L/x)^2} \quad \leftarrow eq.5$$

with $L = 15\,[ft]$, $x = 2$, $d = 11.4\,[ft]$

$$P_1 = \sqrt{(2*(11.4\,[ft] - 15\,[ft]/2))^2 + (11.4\,[ft] - 15\,[ft]/2)^2}$$

$$P_1 = 8.72\,[ft]$$

$$P_6 = 8.72\,[ft]$$

From observation, length P_6 equals length P_1. Therefore, both P_1 and P_6 equal 8.72 feet.

Plug in variables n_c, n_1, P_1, P_2, P_3, P_4, P_5 and P_6 into eq.3, then solve for n_2.

$$n_2 = \left(\frac{(n_c)^{3/2}*(P_1+P_2+P_3+P_4+P_5+P_6) - (n_1)^{3/2}*(P_3+P_4+P_5)}{P_1+P_2+P_6} \right)^{2/3} \leftarrow eq.3$$

with $P_2 = P_4 = 15\,[ft]$, $n_c = 0.0318$, $P_1 = P_6 = 8.72\,[ft]$, $n_1 = 0.0293$, $P_3 = P_5 = 16.77\,[ft]$

$$n_2 = \left(\frac{\begin{array}{c}(0.0318)^{3/2}*(8.72\,[ft]+15\,[ft]+16.77\,[ft]+15\,[ft]+16.77\,[ft]+8.72\,[ft]) \\ -(0.0293)^{3/2}*(16.77\,[ft]+15\,[ft]+16.77\,[ft])\end{array}}{8.72\,[ft]+15\,[ft]+8.72\,[ft]} \right)^{2/3}$$

$$n_2 = 0.0354 \qquad \text{Answer:} \quad \boxed{C}$$

Open Channel Flow #5

<u>Find:</u> S ← the channel slope

<u>Given:</u>

d = 5 [ft] ← water depth

b = 8 [ft] ← base width

Q = 2,312 [ft³/s] ← flow rate

n = 0.013 ← roughness coefficient

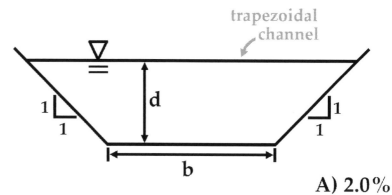

trapezoidal channel

the channel side slopes are 1:1

A) 2.0%
B) 2.3%
C) 2.6%
D) 2.9%

Analysis:

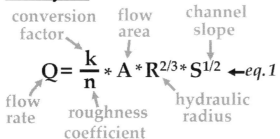

conversion factor
flow area
channel slope

$$Q = \frac{k}{n} * A * R^{2/3} * S^{1/2} \leftarrow eq.1$$

flow rate
roughness coefficient
hydraulic radius

Eq. 1 computes the flow rate using Manning's equation.

$$S = \left(\frac{Q*n}{k*A*R^{2/3}} \right)^2 \leftarrow eq.2$$

Solve Eq. 1 for the channel slope.

$$R = A/P \leftarrow eq.3$$

wetted perimeter

The hydraulic radius, R, equals the cross-sectional area of the channel divided by the wetted perimeter.

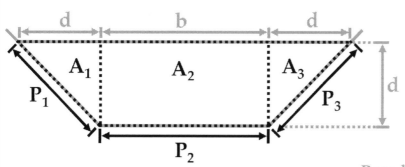

Figure 1

Figure 1 divides the cross-section of the channel into 3 separate areas, and 3 perimeters.

Based on a 1:1 side slope, the slope width equals the water depth.

Water Resources Practice Problems

Open Channel Flow #5 (cont.)

$$A = A_1 + A_2 + A_3 \leftarrow eq.4$$

Eq.4 computes the total area of the channel, the sum of the three individual areas.

$$A_1 = A_3 = 0.5 * d^2 \leftarrow eq.5$$
$$\uparrow$$
$$d = 5 [ft]$$

From Figure 1, the area A_1 equals area A_3, which equals half the depth of the water, squared.

$$A_1 = A_3 = 0.5 * (5 [ft])^2$$

Substitute in the depth, d, into eq.5, then solve for A_1 and A_3.

$$A_1 = A_3 = 12.5 [ft^2]$$

$$A_2 = b * d \leftarrow eq.6$$
$$b = 8 [ft] \qquad d = 5 [ft]$$

Substitute in variables b and d into eq.6, then solve for A_2.

$$A_2 = 8 [ft] * 5 [ft]$$

$$A_2 = 40 [ft^2]$$

$$A_2 = 40 [ft^2]$$
$$\downarrow$$
$$A = A_1 + A_2 + A_3 \leftarrow eq.4$$
$$A_1 = A_3 = 12.5 [ft^2]$$

Plug in the values for A_1, A_2, and A_3, then solve eq.4, for the area.

$$A = 12.5 [ft^2] + 40 [ft^2] + 12.5 [ft^2]$$

$$A = 65 [ft^2]$$

$$P = P_1 + P_2 + P_3 \leftarrow eq.7$$

Eq.7 computes the total wetted perimeter as the sum of the three individual perimeters.

$$P_2 = b = 8 [ft]$$

From Figure 2, it is clear $P_2 = b$.

Open Channel Flow #5 (cont.)

$P=P_1+P_2+P_3 \leftarrow eq.7$

into eq.7, then solve for P.

$P_1=P_3=7.07\,[\text{ft}^2]$

$P=7.07\,[\text{ft}]+8\,[\text{ft}]+7.07\,[\text{ft}]$

$P=22.14\,[\text{ft}]$

$P=22.14\,[\text{ft}]$

$R=A/P \leftarrow eq.3$

Plug in variables A and P into eq.3, then solve for R.

$A=65\,[\text{ft}^2]$

$R=65\,[\text{ft}^2]/22.14\,[\text{ft}]$

$R=2.936\,[\text{ft}]$

$Q=2{,}312\,[\text{ft}^3/\text{s}] \qquad n=0.013$

$S=\left(\dfrac{Q*n}{k*A*R^{2/3}}\right)^2 \leftarrow eq.2$

Plug in the know variables into eq.2, then solve for the channel slope, S.

$k=1.49\,[\text{ft}^{1/3}/\text{s}] \qquad A=65\,[\text{ft}^2] \qquad R=2.936\,[\text{ft}]$

Open Channel Flow #5 (cont.)

$$S = \left(\frac{2{,}312\,[\text{ft}^3/\text{s}] * 0.013}{1.49\,[\text{ft}^{1/3}/\text{s}] * 65\,[\text{ft}^2] * (2.936\,[\text{ft}])^{2/3}} \right)^2$$

$S = 0.0229 * 100\%$ Multiply the channel slope by 100% to convert the slope to a percent.

↑
channel slope
as a decimal

$S = 2.29\%$

Answer: B

Open Channel Flow #6

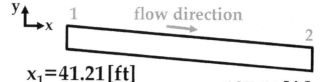

Find: d ← the normal depth of flow

Given:

$n=0.015$ ← roughness coefficient

$x_1=41.21\,[ft]$
$y_1=88.02\,[ft]$

$x_2=195.11\,[ft]$
$y_2=87.84\,[ft]$

$v=3.92\,[ft/s]$ ← velocity of water in the channel

side view of the channel

cross-section of the channel

∇
d

b

$b=6.5\,[ft]$ ← the base width of the channel

A) $0.5\,[ft]$
B) $1.0\,[ft]$
C) $1.5\,[ft]$
D) $2.0\,[ft]$

Analysis:

conversion factor

channel slope

$$V=\frac{k}{n}*R^{2/3}*S^{1/2} \leftarrow eq.1$$

roughness coefficient

hydraulic radius

Eq.1 computes the velocity of the open channel flow.

$A=b*d$

$$R=\frac{A}{P} \leftarrow eq.2$$

$P=b+2*d$

Eq.2 computes the hydraulic radius of an open channel.

$$R=\frac{b*d}{b+2*d}$$

Plug in variables A and P into eq.2, then revise the equation for the hydraulic radius.

$$R=\frac{b*d}{b+2*d}$$

$$V=\frac{k}{n}*R^{2/3}*S^{1/2} \leftarrow eq.1$$

Plug in the hydraulic radius into eq.1, then isolate the hydraulic radius term.

$$V=\frac{k}{n}*\left(\frac{b*d}{b+2*d}\right)^{2/3}*S^{1/2}$$

Water Resources Practice Problems

Open Channel Flow #6 (cont.)

$$\left(\frac{b*d}{b+2*d}\right)^{2/3} = \frac{V*n}{k*S^{1/2}} \leftarrow eq.3$$

LHS   RHS

Eq. 3 identifies LHS and RHS as the left and right hand side of the equation.

$y_2 = 87.84\,[ft]$ $y_1 = 88.02\,[ft]$

$$S = -\frac{y_2 - y_1}{x_2 - x_1} \leftarrow eq.4$$

$x_2 = 195.11\,[ft]$ $x_1 = 41.21\,[ft]$

Eq. 4 computes the slope of the channel. Plug in variables x_1, x_2, y_1 and y_2 into eq. 4, then solve for S

$$S = -\frac{87.84\,[ft] - 88.02\,[ft]}{195.11\,[ft] - 41.21\,[ft]}$$

$$S = -0.001170$$

$v = 3.92\,[ft/s]$

$b = 6.5\,[ft]$ $n = 0.015$

$$\left(\frac{b*d}{b+2*d}\right)^{2/3} = \frac{V*n}{k*S^{1/2}} \leftarrow eq.5$$

$k = 1.49\,[ft^{1/3}/s]$ $S = 0.001170$

Plug in variables b, V, n, k and S, into eq. 3, then solve for d.

$$\left(\frac{6.5\,[ft]*d}{6.5\,[ft]+2*d}\right)^{2/3} = \frac{3.92\,[ft/s]*0.015}{1.49\,[ft^{1/3}/s]*(0.001170)^{1/2}}$$

$$\left(\frac{6.5\,[ft]*d}{6.5\,[ft]+2*d}\right)^{2/3} = 1.1537\,[ft^{2/3}]$$

$$d = 2.00\,[ft]$$

Answer: D

Open Channel Flow #7

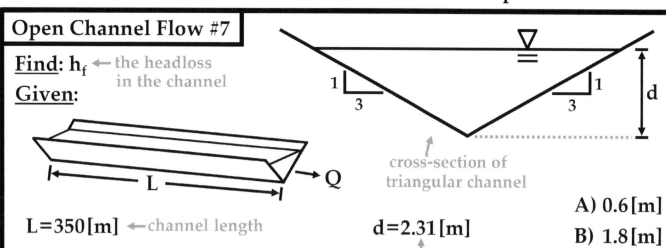

<u>Find:</u> h_f ← the headloss in the channel

<u>Given:</u>

L=350 [m] ← channel length

Q=120.4 [m³/s] ← flow rate

n=0.015 ← roughness coefficient

cross-section of triangular channel

d=2.31 [m] ← water depth

A) 0.6 [m]

B) 1.8 [m]

C) 3.9 [m]

D) 7.4 [m]

Analysis:

$$h_f = L * S \leftarrow eq.1$$

channel length   channel slope

Eq.1 computes the headloss in the open channel.

$$Q = \frac{k}{n} * A * R^{2/3} * S^{1/2} \leftarrow eq.2$$

flow rate   channel slope

Eq.2 computes the flow rate in the channel. Solve eq.2 for the slope.

$$S = \left(\frac{Q*n}{k*A*R^{2/3}} \right)^2 \leftarrow eq.3$$

$$R = \overline{A/P}$$

Substitute in the flow area divided by the wetted perimeter in for the hydraulic radius in eq.3.

$$S = \left(\frac{Q*n*P^{2/3}}{k*A^{5/3}} \right)^2 \leftarrow eq.4$$

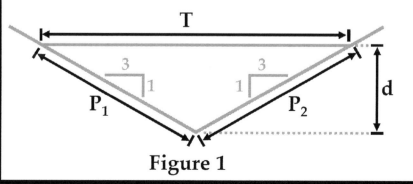

Figure 1

Figure 1 identifies the dimensions needed to compute the area, A, and the wetted perimeter, P.

Water Resources Practice Problems

Open Channel Flow #7 (cont.)

$$A = 0.5 * T * d \leftarrow eq.5$$
$$T = 6 * d$$

Eq.5 computes the are of the cross section as half the depth times the top width.

$$A = 0.5 * (6 * d) * d$$

Based on the side slopes, the top width equals 6 times the depth.

$$A = 3 * d^2 \leftarrow eq.6$$
$$d = 2.31 \, [m]$$

Plug in variable d into eq.6, then solve for A.

$$A = 3 * (2.31 \, [m])^2$$

$$A = 16.01 \, [m^2]$$

$$P = P_1 + P_2 \leftarrow eq.7$$

Eq.7 computes the wetted perimeter of both sides of the channel.

$$P_1 = P_2 = \sqrt{d^2 + (T/2)^2} \leftarrow eq.8$$
$$T = 6 * d$$

Eq.8 computes the wetted perimeter of each side of the channel

$$P_1 = P_2 = \sqrt{d^2 + (3 * d)^2} \leftarrow eq.9$$
$$d = 2.31 \, [m]$$

Plug in variables T and d into eq.9, then solve for P_1 and P_2.

$$P_1 = P_2 = \sqrt{(2.31 \, [m])^2 + (3 * (2.31 \, [m]))^2}$$

$$P_1 = P_2 = 7.305 \, [m]$$

$$P_1 = P_2 = 7.305 \, [m]$$
$$P = P_1 + P_2 \leftarrow eq.7$$

Plug in P_1 and P_2 into eq.7, then solve for P.

$$P = 7.305 \, [m] + 7.305 \, [m]$$

Open Channel Flow #7 (cont.)

$$P = 14.61 \, [m]$$

n = 0.015

Q = 120.4 [m³/s]   P = 14.61 [m]

$$S = \left(\frac{Q * n * P^{2/3}}{k * A^{5/3}} \right)^2 \leftarrow eq.4$$

k = 1.00 [m^{1/3}/s]   A = 16.01 [m²]

Plug in Q, n, P, k and A into eq. 4, then solve for the slope, S.

$$S = \left(\frac{120.4 \, [m^3/s] * 0.015 * (14.61 \, [m])^{2/3}}{1.00 \, [m^{1/3}/s] * (16.01 \, [m^2])^{5/3}} \right)^2$$

$$S = 0.01126$$

S = 0.01126

$$h_f = L * S \leftarrow eq.1$$

L = 350 [m]

Plug in variables L and S into eq. 1, then solve for h_f.

$$h_f = 350 \, [m] * 0.01126$$

$$h_f = 3.94 \, [m]$$

Answer: $\boxed{C}$

Water Resources Practice Problems

Open Channel Flow #8

<u>Find:</u> d_c ← critical depth

<u>Given:</u>

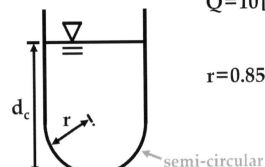

$Q=10\,[m^3/s]$ ← flow rate

$r=0.85\,[m]$ ← radius of the channel bottom

semi-circular channel bottom

A) $1.28\,[m]$

B) $1.70\,[m]$

C) $2.40\,[m]$

D) $3.40\,[m]$

Analysis:

$V=Q/A$

$$\frac{V^2}{g} = \frac{A}{T} \quad \leftarrow eq.1$$

← area ← top width

Eq. 1 holds true during critical flow conditions.

$$\frac{Q^2}{g*A^2} = \frac{A}{T} \quad \leftarrow eq.2$$

Substitute in Q and A, in for the velocity, in eq. 1.

Solve eq. 2 for A.

$$A = \left(\frac{Q^2*T}{g}\right)^{1/3} \quad \leftarrow eq.3$$

$$A = A_1 + A_2 \quad \leftarrow eq.4$$

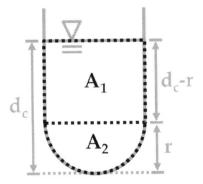

Figure 1

Figure 1 identifies the radius, critical depth and areas A_1 and A_2.

All possible solutions for d_c are greater than the radius of 0.85 meters. Therefore, the flow area, A, will include a rectangular area, A_1, plus the semicircular area, A_2.

Open Channel Flow #8 (cont.)

$$A_1 = (d_c - r) * (2 * r) \leftarrow eq.5$$

r = 0.85 [m]

Eq. 5 computes the area of the rectangle, A_1

$$A_1 = (d_c - 0.85 [m]) * (2 * 0.85 [m])$$

Plug in variable r into eq. 5, then simplify.

$$A_1 = 1.7 [m] * d_c - 1.445 [m^2]$$

$$A_2 = 0.5 * \pi * r^2 \leftarrow eq.6$$

r = 0.85 [m]

Eq. 6 computes the area of the semi-circle, A_2.

$$A_2 = 0.5 * \pi * (0.85 [m])^2$$

Plug in variable r into eq. 6, then solve for A_2.

$$A_2 = 1.1349 [m^2]$$

$A_2 = 1.1349 [m^2]$

$$A = A_1 + A_2 \leftarrow eq.4$$

$A_1 = 1.7 [m] * d_c - 1.445 [m^2]$

Plug in variables A_1 and A_2 into eq. 4, then solve for the area, A.

$$A = 1.7 [m] * d_c - 1.445 [m^2] + 1.1349 [m^2]$$

$$A = 1.7 [m] * d_c - 0.3101 [m^2]$$

$$A = \left(\frac{Q^2 * T}{g} \right)^{1/3} \leftarrow eq.3$$

$A = 1.7 [m] * d_c - 0.3101 [m^2]$

Plug in the area A, into eq. 3, then solve for the critical depth, d_c.

$$1.7 [m] * d_c - 0.3101 [m^2] = \left(\frac{Q^2 * T}{g} \right)^{1/3}$$

Water Resources Practice Problems

Open Channel Flow #8 (cont.)

$$d_c = \frac{\left(\dfrac{Q^2 * T}{g}\right)^{1/3} + 0.3101\,[m^2]}{1.7\,[m]} \quad \leftarrow eq.7$$

$$T = 2 * r \quad \leftarrow eq.8$$

r=0.85 [m]

$$T = 2 * 0.85\,[m]$$

$$T = 1.70\,[m]$$

Eq.8 computes the top width of the channel.

Plug in variable r into eq.8, then solve for T.

Q=10 [m³/s]   T=1.70 [m]

$$d_c = \frac{\left(\dfrac{Q^2 * T}{g}\right)^{1/3} + 0.3101\,[m^2]}{1.7\,[m]} \quad \leftarrow eq.7$$

g=9.81 [m/s²]

Plug in variables Q, T and g into eq.7, then solve for the critical depth, d_c.

$$d_c = \frac{\left(\dfrac{(10\,[m^3/s])^2 * 1.70\,[m]}{9.81\,[m/s^2]}\right)^{1/3} + 0.3101\,[m^2]}{1.7\,[m]}$$

$$d_c = 1.705\,[m]$$

Answer: $\boxed{B}$

Open Channel Flow #9

Find: b ← the base width of the rectangular channel

Given:

d=2.5 [ft] ← normal depth

Q=80 [ft³/s] ← flow rate

E=3.026 [ft] ← total energy of the channel flow (expressed as total head)

y   d

b

A) 4.5 [ft]
B) 5.5 [ft]
C) 6.5 [ft]
D) 7.5 [ft]

vertical datum

Analysis:

$$E = d + \frac{v^2}{2*g} \leftarrow eq.1$$

total energy, elevation head, velocity head

Eq.1 computes the total energy of the channel flow.

$$v = Q/A \leftarrow eq.2$$

flow rate   area of flow

Eq.2 computes the channel velocity.

$$A = b*d \leftarrow eq.3$$

base width   depth of flow in the channel

Eq.3 computes the cross-sectional area of the channel.

$$v = Q/A \leftarrow eq.2$$

$A = b*d$

Substitute in the area term into eq.2.

$$v = Q/(b*d) \leftarrow eq.4$$

$v = Q/(b*d)$

$$E = d + \frac{v^2}{2*g} \leftarrow eq.1$$

Plug in variable v into eq.1.

Water Resources Practice Problems

Open Channel Flow #9 (cont.)

$$E = d + \frac{(Q/(b*d))^2}{2*g} \quad \leftarrow eq.5$$

Solve eq. 5 for b.

$$b = \sqrt{\frac{Q^2}{(E-d)*2*d^2*g}} \quad \leftarrow eq.6$$

Q=80 [ft³/s]

E=3.026 [ft]   d=2.5 [ft]   g=32.2 [ft/s²]

Plug in variables Q, E, d and g into eq. 6, then solve for b.

$$b = \sqrt{\frac{80\,[ft^3/s]}{(3.026\,[ft]-2.5\,[ft])*2*(2.5\,[ft])^2*32.2\,[ft/s^2]}}$$

$$b = 5.50\,[ft]$$

Answer: $\boxed{B}$

Open Channel Flow #10

<u>Find</u>: n ← the roughness coefficient

<u>Given</u>:

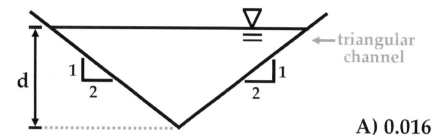

$F_r = 0.903$

← Froude number

← triangular channel

A) 0.016

$d = 1.45 \, [m]$ ← water depth

B) 0.018

$S = 0.005$ ← channel slope

C) 0.020

D) 0.022

<u>Analysis</u>:

conversion factor

channel slope

$$v = \frac{k}{n} * R^{2/3} * S^{1/2} \leftarrow eq.\,1$$

roughness coefficient

hydraulic radius

Eq. 1 is Manning's equation, used to compute the velocity of flow in an open channel.

Solve eq. 1 for the roughness coefficient, n.

$$n = \frac{k}{v} * R^{2/3} * S^{1/2} \leftarrow eq.\,2$$

area

$$R = \frac{A}{P} \leftarrow eq.\,3$$

wetted perimeter

Eq. 3 computes the hydraulic radius.

Figure 1 shows the area and wetted perimeter of the channel.

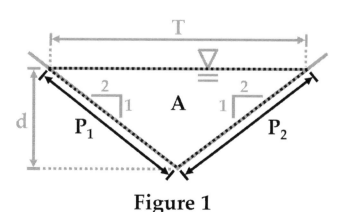

In Figure 1, variable T represents the top width of the free surface of the water in the channel.

Figure 1

Water Resources Practice Problems

Open Channel Flow #10 (cont.)

$$A = 0.5 * d * T \leftarrow eq.4$$

water depth ↗ ↖ top width

Eq.4 computes the area of flow of the triangular channel.

$$T = 4 * d \leftarrow eq.5$$

$d = 1.45 \, [m]$

Eq.5 computes the top width based on 2:1 side slopes.

Plug in variable d into eq.5, then solve for T.

$$T = 4 * 1.45$$

$$T = 5.8$$

$T = 4 * d$

$$A = 0.5 * d * T \leftarrow eq.4$$

Plug in variable T into eq.4, then simplify.

$$A = 0.5 * d * (4 * d)$$

$$A = 2 * d^2 \leftarrow eq.6$$

$d = 1.45 \, [m]$

Plug in variable d into eq.6, then solve for the flow area, A.

$$A = 2 * (1.45 \, [m])^2$$

$$A = 4.205 \, [m^2]$$

$$P = P_1 + P_2 \leftarrow eq.7$$

$P_2 = P_1$

Eq.7 computes the wetted perimeter.

$$P = P_1 + P_1 \leftarrow eq.8$$

Since the side slopes of the channel are equal, then P_1 equals P_2.

Open Channel Flow #10 (cont.)

$$P_1 = \sqrt{d^2 + (2*d)^2} \leftarrow eq.9$$

$$d = 1.45\,[m]$$

Eq. 9 computes the submerged length of one side of the channel.

$$P_1 = \sqrt{(1.45\,[m])^2 + (2*(1.45\,[m]))^2}$$

Plug in variable d into eq. 9, then solve for P_1.

$$P_1 = 3.242\,[m]$$

$$P_1 = 3.242\,[m]$$

$$P = P_1 + P_1 \leftarrow eq.8$$

Plug in variable P_1 into eq. 8, then solve for the wetted perimeter, P.

$$P = 3.242\,[m] + 3.242\,[m]$$

$$P = 6.484\,[m]$$

$$A = 4.205\,[m^2]$$

$$R = \frac{A}{P} \leftarrow eq.3$$

$$P = 6.484\,[m]$$

Plug in variables A and P into eq. 3, then solve for the hydraulic radius, R.

$$R = \frac{4.205\,[m^2]}{6.484\,[m]}$$

$$R = 0.648\,[m]$$

Eq. 10 computes the Froude number.

$$F_r = v * \sqrt{\frac{T}{A*g}} \leftarrow eq.10$$

Solve eq. 10 for the channel velocity, v.

Water Resources Practice Problems

Open Channel Flow #10 (cont.)

$$v = F_r * \sqrt{\dfrac{A*g}{T}} \leftarrow eq.11$$

A=4.205 [m²]   g=9.81 [m/s²]

F_r=0.903   T=5.8 [m]

Plug in variables F_r, A, g, and T into eq.11, then compute v.

$$v = 0.903 * \sqrt{\dfrac{4.205\,[m^2] * 9.81\,[m/s^2]}{5.8\,[m]}}$$

$$v = 2.408\,[m/s]$$

k=1.00   R=0.648 [m]

$$n = \dfrac{k}{v} * R^{2/3} * S^{1/2} \leftarrow eq.2$$

v=2.408 [m/s]   S=0.005

Plug in variables k, v, R and S, then solve for the roughness coefficient, n.

$$n = \dfrac{1.00\,[m^{1/3}/s]}{2.408\,[m/s]} * (0.648\,[m])^{2/3} * (0.005)^{1/2}$$

$$n = 0.022$$

Answer: $\boxed{D}$

Open Channel Flow #11

<u>Find:</u> ΔE ← the change in energy across the hydraulic jump

<u>Given:</u>

$Q = 150\,[\text{ft}^3/\text{s}]$ ← flow rate

$b = 6\,[\text{ft}]$ ← channel width

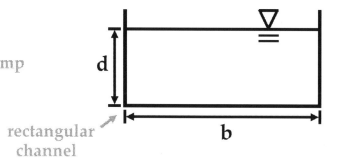

rectangular channel

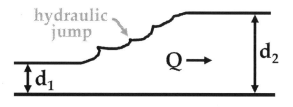

hydraulic jump

$Q \rightarrow$

d_1 d_2

$d_1 = 1.1\,[\text{ft}]$

water depth before the hydraulic jump

A) -1.84 [ft]

B) -3.37 [ft]

C) -5.75 [ft]

D) -9.12 [ft]

Analysis:

$$\Delta E = E_2 - E_1 \leftarrow eq.1$$

energy after the jump   energy before the jump

Eq.1 computes the change in energy across the hydraulic jump.

$$\Delta E = \left(d_2 + \frac{v_2^2}{2*g}\right) - \left(d_1 + \frac{v_1^2}{2*g}\right) \leftarrow eq.2$$

Eq.2 writes out the energy terms found in eq.1.

$$v_1 = Q/A_1 \leftarrow eq.3$$

$A_1 = b*d_1$

Eq.3 calculates velocity v_1 based on the flow rate and area of flow before the jump.

$b = 6\,[\text{ft}]$

$$v_1 = Q/(b*d_1) \leftarrow eq.4$$

$Q = 150\,[\text{ft}^3/\text{s}]$ $d_1 = 1.1\,[\text{ft}]$

Plug in variables Q, b and d_1 into eq.4, then solve for v_1.

$$v_1 = \frac{150\,[\text{ft}^3/\text{s}]}{6\,[\text{ft}] * 1.1\,[\text{ft}]}$$

$$v_1 = 22.73\,[\text{ft/s}]$$

Water Resources Practice Problems

Open Channel Flow #11 (cont.)

$v_1 = 22.73\,[ft/s]$ $d_1 = 1.1\,[ft]$

Use eq. 5 to compute the water depth after the hydraulic jump.

$$d_2 = -0.5 * d_1 + \sqrt{\frac{2 * v_1^2 * d_1}{g} + \frac{d_1^2}{4}} \leftarrow eq.\,5$$

$d_1 = 1.1\,[ft]$ $g = 32.2\,[ft/s^2]$

Plug in the variables d_1 and v_1 into eq. 5, then solve for the depth d_2.

$$d_2 = -0.5 * 1.1\,[ft] + \sqrt{\frac{2 * (22.73\,[ft/s])^2 * 1.1\,[ft]}{32.2\,[ft/s^2]} + \frac{(1.1\,[ft])^2}{4}}$$

$$d_2 = 5.42\,[ft]$$

Eq. 6 calculates velocity v_2 based on the flow rate and area of flow after the jump.

$$v_2 = Q / A_2 \leftarrow eq.\,6$$

$$A_2 = b * d_2$$

$b = 6\,[ft]$

Plug in variables Q, b and d_2 into eq. 4, then solve for v_2.

$$v_2 = Q / (b * d_2) \leftarrow eq.\,4$$

$Q = 150\,[ft^3/s]$ $d_2 = 5.42\,[ft]$

$$v_2 = \frac{150\,[ft^3/s]}{6\,[ft] * 5.42\,[ft]}$$

$$v_2 = 4.61\,[ft/s]$$

$v_2 = 4.61\,[ft/s]$ $d_1 = 1.1\,[ft]$ $v_1 = 22.73\,[ft/s]$

$$\Delta E = \left(d_2 + \frac{v_2^2}{2*g} \right) - \left(d_1 + \frac{v_1^2}{2*g} \right) \leftarrow eq.\,2$$

$d_2 = 5.42\,[ft]$ $g = 32.2\,[ft/s^2]$

Plug in the known variables into eq. 2, then solve ΔE.

Open Channel Flow #11 (cont.)

$$\Delta E = \left(5.42\,[\text{ft}] + \frac{(4.61\,[\text{ft/s}])^2}{2 * 32.2\,[\text{ft/s}^2]}\right) - \left(1.1\,[\text{ft}] + \frac{(22.73\,[\text{ft/s}])^2}{2 * 32.2\,[\text{ft/s}^2]}\right)$$

$$\Delta E = -3.37\,[\text{ft}]$$

Answer: $\boxed{\text{B}}$

Water Resources Practice Problems

Open Channel Flow #12

Find: d_2 ←the water depth at section 2

Given: $b=1.7\,[m]$ ← channel width

total energy is conserved between
section 1 and section 2 in the channel

$d_1=1.21\,[m]$ ← water depth at section 1

$Q=1.55\,[m^3/s]$ ← flow rate

$w_p=0.4\,[m]$ ↑ pier width

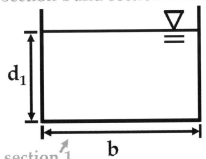

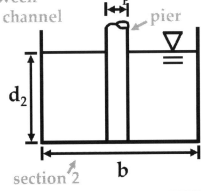

section 1   b

section 2   b

A) 1.15 [m]
B) 1.19 [m]
C) 1.23 [m]
D) 1.26 [m]

Analysis:

$$E_1=E_2 \quad \leftarrow eq.1$$

Eq.1 equate the total energy at section 1 and section 2.

$$d_1+\frac{v_1^2}{2*g}=d_2+\frac{v_2^2}{2*g} \quad \leftarrow eq.2$$

Write out the energy terms from eq.1.

Solve eq.2 for the depth d_2.

$$d_2=d_1+\frac{v_1^2-v_2^2}{2*g} \quad \leftarrow eq.3$$

Eq.4 computes the velocity at section 1, which equals the flow rate divided by the cross-sectional area at section 1.

$$v_1=\frac{Q}{A_1} \quad \leftarrow eq.4$$

$$A_1=b*d_1$$

Plug in the cross-sectional area into eq.4.

$$Q=1.55\,[m^3/s]$$

$$v_1=\frac{Q}{b*d_1} \quad \leftarrow eq.5$$

$$b=1.7\,[m] \quad d_1=1.21\,[m]$$

Plug in variables Q, b and d_1 into eq.5, then solve for velocity v_1.

$$v_1=\frac{1.55\,[m^3/s]}{1.7\,[m]*1.21\,[m]}$$

Open Channel Flow #12 (cont.)

$$v_1 = 0.754 \, [\text{m/s}]$$

$$v_2 = \frac{Q}{A_2} \leftarrow eq.6$$

$$A_2 = b_{eff} * d_1$$

Eq. 6 computes the velocity at section 2, which equals the flow rate divided by the cross-sectional area at section 2.

$$b_{eff} = b - w_p \leftarrow eq.7$$

$$b = 1.7 \, [\text{m}] \qquad w_p = 0.4 \, [\text{m}]$$

Eq. 7 computes the effective base width of the channel at section 2.

$$b_{eff} = 1.7 \, [\text{m}] - 0.4 \, [\text{m}]$$

Plug in variables b and w_p into eq. 7, then solve for b_{eff}.

$$b_{eff} = 1.3 \, [\text{m}]$$

$$Q = 1.55 \, [\text{m}^3/\text{s}]$$

$$v_2 = \frac{Q}{b_{eff} * d_2} \leftarrow eq.8$$

$$b_{eff} = 1.3 \, [\text{m}]$$

Plug in variables Q and b_{eff} into eq. 8, then solve for velocity v_2.

$$v_2 = \frac{1.55 \, [\text{m}^3/\text{s}]}{1.3 \, [\text{m}] * d_2}$$

$$v_2 = 1.1923 \, [\text{m}^2/\text{s}] / d_2$$

$$v_1 = 0.754 \, [\text{m/s}] \qquad v_2 = 1.1923 \, [\text{m}^2/\text{s}] / d_2$$

$$d_2 = d_1 + \frac{v_1{}^2 - v_2{}^2}{2 * g} \leftarrow eq.3$$

$$d_1 = 1.21 \, [\text{m}] \qquad g = 9.81 \, [\text{m/s}^2]$$

Plug in variables d_1, v_1, v_2 and g into eq. 3, then simplify.

$$d_2 = 1.21 \, [\text{m}] + \frac{(0.754 \, [\text{m/s}])^2 - (1.1923 \, [\text{m}^2/\text{s}] / d_2)^2}{2 * 9.81 \, [\text{m/s}^2]}$$

Water Resources Practice Problems

Open Channel Flow #12 (cont.)

$$0 = 19.62 \, [m/s^2] * d_2^3 - 24.31 \, [m^2/s^3] * d_2^2 + 1.422 \, [m^4/s^2] \leftarrow eq. \, 9$$

$d_2 \, [m]$	RHS of eq. 9
A) 1.15 [m] $\longrightarrow$	-0.888 [m⁴/s²]
B) 1.19 [m] $\longrightarrow$	0.059 [m⁴/s²]
C) 1.23 [m] $\longrightarrow$	1.154 [m⁴/s²]
D) 1.26 [m] $\longrightarrow$	2.075 [m⁴/s²]

possible
solutions

Answer: $\boxed{\text{B}}$

Eq. 9 contains only one unknown variable, d_2.

Plug in possible solutions for d_2 into eq. 9. The value of d_2 most nearly correct will cause the right hand side of eq. 9 to be most nearly zero.

Since right hand side of eq. 9 is mostly nearly zero when the depth d_2=1.19 [m], answer B is correct.

Open Channel Flow #13

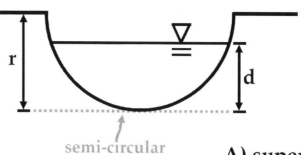

Find: Flow Type

Given:

  $r = 0.79 \, [m]$ ← channel radius

  $d = 0.56 \, [m]$ ← depth of flow

  $S = 1.00\%$ ← channel slope

  $n = 0.013$ ← roughness coefficient

semi-circular channel

A) supercritical

B) subcritical

C) critical

D) not enough information

Analysis:

  if $F_r = 1$ → critical

  if $F_r < 1$ → subcritical

  if $F_r > 1$ → supercritical

Determine the flow type based on the Froude number, F_r.

velocity

top width

$$F_r = v * \sqrt{\frac{T}{A*g}} \leftarrow eq.1$$

Froude number   area   gravitational acceleration

Eq. 1 computes the Froude number.

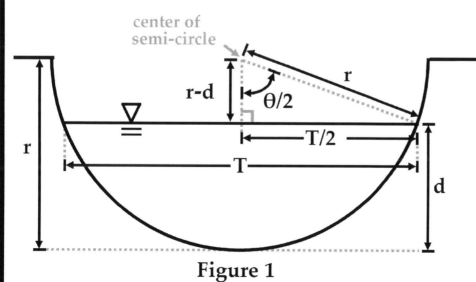

center of semi-circle

$r-d$

$\theta/2$

r

$T/2$

T

r

d

Figure 1 shows the water depth, channel radius and top width of the water.

Figure 1

Water Resources Practice Problems

Open Channel Flow #13 (cont.)

$$T/2 = \sqrt{r^2 - (r-d)^2} \leftarrow eq.2$$

Use right triangle trigonometry and Figure 1 to derive an equation for the top width, T.

Solve eq. 2 for the top width, T.

$$T = 2*\sqrt{r^2 - (r-d)^2} \leftarrow eq.3$$

$r = 0.79\,[m]$ $d = 0.56\,[m]$

Plug in variables r and d into eq. 3, then solve for T.

$$T = 2*\sqrt{(0.79\,[m])^2 - (0.79\,[m]-0.56\,[m])^2}$$

$$T = 1.512\,[m]$$

$$A = 0.5*(\theta - \sin(\theta))*r^2 \leftarrow eq.4$$

angle θ is in radians | channel radius

Eq. 4 computes the flow area.

$$\frac{\theta}{2} = \sin^{-1}\left(\frac{T/2}{r}\right) \leftarrow eq.5$$

Eq. 5 is derived from Figure 1, and calculates angle theta, θ.

Solve eq. 5 for angle theta.

$T = 1.512\,[m]$

$$\theta = 2*\sin^{-1}\left(\frac{T/2}{r}\right) \leftarrow eq.6$$

$r = 0.79\,[m]$

Plug in variables T and r, then solve for θ.

$$\theta = 2*\sin^{-1}\left(\frac{1.512\,[m]/2}{0.79\,[m]}\right)$$

$$\theta = 2.553\,[rad]$$

$\theta = 2.553\,[rad]$ $r = 0.79\,[m]$

$$A = 0.5*(\theta - \sin(\theta))*r^2 \leftarrow eq.4$$

Plug in variables θ and r into eq. 4, then solve for A.

Open Channel Flow #13 (cont.)

$A = 0.5 * (2.553 - \sin(2.553\,[\text{rad}])) * (0.79\,[\text{m}])^2$

$$A = 0.623\,[\text{m}^2]$$

$$v = \frac{k}{n} * R^{2/3} * S^{1/2} \leftarrow eq.\,7$$

velocity — slope — hydraulic radius

Eq. 7 computes the velocity through the channel.

$$k = 1.00\,[\text{m}^{1/3}/\text{s}]$$

In metric units, $k = 1.00\,[\text{m}^{1/3}/\text{s}]$

$$R = 0.5 * \left(1 - \frac{\sin(\theta)}{\theta}\right) * r \leftarrow eq.\,8$$

$r = 0.79\,[\text{m}]$

$\theta = 2.553\,[\text{rad}]$

$$R = 0.5 * \left(1 - \frac{\sin(2.553\,[\text{rad}])}{2.553}\right) * 0.79\,[\text{m}]$$

$$R = 0.3091\,[\text{m}]$$

$k = 1.00\,[\text{m}^{1/3}/\text{s}]$ $S = 0.01$

$$v = \frac{k}{n} * R^{2/3} * S^{1/2} \leftarrow eq.\,7$$

$n = 0.013$ $R = 0.3091\,[\text{m}]$

Plug in variables k, n, R and S into eq. 7, then solve for v.

$$v = \frac{1.00\,[\text{m}^{1/3}/\text{s}]}{0.013} * (0.3091\,[\text{m}])^{2/3} * (0.01)^{1/2}$$

$$v = 3.517\,[\text{m/s}]$$

Water Resources Practice Problems

Open Channel Flow #13 (cont.)

$$F_r = v * \sqrt{\frac{T}{A*g}} \leftarrow eq.1$$

where $v = 3.517\,[\text{m/s}]$, $T = 1.512\,[\text{m}]$, $A = 0.623\,[\text{m}^2]$, $g = 9.81\,[\text{m/s}^2]$

Plug in the known variables into the right hand side of eq.1, then solve for the Froude number.

$$F_r = 3.513\,[\text{m/s}] * \sqrt{\frac{1.512\,[\text{m}]}{0.623\,[\text{m}^2] * 9.81\,[\text{m/s}^2]}}$$

$$F_r = 1.74$$

Since the Froude number is greater than 1, the flow in the channel is supercritical.

~~if $F_r = 1 \rightarrow$ critical~~

~~if $F_r < 1 \rightarrow$ subcritical~~

if $F_r > 1 \rightarrow$ supercritical

Answer: $\boxed{A}$

Open Channel Flow #14

Find: d_c ← the critical depth

Given:

circular pipe

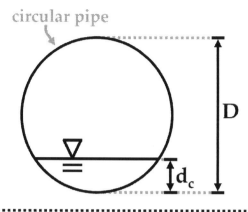

$Q_c = 2.367 * 10^{-4} \ [m^3/s]$

the critical flow rate

$v_c = 0.3163 \ [m/s]$

the critical velocity

$D = 0.078 \ [m]$

the diameter of the pipe

A) 13 [mm]

B) 20 [mm]

C) 26 [mm]

D) 38 [mm]

Analysis:

possible solutions for d_c

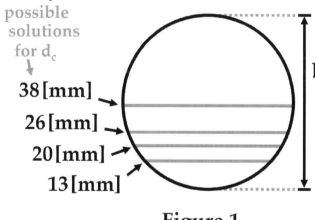

38 [mm]
26 [mm]
20 [mm]
13 [mm]

D = 78 [mm]

Figure 1

Figure 1 shows the four possible solutions for the critical depth, d_c.

Convert the diameter of the pipe from 0.078 meters to 78 millimeters

All 4 possible solutions are less than half the diameter of the pipe.

$$d_c < D/2$$

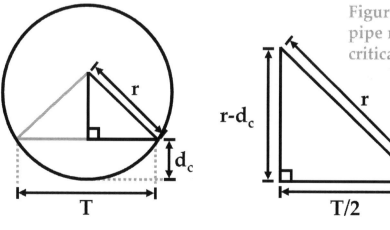

Figure 2   **Figure 3**

Figure 2 shows the top width T, the pipe radius, r, and an arbitrary critical depth d_c.

Figure 3 identifies the side lengths of the right triangle from Figure 2.

Water Resources Practice Problems

critical depth

$$r\text{-}d_c=\sqrt{r^2-(T/2)^2}\ \leftarrow eq.1$$

pipe radius   top width

Eq. 1 relates the the side lengths of the triangle shown in Figure 3.

$$d_c=r-\sqrt{r^2-(T/2)^2}\ \leftarrow eq.2$$

Solve eq. 1 for the critical depth, d_c.

$$r=D/2\ \leftarrow eq.3$$

$D=78\,[mm]$

Plug in variable D into into eq. 3, then solve for r.

$$r=78\,[mm]/2$$

$$r=39\,[mm]$$

velocity   area

$$\frac{v^2}{g}=\frac{A}{T}\ \leftarrow eq.4$$

gravitational acceleration   top width

Use eq. 4 to compute the top width, T. Eq. 4 is valid for critical flow conditions.

$$T=\frac{g*A}{v^2}\ \leftarrow eq.5$$

Solve eq. 4 for the top width, T.

$Q_c=2.367*10^{-4}\,[m^3/s]$

$$A=\frac{Q_c}{v_c}\ \leftarrow eq.6$$

$v_c=0.3163\,[m/s]$

In eq. 5, variables T, A and v refer to the critical top width, area and velocity of the flow.

Eq. 6 computes the flow area.

$$A=\frac{2.367*10^{-4}\,[m^3/s]}{0.3163\,[m/s]}$$

Plug in variables Q_c and v_c into eq. 6, then solve for the area.

$$A=7.486*10^{-4}\,[m^2]$$

Open Channel Flow #14 (cont.)

$$g=9.81\,[\text{m/s}^2] \qquad A=7.486*10^{-4}\,[\text{m}^2]$$

$$T = \frac{g*A}{v^2} \leftarrow eq.5$$

$$v=v_c=0.3163\,[\text{m/s}]$$

Plug in variables g, A and v into eq. 5, then solve for the top width.

$$T = \frac{9.81\,[\text{m/s}^2]*7.486*10^{-4}\,[\text{m}^2]}{(0.3163\,[\text{m/s}])^2}$$

$$T=0.0734\,[\text{m}] * \boxed{\frac{1{,}000\,[\text{mm}]}{1\,[\text{m}]}}$$

Convert the top width from meters to millimeters.

conversion factor

$$T=73.4\,[\text{mm}]$$

$$r=39\,[\text{mm}] \qquad T=73.4\,[\text{mm}]$$

$$d_c=r-\sqrt{r^2-(T/2)^2} \leftarrow eq.2$$

Plug in variables r and T into eq. 2, then solve for d_c.

$$d_c=39\,[\text{mm}]-\sqrt{(39\,[\text{mm}])^2-((73.4\,[\text{mm}])/2)^2}$$

$$d_c=25.8\,[\text{mm}]$$

Answer: $\boxed{C}$

Water Resources Practice Problems

Open Channel Flow #15

<u>Find</u>: E_{min} ← the minimum energy of the channel flow

<u>Given</u>:

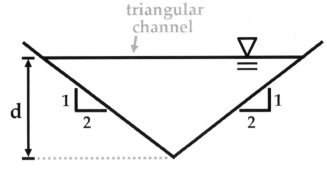

triangular channel

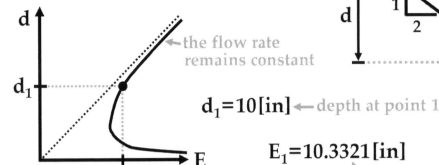

the flow rate remains constant

$d_1 = 10 [in]$ ← depth at point 1

$E_1 = 10.3321 [in]$

energy at point 1

A) 6.68 [in]
B) 7.52 [in]
C) 8.35 [in]
D) 9.19 [in]

Analysis:

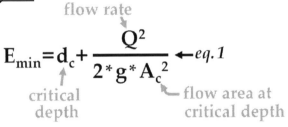

flow rate

$$E_{min} = d_c + \frac{Q^2}{2 * g * A_c^2} \leftarrow eq.1$$

critical depth

flow area at critical depth

Eq. 1 computes the minimum energy of flow in an open channel.

$$E_1 = d_1 + \frac{Q^2}{2 * g * A_1^2} \leftarrow eq.2$$

flow area at depth d_1

Eq. 2 computes the energy E_1 for the given depth of d_1.

Solve eq. 2 for the flow rate Q.

$$Q = \sqrt{(E_1 - d_1) * 2 * g * A_1^2} \leftarrow eq.3$$

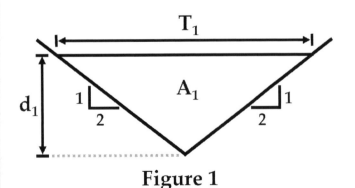

Figure 1

Figure 1 shows a cross-section of the triangular channel, and labels the depth, top width and area corresponding to point 1.

$$A_1 = 0.5 * d_1 * T_1 \leftarrow eq.4$$

Eq. 4 calculates area A_1.

Open Channel Flow #15 (cont.)

$$d_1=10\,[in]$$

$$T_1=4*d_1 \leftarrow eq.5$$

Eq.5 computes the top width of the channel based on a side slope of 2:1.

$$T_1=4*10\,[in]$$

Plug in variable d_1 into eq.5, then solve for T_1.

$$T_1=40\,[in]$$

$$d_1=10\,[in] \qquad T_1=40\,[in]$$

$$A_1=0.5*d_1*T_1 \leftarrow eq.4$$

Plug in variables d_1 and T_1 into eq.4, then solve for A_1.

$$A_1=0.5*10\,[in]*40\,[in]$$

$$A_1=200\,[in^2]$$

$$E_1=10.3321\,[in] \qquad g=386\,[in/s^2]$$

$$Q=\sqrt{(E_1-d_1)*2*g*A_1^2} \leftarrow eq.3$$

$$d_1=10\,[in] \qquad A_1=200\,[in^2]$$

Plug in variables E_1, d_1, g, and A_1, then solve for the flow rate Q.

$$Q=\sqrt{(10.3321\,[in]-10\,[in])*2*386\,[in/s^2]*(200\,[in^2])^2}$$

$$Q=3{,}202\,[in^3/s]$$

$$\frac{Q^2}{g} = \frac{A^3}{T} \leftarrow eq.6$$

Eq.6 relates the flow rate, flow area and top with for critical flow conditions.

$$A=0.5*d*T \leftarrow eq.4$$

$$T=4*d$$

Plug in the equation for the top with into eq.4, then simplify.

Water Resources Practice Problems

$$A = 0.5 * d * (4 * d)$$

$$A = 2 * d^2 \leftarrow eq.7$$

$$Q = 3{,}202 \, [in^3/s] \qquad A = 2 * d_c^2$$

$$\frac{Q^2}{g} = \frac{A^3}{T} \leftarrow eq.8$$

$$g = 386 \, [in/s^2] \qquad T = 4 * d_c$$

Plug in Q, g, A and T into eq.8. Since eq.4 is only valid for the critical flow condition, use the critical depth d_c.

Solve eq.8 for the critical depth d_c.

$$\frac{(3202 \, [in^3/s])^2}{386 \, [in/s^2]} = \frac{(2 * d_c^2)^3}{4 * d_c}$$

The subscript "c" denotes the critical condition. We can also add this subscript "c" to variables Q, A and T, where applicable.

$$d_c = 6.678 \, [in]$$

$$d_c = 6.678 \, [in]$$

$$A_c = 2 * d_c^2 \leftarrow eq.7$$

Plug in the critical depth, then solve for the cross-sectional area, A_c.

$$A_c = 2 * (6.678 \, [in])^2$$

$$A_c = 89.19 \, [in^2]$$

$$Q = 3{,}202 \, [in^3/s]$$

$$d_c = 6.678 \, [in]$$

$$E_{min} = d_c + \frac{Q^2}{2 * g * A_c^2} \leftarrow eq.1$$

$$g = 386 \, [in/s^2] \qquad A_c = 89.19 \, [in^2]$$

Plug in variables d_c, Q, g and A_c into eq.1, then solve for E_{min}.

$$E_{min} = 6.678 \, [in] + \frac{(3{,}202 \, [in^3/s])^2}{2 * 386 \, [in/s] * (89.19 [in^2])^2}$$

$$E_{min} = 8.348 \, [in] \qquad \text{Answer:} \quad \boxed{C}$$

Open Channel Flow #16

<u>Find:</u> Q ← the flow rate

<u>Given:</u>

$F_r=1.00$ ← the Froude number

$b=12\,[ft]$ ← base width

$A=55.7\,[ft^2]$ ← the cross-sectional area
of the water in the channel

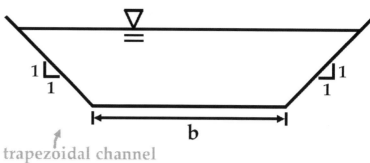

trapezoidal channel
with 1:1 side slope

A) $380\,[ft^3/s]$

B) $425\,[ft^3/s]$

C) $540\,[ft^3/s]$

D) $625\,[ft^3/s]$

<u>Analysis:</u>

$$Q=v*A \leftarrow eq.1$$

Eq.1 computes the flow rate.

velocity   top width

$$F_r=v*\sqrt{\frac{T}{g*A}} \leftarrow eq.2$$

Froude
number   area of channel

gravitational
acceleration

Eq.2 computes the Froude number.

$$v=F_r*\sqrt{\frac{g*A}{T}} \leftarrow eq.3$$

Solve eq.2 for the velocity, v.

$$T=b+2*d \leftarrow eq.4$$

Eq.4 computes the top width of the
water surface, based on a 1:1 side slope.

$$A=0.5*d*(b+T) \leftarrow eq.5$$

Eq.5 computes the cross-sectional
area of the water in the channel.

$$d=2*A/(b+T) \leftarrow eq.6$$

Solve eq.5 for the depth, d.

$$d=2*A/(b+T)$$
$$T=b+2*d \leftarrow eq.4$$

Plug in the equation for depth
into eq.4, then solve for T.

Water Resources Practice Problems

Open Channel Flow #16 (cont.)

$$T=\sqrt{b^2+4*A} \leftarrow eq.7$$

b=12[ft]   A=55.7[ft²]

Plug in variables b and A into eq.7, then solve for T.

$$T=\sqrt{(12[ft])^2+4*55.7[ft^2]}$$

$$T=19.15[ft]$$

g=32.2[ft/s²]   A=55.7[ft²]

$$v=F_r*\sqrt{\frac{g*A}{T}} \leftarrow eq.3$$

F_r=1.00   T=19.15[ft]

Plug in the known values into the right hand side of eq.3, then solve for the velocity.

$$v=1.00*\sqrt{\frac{32.2[ft/s^2]*55.7[ft^2]}{19.15[ft]}}$$

$$v=9.678[ft/s]$$

v=9.678[ft/s]

$$Q=v*A \leftarrow eq.1$$

A=55.7[ft²]

Plug in variables v and A into eq.1, then solve for the flow rate.

$$Q=9.678[ft/s]*55.7[ft^2]$$

$$Q=539.1[ft^3/s]$$

Answer: $\boxed{C}$

Open Channel Flow #17

Find: $L_{1,2}$ ← the length between sections 1 and 2

Given: $Q=93.4\,[ft^3/s]$ ← flow rate

$d_1=2.8\,[ft]$ ← water depth at section 1

$d_2=3.0\,[ft]$ ← water depth at section 2

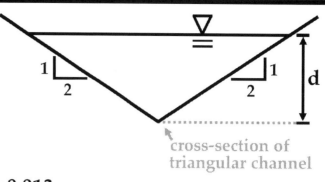

cross-section of triangular channel

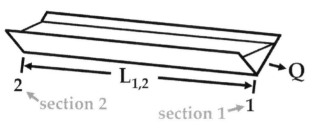

2 ← section 2

section 1 → 1

→ Q

$L_{1,2}$

$n=0.013$
roughness coefficient

$S_o=0.002$
channel bottom slope

A) 200 [ft]

B) 300 [ft]

C) 400 [ft]

D) 500 [ft]

Analysis:

energy at section 1

energy at section 2

$$L_{1,2} \approx \frac{E_1 - E_2}{S_{ave} - S_o} \quad \leftarrow approx.1$$

average slope of EGL between sections 1 and 2

channel slope

Approx. 1 approximates the length between sections 1 and section 2.

velocity at section 1

$$E_1 = d_1 + \frac{v_1^2}{2*g} \quad \leftarrow eq.1$$

Eq. 1 calculates the energy of the flow at section 1.

$$v_1 = Q/A_1 \quad \leftarrow eq.2$$

Eq. 2 calculates the velocity of water at section 1.

$$A_1 = 2*d_1^2 \quad \leftarrow eq.3$$

$d_1=2.8\,[ft]$

Based on a 2:1 side slope, the area of the channel equals 2 times the depth squared.

$$A_1 = 2*(2.8\,[ft])^2$$

Plug in variable d_1 into eq. 3, then solve for A_1.

$$A_1 = 15.68\,[ft^2]$$

Water Resources Practice Problems

Open Channel Flow #17 (cont.)

$Q = 93.4\,[\text{ft}^3/\text{s}]$

$$v_1 = Q/A_1 \leftarrow eq.2$$

$A_1 = 15.68\,[\text{ft}^2]$

Plug in variables Q and A_1 into eq. 2, then solve for v_1.

$$v_1 = 93.4\,[\text{ft}^3/\text{s}]/15.68\,[\text{ft}^2]$$

$$v_1 = 5.957\,[\text{ft/s}]$$

$v_1 = 5.957\,[\text{ft/s}]$

$$E_1 = d_1 + \frac{v_1^2}{2*g} \leftarrow eq.1$$

$d_1 = 2.8\,[\text{ft}]$ $g = 32.2\,[\text{ft/s}^2]$

Plug in variables d_1, v_1 and g into eq. 1, then solve for the energy E_1.

$$E_1 = 2.8\,[\text{ft}] + \frac{(5.957\,[\text{ft/s}])^2}{2*32.2\,[\text{ft/s}^2]}$$

$$E_1 = 3.351\,[\text{ft}]$$

velocity at section 2

$$E_2 = d_2 + \frac{v_2^2}{2*g} \leftarrow eq.4$$

Eq. 4 calculates the energy of the flow at section 2.

$$v_2 = Q/A_2 \leftarrow eq.5$$

Eq. 5 calculates the velocity of water at section 2.

$$A_2 = 2*d_2^2 \leftarrow eq.6$$

$d_2 = 3.0\,[\text{ft}]$

Plug in variable d_2 into eq. 6, then solve for A_2.

$$A_2 = 2*(3.0\,[\text{ft}])^2$$

$$A_2 = 18\,[\text{ft}^2]$$

Open Channel Flow #17 (cont.)

$Q=93.4\,[\text{ft}^3/\text{s}]$

$$v_2 = Q / A_2 \leftarrow eq.5$$

$A_2 = 18\,[\text{ft}^2]$

Plug in variables Q and A_2 into eq.5, then solve for v_2.

$$v_2 = 93.4\,[\text{ft}^3/\text{s}] / 18\,[\text{ft}^2]$$

$$v_2 = 5.189\,[\text{ft}/\text{s}]$$

$v_2 = 5.189\,[\text{ft}/\text{s}]$

$$E_2 = d_2 + \frac{v_2^2}{2*g} \leftarrow eq.4$$

$d_2 = 3.0\,[\text{ft}] \qquad g = 32.2\,[\text{ft}/\text{s}^2]$

Plug in variables d_2, v_2 and g into eq.2, then solve for the energy E_2.

$$E_2 = 3.0\,[\text{ft}] + \frac{(5.189\,[\text{ft}/\text{s}])^2}{2*32.2\,[\text{ft}/\text{s}^2]}$$

$$E_2 = 3.418\,[\text{ft}]$$

$$v_{ave} \approx \frac{k}{n} * R_{ave}^{2/3} * S_{ave}^{1/2} \leftarrow approx.2$$

Approx.2 approximates the average velocity between section 1 and section 2.

$$S_{ave} \approx \left(\frac{v_{ave}*n}{k*R_{ave}^{2/3}} \right)^2 \leftarrow approx.3$$

Solve approx.2 for variable S_{ave}.

$v_2 = 5.189\,[\text{ft}/\text{s}]$

$$v_{ave} \approx 0.5*(v_1 + v_2) \leftarrow approx.4$$

$v_1 = 5.957\,[\text{ft}/\text{s}]$

Plug in velocities v_1 and v_2 into approx.4, then solve for v_{ave}.

$$v_{ave} \approx 0.5*(5.957\,[\text{ft}/\text{s}] + 5.189\,[\text{ft}/\text{s}])$$

$$v_{ave} \approx 5.573 \, [\text{ft/s}]$$

$$R_{ave} \approx 0.5 * (R_1 + R_2) \leftarrow approx.5$$

Approx. 5 approximates the average hydraulic radius between sections 1 and 2.

$$R_1 = A_1 / P_1 \leftarrow eq.7$$

Use eq. 7 to compute the hydraulic radius at section 1.

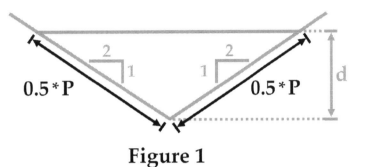

0.5*P   0.5*P   d

Figure 1

Since the side slopes are both 2:1, the submerged length along each side slope equals half the wetted perimeter.

$$P_1 = 2 * \sqrt{d_1^2 + (2 * d_1)^2} \leftarrow eq.8$$

$$d_1 = 2.8 \, [\text{ft}]$$

Eq. 8 computes the wetted perimeter at section 1. Plug in d_1 into eq. 8, then solve for P_1.

$$P_1 = 2 * \sqrt{(2.8 \, [\text{ft}])^2 + (2 * 2.8 \, [\text{ft}])^2}$$

$$P_1 = 12.522 \, [\text{ft}]$$

$$A_1 = 15.68 \, [\text{ft}^2]$$

$$R_1 = A_1 / P_1 \leftarrow eq.7$$

$$P_1 = 12.522 \, [\text{ft}]$$

Plug in variables A_1 and P_1 into eq. 7, then solve for the hydraulic radius at section 1, R_1.

$$R_1 = 15.68 \, [\text{ft}^2] / 12.522 \, [\text{ft}]$$

$$R_1 = 1.252 \, [\text{ft}]$$

Open Channel Flow #17 (cont.)

$$R_2 = A_2/P_2 \leftarrow eq.9$$

Eq. 9 computes the hydraulic radius at section 2.

$$P_2 = 2 * \sqrt{d_2{}^2 + (2*d_2)^2} \leftarrow eq.10$$

$$d_2 = 3.0 \, [ft]$$

Eq. 10 computes the wetted perimeter at section 2. Plug in d_2 into eq. 10, then solve for P_2.

$$P_2 = 2 * \sqrt{(3.0\,[ft])^2 + (2*3.0\,[ft])^2}$$

$$P_2 = 13.416 \, [ft]$$

$$A_2 = 18 \, [ft^2]$$

$$R_2 = A_2/P_2 \leftarrow eq.9$$

$$P_2 = 13.416 \, [ft]$$

Plug in variables A_1 and P_1 in eq. 9, then solve for the hydraulic radius at section 2, R_2.

$$R_2 = 18 \, [ft^2] / 12.522 \, [ft]$$

$$R_2 = 1.342 \, [ft]$$

$$R_2 = 1.342 \, [ft]$$

$$R_{ave} \approx 0.5 * (R_1 + R_2) \leftarrow approx.5$$

$$R_1 = 1.252 \, [ft]$$

Plug in R_1 and R_2 into approx. 5, to approximate the average hydraulic radius between sections 1 and 2.

$$R_{ave} \approx 0.5 * (1.252 \, [ft] + 1.342 \, [ft])$$

$$R_{ave} \approx 1.297 \, [ft]$$

$$v_{ave} \approx 5.573 \, [ft/s] \qquad n = 0.013$$

$$S_{ave} \approx \left(\frac{v_{ave} * n}{k * R_{ave}{}^{2/3}} \right)^2 \leftarrow approx.3$$

$$k = 1.49 \, [ft^{1/3}/s] \qquad R_{ave} \approx 1.297 \, [ft]$$

Plug in variables v_{ave}, n, and R_{ave} into approx. 3, then solve for S_{ave}.

Open Channel Flow #17 (cont.)

$$S_{ave} \approx \left(\frac{5.573\,[ft/s] * 0.013}{1.49\,[ft^{1/3}/s] * (1.297\,[ft])^{2/3}} \right)^2$$

$$S_{ave} \approx 0.001671$$

$E_1 = 3.351\,[ft] \qquad E_2 = 3.418\,[ft]$

$$L_{1,2} \approx \frac{E_1 - E_2}{S_{ave} - S_o} \leftarrow approx.\,1$$

$S_{ave} \approx 0.001671 \qquad S_o = 0.002$

Plug in variables E_1, E_2, S_{ave} and S_o into approx. 1, then solve for $L_{1,2}$.

$$L_{1,2} \approx \frac{3.351\,[ft] - 3.418\,[ft]}{0.001671 - 0.002}$$

$$L_{1,2} \approx 203.6\,[ft]$$

Answer: $\boxed{A}$

Open Channel Flow #18

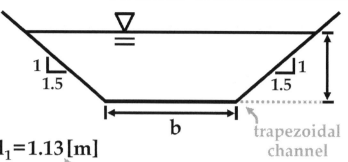

Find: d_2 ← the depth downstream of the hydraulic jump

Given:

$Q=28.4\,[m^3/s]$ ← flow rate

$b=2.1\,[m]$ ← channel width

$d_1=1.13\,[m]$

water depth before the hydraulic jump

$\Delta E=2.49\,[m]$

energy loss across the jump

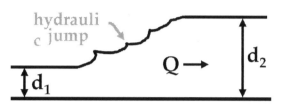

trapezoidal channel

A) 3.31 [m]

B) 4.43 [m]

C) 5.85 [m]

D) 6.67 [m]

Analysis:

$$\Delta E = E_2 - E_1 \leftarrow eq.1$$

Eq. 1 computes the change in energy across the hydraulic jump.

$$\Delta E = \left(d_2+\frac{v_2^2}{2^*g}\right) - \left(d_1+\frac{v_1^2}{2^*g}\right) \leftarrow eq.2$$

Write out the energy terms in eq. 1

$$d_2+\frac{v_2^2}{2^*g} = \Delta E + d_1 + \frac{v_1^2}{2^*g} \leftarrow eq.3$$

Since v_2 is a function of d_2, isolate the terms in eq. 2 containing d_2 and v_2.

$$v_1=\frac{Q}{A_1} \leftarrow eq.4$$

Eq. 4 computes the velocity upstream of the hydraulic jump.

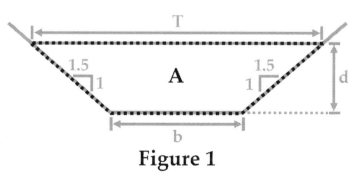

Figure 1

Figure 1 identifies the variables used to compute the area of the channel.

$$A_1=0.5^*d_1^*(b+T_1) \leftarrow eq.5$$

$$T_1 = b + 3^*d_1$$

Plug in the top width of the channel, T, into eq. 5.

Water Resources Practice Problems

Open Channel Flow #18 (cont.)

$$A_1 = 0.5 * d_1 * (b + (b + 3 * d_1))$$

$$b = 2.1 \, [m]$$

$$A_1 = d_1 * b + 1.5 * d_1^2 \leftarrow eq.6$$

$$d_1 = 1.13 \, [m]$$

Plug in variables d_1 and b into eq.6, then solve for the area A_1.

$$A_1 = 1.13 \, [m] * 2.1 \, [m] + 1.5 * (1.13 \, [m])^2$$

$$A_1 = 4.288 \, [m^2]$$

$$Q = 28.4 \, [m^3/s]$$

$$v_1 = \frac{Q}{A_1} \leftarrow eq.4$$

$$A_1 = 4.288 \, [m^2]$$

Substitute in the flow rate and area A_1 into eq.4, then solve for the velocity v_1.

$$v_1 = \frac{28.4 \, [m^3/s]}{4.288 \, [m^2]}$$

$$v_1 = 6.623 \, [m/s]$$

$$v_2 = \frac{Q}{A_2} \leftarrow eq.7$$

$$A_2 = d_2 * b + 1.5 * d_2^2$$

Eq.7 computes the velocity downstream of the hydraulic jump.

Plug in the equation for A_2 into eq.7.

$$v_2 = \frac{Q}{d_2 * b + 1.5 * d_2^2}$$

$$v_2 = \frac{Q}{d_2 * b + 1.5 * d_2^2}$$

Plug in the revised equation for the velocity after the hydraulic jump into eq.3.

$$d_2 + \frac{v_2^2}{2 * g} = \Delta E + d_1 + \frac{v_1^2}{2 * g} \leftarrow eq.3$$

Open Channel Flow #18 (cont.)

Plug in the known values into eq. 3.

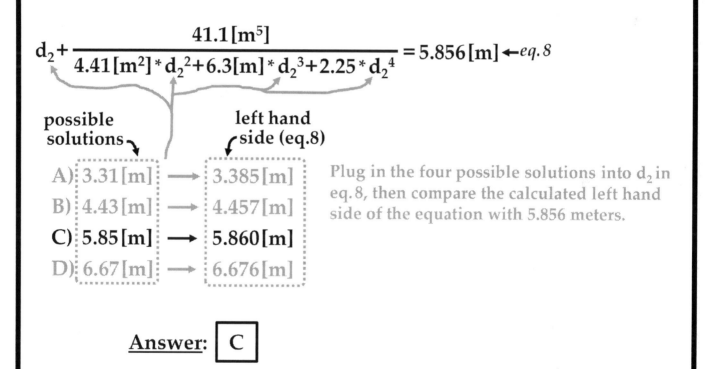

$$Q=28.4\,[m^3/s] \quad d_1=1.13\,[m] \quad v_1=6.623\,[m/s]$$

$$d_2+\frac{1}{2*g}*\left(\frac{Q}{d_2*b+1.5*d_2^2}\right)^2=\Delta E+d_1+\frac{v_1^2}{2*g} \leftarrow eq.\,3$$

$$g=9.81\,[m/s^2] \quad b=2.1\,[m] \quad \Delta E=2.49\,[m] \quad g=9.81\,[m/s^2]$$

$$d_2+\frac{1}{2*9.81\,[m/s^2]}*\left(\frac{28.4\,[m^3/s]}{d_2*2.1[m]+1.5*d_2^2}\right)^2$$

$$=2.49\,[m]+1.13\,[m]+\frac{(6.623\,[m/s])^2}{2*9.81\,[m/s^2]}$$

$$d_2+\frac{41.1\,[m^5]}{4.41\,[m^2]*d_2^2+6.3[m]*d_2^3+2.25*d_2^4}=5.856\,[m]\leftarrow eq.\,8$$

possible solutions

left hand side (eq.8)

A) 3.31 [m] ⟶ 3.385 [m]

B) 4.43 [m] ⟶ 4.457 [m]

C) 5.85 [m] ⟶ 5.860 [m]

D) 6.67 [m] ⟶ 6.676 [m]

Plug in the four possible solutions into d_2 in eq. 8, then compare the calculated left hand side of the equation with 5.856 meters.

Answer: C

Water Resources Practice Problems

Open Channel Flow #19

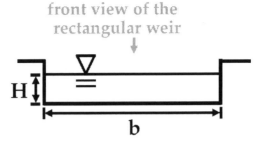

front view of the rectangular weir

Find: Q ← the flow rate

Given: N=2 ← number of contractions

b=1.50 [m] ← actual width of the weir

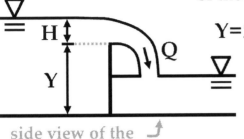

side view of the rectangular weir

Y=2.81 [m] ← height of the weir invert

H=0.15 [m]

height of the water above the weir invert

A) 0.04 [m³/s]

B) 0.15 [m³/s]

C) 0.34 [m³/s]

D) 0.83 [m³/s]

Analysis:

Eq. 1 computes the flow rate through a rectangular weir.

coefficient

gravitational acceleration

$$Q=(2/3)*C_1*b_{eff}*\sqrt{2*g}*H^{3/2} \leftarrow eq.1$$

flow rate

effective weir width

water height above weir invert

H=0.15 [m]

$$C_1 \approx 0.602+0.083*\frac{H}{Y} \leftarrow approx.1$$

Y=2.81 [m]

Approx. 1 approximates the coefficient C_1.

Plug in variables H and Y into approx. 1, then solve for C_1.

$$C_1 \approx 0.602+0.083*\frac{0.15\,[m]}{2.81\,[m]}$$

$$C_1 \approx 0.606$$

N=2

Eq. 2 computes the effective weir width.

$$b_{eff}=b-0.1*N*H \leftarrow eq.2$$

b=1.50 [m]   H=0.15 [m]

Plug in variables b, N and H into eq. 2, then solve for b_{eff}.

$$b_{eff}=1.50\,[m]-0.1*2*0.15\,[m]$$

Open Channel Flow #19 (cont.)

$$b_{eff} = 1.47 \, [m]$$

$C_1 \approx 0.606$ $g = 9.81 \, [m/s^2]$

$$Q = (2/3) * C_1 * b_{eff} * \sqrt{2 * g} * H^{3/2} \leftarrow eq.\,1$$

$b_{eff} = 1.47 \, [m]$ $H = 0.15 \, [m]$

Plug in variables C_1, b_{eff}, g and H into eq. 1, then solve for the flow rate over the weir.

$$Q = (2/3) * 0.606 * 1.47 \, [m] * \sqrt{2 * 9.81 \, [m/s^2]} * (0.15 \, [m])^{3/2}$$

$$Q = 0.1528 \, [m^3/s]$$

Answer: $\boxed{B}$

Water Resources Practice Problems

Open Channel Flow #20

Find: N ← number of contractions

Given:

$b=3.10\,[ft]$ ← actual width of the weir

$H=0.77\,[ft]$

height of the water above the weir invert

$Q=6.9197\,[ft^3/s]$ ← flow rate across the weir

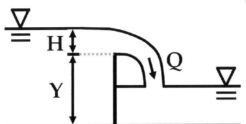

side view of the rectangular weir

$Y=6.50\,[ft]$

height of the weir invert

A) 0

B) 1

C) 2

D) not enough information

Analysis:

actual weir width   contractions

$$b_{eff}=b-0.1*N*H \leftarrow eq.1$$

effective weir width   water height above weir invert

Eq.1 computes the effective width of the rectangular weir.

Solve eq.1 for the number of contractions, N.

$$N=\frac{b-b_{eff}}{0.1*H} \leftarrow eq.2$$

Eq.3 calculates the flow rate as a function of the effective weir width.

$$Q=(2/3)*C_1*b_{eff}*\sqrt{2*g}*H^{3/2} \leftarrow eq.3$$

Solve eq.3 for b_{eff}.

$$b_{eff}=\frac{1.5*Q}{C_1*\sqrt{2*g}*H^{3/2}} \leftarrow eq.4$$

Use eq.5 to solve for the coefficient C_1.

Plug in variables H and Y into eq.5, then solve for C_1.

$H=0.77\,[ft]$

$$C_1=\left(0.6035+0.0813*\frac{H}{Y}+\frac{0.000295\,[ft]}{Y}\right)*\left(1+\frac{0.00361\,[ft]}{H}\right)^{3/2} \leftarrow eq.5$$

$Y=6.50\,[ft]$ $H=0.77\,[ft]$

Open Channel Flow #20 (cont.)

$$C_1 = \left(0.6035 + 0.0813 * \frac{0.77\,[\text{ft}]}{6.50\,[\text{ft}]} + \frac{0.000295\,[\text{ft}]}{6.50\,[\text{ft}]}\right) * \left(1 + \frac{0.00361\,[\text{ft}]}{0.77\,[\text{ft}]}\right)^{3/2}$$

$$C_1 = 0.6175$$

Plug in variables Q, C_1, g and H into eq. 4, then solve for b_{eff}.

$$b_{eff} = \frac{1.5 * Q}{C_1 * \sqrt{2 * g} * H^{3/2}} \leftarrow eq.4$$

Q=6.9197 [ft³/s]

H=0.77 [ft]

C_1=0.6175   g=32.2 [ft/s²]

$$b_{eff} = \frac{1.5 * 6.9197\,[\text{ft}^3/\text{s}]}{0.6175 * \sqrt{2 * 32.2\,[\text{ft/s}^2]} * (0.77\,[\text{ft}])^{3/2}}$$

$$b_{eff} = 3.10\,[\text{ft}]$$

b=3.10 [ft] b_{eff}=3.10 [ft]

$$N = \frac{b - b_{eff}}{0.1 * H} \leftarrow eq.2$$

H=0.77 [ft]

Plug in variables b, b_{eff} and H into eq.2, then solve for the number of contractions in the weir, N.

$$N = \frac{3.10\,[\text{ft}] - 3.10\,[\text{ft}]}{0.1 * 0.77\,[\text{ft}]}$$

$$N = 0$$

Answer: $\boxed{\text{A}}$

Water Resources Practice Problems

Open Channel Flow #21

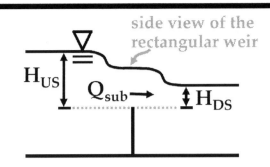

side view of the rectangular weir

Find: H_{DS} ← the height of the water surface above the weir invert, downstream of the weir

Given:

$b=250\,[mm]$ ← actual width of the weir

$N=1$ ← number of contractions

$C=0.61$ ← weir coefficient

$Q_{sub}=0.0192\,[m^3/s]$ ← submerged flow rate

$Q_{free}=0.0227\,[m^3/s]$ ← "free flow" flow rate

front view of the rectangular weir

A) 49 [mm]

B) 71 [mm]

C) 142 [mm]

D) 314 [mm]

Analysis:

downstream water surface elevation above weir invert

$$Q_{sub}= Q_{free} * \left(1-\left(\frac{H_{DS}}{H_{US}}\right)^{3/2}\right)^{0.385} \leftarrow eq.1$$

upstream water surface elevation above weir invert

Eq. 1 computes the submerged flow rate through the weir.

$$H_{DS}=H_{US} * \left(1-\left(\frac{Q_{sub}}{Q_{free}}\right)^{2.597}\right)^{2/3} \leftarrow eq.2$$

Solve eq. 1 for the height of the water surface above the weir invert, downstream of the weir.

$$Q_{free}=(2/3) * C_1 * b_{eff} * \sqrt{2*g} * H_{US}^{3/2} \leftarrow eq.3$$

effective weir width

Eq. 3 calculates Q_{free}.

Solve eq. 3 for H_{US}. Add a subscript "i" to H_{US} and b_{eff}, to denote the ith iteration.

$Q_{free}=0.0227\,[m^3/s]$

$$H_{US,i}=\left(\frac{3*Q_{free}}{2*C_1*b_{eff,i}*\sqrt{2*g}}\right)^{2/3} \leftarrow eq.4$$

$C_1=0.61$

$g=9.81\,[m/s^2]$

$b_{eff,1}=b=0.25\,[m]$

For eq. 4, first assume $b_{eff,1}=b$. Plug in the known variables and solve for $H_{US,1}$.

The variable b_{eff} converts from 250 millimeters to 0.25 meters.

$$H_{US,1}=\left(\frac{3*0.0227\,[m^3/s]}{2*0.61*0.25\,[m]*\sqrt{2*9.81\,[m/s^2]}}\right)^{2/3}$$

Open Channel Flow #21 (cont.)

$$H_{US,1}=0.1365\,[m]$$

$H_{US,1}=0.1365\,[m]$ $Q_{sub}=0.0192\,[m^3/s]$

$$H_{DS,i}=H_{US,i}*\left(1-\left(\frac{Q_{sub}}{Q_{free}}\right)^{2.597}\right)^{2/3}\leftarrow eq.\,2$$

$Q_{free}=0.0227\,[m^3/s]$

Add the same subscript "i" to H_{DS} and H_{US} in eq. 2, then plug in variables $H_{US,1}$, Q_{sub}, and Q_{free} and solve for $H_{DS,1}$.

$$H_{DS,1}=0.1365\,[m]*\left(1-\left(\frac{0.0192\,[m^3/s]}{0.0227\,[m^3/s]}\right)^{2.597}\right)^{2/3}$$

$$H_{DS,1}=0.0681\,[m]*\frac{1{,}000\,[mm]}{1\,[m]}$$

Convert the downstream head, H_{DS}, back to units of millimeters.

conversion factor

$$H_{DS,1}=68.1\,[mm]$$

A) 49 [mm]

B) 71 [mm]

C) 142 [mm]

D) 314 [mm]

possible solutions for H_{DS}

Perform a second iteration for a more accurate calculation of H_{DS}.

$b=0.25\,[m]$ $N=1$

$$b_{eff}=b-0.1*N*H_{US}\leftarrow eq.\,5$$

$H_{US}=0.1365\,[m]$

Eq. 5 computes the effective weir width

Plug in variables b, N and H_{US} into eq. 5, then solve for b_{eff}.

$$b_{eff}=0.25\,[m]-0.1*1*0.1365\,[m]$$

$$b_{eff}=0.2364\,[m]$$

Water Resources Practice Problems

Open Channel Flow #21 (cont.)

$Q_{free}=0.0227\,[\text{m}^3/\text{s}]$

$$H_{US,i}=\left(\frac{3*Q_{free}}{2*C_1*b_{eff,i}*\sqrt{2*g}}\right)^{2/3} \leftarrow eq.\,4$$

$C_1=0.61$
$b_{eff,2}=0.2364\,[\text{m}]$
$g=9.81\,[\text{m/s}^2]$

For i=2, plug in variables Q_{free}, C_1, $b_{eff},2$ and g into eq. 4, then solve for the upstream head $H_{US,2}$.

$$H_{US,2}=\left(\frac{3*0.0227\,[\text{m}^3/\text{s}]}{2*0.61*0.2364\,[\text{m}]*\sqrt{2*9.81\,[\text{m/s}^2]}}\right)^{2/3}$$

$$H_{US,2}=0.1416\,[\text{m}]$$

$H_{US,2}=0.1416\,[\text{m}]$ $Q_{sub}=0.0192\,[\text{m}^3/\text{s}]$

$$H_{DS,i}=H_{US,i}*\left(1-\left(\frac{Q_{sub}}{Q_{free}}\right)^{2.597}\right)^{2/3} \leftarrow eq.\,2$$

$Q_{free}=0.0227\,[\text{m}^3/\text{s}]$

Plug in variables $H_{US,1}$, Q_{sub}, and Q_{free} into eq.2, then solve for $H_{DS,i}$, for this second iteration where i=2.

$$H_{DS,2}=0.1416\,[\text{m}]*\left(1-\left(\frac{0.0192\,[\text{m}^3/\text{s}]}{0.0227\,[\text{m}^3/\text{s}]}\right)^{2.597}\right)^{2/3}$$

$$H_{DS,1}=0.0707\,[\text{m}]*\frac{1,000\,[\text{mm}]}{1\,[\text{m}]}$$

conversion factor

Convert the downstream head, H_{DS}, back to units of millimeters.

$$H_{DS,1}=70.7\,[\text{mm}]$$

Answer: B

Pressure Flow #1

<u>Find:</u> h_f ← the headloss through the pipe

smooth pipe

<u>Given:</u>

$D=100\,[mm]$ ← pipe diameter

$T=20^\circ C$ ← water temperature

$v=1.6\,[m/s]$ ← fluid velocity

$L=40\,[m]$

pipe length

Q → [pipe diagram] D

L

pipe is flowing full of water

A) 0.51 [m]
B) 0.85 [m]
C) 1.72 [m]
D) 2.87 [m]

Analysis:

$$h_f = \frac{f*L*v^2}{2*g*D} \leftarrow eq.1$$

friction factor, pipe length, headloss, fluid velocity, gravitational acceleration, diameter

Eq.1 computes the headloss through a pipe using the Darcy equation.

$$D=100\,[mm]*\frac{1\,[m]}{1,000\,[mm]} \leftarrow eq.2$$

Eq.2 converts the diameter to units of meters.

$$D=0.1\,[m]$$

$$f=f(Re,\varepsilon/D) \leftarrow eq.3$$

Reynolds Number, Relative Roughness

Eq.3 shows the friction factor is a function of the Reynolds Number of the relative roughness.

$$Re=\frac{D_e*v}{\nu} \leftarrow eq.4$$

equivalent diameter, fluid velocity, Reynolds Number, kinematic viscosity

Eq.4 computes Reynolds Number.

water 20°C $\bigg\}$ $\nu=1.007*10^{-6}\,[m^2/s] \leftarrow eq.5$

Eq.5 shows the kinematic viscosity is based on the water temperature.

Water Resources Practice Problems

Pressure Flow #1 (cont.)

$$\boxed{D_e = D} = 0.1\,[m] \leftarrow eq.\,6$$

true for a
circular pipe

Eq. 6 computes the equivalent diameter, which equals the pipe diameter for circular pipes.

$D_e = 0.1\,[m]$　　$v = 1.6\,[m/s]$

$$Re = \frac{D_e * v}{\nu} \leftarrow eq.\,4$$

$\nu = 1.007 * 10^{-6}\,[m^2/s]$

Plug in variables D_e, v and ν into eq. 4, then solve for Re.

$$Re = \frac{0.1\,[m] * 1.6\,[m/s]}{1.007 * 10^{-6}\,[m^2/s]}$$

$$Re = 158,888$$

Reynolds Number has no units.

relative
roughness

$$\varepsilon/D = 0 \leftarrow eq.\,7$$

assumption for
"smooth pipe"

The problem states the pipe is a smooth pipe, therefore the relative roughness is assumed to be zero.

Based on the Reynolds Number and relative roughness, use the Moody Diagram in Figure 1 to identify the friction factor, f.

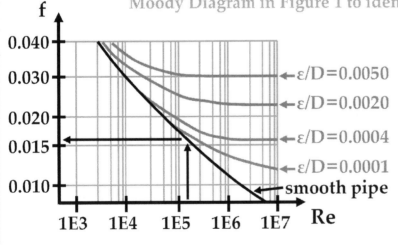

In Figure 1, start on the horizontal axis, at the value of the Reynolds Number. Then sketch up to the line representing the relative roughness. Lastly, trace left to the vertical axis and read the friction factor.

Figure 1

$$f = 0.016$$

From Figure 1, the friction factor is approximately 0.016.

Pressure Flow #1 (cont.)

The frication factor can also be determined using table data. Eq.8 uses linear interpolation to compute the friction factor for a smooth pipe having a Reynolds Number between 150,000 and 200,000.

$$f_{Re,0} = f_{1.5E5,0} + \frac{Re - 1.5*10^5}{2.0*10^5 - 1.5*10^5} * (f_{2E5,0} - f_{1.5E5,0}) \leftarrow eq.8$$

Re=158,888

$f_{2E5,0} = 0.0156$

$f_{1.5E5,0} = 0.0166$

$f_{1.5E5,0} = 0.0166$

$$f_{158,888,0} = 0.0166 + \frac{158,888 - 1.5*10^5}{2.0*10^5 - 1.5*10^5} * (0.0156 - 0.0166)$$

$$f = f_{158,888,0} = 0.0164$$

The two values of friction factor are sufficiently close enough to each other.

$$h_f = \frac{f*L*v^2}{2*g*D} \leftarrow eq.1$$

L=40[m]

v=1.6[m/s]

f=0.0164

g=9.81[m/s²]

D=0.1[m]

Plug in variables f, L, v, g and D into eq.1 then solve for h_f.

$$h_f = \frac{0.0164*40[m]*(1.6[m/s])^2}{2*9.81[m/s^2]*0.1[m]}$$

$$h_f = 0.856[m]$$

Answer: $\boxed{B}$

Water Resources Practice Problems

Find: h_f ← the headloss through the pipe

Given:

$d_n = 6 \,[in]$ ← nominal pipe diameter

$Q = 1.2 \,[ft^3/s]$ ← flow rate

$L = 600 \,[ft]$ ← pipe length

$T = 45° \,F$
↑
water temperature

schedule 40
steel pipe

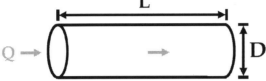

L

$Q \rightarrow$ $\rightarrow$ D

pipe is flowing
full of water

A) 2.0 [ft]

B) 3.6 [ft]

C) 5.7 [ft]

D) 11.9 [ft]

Analysis:

headloss

friction factor

pipe length

$$h_f = \frac{f * L * v^2}{2 * g * D} \quad \leftarrow eq.1$$

gravitational acceleration

diameter

fluid velocity

Eq.1 computes the headloss through a pipe using the Darcy equation.

Eq.1 assumes the diameter, D, is the inside diameter of the pipe.

(inside) diameter

wall thickness

$$D = D_o - 2 * t \quad \leftarrow eq.2$$

outside pipe diameter

Eq.2 computes the diameter based on the outside diameter and wall thickness, based on the given nominal pipe diameter and material.

$\left. \begin{array}{l} d_n = 6\,[in] \\ \text{schedule } 40 \end{array} \right\}$ $\begin{array}{l} D_o = 6.625\,[in] \\ t = 0.280\,[in] \end{array}$

Look up the outside pipe diameter and the wall thickness

$D_o = 6.625\,[in]$ $t = 0.280\,[in]$

$$D = D_o - 2 * t \quad \leftarrow eq.2$$

Plug in variables D_o and t into eq.2, then solve for D.

$$D = 6.625\,[in] - 2 * 0.280\,[in]$$

$$D = 6.065\,[in]$$

flow rate   cross-sectional area

$$v = Q/A \quad \leftarrow eq.3$$

Eq.3 computes the velocity of water through the pipe.

Pressure Flow #2 (cont.)

D = 6.065 [in]

$$A = \frac{\pi * D^2}{4} \leftarrow eq.4$$

Eq. 4 computes the cross-sectional area of the pipe.

$$A = \frac{\pi * (6.065\,[in])^2}{4}$$

Plug in the diameter into eq.4, then solve for the cross-sectional area.

$$A = 28.89\,[in^2] * \left(\frac{1\,[ft]}{12\,[in]}\right)^2 \leftarrow eq.5$$

Eq. 5 converts the cross-sectional area to units of feet squared.

$$A = 0.2006\,[ft^2]$$

Q = 1.2 [ft³/s]   A = 0.2006 [ft²]

$$v = Q/A \leftarrow eq.3$$

Plug in the flow rate and area into eq.3, then solve for the velocity.

$$v = \frac{1.2\,[ft^3/s]}{0.2006\,[ft^2]}$$

$$v = 5.98\,[ft/s]$$

$$f = f(Re, \varepsilon/D) \leftarrow eq.6$$

Reynolds   Relative
Number   Roughness

Eq. 6 shows the friction factor is a function of the Reynolds Number of the relative roughness.

equivalent
diameter   fluid velocity

$$Re = \frac{D_e * v}{\nu} \leftarrow eq.7$$

Reynolds   kinematic
Number   viscosity

Eq. 7 computes Reynolds Number.

water
45° F   } $\nu = 1.537 * 10^{-5}\,[ft^2/s] \leftarrow eq.8$

Eq. 8 shows the kinematic viscosity of water, based on the temperature.

Pressure Flow #2 (cont.)

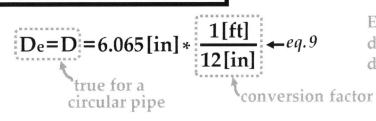

$$D_e = D = 6.065 \, [in] * \frac{1 \, [ft]}{12 \, [in]} \leftarrow eq. 9$$

true for a
circular pipe

conversion factor

Eq. 9 computes the equivalent diameter, which equals the pipe diameter for circular pipes.

$$D_e = D = 0.5054 \, [ft]$$

Convert the diameter to feet.

$D_e = 0.5054 \, [ft]$ $v = 5.98 \, [ft/s]$

$$Re = \frac{D_e * v}{\nu} \leftarrow eq. 7$$

$\nu = 1.537 * 10^{-5} \, [ft^2/s]$

Plug in variables D_e, v and ν into eq. 7, then solve for Re.

$$Re = \frac{0.5054 \, [ft] * 5.98 \, [ft/s]}{1.537 * 10^{-5} \, [ft^2/s]}$$

$$Re = 196,636$$

Eq. 10 computes the relative roughness of the pipe. The roughness of the pipe depends on the material.

true for steel pipe

$\varepsilon = 2 * 10^{-4} \, [ft]$

$$\frac{\varepsilon}{D} = \frac{2 * 10^{-4} \, [ft]}{0.5054 \, [ft]} = 3.96 * 10^{-4} \leftarrow eq. 10$$

$D = 0.5054 \, [ft]$

Use the Moody Diagram in Figure 1 to determine the friction factor, based on the Reynolds Number and the relative roughness of the pipe.

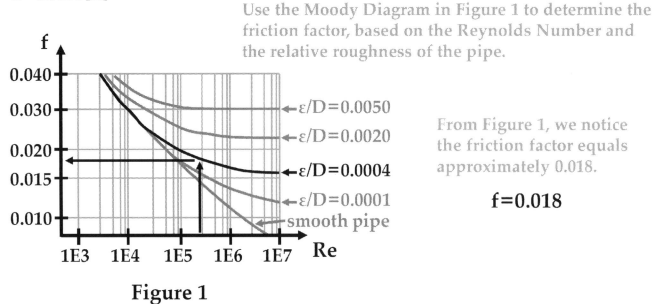

From Figure 1, we notice the friction factor equals approximately 0.018.

$$f = 0.018$$

Figure 1

Pressure Flow #2 (cont.)

$$h_f = \frac{f * L * v^2}{2 * g * D} \leftarrow eq.1$$

L=600[ft]

f=0.018

v=5.98[ft/s]

g=32.2[ft/s²]

D=0.5054[ft]

Plug in variables f, L, v, g and D into eq. 1 then solve for h_f.

$$h_f = \frac{0.018 * 600[ft] * (5.98[ft/s])^2}{2 * 32.2[ft/s^2] * 0.5054[ft]}$$

$$h_f = 11.87[ft]$$

Answer: $\boxed{D}$

Water Resources Practice Problems

Pressure Flow #3

<u>Find</u>: T ← the water temperature

<u>Given</u>:

D=1.0 [ft] ← pipe diameter

Q=2000 [gal/min] ← flow rate

L=600 [ft] ← pipe length

f=0.017 ← friction factor

Re=466,400 ← Reynolds Number

steel pipe

pipe is flowing
full of water

A) 40°F

B) 50°F

C) 60°F

D) 70°F

Analysis:

equivalent diameter — fluid velocity

$$Re = \frac{D_e * v}{\nu} \leftarrow eq.1$$

Reynolds Number — kinematic viscosity

Eq. 1 solves for the Reynolds Number.

$$\nu = \frac{D_e * v}{Re} \leftarrow eq.2$$

Solve eq. 1 for the kinematic viscosity.

D=1.0 [ft]

$$D_e = D \leftarrow eq.3$$

$$D_e = 1.0 [ft]$$

Eq. 3 shows that the equivalent diameter for a fully-flowing circular pipe equals the pipe diameter.

flow rate

$$v = \frac{Q}{A} \leftarrow eq.4$$

cross-section area of the pipe

Eq.4 computes the velocity of water in the pipe based on the flow rate and cross-sectional area.

$$Q = 2,000 \left[\frac{gal}{min}\right] * \frac{1}{7.48}\left[\frac{ft^3}{gal}\right] * \frac{1}{60}\left[\frac{min}{s}\right] \leftarrow eq.5$$

conversion factors

Eq. 5 converts the flow rate to cubic feet per second.

$$Q = 4.456 [ft^3/s]$$

Pressure Flow #3 (cont.)

$D = 1.0 \, [\text{ft}]$

$$A = \frac{\pi * D^2}{4} \leftarrow eq.6$$

Eq. 6 computes the cross-sectional area of the pipe.

Plug in the diameter into eq. 6, then solve for the cross-sectional area.

$$A = \frac{\pi * (1.0 \, [\text{ft}])^2}{4}$$

$$A = 0.785 \, [\text{ft}^2]$$

$Q = 4.456 \, [\text{ft}^3/\text{s}]$

$$v = \frac{Q}{A} \leftarrow eq.4$$

$A = 0.785 \, [\text{ft}^2]$

Plug in variables Q and A into eq. 4, then solve for the velocity.

$$v = \frac{4.456 \, [\text{ft}^3/\text{s}]}{0.785 \, [\text{ft}^2]}$$

$$v = 5.676 \, [\text{ft/s}]$$

$D_e = 1.0 \, [\text{ft}]$ $v = 5.676 \, [\text{ft/s}]$

$$\nu = \frac{D_e * v}{Re} \leftarrow eq.2$$

$Re = 466,400$

Plug in variables De, v and Re into eq. 2, then solve for ν.

$$\nu = \frac{1.0 \, [\text{ft}] * 5.676 \, [\text{ft/s}]}{466,400}$$

$$\nu = 1.217 * 10^{-5} \, [\text{ft}^2/\text{s}]$$
$$\downarrow$$
$$T = 60° \, F$$

Based on water property tables, water has a kinematic viscosity of $1.217*10^{-5} \, [\text{ft}^2/\text{s}]$ at 60° F.

Answer: $\boxed{C}$

Water Resources Practice Problems

Pressure Flow #4

<u>Find:</u> h_f ← the headloss through the culvert

concrete box culvert is flowing full of water

<u>Given:</u>

$Q=1.7\,[m^3/s]$ ← flow rate

$\mu=9*10^{-4}\,[Pa*s]$ ← absolute viscosity

$L=100\,[m]$ ← culvert length

$h=0.7\,[m]$ $w=0.9\,[m]$

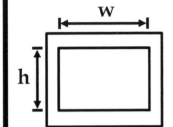   

culvert dimensions

concrete

drawing is not to scale

A) 1 [m]

B) 2 [m]

C) 3 [m]

D) 4 [m]

Analysis:

friction factor

pipe length

headloss

$$h_f=\frac{f*L*v^2}{2*g*D} \leftarrow eq.1$$

gravitational acceleration

diameter

fluid velocity

Eq. 1 computes the headloss through a pipe using the Darcy equation.

Since there is no 'diameter' to a box culvert, we'll compute the equivalent diameter using Eq. 2.

$h=0.7\,[m]$ $w=0.9\,[m]$

$$D=D_e=\frac{2*h*w}{h+w} \leftarrow eq.2$$

Plug in variables h and w into eq. 2, then solve for D and D_e.

$$D=D_e=\frac{2*0.7\,[m]*0.9\,[m]}{0.7\,[m]+0.9\,[m]}$$

$$D=D_e=0.7875\,[m]$$

flow rate

$Q=1.7\,[m^3/s]$

velocity

$$v=\frac{Q}{A}=\frac{Q}{h*w} \leftarrow eq.3$$

$A=h*w$ $h=0.7\,[m]$ $w=0.9\,[m]$

Eq. 3 computes the velocity through the culvert.

Plug in variables Q, h and w into eq. 3, then solve for v.

$$v=\frac{1.7\,[m^3/s]}{0.7\,[m]*0.9\,[m]}$$

Pressure Flow #4 (cont.)

$$v=2.698\,[\text{m/s}]$$

$$f=f(\text{Re},\varepsilon/D) \leftarrow eq.4$$

Reynolds Number   Relative Roughness

Eq. 4 shows the friction factor is a function of the Reynolds Number of the relative roughness.

$v=2.698\,[\text{m/s}]$

$D_e=0.7875\,[\text{m}]$

$\varrho=1,000\,[\text{kg/m}^3]$

$$\text{Re}=\frac{D_e*v*\varrho}{\mu} \leftarrow eq.5$$

Reynolds Number

absolute viscosity

$\mu=9*10^{-4}\,[\text{Pa*s}]$

Eq. 5 computes Reynolds Number, where ϱ represents the fluid density

The units of absolute viscosity [Pa*s] is converted to [kg/(s*m)].

$$\text{Re}=\frac{0.7875\,[\text{m}]*2.698\,[\text{m/s}]*1,000\,[\text{kg/m}^3]}{9*10^{-4}\,[\text{kg/(s*m)}]}$$

$$\text{Re}=2.36*10^6$$

$\varepsilon=0.0012\,[\text{m}] \leftarrow$ true for concrete

$$\frac{\varepsilon}{D}=\frac{0.0012\,[\text{m}]}{0.7875\,[\text{m}]}=0.00152 \leftarrow eq.6$$

$D=0.7875\,[\text{m}]$

Eq. 6 computes the relative rough-ness by dividing the roughness of concrete by the effective diameter.

Use the Moody Diagram in Figure 1 to determine the friction factor, based on the Reynolds Number and the relative roughness of the pipe.

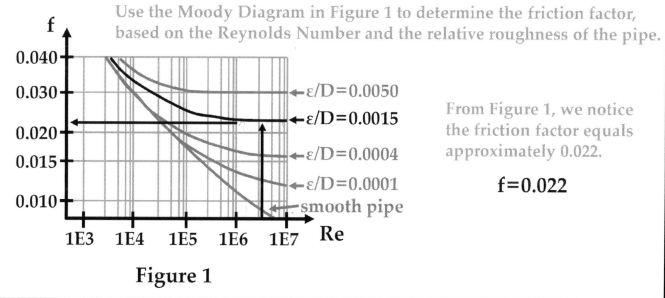

Figure 1

From Figure 1, we notice the friction factor equals approximately 0.022.

$$f=0.022$$

Water Resources Practice Problems

Pressure Flow #4 (cont.)

$$h_f = \frac{f * L * v^2}{2 * g * D} \leftarrow eq.1$$

L=100 [m]
f=0.022
v=2.698 [m/s]
g=9.81 [m/s²]
D=0.7875 [m]

Plug in variables f, L, v, g and D into eq. 1, then solve for h_f.

$$h_f = \frac{0.022 * 100\,[ft] * (2.698\,[ft/s])^2}{2 * 9.81\,[m/s^2] * 0.7875\,[m]}$$

$$h_f = 1.036\,[m]$$

Answer: $\boxed{A}$

Pressure Flow #5

Find: D ← the minimum allowable pipe diameter

Given:

C=100 ← roughness coefficient

$h_f \leq 5$ [ft] ← maximum allowable headloss through the pipe

Q=0.24 [ft³/s] ← flow rate

L=2,000 [ft] ← pipe length

pipe is flowing full of water

A) 4 [in]

B) 6 [in]

C) 8 [in]

D) 10 [in]

Analysis:

Eq. 1 computes the headloss through a pipe using the Hazen-Williams equation.

headloss [ft] — pipe length [ft] — flow rate [gal/min]

$$h_f = \frac{10.44 * L * Q^{1.85}}{C^{1.85} * D^{4.87}} \leftarrow eq. 1$$

roughness coefficient — pipe diameter [in]

In eq. 1, the units for variables h_f, L, Q and D are specified.

Solve eq. 1 for the diameter, D.

$$D = \left(\frac{10.44 * L * Q^{1.85}}{C^{1.85} * h_f} \right)^{1/4.87} \leftarrow eq. 2$$

Since we're asked to find the minimum diameter for $h_f \leq 5$ feet, we should find the minimum diameter, by setting $h_f=5$, solve for diameter, then round up to the next largest diameter.

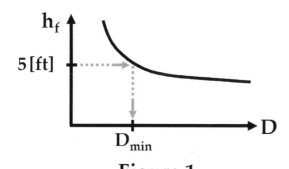

Figure 1

Figure 1 shows that the larger diameter, the less headloss.

conversion factors

$$Q = 0.24 \left[\frac{ft^3}{s} \right] * 7.48 \left[\frac{gal}{ft^3} \right] * 60 \left[\frac{s}{min} \right] \leftarrow eq. 3$$

Q=107.7 [gal/min]

Eq. 3 converts the flow rate to units of gallons per minute.

Water Resources Practice Problems

Pressure Flow #5 (cont.)

$$L=2{,}000\,[\text{ft}] \quad Q=107.7\,[\text{gal/min}]$$

$$D_{min}=\left(\frac{10.44 * L * Q^{1.85}}{C^{1.85} * h_f}\right)^{0.2053} \leftarrow eq.\,4$$

$$C=100 \qquad h_f=5\,[\text{ft}]$$

$$D_{min}=\left(\frac{10.44 * 2{,}000 * (107.7)^{1.85}}{(100)^{1.85} * 5}\right)^{0.2053}$$

$$D_{min}=5.70\,[\text{in}]$$

$$D=6\,[\text{in}]$$

Answer: $\boxed{\text{B}}$

Eq. 4 computes the minimum diameter of the pipe.

When using the Hazen-Williams equation, it is important that all factors have the correct units.

Drop the units from the right hand side of the equation and remember the minimum diameter will be in units of inches.

Of the possible solutions, the smallest diameter larger than 5.70 inches is 6 inches.

Pressure Flow #6

<u>Find:</u> $h_{f,2}$ ← the headloss in the pipe
at a flow rate of Q_2

<u>Given:</u>

$Q_1=100[gal/min]$ ← flow rate 1

$Q_2=200[gal/min]$ ← flow rate 2

pipe is flowing
full of water

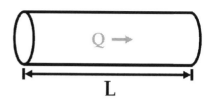

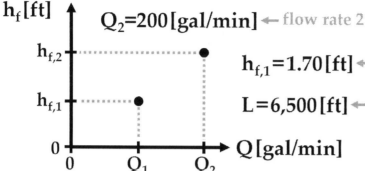

$h_{f,1}=1.70[ft]$ ← headloss 1

$L=6,500[ft]$ ← pipe length

A) 2.4[ft]

B) 3.4[ft]

C) 6.5[ft]

D) 9.8[ft]

Analysis:

$$h_f = \frac{10.44 * L * Q^{1.85}}{C^{1.85} * D^{4.87}} \leftarrow eq.1$$

headloss [ft], pipe length [ft], flow rate [gal/min], roughness coefficient, pipe diameter [in]

Eq.1 computes the headloss through a pipe using the Hazen-Williams equation.

Since the length, roughness and diameter are constant values, we can simplify eq.1 with eq.2.

$$h_f = x * Q^{1.85} \leftarrow eq.2 \rightarrow x = 0.00034$$

Solve eq.2 for x.

$$x = \frac{h_f}{Q^{1.85}} \leftarrow eq.3$$

Since it is assumed the value of x is constant, then eq.3 can be used for any pair of headloss and flow rate.

$$x = \frac{h_{f,1}}{Q_1^{1.85}} = \frac{h_{f,2}}{Q_2^{1.85}} \leftarrow eq.4$$

Eq.4 expands eq.3 to include 2 flow rates, identified by subscripts 1 and 2.

$h_{f,1}=1.70[ft]$ $Q_2=200[gal/min]$

$$h_{f,2} = \frac{h_{f,1} * Q_2^{1.85}}{Q_1^{1.85}} \leftarrow eq.5$$

$Q_1=100[gal/min]$

Solve eq.4 for $h_{f,2}$, plug in variables $h_{f,1}$, Q_1 and Q_2, then solve for $f_{h,2}$.

$$h_{f,2} = \frac{1.70 * (200)^{1.85}}{(100)^{1.85}} = 6.13[ft]$$

<u>Answer:</u> C

Water Resources Practice Problems

Pressure Flow #7

Find: C ← the roughness coefficient

Given: use the equivalent length method

$D = 4\,[in]$ ← pipe diameter

$h_f = 1.66\,[ft]$ ← total headloss

$Q = 100\,[gal/min]$ ← flow rate

$L_1 + L_2 + L_3 + L_4 = 48\,[ft]$ ← total length of piping

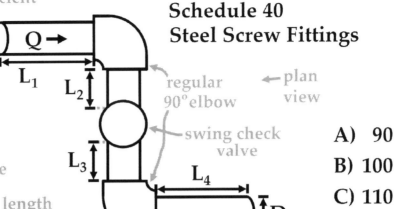

Schedule 40 Steel Screw Fittings

regular 90° elbow

← plan view

swing check valve

A) 90

B) 100

C) 110

D) 120

Analysis:

Eq. 1 computes the headloss through a pipe using the Hazen-Williams equation.

$$h_f = \frac{10.44 * L * Q^{1.85}}{C^{1.85} * D^{4.87}} \leftarrow eq.1$$

headloss [ft] — pipe length [ft] — flow rate [gal/min]

roughness coefficient — pipe diameter [in]

Solve eq.1 for the roughness coefficient.

In eq. 2, add a subscript t to the length term to represent the total length.

$$C = \left(\frac{10.44 * L_t * Q^{1.85}}{h_f * D^{4.87}}\right)^{0.5405} \leftarrow eq.2$$

total length

Eq.3 computes the total length of the pipe, including the equivalent length to account for minor losses through the fittings.

$$L_t = L_1 + L_2 + L_3 + L_4 + L_e \leftarrow eq.3$$

total length — total length of piping — equivalent length

effective length through a 4 inch swing check valve and 90° elbow

Eq. 4 computes the equivalent length.

$$L_e = L_{4'',CV} + 2 * L_{4'',90° \text{ elbow}} \leftarrow eq.4$$

$L_{4'',CV} = 38.0\,[ft]$ $L_{4'',90° \text{ elbow}} = 13.0\,[ft]$

Plug in the values of $L_{4'',CV}$ and $L_{4'',90° \text{ elbow}}$ into eq.4, then solve for variable L_e.

Pressure Flow #7 (cont.)

$$L_e = 38.0\,[ft] + 2 * 13.0\,[ft]$$

$$L_e = 64\,[ft]$$

$\overbrace{L_1 + L_2 + L_3 + L_4 = 48\,[ft]}$ $L_e = 64\,[ft]$

$$L_t = L_1 + L_2 + L_3 + L_4 + L_e \leftarrow eq.3$$

Plug in the total length of piping and variable L_e into eq.3, then solve for the total length.

$$L_t = 48\,[ft] + 64\,[ft]$$

$$L_t = 112\,[ft]$$

$L_t = 112\,[ft]$ $Q = 100\,[gal/min]$

$$C = \left(\frac{10.44 * L_t * Q^{1.85}}{h_f * D^{4.87}} \right)^{0.5405} \leftarrow eq.2$$

$h_f = 1.66\,[ft]$ $D = 4\,[in]$

Plug in variables L_t, Q, h_f and D into eq. 2, then solve for C.

$$C = \left(\frac{10.44 * 112 * (100)^{1.85}}{1.66 * (4)^{4.87}} \right)^{0.5405}$$

Drop the units from the right hand side of the equation, and remember the roughness coefficient, C, is unitless.

$$C = 90.02$$

Answer: $\boxed{A}$

Water Resources Practice Problems

Pressure Flow #8

Find: D ← the diameter of the pipe and fittings

Given:

$Q = 0.14 \, [\text{ft}^3/\text{s}]$ ← flow rate

$f = 0.014$ ← friction factor

$h_{L,m} = 0.5584 \, [\text{in}]$ ← minor headloss

tee fitting

cap (no flow)

D

45° elbow fitting

Q

D	$L_{e,tee}$	$L_{e,45° elbow}$
1 [in]	3.2 [ft]	1.3 [ft]
2 [in]	7.7 [ft]	2.7 [ft]
3 [in]	11.9 [ft]	4.1 [ft]
4 [in]	17.0 [ft]	5.5 [ft]

table showing equivalent lengths for both fittings

A) 1 [in]

B) 2 [in]

C) 3 [in]

D) 4 [in]

Analysis:

minor headloss

friction factor

equivalent pipe length

fluid velocity

$$h_{f,m} = \frac{f * L_e * v^2}{2 * g * D} \leftarrow eq.1$$

gravitational acceleration

diameter

Eq. 1 computes the minor headloss through a pipe fitting using the equivalent length, L_e.

$$L_e = \frac{2 * g * D * h_{f,m}}{f * v^2} \leftarrow eq.2$$

Solve eq. 1 for the equivalent length.

Assume the diameter is 3 inches then solve for both sides of eq. 2 to check this assumption.

flow rate

$$v = Q/A \leftarrow eq.3$$

velocity

cross-sectional area

Eq. 3 computes the fluid velocity.

$D = 3 \, [\text{in}]$ ← assumed

$$A_{D=3[in]} = \frac{\pi * D^2}{4} \leftarrow eq.4$$

Eq. 4 computes the cross-sectional area assuming the diameter is 3 inches.

$$A_{D=3[in]} = \frac{\pi * (3 \, [\text{in}])^2}{4}$$

Plug in variable D into eq. 4, then solve for the area.

conversion factor

$$A_{D=3[in]} = 7.069 \, [\text{in}^2] * \left(\frac{1 \, [\text{ft}]}{12 \, [\text{in}]} \right)^2 \leftarrow eq.5$$

Eq. 5 converts the area to units of feet squared.

Pressure Flow #8 (cont.)

$$A_{D=3[in]}=0.0491\,[ft^2]$$

$Q=0.14\,[ft^3/s]$

$$v_{D=3[in]}=Q/A_{D=3[in]} \leftarrow eq.6$$

$A_{D=3[in]}=0.0491\,[ft^2]$

Eq.6 is a modification of eq.3, for a 3 inch diameter pipe. Plug in variables Q and $A_{D=2[in]}$ into eq.6, then solve for $v_{D=3[in]}$.

$$v_{D=3[in]}=\frac{0.14\,[ft^3/s]}{0.0491\,[ft^2]}$$

$$v_{D=3[in]}=2.851\,[ft/s]$$

total equivalent length from fittings

$$L_e=L_{e,tee}+L_{e,45°elbow} \leftarrow eq.7$$

equivalent length from the tee and 45° elbow

Eq.7 computes the sum of the equivalent lengths from both fittings.

$L_{e,tee,3''}=11.9\,[in]$ $L_{e,45°elbow,3''}=4.1\,[in]$

$$L_{e,3''}=L_{e,tee,3''}+L_{e,45°elbow,3''} \leftarrow eq.8$$

Eq.8 computes the sum of the equivalent lengths, specifically for the 3 inch diameter fittings.

$$L_{e,3''}=11.9\,[in]+4.1\,[in]$$

$$L_{e,3''}=16.0\,[in]$$

assumed diameter   conversion factor

$$D=3\,[in]*\frac{1\,[ft]}{12\,[in]}$$

Convert the assumed diameter to feet.

$$D=0.25\,[ft]$$

Water Resources Practice Problems

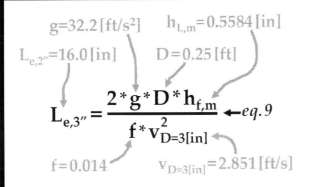

Eq. 9 is a modification of eq. 2 for a 3 inch diameter pipe.

$$L_{e,3''} = \frac{2 * g * D * h_{f,m}}{f * v_{D=3[in]}^2} \leftarrow eq.\ 9$$

Plug in variables L_e, g, D, $h_{f,m}$, f and v into eq. 9 and check to see if the right hand side equals the left hand side of the equation.

$$16.0\,[in] = \frac{2 * 32.2\,[ft/s^2] * 0.25\,[ft] * 0.5584\,[in]}{0.014 * (2.851\,[ft/s])^2}$$

$$16.0\,[in] \neq 79.0\,[in]$$

$$D \neq 3\,[in]$$

Since 16 inches is much smaller than 79.0 inches, we know the diameter is not 3 inches. We'll choose a smaller diameter and try again.

D=2 [in] ← assumed

$$A_{D=2[in]} = \frac{\pi * D^2}{4} \leftarrow eq.\ 10$$

Assuming the diameter is 2 inches, use eq. 10 to compute the cross-sectional area.

$$A_{D=2[in]} = \frac{\pi * (2\,[in])^2}{4}$$

Plug in variable D into eq. 4, then solve for the area.

$$A_{D=2[in]} = 3.142\,[in^2] * \left(\frac{1\,[ft]}{12\,[in]}\right)^2 \leftarrow eq.\ 11$$

← conversion factor

Eq. 11 converts the area to units of feet squared.

$$A_{D=2[in]} = 0.0218\,[ft^2]$$

Q=0.14 [ft³/s]

$$v_{D=2[in]} = Q / A_{D=2[in]} \leftarrow eq.\ 12$$

$A_{D=2[in]} = 0.0218\,[ft^2]$

Eq. 12 is a modification of eq. 3, for a 2 inch diameter pipe. Plug in variables Q and $A_{D=2[in]}$ into eq 6, then solve for $v_{D=2[in]}$.

Pressure Flow #8 (cont.)

$$v_{D=2[in]} = \frac{0.14\,[ft^3/s]}{0.0218\,[ft^2]}$$

$$v_{D=2[in]} = 6.42\,[ft/s]$$

$L_{e,tee,2''} = 7.7\,[in]$ $L_{e,45° \, elbow,2''} = 2.7\,[in]$

$$L_{e,2''} = L_{e,tee,2''} + L_{e,45° \, elbow,2''} \leftarrow eq.\,13$$

Eq. 13 computes the sum of the equivalent lengths for the 2 inch diameter pipe.

$$L_{e,2''} = 7.7\,[in] + 2.7\,[in]$$

$$L_{e,2''} = 10.4\,[in]$$

assumed diameter   conversion factor

$$D = 2\,[in] * \frac{1\,[ft]}{12\,[in]} \leftarrow eq.\,14$$

Eq. 14 converts the assumed diameter to feet.

$$D = 0.167\,[ft]$$

$g = 32.2\,[ft/s^2]$ $h_{L,m} = 0.5584\,[in]$

$L_{e,2''} = 10.4\,[in]$ $D = 0.167\,[ft]$

Eq. 15 is a modification of eq. 2 for a 2 inch diameter pipe.

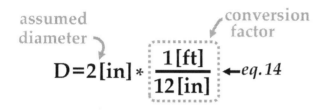

$$L_{e,2''} = \frac{2 * g * D * h_{f,m}}{f * v_{D=2[in]}^2} \leftarrow eq.\,15$$

$f = 0.014$ $v_{D=2[in]} = 6.42\,[ft/s]$

Plug in variables L_e, g, D, $h_{f,m}$, f and v into eq. 15 and check to see if the right hand side equals the left hand side of the equation.

$$10.4\,[in] = \frac{2 * 32.2\,[ft/s^2] * 0.167\,[in] * 0.5584\,[in]}{0.014 * (6.42\,[ft/s])^2}$$

$$10.4\,[in] \approx 10.41\,[in]$$

Since 10.4 inches is very close to 10.41 inches we know the diameter is 2 inches.

$$D = 2\,[in] \qquad \underline{Answer:} \quad \boxed{B}$$

Water Resources Practice Problems

Pressure Flow #9

Find: K_M ← the minor headloss coefficient of the meter

Given:

$Q = 313\,[gal/min]$ ← the flow rate

$D = 4\,[in]$ ← the diameter of the pipe and meter

$h_{L,meter} = 4.31\,[lb_m/in^2]$

the minor headloss caused by the meter

meter

$Q \rightarrow$ ⌀ D

A) 4.3 [ft]
B) 6.2 [ft]
C) 8.1 [ft]
D) 10.0 [ft]

Analysis:

minor headloss coefficient from the meter

velocity

$$h_{L,meter} = \frac{K_M * v^2}{2 * g} \leftarrow eq.1$$

minor headloss from the meter

gravitational acceleration

Eq.1 computes the minor headloss from the meter.

Solve eq.1 for the minor headloss coefficient from the meter.

✓

$$K_M = \frac{h_{L,meter} * 2 * g}{v^2} \leftarrow eq.2$$

flow rate

$$v = \frac{Q}{A} \leftarrow eq.3$$

cross-sectional area of the pipe

Eq.3 computes the velocity

$$Q = 313 \left[\frac{gal}{min}\right] * \frac{1}{7.48}\left[\frac{ft^3}{gal}\right] * \frac{1}{60}\left[\frac{min}{s}\right]$$

conversion factors

Convert the flow rate to cubic feet per second.

$$Q = 0.697\,[ft^3/s]$$

$D = 4\,[in]$

$$A = \frac{\pi * D^2}{4} \leftarrow eq.4$$

Eq.4 computes the cross-sectional area of the pipe.

Plug in the diameter into eq.4, then solve for the cross-sectional area.

Pressure Flow #9 (cont.)

$$A = \frac{\pi * (4\,[in])^2}{4}$$

$$A = 12.566\,[in^2] * \left(\frac{1\,[ft]}{12\,[in]}\right)^2 \leftarrow eq.5$$

conversion factor

Convert the cross-sectional area to units of feet squared.

$$A = 0.0873\,[ft^2]$$

$Q = 0.697\,[ft^3/s]$

$$v = \frac{Q}{A} = \frac{0.697\,[ft^3/s]}{0.0873\,[ft^2]} \leftarrow eq.3$$

$A = 0.0873\,[ft^2]$

Plug in variables Q and A into eq.3, then solve for v.

Eq.6 converts the headloss to units of length by dividing by the density of water

$$v = 7.983\,[ft/s]$$

$$h_{L,meter} = 4.31\left[\frac{lb_m}{in^2}\right] * \frac{1}{62.4}\left[\frac{ft^3}{lb_m}\right] * \left(12\left[\frac{in}{ft}\right]\right)^2 \leftarrow eq.6$$

water density   conversion factor

$$h_{L,meter} = 9.946\,[ft]$$

$h_{L,meter} = 9.946\,[ft]$ $g = 32.2\,[ft/s^2]$

$$K_M = \frac{h_{L,meter} * 2 * g}{v^2} \leftarrow eq.2$$

$v = 7.983\,[ft/s]$

Substitute in variables $h_{L,meter}$, g and v into eq.2, then solve for K_M.

$$K_M = \frac{9.946\,[ft] * 2 * 32.2\,[ft/s^2]}{(7.983\,[ft/s])^2}$$

$$K_M = 10.05$$

Answer: $\boxed{D}$

Water Resources Practice Problems

Pressure Flow #10

Find: D_2 ← the diameter of the smaller pipe

Given:

$Q = 0.041 \, [\text{m}^3/\text{s}]$ ← the flow rate

$D_1 = 315 \, [\text{mm}]$ ← the diameter of the larger pipe

$h_{L,m} = 0.252 \, [\text{m}]$ ← the minor headloss

$K_{contraction} = 0.37$
$K_{90 \text{ elbow}} = 0.41$ ⎫ minor headloss coefficients

D_1 D_2

$Q \rightarrow$

sudden contraction

$90°$ elbow

A) 110 [mm]
B) 140 [mm]
C) 160 [mm]
D) 190 [mm]

Analysis:

$$D_2 = \sqrt{\frac{4 * A_2}{\pi}} \leftarrow eq.1$$

diameter of the smaller pipe — area of the smaller pipe

Eq.1 computes the diameter of the smaller pipe.

$$A_2 = \frac{Q}{v_2} \leftarrow eq.2$$

area of the smaller pipe — flow rate — velocity through the smaller pipe

Eq.2 computes the cross-sectional area of the smaller pipe.

$$h_{L,m} = h_{L,contraction} + 2 * h_{L,90° \text{ elbow}} \leftarrow eq.3$$

minor headloss — minor headloss through the contraction and $90°$ elbows

Eq.3 computes the minor headloss in the pipe system.

Eq.4 expands the minor headloss terms from the right hand side of eq.3.

$$h_{L,m} = K_{contraction} * \frac{v_2{}^2}{2*g} + 2 * K_{90°elbow} * \frac{v_2{}^2}{2*g} \leftarrow eq.4$$

velocity through the smaller pipe

$$v_2 = \sqrt{\frac{h_{L,m} * 2 * g}{K_{contraction} + 2 * K_{90°elbow}}} \leftarrow eq.5$$

$h_{L,m} = 0.252 \, [\text{m}]$ $g = 9.81 \, [\text{m/s}^2]$

$K_{contraction} = 0.37$ $K_{90°elbow} = 0.41$

The velocity of the smaller pipe is used to compute minor head-loss for contraction fittings.

Plug in variables $h_{L,m}$, g, $K_{90° \text{ elbow}}$, $K_{contraction}$ and then solve for v_2.

Pressure Flow #10 (cont.)

$$v_2 = \sqrt{\frac{0.252\,[m] * 2 * 9.81\,[m/s^2]}{0.37 + 2 * 0.41}}$$

$$v_2 = 2.038\,[m/s]$$

$$Q = 0.041\,[m^3/s]$$

$$A_2 = \frac{Q}{v_2} \leftarrow eq.\,2$$

$$v_2 = 2.038\,[m/s]$$

Plug in variables Q and v_2 into eq.2, then solve for A_2.

$$A_2 = \frac{0.041\,[m^3/s]}{2.038\,[m/s]}$$

$$A_2 = 0.0201\,[m^2]$$

$$A_2 = 0.0201\,[m^2]$$

$$D_2 = \sqrt{\frac{4 * A_2}{\pi}} \leftarrow eq.\,1$$

Plug in variable A_2 into eq.1, then solve for D_2.

$$D_2 = \sqrt{\frac{4 * 0.0201\,[m^2]}{\pi}}$$

conversion factor

$$D_2 = 0.160\,[m] * \frac{1,000\,[mm]}{1\,[m]}$$

Convert the diameter to millimeters.

$$D_2 = 160\,[mm]$$

Answer: $\boxed{C}$

Water Resources Practice Problems

Pressure Flow #11

<u>**Find: n**</u> ← the number of pipes

<u>**Given:**</u>

L=20,000 [ft] ← pipe length

D=1.5 [ft] ← pipe diameter

A=1.767 [ft^2] ← flow area

Q_T=12 [ft^3/s] ← total flow rate
(through all n pipes)

C=100 ← roughness coefficient

$h_{f,max}$=25 [ft] ← max allowable headloss

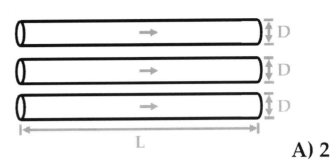

minimize the number of pipes without exceeding the maximum allowable headloss

A) 2

B) 3

C) 4

D) 5

- -

Analysis:

pipe length [ft]   velocity [ft/s]

headloss [ft]

$$h_f = \frac{3.022 * L * v^{1.85}}{C^{1.85} * D^{1.165}} \leftarrow eq.1$$

roughness coefficient   pipe diameter [ft]

Eq. 1 computes the headloss through a pipe using the Hazen-Williams equation.

$$v = \left(\frac{h_f * C^{1.85} * D^{1.165}}{3.022 * L} \right)^{0.5405} \leftarrow eq.2$$

Solve eq. 1 for the velocity, v.

$h_{f,max}$=25 [ft]   D=1.5 [ft]

$$v \leq \left(\frac{h_{f,max} * C^{1.85} * D^{1.165}}{3.022 * L} \right)^{0.5405} \leftarrow ieq.1$$

C=100   L=20,000 [ft]

Substitute in the maximum allowable headloss and replace the equal sign with an 'at most' symbol into eq. 2.

Plug in variables $h_{f,max}$, D, C and L into ieq. 1, then drop the units and solve for the maximum allowable velocity, in feet per second.

$$v \leq \left(\frac{25 * (100)^{1.85} * (1.5)^{1.165}}{3.022 * (20,000)} \right)^{0.5405}$$

$$v \leq 1.914 \text{ [ft/s]}$$

Pressure Flow #11 (cont.)

$$v = Q/A \leftarrow eq.3$$

Eq. 3 computes the velocity of flow based on flow rate and flow area.

$$Q_T = 12 \, [ft^3/s]$$

$$Q_n = Q_T/n \leftarrow eq.4$$

$$n = 2,3,4,5$$

Eq. 4 computes the flow rate through each pipe, assuming there are n pipes.

$$Q_2 = 12 \, [ft^3/s]/2 = 6 \, [ft^3/s]$$

$$Q_3 = 12 \, [ft^3/s]/3 = 4 \, [ft^3/s]$$

$$Q_4 = 12 \, [ft^3/s]/4 = 3 \, [ft^3/s]$$

$$Q_5 = 12 \, [ft^3/s]/5 = 2.4 \, [ft^3/s]$$

Plug in variable Q_T and the four possible values of n, then solve for Q_n.

$$v_n = Q_n/A \leftarrow eq.5$$

$$A = 1.767 \, [ft^2]$$

Eq. 5 computes the velocity of flow through n pipes.

Plug in variables Q_n and A into eq. 5, then solve for v_n.

$$v_2 = 6 \, [ft^3/s]/1.767 \, [ft^2] = 3.396 \, [ft/s]$$

$$v_3 = 4 \, [ft^3/s]/1.767 \, [ft^2] = 2.264 \, [ft/s]$$

$$v_4 = 3 \, [ft^3/s]/1.767 \, [ft^2] = 1.698 \, [ft/s]$$

$$v_5 = 2.4 \, [ft^3/s]/1.767 \, [ft^2] = 1.358 \, [ft/s]$$

$$v_4, v_5 \leq 1.914 \, [ft/s]$$

Only n=4 and n=5 satisfy the max headloss requirement:

$$n = 4$$

Answer: $\boxed{C}$

Water Resources Practice Problems

Pressure Flow #12

Find: Q_2 ← the flow rate at time 2

Given:

$D_1 = 4 [in]$ ← pipe diameter at time 1

$D_2 = 3 [in]$ ← pipe diameter at time 2

the pipe diameter decreases over time

$h_{f,1} = h_{f,2}$ ← headloss and friction factor remain constant

$f_1 = f_2$

$L = 6,000 [ft]$ ← length

$\nu = 1*10^{-6} [m^2/s]$ ← kinematic viscosity

$Q_1 = 0.20 [ft^3/s]$ ← flow rate at time 1

water flows from tank 1 to tank 2

tank 1

smooth pipe

$Q \rightarrow$

tank 2

A) $0.100 [ft^3/s]$

B) $0.125 [ft^3/s]$

C) $0.133 [ft^3/s]$

D) $0.150 [ft^3/s]$

Analysis:

$Q_2 = v_2 * A_2$ ← eq.1

flow rate

cross-sectional area of the pipe

velocity

Eq. 1 computes the flow rate through the pipe at time 2.

$A_2 = \dfrac{\pi * D_2^2}{4}$ ← eq.2

$D_2 = 3 [in]$

Eq. 2 computes the cross-sectional area of the pipe at time 2.

$A_2 = \dfrac{\pi * (3 [in])^2}{4}$

Plug in the diameter D_2 into eq. 2, then solve for the cross-sectional area at time 2.

$A_2 = 7.069 [in^2] * \left(\dfrac{1 [ft]}{12 [in]} \right)^2$ ← eq.3

conversion factor

Eq. 3 converts the cross-sectional area to units of feet squared.

$A_2 = 0.04909 [ft^2]$

$h_f = \dfrac{f * L * v^2}{2 * g * D}$ ← eq.4

friction factor

pipe length

fluid velocity

headloss

diameter

gravitational acceleration

Eq. 4 computes the headloss through a pipe, using the Darcy equation.

$v_2 = \sqrt{\dfrac{h_{f,2} * 2 * g * D_2}{f_2 * L}}$ ← eq.5

Solve eq. 4 for the velocity, and add a subscript "2" to the velocity, headloss, friction factor, and diameter terms.

Pressure Flow #12 (cont.)

$$f_1 = f_2 = f(Re, \varepsilon/D) \leftarrow eq.6$$

Reynolds Number — Relative Roughness

Eq. 6 shows the friction factor is a function of the Reynolds Number of the relative roughness.

Eq. 7 computes Reynolds Number.

equivalent diameter — fluid velocity

$$Re = \frac{D_{e,1} * v_1}{\nu} \leftarrow eq.7$$

Reynolds Number — kinematic viscosity

Add a subscript "1" to the equivalent diameter and velocity terms in eq. 7.

$$\nu = 1*10^{-6} \left[\frac{m^2}{s}\right] * \left(3.281 \left[\frac{ft}{m}\right]\right)^2 \leftarrow eq.8$$

Eq. 8 converts the kinematic viscosity to English units.

$$\nu = 1.0765 * 10^{-5} \left[\frac{ft^2}{s}\right]$$

$$v_1 = \frac{Q_1}{A_1} = \frac{4*Q_1}{\pi * D_1^2} \leftarrow eq.9$$

Eq. 9 computes the velocity through the pipe at time 1.

$$A_1 = \frac{\pi * D_1^2}{4}$$

conversion factor

$$D_1 = 4[in] * \frac{1}{12}\left[\frac{ft}{in}\right] \leftarrow eq.10$$

Eq. 10 converts the diameter at time 1 to feet.

$$D_1 = 0.333 [ft]$$

$$Q_1 = 0.20 [ft^3/s]$$

$$v_1 = \frac{4*Q_1}{\pi * D_1^2} \leftarrow eq.9$$

Plug in variables Q_1 and D_1 into eq. 9, then solve for v_1.

$$D_1 = 0.333 [ft]$$

Water Resources Practice Problems

$$v_1 = \frac{4 * 0.20 \, [\text{ft}^3/\text{s}]}{\pi * (0.333 \, [\text{ft}])^2}$$

$$v_1 = 2.296 \, [\text{ft/s}]$$

$D_{e,1} = D_1 = 0.333 \, [\text{ft}]$ $v_1 = 2.296 \, [\text{ft/s}]$

$$Re = \frac{D_{e,1} * v_1}{\nu} \leftarrow eq.7$$

$\nu = 1.0765 * 10^{-5} \, [\text{ft}^2/\text{s}]$

Plug in variables D_1, v_1 and ν into eq.7, then solve for Re.

$$Re = \frac{0.333 \, [\text{ft}] * 2.296 \, [\text{ft/s}]}{1.0765 * 10^{-5} \, [\text{ft}^2/\text{s}]}$$

$$Re = 71{,}024$$

$Re = 71{,}024$ "smooth"

$$f_1 = f_2 = f(Re, \varepsilon/D) \leftarrow eq.6$$

$$f_1 = f_2 = 0.0124$$

Based on a Reynolds Number of 71,024, a smooth pipe will have a friction factor equal to 0.0124

$L = 6{,}000 \, [\text{ft}]$ $v_1 = 2.296 \, [\text{ft/s}]$

$f_1 = 0.0124$

$$h_{f,1} = \frac{f_1 * L * v_1^2}{2 * g * D_1} \leftarrow eq.11$$

$g = 32.2 \, [\text{ft/s}^2]$ $D_1 = 0.333 \, [\text{ft}]$

Add the subscripts "1" to variables h_f, f, v and D in eq.4, then plug in the known variables into eq.11, then solve for $h_{f,1}$.

$$h_{f,1} = \frac{0.0124 * 6{,}000 \, [\text{ft}] * (2.296 \, [\text{ft/s}])^2}{2 * 32.2 \, [\text{ft/s}^2] * (0.333 \, [\text{ft}])}$$

Pressure Flow #12 (cont.)

$$h_{f,1} = 18.29 \, [ft]$$

$$D_2 = 3 \, [in] * \frac{1}{12} \left[\frac{ft}{in} \right] \leftarrow eq. 12$$

Eq. 12 converts the diameter at time 2 to feet.

$$D_2 = 0.25 \, [ft]$$

$$g = 32.2 \, [ft/s^2]$$

$$h_{f,2} = 18.29 \, [ft] \qquad D_2 = 0.25 \, [ft]$$

$$v_2 = \sqrt{\frac{h_{f,2} * 2 * g * D_2}{f_2 * L}} \leftarrow eq. 5$$

$$f_2 = 0.0124 \qquad L = 6,000 \, [ft]$$

Plug in the known values into the right hand side of eq. 5, then solve for v_2.

$$v_2 = \sqrt{\frac{18.29 \, [ft] * 2 * 32.2 \, [ft/s^2] * 0.25 \, [ft]}{0.0124 * 6,000 \, [ft]}}$$

$$v_2 = 1.989 \, [ft/s]$$

$$v_2 = 1.989 \, [ft/s]$$

$$Q_2 = v_2 * A_2 \leftarrow eq. 1$$

$$A_2 = 0.04909 \, [ft^2]$$

Plug in variables v_2 and A_2 into eq. 1, then solve for Q_2.

$$Q_2 = 1.989 \, [ft/s] * 0.04909 \, [ft^2]$$

$$Q_2 = 0.098 \, [ft^3/s]$$

Answer: $\boxed{A}$

Water Resources Practice Problems

Pressure Flow #13

Find: L ← the pipe length

Given:

$D=6\,[in]$ ← the pipe diameter

$C=110$ ← the roughness coefficient

$Elev_A=45.5\,[ft]$ ← the water surface elevation at the tank

$Elev_B=38.6\,[ft]$ ← the elevation at the end of the pipe

$Q=0.358\,[ft^3/s]$ ← the flow rate through the pipe

neglect minor losses

A) 1,000 [ft]
B) 2,000 [ft]
C) 3,000 [ft]
D) 4,000 [ft]

— $Elev_A$

tank

L   D

Q

— $Elev_B$

Analysis:

total head at the tank   total head at the end of the pipe

$$h_{t,A}=h_{t,B}+h_f \leftarrow eq.1$$

major headloss

Eq.1 shows the total head at the tank equals the total head at the end of the pipe plus the headloss experienced by the water flowing through the pipe.

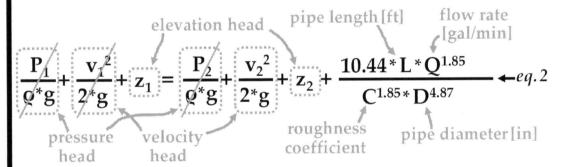

elevation head   pipe length [ft]   flow rate [gal/min]

$$\frac{\cancel{P_1}}{\varrho^*g}+\frac{v_1^2}{2^*g}+z_1=\frac{\cancel{P_2}}{\varrho^*g}+\frac{v_2^2}{2^*g}+z_2+\frac{10.44*L*Q^{1.85}}{C^{1.85}*D^{4.87}} \leftarrow eq.2$$

pressure head   velocity head   roughness coefficient   pipe diameter [in]

Eq. 2 expands the terms in eq. 1.

[ft]   [ft/s]   [in]

$$L=\left(z_A-z_B-\frac{v_2^2}{2^*g}\right)*\left(\frac{C^{1.85}*D^{4.87}}{10.44*Q^{1.85}}\right) \leftarrow eq.3$$

[ft/s²]   [gal/min]   conversion factors

In eq. 2, the pressure heads, and the velocity head at the tank, equal 0.

Eq. 3 simplifies eq. 2, by solving for the pipe length, and identifying the units for each variable.

$$Q=0.358\left[\frac{ft^3}{s}\right]*7.48\left[\frac{gal}{ft^3}\right]*60\left[\frac{s}{min}\right] \leftarrow eq.4$$

Eq. 4 converts the flow rate to gallons per minute

$$Q=160.7\,[gal/min]$$

Pressure Flow #13 (cont.)

$z_A = Elev_A = 45.5 \, [ft] \leftarrow eq.5$

Eq.5 and eq.6 identify the water elevation at the tank and at the end of the pipe.

$z_B = Elev_B = 38.6 \, [ft] \leftarrow eq.6$

$v_2 = Q/A \leftarrow eq.7$

Eq.7 computes the velocity through the pipe

$D = 6 \, [in]$

$A = \dfrac{\pi * D^2}{4} \leftarrow eq.8$

Eq.8 computes the cross-sectional area of the pipe.

$A = \dfrac{\pi * (6 \, [in])^2}{4} * \left(\dfrac{1}{12} \left[\dfrac{ft}{in} \right] \right)^2$

Plug in the pipe diameter into eq.8, then solve for the area.

conversion factor

$A = 0.1963 \, [ft^2]$

$Q = 0.358 \, [ft^3/s] \quad A = 0.1963 \, [ft^2]$

$v_2 = Q/A \leftarrow eq.7$

Plug in variables Q and A into eq.7, then solve for v_2.

$v_2 = \dfrac{0.358 \, [ft^3/s]}{0.1963 \, [ft^2]}$

$v_2 = 1.824 \, [ft/s]$

$v_2 = 1.824 \, [ft/s]$

$z_A = 45.5 \, [ft] \qquad C = 110 \quad D = 6 \, [in]$

Plug in the variables z_A, z_B, v_2, g, Q, C and D into eq.3, then solve for L.

$L = \left(z_A - z_B - \dfrac{v_2^2}{2*g} \right) * \left(\dfrac{C^{1.85} * D^{4.87}}{10.44 * Q^{1.85}} \right) \leftarrow eq.3$

$z_B = 38.6 \, [ft] \qquad g = 32.2 \, [ft/s^2] \qquad Q = 160.7 \, [gal/min]$

Water Resources Practice Problems

The units have been removed from the headloss term of the equation.

$$L = \left(45.5\,[\text{ft}] - 38.6\,[\text{ft}] - \frac{(1.824\,[\text{ft/s}])^2}{2 * 32.2\,[\text{ft/s}^2]}\right) * \left(\frac{(110)^{1.85} * (6)^{4.87}}{10.44 * (160.7)^{1.85}}\right)$$

$$L = 2{,}004\,[\text{ft}]$$

Answer: $\boxed{\text{B}}$

Pressure Flow #14

<u>Find:</u> $Elev_C$ ← the water surface elevation at point C

<u>Given:</u>

$D_B = D_C = 250\,[mm]$ ← diameter at B and C

$D_A = 450\,[mm]$ ← diameter at A

$P_{g,C} = 0\,[Pa]$ ← gauge pressure at points B and C

$P_{g,B} = 1.962 * 10^5\,[Pa]$

$v_A = 1.00\,[m/s]$ ← velocity at point A

$Elev_A = Elev_B = 44.5\,[m]$ ← invert elevation at points A and B

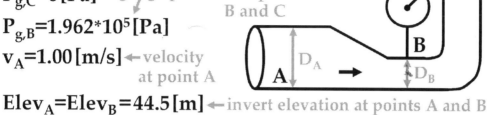

$Elev_C$ → constant water surface elevation at top of pipe, as water barely spills over

pressure gauge

assume headloss is negligible

A) 59 [m]

B) 60 [m]

C) 61 [m]

D) 65 [m]

<u>Analysis:</u>

Eq.1 equates the total head at point B equal to the total head at point C, using Bernoulli's equation.

elevation head

$$\underbrace{\frac{P_B}{\varrho^* g}} + \underbrace{\frac{v_B^2}{2^* g}} + \underbrace{z_B} = \underbrace{\frac{P_C}{\varrho^* g}} + \underbrace{\frac{v_C^2}{2^* g}} + \underbrace{z_C} \leftarrow eq.1$$

pressure head   velocity head

$P_C = P_{g,C} = 0\,[Pa]$

The gauge pressure at point C equals zero.

$v_C = 0\,[m/s]$

The velocity at point C equals zero.

Plug in variables P_C and v_C into eq.1, then solve for z_C, the elevation head at point C.

$P_C = 0\,[Pa]$

$z_B = Elev_B$ $v_C = 0\,[m/s]$

$$\frac{P_B}{\varrho^* g} + \frac{v_B^2}{2^* g} + z_B = \frac{P_C}{\varrho^* g} + \frac{v_C^2}{2^* g} + z_C \leftarrow eq.1$$

$z_C = Elev_C$

$$\frac{P_B}{\varrho^* g} + \frac{v_B^2}{2^* g} + Elev_B = \frac{0\,[Pa]}{\varrho^* g} + \frac{(0\,[m/s])^2}{2^* g} + Elev_C$$

$$Elev_C = Elev_B + \frac{P_B}{\varrho^* g} + \frac{v_B^2}{2^* g} \leftarrow eq.2$$

Water Resources Practice Problems

Pressure Flow #14 (cont.)

Eq.3 shows that a Pascal equals a meter kilogram per second squared.

$$P_{g,B}=1.962*10^5\,[Pa]*1\left[\frac{kg}{Pa*m*s^2}\right] \leftarrow eq.3$$

conversion factor

$$P_B=P_{g,B}=1.962*10^5\left[\frac{kg}{m*s^2}\right]$$

flow rate   velocity   area

$$Q=v_A*A_A=v_B*A_B \leftarrow eq.4$$

point A   point B

Eq.4 computes the flow rate through the pipe based on the area and velocity at points A and B.

$$v_B=v_A*\frac{A_A}{A_B} \leftarrow eq.5$$

Solve eq.4 for the velocity at B.

$$D_B=250\,[mm]*\frac{1}{1,000}\left[\frac{m}{mm}\right]=0.25\,[m] \leftarrow eq.6$$

Eq.6 converts the diameter at point B to meters.

$D_B=0.25\,[m]$

$$A_B=\frac{\pi*D_B^2}{4} \leftarrow eq.7$$

Eq.7 computes the area of the pipe at point B.

$$A_B=\frac{\pi*(0.25\,[m])^2}{4}$$

Plug in variable D_B into eq.7, then solve for A_B.

$$A_B=0.04909\,[m^2]$$

Eq.8 converts the diameter at point A to meters.

$$D_A=450\,[mm]*\frac{1}{1,000}\left[\frac{m}{mm}\right]=0.45\,[m] \leftarrow eq.8$$

Eq.9 computes the area of the pipe at point A.

$D_A=0.45\,[m]$

$$A_A=\frac{\pi*D_A^2}{4} \leftarrow eq.9$$

Plug in variable D_A into eq.9, then solve for A_A.

Pressure Flow #14 (cont.)

$$A_A = \frac{\pi * (0.45\,[m])^2}{4}$$

$$A_A = 0.15904\,[m^2]$$

$v_A = 1.00\,[m/s]$ $A_A = 0.15904\,[m^2]$

$$v_B = v_A * \frac{A_A}{A_B} \leftarrow eq.5$$

$A_B = 0.04909\,[m^2]$

Plug in variables v_A, A_A and A_B into eq.5, then solve for v_B.

$$v_B = 1.00\,[m/s] * \frac{0.15904\,[m^2]}{0.04909\,[m^2]}$$

$$v_B = 3.240\,[m/s]$$

Plug in variables $Elev_B$, P_B, v_B, ϱ and g into eq.2, then solve for $Elev_C$.

$P_B = 1.962 * 10^5 \left[\dfrac{kg}{m * s^2}\right]$

$Elev_B = 44.5\,[m]$ $v_B = 3.240\,[m/s]$

$$Elev_C = Elev_B + \frac{P_B}{\varrho * g} + \frac{v_B{}^2}{2 * g} \leftarrow eq.2$$

$\varrho = 1,000\,[kg/m^3]$ $g = 9.81\,[m/s^2]$

$$Elev_C = 44.5\,[m] + \frac{1.962 * 10^5 \left[\dfrac{kg}{m * s^2}\right]}{1,000\,[kg/m^3] * 9.81\,[m/s^2]} + \frac{(3.240\,[m/s])^2}{2 * 9.81\,[m/s^2]}$$

$$Elev_C = 65.04\,[m]$$

Answer: $\boxed{D}$

Water Resources Practice Problems

Pressure Flow #15

<u>Find:</u>$h_{f,AB}$ ← the headloss between points A and B

<u>Given:</u>

$P_{g,A}=3.096*10^5 [Pa]$ ← the gauge pressure at points A and B

$P_{g,B}=3.057*10^5 [Pa]$

$\Delta v_{AB}=0 [m/s]$

$\Delta z_{AB}=0 [m]$

constant velocity and elevation at points A and B

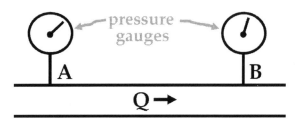
pressure gauges
A   Q→   B

A) 0.1 [m]
B) 0.2 [m]
C) 0.3 [m]
D) 0.4 [m]

Analysis:

$$h_{T,A}=h_{T,B}+h_{f,AB} \leftarrow eq.1$$

total head at point A and B   headloss

Eq.1 computes the total head at point A based on the total head at point B and the headloss between points A and B.

elevation head   headloss

$$\frac{P_A}{\varrho*g}+\frac{v_A^2}{2*g}+z_A = \frac{P_B}{\varrho*g}+\frac{v_B^2}{2*g}+z_B + h_{f,AB} \leftarrow eq.2$$

pressure head   velocity head

Eq.2 writes out the total head terms from eq.1.

Cancel the velocity head and elevation head terms because there is no difference in elevation or velocity at points A and B.

$P_{g,A}=3.096*10^5 [Pa]$ $P_{g,B}=3.057*10^5 [Pa]$

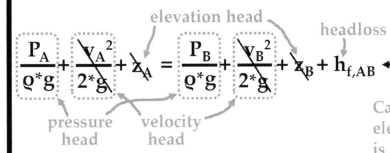

$$h_{f,AB}=\frac{P_A-P_B}{\varrho*g} \leftarrow eq.3$$

$\varrho=1000 [kg/m^3]$ $g=9.81 [m/s^2]$

Eq.3 computes solves eq.2 for the headloss

Plug in P_A, P_B, ϱ, and g into eq. 3, then solve for $h_{f,AB}$.

$$h_{f,AB}=\frac{3.096*10^5 [Pa]-3.057*10^5 [Pa]}{1000 [kg/m^3]*9.81 [m/s^2]}$$

Pressure Flow #15 (cont.)

$$h_{f,AB} = 0.398 \left[\frac{Pa*m^2*s^2}{kg} \right] * 1 \left[\frac{kg}{Pa*m*s^2} \right]$$

Convert the headloss to units of meters.

conversion factor

$$h_{f,AB} = 0.398 \,[m]$$

Answer: $\boxed{D}$

Water Resources Practice Problems

Network Flows #1

Find: Q ← the flow rate

Given:

$L_1 = 350 \, [\text{ft}]$
$L_2 = 550 \, [\text{ft}]$ ← pipe lengths

$\text{Elev}_1 = 247.8 \, [\text{ft}]$
$\text{Elev}_2 = 181.9 \, [\text{ft}]$ ← water surface elevations

$D_1 = 4 \, [\text{in}]$
$D_2 = 12 \, [\text{in}]$ ← pipe diameters

$f_1 = 0.016$
$f_2 = 0.020$ ← friction factors

water flows from tank 1 to tank 2

Elev 1 — tank 1 — pipe 1 — Elev 2 — tank 2 — Q → pipe 2

A) $0.08 \, [\text{ft}^3/\text{s}]$

B) $0.22 \, [\text{ft}^3/\text{s}]$

C) $0.64 \, [\text{ft}^3/\text{s}]$

D) $1.38 \, [\text{ft}^3/\text{s}]$

Analysis:

headloss — friction factors — $v_1 = Q/A_1$ — pipe lengths — water surface elevations — gravitational acceleration — pipe diameters — $v_2 = Q/A_2$

$$h_f = \text{Elev}_1 - \text{Elev}_2 = \frac{f_1 * L_1 * v_1^2}{2 * g * D_1} + \frac{f_2 * L_2 * v_2^2}{2 * g * D_2} \leftarrow eq.1$$

Eq. 1 computes the total headloss between tank 1 and tank 2.

Plug in the flow rate and pipe area in for the velocities in eq. 1.

flow rate through the pipes

$$\text{Elev}_1 - \text{Elev}_2 = \frac{f_1 * L_1 * Q^2}{2 * g * D_1 * A_1^2} + \frac{f_2 * L_2 * Q^2}{2 * g * D_2 * A_2^2} \leftarrow eq.2$$

cross-sectional areas of the pipes

Solve eq. 2 for the flow rate.

$$Q = \sqrt{\frac{2 * g * (\text{Elev}_1 - \text{Elev}_2)}{\left(\dfrac{f_1 * L_1}{D_1 * A_1^2} + \dfrac{f_2 * L_2}{D_2 * A_2^2} \right)}} \leftarrow eq.3$$

$D_1 = 4 \, [\text{in}]$

$$A_1 = \frac{\pi * D_1^2}{4} \leftarrow eq.4$$

Eq. 4 computes the cross-sectional area of pipe 1. Plug in variable D_1 into eq. 4, then solve for A_1.

$$A_1 = \frac{\pi * (4 \, [\text{in}])^2}{4} * \left(\frac{1}{12} \left[\frac{\text{ft}}{\text{in}} \right] \right)^2$$

conversion factor

Convert the area A_1 to feet squared.

Network Flows #1 (cont.)

$$A_1 = 0.0873\,[\text{ft}^2]$$

$$A_2 = \frac{\pi * D_2^{\;2}}{4} \leftarrow eq.5$$

$D_2 = 12\,[\text{in}]$

Eq. 5 computes the cross-sectional area of pipe 2. Plug in variable D_2 into eq. 5, then solve for A_2.

$$A_2 = \frac{\pi * (12\,[\text{in}])^2}{4} * \left(\frac{1}{12}\left[\frac{\text{ft}}{\text{in}}\right]\right)^2$$

conversion factor

Convert the area A_2 to feet squared.

$$A_2 = 0.7854\,[\text{ft}^2]$$

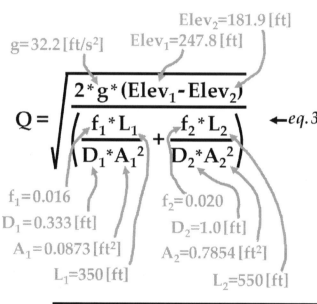

$\text{Elev}_2 = 181.9\,[\text{ft}]$

$g = 32.2\,[\text{ft/s}^2]$ $\text{Elev}_1 = 247.8\,[\text{ft}]$

Plug in all the known variables into the right hand side of eq. 3, then solve for Q.

$$Q = \sqrt{\frac{2*g*(\text{Elev}_1 - \text{Elev}_2)}{\left(\dfrac{f_1 * L_1}{D_1 * A_1^{\;2}} + \dfrac{f_2 * L_2}{D_2 * A_2^{\;2}}\right)}} \leftarrow eq.3$$

$f_1 = 0.016$
$D_1 = 0.333\,[\text{ft}]$
$A_1 = 0.0873\,[\text{ft}^2]$
$L_1 = 350\,[\text{ft}]$

$f_2 = 0.020$
$D_2 = 1.0\,[\text{ft}]$
$A_2 = 0.7854\,[\text{ft}^2]$
$L_2 = 550\,[\text{ft}]$

$$Q = \sqrt{\frac{2*32.2\,[\text{ft/s}^2]*(247.8\,[\text{ft}] - 181.9\,[\text{ft}])}{\left(\dfrac{0.016*350\,[\text{ft}]}{0.333\,[\text{ft}]*(0.0873\,[\text{ft}^2])^2} + \dfrac{0.020*550\,[\text{ft}]}{1.0\,[\text{ft}]*(0.7854\,[\text{ft}^2])^2}\right)}}$$

$$Q = 1.38\,[\text{ft}^3/\text{s}]$$

Answer: $\boxed{\text{D}}$

Water Resources Practice Problems

Network Flows #2

Find: Q_c ← the flow rate through pipe C

Given:

$Q_A = 20\,[\text{ft}^3/\text{s}]$ ← the flow rate through pipe A

$\left.\begin{array}{l} L_B = 1{,}200\,[\text{ft}] \\ L_C = 2{,}000\,[\text{ft}] \end{array}\right\}$ ← pipe lengths

$\left.\begin{array}{l} C_B = 100 \\ C_C = 105 \end{array}\right\}$ ← roughness coefficient

$\left.\begin{array}{l} D_B = 1.5\,[\text{ft}] \\ D_C = 2.5\,[\text{ft}] \end{array}\right\}$ ← pipe diameters

pipe schematic (not to scale)

Q_A Q_B Q_C Q_D

ignore minor losses

A) $5\,[\text{ft}^3/\text{s}]$

B) $8\,[\text{ft}^3/\text{s}]$

C) $12\,[\text{ft}^3/\text{s}]$

D) $15\,[\text{ft}^3/\text{s}]$

Analysis:

$Q_C = v_C * A_C$ ← eq.1

flow rate in pipe C · velocity in pipe C · cross-sectional area in pipe C

Eq.1 computes the flow rate in pipe C.

$D_C = 2.5\,[\text{ft}]$

$A_C = \dfrac{\pi * D_C^2}{4}$ ← eq.2

Eq.2 computes the cross-sectional area of pipe C. Plug in variable D_C into eq.2, then solve for A_C.

$A_C = \dfrac{\pi * (2.5\,[\text{ft}])^2}{4} = 4.909\,[\text{ft}^2]$

flow rate through pipes A, B and C

$Q_A = Q_B + Q_C$ ← eq.3

$Q_B = v_B * A_B$ $Q_C = v_C * A_C$

Eq.3 computes the flow rate through pipe A, which we'll use to find the velocity in pipe C.

Substitute the velocity times the pipe area in for the flow rate for pipes B and C, in eq.3.

$Q_A = v_B * A_B + v_C * A_C$ ← eq.4

$h_{f,B} = h_{f,C}$ ← eq.5

Eq.5 shows the headloss across pipe B equals the headloss across pipe C.

Network Flows #2 (cont.)

Eq. 6 writes out the Hazen-Williams headloss equation for pipes B and C.

pipe length [ft]   fluid velocity [ft/s]

$$\frac{3.022 * L_B * v_B^{1.85}}{C_B^{1.85} * D_B^{1.17}} = \frac{3.022 * L_C * v_C^{1.85}}{C_C^{1.85} * D_C^{1.17}} \leftarrow eq.6$$

roughness coefficient   pipe diameter [ft]

Solve eq. 6 for the velocity through pipe B as a function of the velocity through pipe C.

$L_C = 2,000$ [ft] $C_B = 100$ $D_B = 1.5$ [ft]

Plug in variables L_C, C_B, D_B, L_B, C_C and D_C into eq.7 then solve for v_B.

$$v_B = \left(\frac{L_C * v_C^{1.85} * C_B^{1.85} * D_B^{1.17}}{L_B * C_C^{1.85} * D_C^{1.17}} \right)^{0.5405} \leftarrow eq.7$$

$L_B = 1,200$ [ft] $C_C = 105$ $D_C = 2.5$ [ft]

Drop the units from the right hand side of eq.7 and remember the velocity is in feet per second.

$$v_B = \left(\frac{2,000 * v_C^{1.85} * (100)^{1.85} * (1.5)^{1.17}}{1,200 * (105)^{1.85} * (2.5)^{1.17}} \right)^{0.5405}$$

$$v_B = 0.9087 * v_C$$

$D_B = 1.5$ [ft]

$$A_B = \frac{\pi * D_B^2}{4} \leftarrow eq.8$$

Eq. 8 computes the cross-sectional area of pipe B. Plug in variable D_B into eq.8, then solve for A_B.

$$A_B = \frac{\pi * (1.5\,[ft])^2}{4} = 1.767\,[ft^2]$$

$v_B = 0.9087 * v_C$ $A_C = 4.909$ [ft²]

$$Q_A = v_B * A_B + v_C * A_C \leftarrow eq.4$$

$Q_A = 20$ [ft³/s] $A_B = 1.767$ [ft²]

Plug in variables Q, v_B, A_B, and A_C into eq.4, then solve for the velocity through pipe C.

Network Flows #2 (cont.)

$$20\,[\text{ft}^3/\text{s}]=0.9087*v_C*1.767\,[\text{ft}^2]+v_C*4.909\,[\text{ft}^2]$$

$$v_C=3.07\,[\text{ft/s}]$$

$$v_C=3.07\,[\text{ft/s}]\qquad A_C=4.909\,[\text{ft}^2]$$

$$Q_C=v_C*A_C \leftarrow eq.1$$

Plug in v_C and A_C into eq.1, then solve for Q_C.

$$Q_C=3.07\,[\text{ft/s}]*4.909\,[\text{ft}^2]$$

$$Q_C=15.07\,[\text{ft}^3/\text{s}]$$

Answer: $\boxed{D}$

Network Flows #3

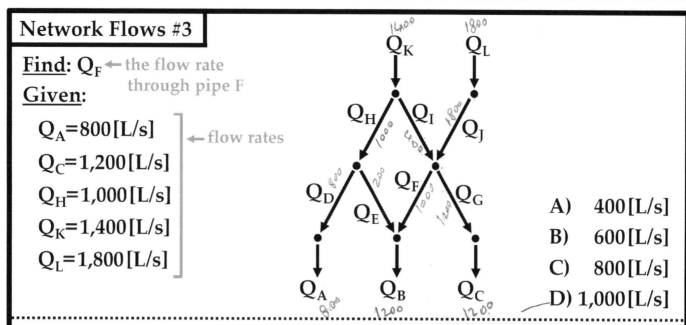

Find: Q_F ← the flow rate through pipe F

Given:

$Q_A = 800\,[L/s]$ ← flow rates
$Q_C = 1,200\,[L/s]$
$Q_H = 1,000\,[L/s]$
$Q_K = 1,400\,[L/s]$
$Q_L = 1,800\,[L/s]$

A) 400 [L/s]

B) 600 [L/s]

C) 800 [L/s]

D) 1,000 [L/s]

Analysis:

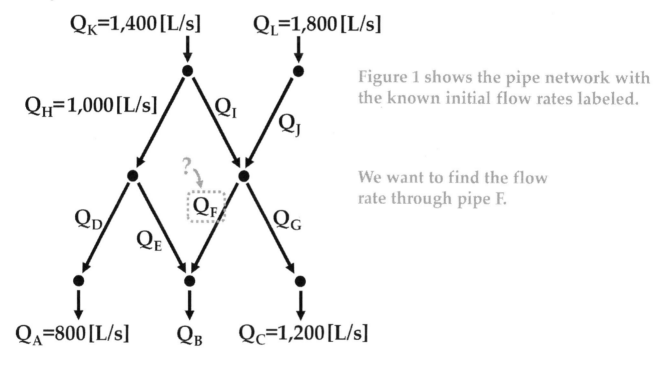

Figure 1 shows the pipe network with the known initial flow rates labeled.

We want to find the flow rate through pipe F.

Figure 1

$$Q_F = Q_B - Q_E \quad \leftarrow eq.1$$

Eq.1 computes the flow rate through pipe F.

total outflows   total inflows

$$\overbrace{Q_A + Q_B + Q_C} = \overbrace{Q_K + Q_L} \quad \leftarrow eq.2$$

Eq.2 computes the mass balance across the entire network.

Network Flows #3 (cont.)

$Q_K=1,400\,[L/s]$ $Q_A=800\,[L/s]$

$$Q_B=Q_K+Q_L-Q_A-Q_C \leftarrow eq.3$$

$Q_L=1,800\,[L/s]$ $Q_C=1,200\,[L/s]$

Solve eq. 2 for Q_B.

Plug in variables Q_K, Q_L, Q_A and Q_C into eq. 3, then solve for Q_B.

$$Q_B=1,400\,[L/s]+1,800\,[L/s]-800\,[L/s]-1,200\,[L/s]$$

$$Q_B=1,200\,[L/s]$$

$$Q_E=Q_H-Q_D \leftarrow eq.4$$

Eq. 4 computes the flow rate through pipe E.

$Q_A=800\,[L/s]$

$$Q_D=Q_A \leftarrow eq.5$$

Eq. 5 computes the flow rate through pipe D.

$$Q_D=800\,[L/s]$$

$Q_H=1,000\,[L/s]$ $Q_D=800\,[L/s]$

$$Q_E=Q_H-Q_D \leftarrow eq.4$$

Plug in variables Q_H and Q_D into eq. 4, then solve for Q_E.

$$Q_E=1,000\,[L/s]-800\,[L/s]$$

$$Q_E=200\,[L/s]$$

$Q_B=1,200\,[L/s]$ $Q_E=200\,[L/s]$

$$Q_F=Q_B-Q_E \leftarrow eq.1$$

Plug in variables Q_B and Q_E into eq. 1, then solve for Q_F.

$$Q_F=1,200\,[L/s]-200\,[L/s]$$

$$Q_F=1,000\,[L/s]$$ Answer: $\boxed{D}$

Network Flows #4

<u>Find:</u> C_A ← the roughness coefficient through pipe A

<u>Given:</u>

pipes A, B and C are connected in series

Q → pipe A pipe B pipe C

$Q=2,000\,[\text{gal/min}]$ ← flow rate

$C_B=100$
$C_C=105$ ← the roughness coefficient through pipes B and C

$h_f=10.5\,[\text{ft}]$
headloss through pipes A, B and C

$L_A=500\,[\text{ft}]$
$L_B=500\,[\text{ft}]$ ← pipe lengths
$L_C=800\,[\text{ft}]$

$D_A=12\,[\text{in}]$
$D_B=18\,[\text{in}]$ ← pipe diameters
$D_C=24\,[\text{in}]$

A) 90
B) 95
C) 100
D) 105

Analysis:

$$h_f=h_{f,A}+h_{f,B}+h_{f,C} \leftarrow eq.1$$

Eq.1 computes the headloss through pipes A, B and C.

Write out the headloss terms on the right hand side of eq.1 using Hazen-Williams headloss equation.

$$h_f=\frac{3.022*L_A*v_A^{1.85}}{C_A^{1.85}*D_A^{1.17}}+\frac{3.022*L_B*v_B^{1.85}}{C_B^{1.85}*D_B^{1.17}}+\frac{3.022*L_C*v_C^{1.85}}{C_C^{1.85}*D_C^{1.17}} \leftarrow eq.2$$

In eq.2, L=pipe length [ft]
v=water velocity [ft/s]
D=pipe diameter [ft]
C=roughness coefficient

Solve eq.2 for C_A.

$$C_A=\left(\frac{3.022*L_A*v_A^{1.85}}{\left(\frac{3.022*L_B*v_B^{1.85}}{C_B^{1.85}*D_B^{1.17}}+\frac{3.022*L_C*v_C^{1.85}}{C_C^{1.85}*D_C^{1.17}}\right)*D_A^{1.17}}\right)^{0.5405} \leftarrow eq.3$$

$$D_A=12\,[\text{in}]*\frac{1}{12}\left[\frac{\text{ft}}{\text{in}}\right] \rightarrow D_A=1.0\,[\text{ft}] \leftarrow eq.4$$

Eq.4, eq.5 and eq.6 convert the pipe diameters to feet.

conversion factors

$$D_B=18\,[\text{in}]*\frac{1}{12}\left[\frac{\text{ft}}{\text{in}}\right] \rightarrow D_B=1.5\,[\text{ft}] \leftarrow eq.5$$

Water Resources Practice Problems

Network Flows #4 (cont.)

$$D_C = 24\,[\text{in}] * \frac{1}{12}\left[\frac{\text{ft}}{\text{in}}\right] \rightarrow D_C = 2.0\,[\text{ft}] \leftarrow eq.6$$

conversion factor

$D_A = 1.0\,[\text{ft}]$

$$A_A = \frac{\pi * D_A^2}{4} = \frac{\pi * (1.0\,[\text{ft}])^2}{4} \leftarrow eq.7$$

$$A_A = 0.7854\,[\text{ft}^2]$$

Eq.7 computes the cross-sectional area of pipe A. Plug in variable D_A into eq.7, then solve for A_A.

$D_B = 1.5\,[\text{ft}]$

$$A_B = \frac{\pi * D_B^2}{4} = \frac{\pi * (1.5\,[\text{ft}])^2}{4} \leftarrow eq.8$$

$$A_B = 1.767\,[\text{ft}^2]$$

Eq.8 computes the cross-sectional area of pipe B. Plug in variable D_B into eq.8, then solve for A_B.

$D_C = 2.0\,[\text{ft}]$

$$A_C = \frac{\pi * D_C^2}{4} = \frac{\pi * (2.0\,[\text{ft}])^2}{4} \leftarrow eq.9$$

$$A_C = 3.142\,[\text{ft}^2]$$

Eq.9 computes the cross-sectional area of pipe C. Plug in variable D_C into eq.9, then solve for A_C.

Eq.10 converts the flow rate to units of cubic feet per second.

$$Q = 2{,}000\left[\frac{\text{gal}}{\text{min}}\right] * \frac{1}{7.48}\left[\frac{\text{ft}^3}{\text{gal}}\right] * \frac{1}{60}\left[\frac{\text{min}}{\text{s}}\right] \leftarrow eq.10$$

$$Q = 4.456\,[\text{ft}^3/\text{s}]$$

$Q = 4.456\,[\text{ft}^3/\text{s}]$

$$v_A = \frac{Q}{A_A} = \frac{4.456\,[\text{ft}^3/\text{s}]}{0.7854\,[\text{ft}^2]} \leftarrow eq.11$$

$A_A = 0.7854\,[\text{ft}^2]$

Eq.11 computes the velocity through pipe A.

Network Flows #4 (cont.)

$$v_A = 5.674 \, [\text{ft/s}]$$

$Q = 4.456 \, [\text{ft}^3/\text{s}]$

$$v_B = \frac{Q}{A_B} = \frac{4.456 \, [\text{ft}^3/\text{s}]}{1.767 \, [\text{ft}^2]} \leftarrow eq. 12$$

$A_B = 1.767 \, [\text{ft}^2]$

Eq. 12 computes the velocity through pipe B.

$$v_B = 2.522 \, [\text{ft/s}]$$

$Q = 4.456 \, [\text{ft}^3/\text{s}]$

$$v_C = \frac{Q}{A_C} = \frac{4.456 \, [\text{ft}^3/\text{s}]}{3.142 \, [\text{ft}^2]} \leftarrow eq. 13$$

$A_C = 3.142 \, [\text{ft}^2]$

Eq. 13 computes the velocity through pipe C.

$$v_C = 1.418 \, [\text{ft/s}]$$

Plug in all the variables into the right hand side of eq. 3, then solve for C_A.

$h_f = 10.5 \, [\text{ft}]$ $v_B = 2.522 \, [\text{ft/s}]$ $v_A = 5.674 \, [\text{ft/s}]$ $L_A = 500 \, [\text{ft}]$ $v_C = 1.418 \, [\text{ft/s}]$

$$C_A = \left(\frac{3.022 * L_A * v_A^{1.85}}{h_f - \left(\frac{3.022 * L_B * v_B^{1.85}}{C_B^{1.85} * D_B^{1.17}} + \frac{3.022 * L_C * v_C^{1.85}}{C_C^{1.85} * D_C^{1.17}} \right) * D_A^{1.17}} \right)^{0.5405} \leftarrow eq. 3$$

cancels out

$C_B = 100$ $D_B = 1.5 \, [\text{ft}]$ $L_C = 800 \, [\text{ft}]$ $D_A = 1.0 \, [\text{ft}]$
$L_B = 500 \, [\text{ft}]$ $C_C = 105$ $D_C = 2.0 \, [\text{ft}]$

$$C_A = \left(\frac{3.022 * 500 * (5.674)^{1.85}}{10.5 - \left(\frac{3.022 * 500 * (2.522)^{1.85}}{(100)^{1.85} * (1.5)^{1.17}} + \frac{3.022 * 800 * (1.418)^{1.85}}{(105)^{1.85} * (2)^{1.17}} \right)} \right)^{0.5405}$$

$$C_A = 89.99 \quad \underline{\text{Answer:}} \quad \boxed{\text{A}}$$

Water Resources Practice Problems

Network Flows #5

<u>Find:</u> Q_C ← the flow rate through pipe C

<u>Given:</u>

$D_A = 6 \, [\text{in}]$ ← pipe diameters
$D_D = 12 \, [\text{in}]$
$D_B, D_C, D_E = 8 \, [\text{in}]$
$L = 250 \, [\text{ft}]$ ← the length of each pipe
$f = 0.018$ ← the friction factor of each pipe
$Q = 1,600 \, [\text{gal/min}]$ ← the flow rate through the pipe network

$3.565 \, ft^3/s$

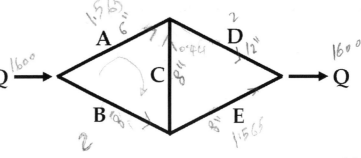

A) $0.88 \, [\text{ft}^3/\text{s}]$
B) $0.94 \, [\text{ft}^3/\text{s}]$
C) $1.02 \, [\text{ft}^3/\text{s}]$
D) $1.10 \, [\text{ft}^3/\text{s}]$

Analysis:

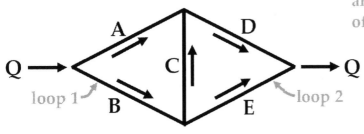

Figure 1

Figure 1 shows the pipe network with arrows showing the assumed direction of flow through each pipe.

We'll identify the left loop as 'loop 1' and the right loop as 'loop 2.'

possible solutions for flow rate Q_C

A) $0.88 \, [\text{ft}^3/\text{s}]$
B) $0.94 \, [\text{ft}^3/\text{s}]$
C) $1.02 \, [\text{ft}^3/\text{s}]$
D) $1.10 \, [\text{ft}^3/\text{s}]$

first guess for Q_C

← $Q_{C,1} = 0.98 \, [\text{ft}^3/\text{s}]$

first iteration

We'll first assume a flow rate of 0.98 cubic feet per second in pipe C because it is larger than 2 of the possible answers and smaller than the other two possible answers.

Assuming $Q_C = 0.98$ cubic feet per second, we can compute the flow rates through pipes A and B.

$\Sigma h_f = 0 = h_{f,A,1} - h_{f,B,1} - h_{f,C,1}$ ← eq.1

Eq.1 shows the headloss around a loop in a balanced pipe network equals zero.

headloss

$h_f = \dfrac{f * L * v^2}{2 * g * D}$ ← eq.2

friction factor · pipe length · velocity · gravitational acceleration · pipe diameter · $v = Q/A$

Eq.2 shows Darcy's headloss equation.

Network Flows #5 (cont.)

headloss   flow rate

$$h_f = \frac{f*L*Q^2}{2*g*D*A^2} \leftarrow eq.3$$

cross-sectional
area of the pipe

Eq. 3 identifies the headloss is a
function of the flow rate squared.

$$D_A = 6\,[in] * \frac{1}{12}\left[\frac{ft}{in}\right] = 0.5\,[ft] \leftarrow eq.4$$

conversion factor

Eq. 4 computes the
diameter of pipe A.

$D_A = 0.5\,[ft]$

$$A_A = \frac{\pi * D_A^2}{4} = \frac{\pi * (0.5\,[ft])^2}{4} \leftarrow eq.5$$

Eq. 5 computes the cross-sectional
area of pipe A. Plug in variable
D_A into eq.5, then solve for A_A.

$$A_A = 0.1963\,[ft^2]$$

$f=0.018$ $L=250\,[ft]$

$$h_{f,A} = \frac{f*L*Q_A^2}{2*g*D_A*A_A^2} \leftarrow eq.6$$

$g=32.2\,[ft/s^2]$ $A_A=0.1963\,[ft^2]$
$D_A=0.5\,[ft]$

Plug in variables f, L, g, D_A, and
A_A into eq.6, then solve for $h_{f,A}$
as a function of Q_A.

$$h_{f,A} = \frac{0.018*250\,[ft]*Q_A^2}{2*32.2[ft/s^2]*0.5\,[ft]*(0.1963[ft^2])^2} = 3.627\,[s^2/ft^5]*Q_A^2$$

$$D_D = 12\,[in] * \frac{1}{12}\left[\frac{ft}{in}\right] = 1.0\,[ft] \leftarrow eq.7$$

conversion factor

Eq. 7 computes the
diameter of pipe D.

$D_D = 1.0\,[ft]$

$$A_D = \frac{\pi * D_D^2}{4} = \frac{\pi * (1.0\,[ft])^2}{4} \leftarrow eq.8$$

Eq. 8 computes the cross-sectional
area of pipe D. Plug in variable
D_D into eq.8, then solve for A_D.

$$A_D = 0.7854\,[ft^2]$$

Water Resources Practice Problems

Network Flows #5 (cont.)

$$h_{f,D} = \frac{f * L * Q_D^2}{2 * g * D_D * A_D^2} \leftarrow eq.\,9$$

where $f = 0.018$, $L = 250\,[ft]$, $g = 32.2\,[ft/s^2]$, $D_D = 1.0\,[ft]$, $A_D = 0.7854\,[ft^2]$

Plug in variables f, L, g, D_D, and A_D into eq. 9, then solve for $h_{f,D}$ as a function of Q_D.

$$h_{f,D} = \frac{0.018 * 250\,[ft] * Q_D^2}{2 * 32.2\,[ft/s^2] * 1.0\,[ft] * (0.7854\,[ft^2])^2} = 0.1133\,[s^2/ft^5] * Q_D^2$$

$$D_B = 8\,[in] * \boxed{\frac{1}{12}\left[\frac{ft}{in}\right]} = 0.667\,[ft] \leftarrow eq.\,10$$

conversion factor

Eq. 10 computes the diameter of pipe B.

$$A_B = \frac{\pi * D^2}{4} = \frac{\pi * (0.667\,[ft])^2}{4} \leftarrow eq.\,11$$

where $D_B = 0.667\,[ft]$

Eq. 11 computes the cross-sectional area of pipe B.

$$A_B = 0.3494\,[ft^2]$$

$$h_{f,B} = \frac{f * L * Q_B^2}{2 * g * D_B * A_B^2} \leftarrow eq.\,12$$

where $f = 0.018$, $L = 250\,[ft]$, $g = 32.2\,[ft/s^2]$, $D_B = 0.667\,[ft]$, $A_B = 0.3494\,[ft^2]$

Plug in variables f, L, g, D_B, and A_B into eq. 12, then solve for $h_{f,B}$ as a function of Q_B.

$$h_{f,B} = \frac{0.018 * 250\,[ft] * Q_B^2}{2 * 32.2\,[ft/s^2] * 0.667\,[ft] * (0.3494\,[ft^2])^2} = 0.8581\,[s^2/ft^5] * Q_B^2$$

$$h_{f,C} = 0.8581 * Q_C^2 \leftarrow eq.\,13$$

$$h_{f,E} = 0.8581 * Q_E^2 \leftarrow eq.\,14$$

Since pipes C and E share the same diameter as pipe B. The headloss through pipes C and E is shown in eq. 13 and eq. 14.

Network Flows #5 (cont.)

$h_{f,A} = 3.627\,[s^2/ft^5] * Q_A^2$

$$h_{f,A} = h_{f,B} + h_{f,C} \leftarrow eq.\,15$$

Substitute in the variables $h_{f,A}$, $h_{f,B}$ and $h_{f,C}$ into eq. 15, then simplify.

$h_{f,B} = 0.8581\,[s^2/ft^5] * Q_B^2$

$h_{f,C} = 0.8581\,[s^2/ft^5] * Q_C^2$

$$3.627\,[s^2/ft^5] * Q_A^2 = 0.8581\,[s^2/ft^5] * Q_B^2 + 0.8581\,[s^2/ft^5] * Q_C^2$$

headloss through pipe A

headloss through pipes B and C

$$3.627\,[s^2/ft^5] * Q_A^2 = 0.8581\,[s^2/ft^5] * (Q_B^2 + Q_C^2) \leftarrow eq.\,16$$

$$Q = Q_A + Q_B \leftarrow eq.\,17$$

Eq. 17 computes the total flow through the pipe network.

$$Q_A = Q - Q_B \leftarrow eq.\,18$$

Solve eq. 17 for Q_A.

conversion factor

$$Q = 1{,}600\left[\frac{gal}{min}\right] * \frac{1}{7.48}\left[\frac{ft^3}{gal}\right] * \frac{1}{60}\left[\frac{min}{s}\right] \leftarrow eq.\,19$$

$$Q = 3.565\,[ft^3/s]$$

Eq. 19 converts the flow rate to units of cubic feet per second.

$Q = 3.565\,[ft^3/s]$

$$Q_A = Q - Q_B$$

$$Q_A = 3.565\,[ft^3/s] - Q_B$$

Plug in variables Q_A and Q_C into eq. 16, then solve for Q_B.

$Q_A = 3.565\,[ft^3/s] - Q_B$

$Q_{C,1} = 0.98\,[ft^3/s] \leftarrow$ assumed flow rate

$$3.627\,[s^2/ft^5] * Q_A^2 = 0.8581\,[s^2/ft^5] * (Q_B^2 + Q_C^2) \leftarrow eq.\,16$$

Water Resources Practice Problems

Network Flows #5 (cont.)

Use the quadratic formula to solve for flow rate Q_B.

$$3.627\,[s^2/ft^5]*(3.565\,[ft^3/s]-Q_B)^2 = 0.8581\,[s^2/ft^5]*(Q_B{}^2+(0.98\,[ft^3/s])^2)$$

$$Q_{B,1}=2.334\,[ft^3/s]$$

Add a subscript 1 to Q_B to identify this value for the first iteration.

$Q=3.565\,[ft^3/s]$ $Q_{B,1}=2.334\,[ft^3/s]$

$$Q_{A,1}=Q-Q_{B,1} \leftarrow eq.\,18$$

Plug in variables Q and $Q_{B,1}$ into eq.18, then solve $Q_{A,1}$.

$$Q_{A,1}=3.565\,[ft^3/s]-2.334\,[ft^3/s]$$

$$Q_{A,1}=1.231\,[ft^3/s]$$

$Q_{A,1}=1.231\,[ft^3/s]$ $Q_{C,1}=0.98\,[ft^3/s]$

$$Q_{D,1}=Q_{A,1}+Q_{C,1} \leftarrow eq.\,20$$

Eq.20 computes the flow rate through pipe D for iteration 1.

$$Q_{D,1}=1.231\,[ft^3/s]+0.98\,[ft^3/s]$$

Plug in variables $Q_{A,1}$ and $Q_{C,1}$ into eq.20, then solve for $Q_{D,1}$.

$$Q_{D,1}=2.211\,[ft^3/s]$$

$Q_{B,1}=2.334\,[ft^3/s]$ $Q_{C,1}=0.98\,[ft^3/s]$

$$Q_{E,1}=Q_{B,1}-Q_{C,1} \leftarrow eq.\,21$$

Eq.21 computes the flow rate through pipe E for iteration 1.

$$Q_{E,1}=2.334\,[ft^3/s]-0.98\,[ft^3/s]$$

Plug in variables $Q_{B,1}$ and $Q_{C,1}$ into eq.21, then solve for $Q_{E,1}$.

$$Q_{E,1}=1.354\,[ft^3/s]$$

$h_{f,C}=0.8581\,[s^2/ft^5]*Q_C{}^2$ $h_{f,E}=0.8581\,[s^2/ft^5]*Q_E{}^2$

$$h_{f,C}+h_{f,D}=h_{f,E} \leftarrow eq.\,22$$

Plug in variables $h_{f,C}$, $h_{f,D}$ and $h_{f,E}$ into eq.22, then simplify.

$h_{f,D}=0.1133\,[s^2/ft^5]*Q_D{}^2$

Network Flows #5 (cont.)

Add subscript 1 to the flow rates in eq. 23, then plug in the assumed flow rates for the first iteration and compare the headlosses.

$Q_{C,1}=0.98\,[\text{ft}^3/\text{s}]$

$Q_{D,1}=2.211\,[\text{ft}^3/\text{s}]$

$Q_{E,1}=1.354\,[\text{ft}^3/\text{s}]$

$$0.8581\,[\text{s}^2/\text{ft}^5]*Q_{C,1}{}^2+0.1133\,[\text{s}^2/\text{ft}^5]*Q_{D,1}{}^2 \overset{?}{=} 0.8581\,[\text{s}^2/\text{ft}^5]*Q_{E,1}{}^2 \quad \leftarrow eq.\,23$$

$$0.8581\,[\text{s}^2/\text{ft}^5]*(0.98\,[\text{ft}^3/\text{s}])^2+0.1133\,[\text{s}^2/\text{ft}^5]*(2.211\,[\text{ft}^3/\text{s}])^2$$

$$\overset{?}{=}0.8581\,[\text{s}^2/\text{ft}^5]*(1.354\,[\text{ft}^3/\text{s}])^2$$

$$1.378\,[\text{ft}]<1.573\,[\text{ft}] \quad \leftarrow ieq.\,1$$

For the first iteration, there is more headloss through pipe E than through pipes C and D.

$$Q_{C,2}>Q_{C,1}=0.98\,[\text{ft}^3/\text{s}]$$

Therefore the true flow rate through pipe C is greater than 0.98 cubic feet per second.

possible solutions
for flow rate Q_C

A) 0.88 [ft³/s]

B) 0.94 [ft³/s]

C) 1.02 [ft³/s] $\quad\leftarrow Q_{C,2}=1.02\,[\text{ft}^3/\text{s}]$

D) 1.10 [ft³/s]

second guess
for Q_C

second
iteration

Next we'll assume a flow rate of 1.02 cubic feet per second in pipe C, and calculate headlosses.

$Q_A=3.565\,[\text{ft}^3/\text{s}]-Q_B$

Plug in variables Q_A and $Q_{C,2}$ into eq. 16, then solve for flow rate Q_B.

$$3.627\,[\text{s}^2/\text{ft}^5]*Q_A{}^2=0.8581\,[\text{s}^2/\text{ft}^5]*(Q_B{}^2+Q_C{}^2) \quad \leftarrow eq.\,16$$

$Q_{C,2}=1.02\,[\text{ft}^3/\text{s}] \quad \leftarrow$ assumed
flow rate

$$3.627\,[\text{s}^2/\text{ft}^5]*(3.565\,[\text{ft}^3/\text{s}]-Q_B)^2=0.8581\,[\text{s}^2/\text{ft}^5]*(Q_B{}^2+(1.02\,[\text{ft}^3/\text{s}])^2)$$

Network Flows #5 (cont.)

$$Q_{B,2}=2.328\,[\text{ft}^3/\text{s}]$$

Add a subscript 2 to Q_B to identify the second iteration.

$Q=3.565\,[\text{ft}^3/\text{s}]$ $Q_{B,2}=2.328\,[\text{ft}^3/\text{s}]$

$$Q_{A,2}=Q-Q_{B,2} \leftarrow eq.\,23$$

Plug in variables Q and $Q_{B,2}$ into eq. 23, then solve $Q_{A,2}$.

$$Q_{A,2}=3.565\,[\text{ft}^3/\text{s}]-2.328\,[\text{ft}^3/\text{s}]$$

$$Q_{A,2}=1.237\,[\text{ft}^3/\text{s}]$$

$Q_{A,2}=1.237\,[\text{ft}^3/\text{s}]$ $Q_{C,2}=1.02\,[\text{ft}^3/\text{s}]$

$$Q_{D,2}=Q_{A,2}+Q_{C,2} \leftarrow eq.\,24$$

Eq. 24 computes the flow rate through pipe D for iteration 2.

$$Q_{D,2}=1.237\,[\text{ft}^3/\text{s}]+1.02\,[\text{ft}^3/\text{s}]$$

Plug in variables $Q_{A,2}$ and $Q_{C,2}$ into eq. 24, then solve for $Q_{D,2}$.

$$Q_{D,2}=2.257\,[\text{ft}^3/\text{s}]$$

$Q_{B,2}=2.328\,[\text{ft}^3/\text{s}]$ $Q_{C,2}=1.02\,[\text{ft}^3/\text{s}]$

$$Q_{E,2}=Q_{B,2}-Q_{C,2} \leftarrow eq.\,25$$

Eq. 25 computes the flow rate through pipe E for iteration 2.

$$Q_{E,2}=2.328\,[\text{ft}^3/\text{s}]-1.02\,[\text{ft}^3/\text{s}]$$

Plug in variables $Q_{B,2}$ and $Q_{C,2}$ into eq. 25, then solve for $Q_{E,2}$.

$$Q_{E,2}=1.308\,[\text{ft}^3/\text{s}]$$

Plug in the assumed flow rates for the second iteration into eq. 26, then compute the headlosses for loop 2.

$Q_{C,2}=1.02\,[\text{ft}^3/\text{s}]$ $Q_{D,2}=2.257\,[\text{ft}^3/\text{s}]$ $Q_{E,2}=1.308\,[\text{ft}^3/\text{s}]$

$$0.8581\,[\text{s}^2/\text{ft}^5]*Q_{C,2}^2+0.1133\,[\text{s}^2/\text{ft}^5]*Q_{D,2}^2 = 0.8581\,[\text{s}^2/\text{ft}^5]*Q_{E,2}^2 \leftarrow eq.\,26$$

?

Network Flows #5 (cont.)

$$1.470 \, [\text{ft}] \approx 1.468 \, [\text{ft}]$$

$$Q_C = 1.02 \, [\text{ft}^3/\text{s}]$$

Answer: $\boxed{\text{C}}$

The headloss through pipes C and D is approximately the same as the headloss through pipe E. Therefore, Q_C equals 1.02 cubic feet per second.

Water Resources Practice Problems

Network Flows #6

Find: Q_{AB} ← the flow rate through pipe AB

Given:

$C_{AB} = C_{AC} = 90$ ← roughness coefficient
$C_{DB} = C_{CD} = 110$

$L = 200 \, [ft]$ ← length of each pipe

$D_{AB} = 4 \, [in]$ ← pipe diameter
$D_{CD} = 8 \, [in]$
$D_{DB} = D_{AC} = 6 \, [in]$

$Q_{A,in} = 500 \, [gal/min]$
$Q_{B,out} = 200 \, [gal/min]$
$Q_{D,out} = 300 \, [gal/min]$

A) 124 [gal/min]
B) 137 [gal/min]
C) 150 [gal/min]
D) 163 [gal/min]

Analysis:

$$\Sigma h_f = 0 = h_{f,AB} - h_{f,AC} - h_{f,CD} - h_{f,DB} \quad \leftarrow eq.1$$

headloss across individual pipes

Eq.1 computes the headloss around a loop in the pipe network.

$$h_f = \frac{10.44 * L * Q^{1.85}}{C^{1.85} * D^{4.87}} \quad \leftarrow eq.2$$

headloss [ft] — pipe length [ft] — flow rate [gal/min]

roughness — pipe diameter [in]

Eq.2 computes the headloss through a pipe using the Hazen-Williams equation.

$$h_{f,AB} = \frac{10.44 * L_{AB} * Q_{AB}^{1.85}}{C_{AB}^{1.85} * D_{AB}^{4.87}} \quad \leftarrow eq.3$$

$L_{AB} = 200 \, [ft]$

$C_{AB} = 90$ $\quad D_{AB} = 4 \, [in]$

Eq.3 computes the headloss across pipe AB.

Plug in variables L_{AB}, C_{AB} and D_{AB} into eq.3, then solve for $h_{f,AB}$ as a function of Q_{AB}.

$$h_{f,AB} = \frac{10.44 * 200 * Q_{AB}^{1.85}}{(90)^{1.85} * (4)^{4.87}}$$

$$h_{f,AB} = 5.920 * 10^{-4} * Q_{AB}^{1.85} \quad \leftarrow eq.4$$

For eq. 4, 6, 8 and 10 remember the units of h_f are 'feet' and the units of Q are 'gallons per minute'.

Network Flows #6 (cont.)

$$h_{f,AC} = \frac{10.44 * L_{AC} * Q_{AC}^{1.85}}{C_{AC}^{1.85} * D_{AC}^{4.87}} \leftarrow eq.5$$

$L_{AC}=200[ft]$ $C_{AC}=90$ $D_{AC}=6[in]$

Eq.5 computes the headloss across pipe AC.

Plug in variables L_{AC}, C_{AC} and D_{AC} into eq.5, then solve for $h_{f,AC}$ as a function of Q_{AC}.

$$h_{f,AC} = \frac{10.44 * 200 * Q_{AC}^{1.85}}{(90)^{1.85} * (6)^{4.87}}$$

$$h_{f,AC} = 8.218*10^{-5} * Q_{AC}^{1.85} \leftarrow eq.6$$

$$h_{f,CD} = \frac{10.44 * L_{CD} * Q_{CD}^{1.85}}{C_{CD}^{1.85} * D_{CD}^{4.87}} \leftarrow eq.7$$

$L_{CD}=200[ft]$ $C_{CD}=110$ $D_{CD}=8[in]$

Eq.7 computes the headloss across pipe CD.

Plug in variables L_{CD}, C_{CD} and D_{CD} into eq.7, then solve for $h_{f,CD}$ as a function of Q_{CD}.

$$h_{f,CD} = \frac{10.44 * 200 * Q_{CD}^{1.85}}{(110)^{1.85} * (8)^{4.87}}$$

$$h_{f,CD} = 1.397*10^{-5} * Q_{CD}^{1.85} \leftarrow eq.8$$

$$h_{f,DB} = \frac{10.44 * L_{DB} * Q_{DB}^{1.85}}{C_{DB}^{1.85} * D_{DB}^{4.87}} \leftarrow eq.9$$

$L_{DB}=200[ft]$ $C_{DB}=110$ $D_{DB}=6[in]$

Eq.9 computes the headloss across pipe DB.

Plug in variables L_{DB}, C_{DB} and D_{DB} into eq.9, then solve for $h_{f,DB}$ as a function of Q_{DB}.

$$h_{f,DB} = \frac{10.44 * 200 * Q_{DB}^{1.85}}{(110)^{1.85} * (6)^{4.87}}$$

$$h_{f,DB} = 5.670*10^{-5} * Q_{DB}^{1.85} \leftarrow eq.10$$

Water Resources Practice Problems

Network Flows #6 (cont.)

Plug in the equations for the head-losses through each pipe into eq. 1.

$h_{f,AB} = 5.920*10^{-4}*Q_{AB}^{1.85}$ $h_{f,CD} = 1.397*10^{-5}*Q_{CD}^{1.85}$

$$0\,[ft] = h_{f,AB} - h_{f,AC} - h_{f,CD} - h_{f,DB} \quad \leftarrow eq.\,1$$

$h_{f,AC} = 8.218*10^{-5}*Q_{AC}^{1.85}$ $h_{f,DB} = 5.670*10^{-5}*Q_{DB}^{1.85}$

$$0\,[ft] = 5.920*10^{-4}*Q_{AB}^{1.85} - 8.218*10^{-5}*Q_{AC}^{1.85}$$
$$-1.397*10^{-5}*Q_{CD}^{1.85} - 5.670*10^{-5}*Q_{DB}^{1.85} \leftarrow eq.\,11$$

$$Q_{A,in} = Q_{AB} + Q_{AC} \leftarrow eq.\,12$$

Eq. 12 computes the flow rate into the network at node A.

$Q_{A,in} = 500\,[gal/min]$

$$Q_{AC} = Q_{A,in} - Q_{AB} \leftarrow eq.\,13$$

Solve eq. 12 for Q_{AC}.

$$Q_{AC} = 500\,[gal/min] - Q_{AB}$$

Plug in variable $Q_{A,in}$ into eq. 13, then solve for Q_{AC}.

$Q_{AC} = 500\,[gal/min] - Q_{AB}$

$$Q_{CD} = Q_{AC} \leftarrow eq.\,14$$

Eq. 14 computes the flow rate through pipe CD. Substitute variable Q_{AC} into eq. 14.

$$Q_{CD} = 500\,[gal/min] - Q_{AB} \leftarrow eq.\,15$$

$Q_{CD} = 500\,[gal/min] - Q_{AB}$ $Q_{D,out} = 300\,[gal/min]$

$$Q_{DB} = Q_{CD} - Q_{D,out} \leftarrow eq.\,16$$

Eq. 16 computes the flow rate through pipe DB. Plug in variables Q_{CD} and $Q_{D,out}$ into eq. 15.

$$Q_{DB} = 500\,[gal/min] - Q_{AB} - 300\,[gal/min]$$

$$Q_{DB} = 200\,[gal/min] - Q_{AB} \leftarrow eq.\,17$$

Network Flows #6 (cont.)

Drop the units on the right hand side of eq.11, and remember the flow rate is in 'gallons per minute'.

Plug in variables Q_{AC}, Q_{CD} and Q_{DB} into eq.11. This results in one equation and one unknown variable, Q_{AB}.

$$Q_{AC} = 500 \, [gal/min] - Q_{AB}$$

$$0 \, [ft] = 5.920 * 10^{-4} * Q_{AB}^{1.85} - 8.218 * 10^{-5} * Q_{AC}^{1.85}$$

$$-1.397 * 10^{-5} * Q_{CD}^{1.85} - 5.670 * 10^{-5} * Q_{DB}^{1.85} \quad \leftarrow eq.11$$

$$Q_{CD} = 500 \, [gal/min] - Q_{AB} \qquad Q_{DB} = 200 \, [gal/min] - Q_{AB}$$

$$0 \, [ft] = 5.920 * 10^{-4} * Q_{AB}^{1.85} - 8.218 * 10^{-5} * (500 - Q_{AB})^{1.85}$$

$$-1.397 * 10^{-5} * (500 - Q_{AB})^{1.85} - 5.670 * 10^{-5} * (200 - Q_{AB})^{1.85} \quad \leftarrow eq.18$$

Q_{AB}	RHS of eq.18
A) 124 [gal/min] →	-1.34 [ft]
B) 137 [gal/min] →	**-0.04 [ft]**
C) 150 [gal/min] →	1.31 [ft]
D) 163 [gal/min] →	2.72 [ft]

Compute the right hand side of eq.18 using the 4 possible solutions for Q_{AB}.

Since $Q_{AB} = 137$ gallons per minute results in a total headloss most nearly 0 feet, the answer is B.

Answer: | B |

Water Resources Practice Problems

Network Flows #7

<u>Find:</u> $h_{T,J}$ ←total head at junction

<u>Given:</u> $WSEL_A$=200[ft] ⎫
$WSEL_B$=180[ft] ⎬ water surface elevations
$WSEL_C$=140[ft] ⎭

Pipe	L	f	D
AJ	400[ft]	0.015	6[in]
BJ	400[ft]	0.015	6[in]
CJ	800[ft]	0.020	12[in]

the length, friction factor and diameter of each pipe

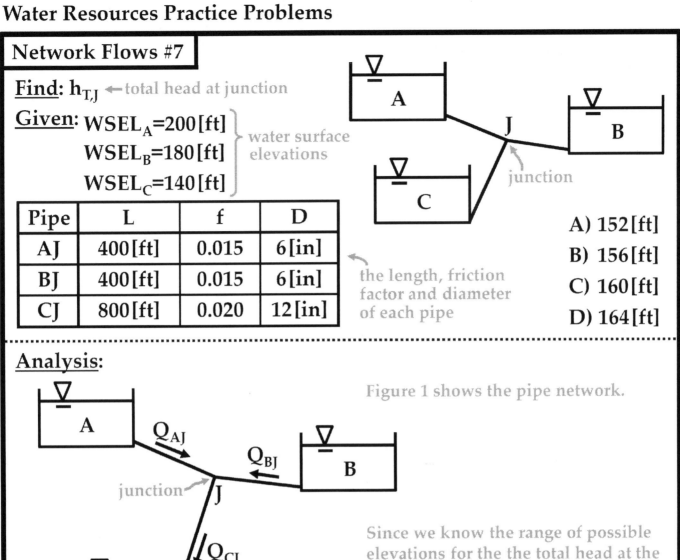

junction

A) 152[ft]
B) 156[ft]
C) 160[ft]
D) 164[ft]

Analysis:

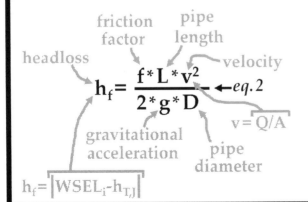

Figure 1

Figure 1 shows the pipe network.

Since we know the range of possible elevations for the the total head at the junction, Figure 1 shows the flow direction through each pipe.

$$0=Q_{AJ}+Q_{BJ}-Q_{CJ} \quad \leftarrow eq.1$$

Eq.1 computes the flow rate into the junction, which should equal 0, based on the conservation of mass.

friction factor | pipe length
headloss | velocity

$$h_f= \frac{f*L*v^2}{2*g*D} \quad \leftarrow eq.2$$

$v=Q/A$

gravitational acceleration | pipe diameter

$h_f=|WSEL_i - h_{T,J}|$

Eq.2 computes headloss using the Darcy headloss equation.

Substitute for variables v and h_f into eq.2, then solve for the flow rate.

Network Flows #7 (cont.)

water surface
elevation at
location i

flow rate

cross-sectional
area of the pipe

$$\left|WSEL_i - h_{T,J}\right| = \frac{f*L*(Q/A)^2}{2*g*D} \leftarrow eq.3$$

total head at
the junction

$$A = \frac{\pi*D^2}{4}$$

Plug in the cross sectional
area of a pipe into eq.3, and
continue to solve for Q.

$$\left|WSEL_i - h_{T,J}\right| = \frac{f*L*\left(\frac{4*Q}{\pi*D^2}\right)^2}{2*g*D}$$

$$Q = \sqrt{\frac{(\left|WSEL_i - h_{T,J}\right|)*g*D^5*\pi^2}{8*f*L}} \leftarrow eq.4$$

Add the appropriate subscripts into
eq.4 to specify the specific pipe.

$$Q_{AJ} = \sqrt{\frac{(\left|WSEL_A - h_{T,J}\right|)*g*D_{AJ}^5*\pi^2}{8*f_{AJ}*L_{AJ}}} \leftarrow eq.5$$

Eq.5 computes the
flow rate in pipe AJ

$$Q_{BJ} = \sqrt{\frac{(\left|WSEL_B - h_{T,J}\right|)*g*D_{BJ}^5*\pi^2}{8*f_{BJ}*L_{BJ}}} \leftarrow eq.6$$

Eq.6 computes the
flow rate in pipe BJ

$$Q_{CJ} = \sqrt{\frac{(\left|WSEL_C - h_{T,J}\right|)*g*D_{CJ}^5*\pi^2}{8*f_{CJ}*L_{CJ}}} \leftarrow eq.7$$

Eq.7 computes the
flow rate in pipe CJ

$$D_{AJ} = D_{BJ} = 6[in]*\frac{1}{12}\left[\frac{ft}{in}\right] = 0.50[ft] \leftarrow eq.8$$

Eq.8 and eq.9 convert
the pipe diameters to
feet.

conversion factors

$$D_{CJ} = 12[in]*\frac{1}{12}\left[\frac{ft}{in}\right] = 1.00[ft] \leftarrow eq.9$$

Water Resources Practice Problems

Network Flows #7 (cont.)

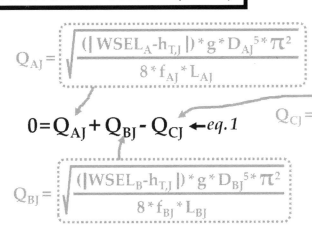

Plug in the expressions for Q_{AJ}, Q_{BJ} and Q_{CJ} into eq.1.

$$Q_{AJ} = \sqrt{\frac{(|WSEL_A - h_{T,J}|) * g * D_{AJ}^5 * \pi^2}{8 * f_{AJ} * L_{AJ}}}$$

$$0 = Q_{AJ} + Q_{BJ} - Q_{CJ} \leftarrow eq.1$$

$$Q_{CJ} = \sqrt{\frac{(|h_{T,J} - WSEL_C|) * g * D_{CJ}^5 * \pi^2}{8 * f_{CJ} * L_{CJ}}}$$

$$Q_{BJ} = \sqrt{\frac{(|WSEL_B - h_{T,J}|) * g * D_{BJ}^5 * \pi^2}{8 * f_{BJ} * L_{BJ}}}$$

Plug in the known variables into the right hand side of eq. 10 and simplify.

$WSEL_A = 200\,[ft]$ $D_{AJ} = 0.50\,[ft]$ $g = 32.2\,[ft/s^2]$ $WSEL_B = 180\,[ft]$ $D_{BJ} = 0.50\,[ft]$

$$0 = \sqrt{\frac{(WSEL_A - h_{T,J}) * g * D_{AJ}^5 * \pi^2}{8 * f_{AJ} * L_{AJ}}} + \sqrt{\frac{(WSEL_B - h_{T,J}) * g * D_{BJ}^5 * \pi^2}{8 * f_{BJ} * L_{BJ}}}$$

$f_{AJ} = 0.015$ $L_{AJ} = 400\,[ft]$ $f_{BJ} = 0.015$ $L_{BJ} = 400\,[ft]$

$WSEL_C = 140\,[ft]$ $g = 32.2\,[ft/s^2]$ $D_{CJ} = 1.00\,[ft]$

$$- \sqrt{\frac{(h_{T,J} - WSEL_C) * g * D_{CJ}^5 * \pi^2}{8 * f_{CJ} * L_{CJ}}} \leftarrow eq.10$$

$f_{CJ} = 0.020$ $L_{CJ} = 800\,[ft]$

$$0 = \sqrt{\frac{(200\,[ft] - h_{T,J}) * 32.2\,[ft/s^2] * (0.50\,[ft])^5 * \pi^2}{8 * 0.015 * 400\,[ft]}}$$

$$+ \sqrt{\frac{(180\,[ft] - h_{T,J}) * 32.2\,[ft/s^2] * (0.50\,[ft])^5 * \pi^2}{8 * 0.015 * 400\,[ft]}}$$

$$- \sqrt{\frac{(h_{T,J} - 140\,[ft]) * 32.2\,[ft/s^2] * (1.00\,[ft])^5 * \pi^2}{8 * 0.020 * 800\,[ft]}}$$

Network Flows #7 (cont.)

$$0 = \sqrt{(200\,[\text{ft}] - h_{T,J}) * 0.207\,[\text{ft}^5/\text{s}^2]}$$

$$+ \sqrt{(180\,[\text{ft}] - h_{T,J}) * 0.207\,[\text{ft}^5/\text{s}^2]}$$

$$- \sqrt{(h_{T,J} - 140\,[\text{ft}]) * 2.483\,[\text{ft}^5/\text{s}^2]} \quad \leftarrow eq.\,11$$

A) 152 [ft]

B) 156 [ft]

C) 160 [ft] $\leftarrow h_{T,J,1} = 158\,[\text{ft}]$

D) 164 [ft]

↑ first iteration

Of the four possible solutions, we'll split the difference and try $h_{T,J}$ equal to 158 feet on the first iteration.

Plug in $WSEL_{J,1}$ into eq.11, then solve for the right hand side of eq.11.

$$0\,[\text{ft}] \underset{?}{=} \sqrt{(200\,[\text{ft}] - h_{T,J}) * 0.207\,[\text{ft}^5/\text{s}^2]}$$

$$+ \sqrt{(180\,[\text{ft}] - h_{T,J}) * 0.207\,[\text{ft}^5/\text{s}^2]}$$

$$- \sqrt{(h_{T,J} - 140\,[\text{ft}]) * 2.483\,[\text{ft}^5/\text{s}^2]} \quad \leftarrow eq.\,11$$

$h_{T,J,1} = 158\,[\text{ft}]$

$$0\,[\text{ft}] \underset{?}{=} \sqrt{(200\,[\text{ft}] - 158\,[\text{ft}]) * 0.207\,[\text{ft}^5/\text{s}^2]}$$

$$+ \sqrt{(180\,[\text{ft}] - 158\,[\text{ft}]) * 0.207\,[\text{ft}^5/\text{s}^2]}$$

$$- \sqrt{(158\,[\text{ft}] - 140\,[\text{ft}]) * 2.483\,[\text{ft}^5/\text{s}^2]}$$

$$0\,[\text{ft}] > -1.60\,[\text{ft}]$$

↑ this assumes $h_{T,J,1} = 158\,[\text{ft}]$

Since the right hand side of eq.11 is negative, the flow rate through pipe CJ is too large, and 158 feet is too high of a value for $h_{T,J}$.

A) 152 [ft]

B) 156 [ft] $\leftarrow h_{T,J,2} = 154\,[\text{ft}]$

~~C) 160 [ft]~~

~~D) 164 [ft]~~

↑ second iteration

For our second iteration, we'll try $h_{T,J,2}$ equal to 154 feet.

Water Resources Practice Problems

Network Flows #7 (cont.)

Plug in $WSEL_{J,2}$ into eq.11, then solve for the right hand side of eq.11.

$$0[ft] \overset{?}{=} \sqrt{(200[ft]-h_{T,J}) * 0.207[ft^5/s^2]}$$

$$+ \sqrt{(180[ft]-h_{T,J}) * 0.207[ft^5/s^2]}$$

$$- \sqrt{(h_{T,J}-140[ft]) * 2.483[ft^5/s^2]} \leftarrow eq.11$$

$WSEL_{J,2}=154[ft]$

$$0[ft] \overset{?}{=} \sqrt{(200[ft]-154[ft]) * 0.207[ft^5/s^2]}$$

$$+ \sqrt{(180[ft]-154[ft]) * 0.207[ft^5/s^2]}$$

$$- \sqrt{(154[ft]-140[ft]) * 2.483[ft^5/s^2]}$$

$$0[ft] > -0.49[ft]$$

this assumes
$h_{T,J,2}=154[ft]$

Since the right hand side of eq.11 is negative, the flow rate through pipe CJ is still too large, and we know $h_{T,J}$ is less than 154 feet.

$$h_{T,J}=152[ft]$$

The only total head at the junction less than 154 feet is 152 feet.

Answer: $\boxed{A}$

Network Flows #8

<u>Find:</u> D_{AJ} ← the diameter of pipe AJ

<u>Given:</u> $L = 500\,[m]$ ← length of all pipes

$h_{T,J} = 62\,[m]$ ← total head at the junction

$WSEL_A = 88\,[m]$ ⎫
$WSEL_B = 38\,[m]$ ⎬ water surface elevations
$WSEL_C = 18\,[m]$ ⎭

$D_{BJ} = 180\,[mm]$ ⎫ the diameter of
$D_{CJ} = 180\,[mm]$ ⎭ pipes BJ and CJ

junction J

A

B

C

$f = 0.018$

the friction factor of all pipes

A) 200 [mm]

B) 250 [mm]

C) 300 [mm]

D) 350 [mm]

Analysis:

$$h_f = \frac{f * L * v^2}{2 * g * D} \quad ← eq.1$$

headloss / friction factor / pipe length / velocity / gravitational acceleration / pipe diameter

$v = Q/A$

Eq.1 computes headloss using the Darcy headloss equation. Plug in variables v and h_f.

$$h_f = |WSEL_i - h_{T,J}|$$

$$A = \frac{\pi * D^2}{4}$$

water surface elevation at point i / cross-sectional area of the pipe

$$|WSEL_i - h_{T,J}| = \frac{f * L * (Q/A)^2}{2 * g * D} \quad ← eq.2$$

total head at the junction

Plug in the cross sectional area of a pipe into eq.2, and solve for the diameter, D.

$$|WSEL_i - h_{T,J}| = \frac{f * L * Q^2 * 16}{2 * g * D * \pi^2 * D^4} \quad ← eq.3$$

$$D_{AJ} = \left(\frac{8 * f_{AJ} * L_{AJ} * Q_{AJ}^2}{(|WSEL_A - h_{T,J}|) * g * \pi^2} \right)^{0.2} \quad ← eq.4$$

Add subscripts A and AJ to eq.4 to specify reservoir A and pipe AJ.

$$0 = Q_{AJ} - Q_{BJ} - Q_{CJ} \quad ← eq.5$$

Eq.5 shows the flow rate into the junction equals the flow rate out of the junction.

Network Flows #8 (cont.)

Solve eq. 5 for Q_{AJ}.

$$Q_{AJ}=Q_{BJ}+Q_{CJ} \leftarrow eq.6$$

Eq. 7 and eq. 8 solve for the flow rate through pipes BJ and CJ.

$$Q_{BJ}=\sqrt{\frac{(|h_{TJ}-WSEL_B|)*g*D_{BJ}^{5}*\pi^2}{8*f_{BJ}*L_{BJ}}} \leftarrow eq.7$$

In eq. 7 and eq. 8 the total head at the junction is subtracted from the water surface elevation at each reservoir.

$$Q_{CJ}=\sqrt{\frac{(|h_{TJ}-WSEL_C|)*g*D_{CJ}^{5}*\pi^2}{8*f_{CJ}*L_{CJ}}} \leftarrow eq.8$$

Eq. 9 and eq. 10 convert the pipe diameters to meters.

$$D_{BJ}=D_{CJ}=180\,[mm]*\boxed{\frac{1}{1,000}\left[\frac{m}{mm}\right]}=0.18\,[m] \leftarrow eq.9$$

conversion factors

Plug in variables W_{TJ}, $WSEL_B$, g, D_{BJ}, f_{BJ} and L_{BJ} into eq. 7, then solve for Q_{BJ}.

$W_{TJ}=62\,[m]$ $WSEL_B=38\,[m]$ $D_{BJ}=0.18\,[m]$

$$Q_{BJ}=\sqrt{\frac{(W_{TJ}-WSEL_B)*g*D_{BJ}^{5}*\pi^2}{8*f_{BJ}*L_{BJ}}} \leftarrow eq.7$$

$f_{BJ}=0.018$ $L_{BJ}=500\,[m]$ $g=9.81\,[m/s^2]$

$$Q_{BJ}=\sqrt{\frac{(62\,[m]-38\,[m])*9.81\,[m/s^2]*(0.18\,[m])^5*\pi^2}{8*0.018*500\,[m]}}$$

$$Q_{BJ}=0.0781\,[m^3/s]$$

$W_{TJ}=62\,[m]$ $WSEL_C=18\,[m]$ $D_{CJ}=0.18\,[m]$

Plug in variables W_{TJ}, $WSEL_C$, g, D_{CJ}, f_{CJ} and L_{CJ} into eq. 8, then solve for Q_{CJ}.

$$Q_{CJ}=\sqrt{\frac{(W_{TJ}-WSEL_C)*g*D_{CJ}^{5}*\pi^2}{8*f_{CJ}*L_{CJ}}} \leftarrow eq.8$$

$f_{CJ}=0.018$ $L_{CJ}=500\,[m]$ $g=9.81\,[m/s^2]$

Network Flows #8 (cont.)

$$Q_{CJ} = \sqrt{\frac{(62\,[m] - 18\,[m]) * 9.81\,[m/s^2] * (0.18\,[m])^5 * \pi^2}{8 * 0.018 * 500\,[m]}}$$

$$Q_{CJ} = 0.1057\,[m^3/s]$$

$Q_{BJ} = 0.0781\,[m^3/s]$ $\qquad$ $Q_{CJ} = 0.1057\,[m^3/s]$

$$Q_{AJ} = Q_{BJ} + Q_{CJ} \quad \leftarrow eq.6$$

Plug in variables Q_{BJ} and Q_{CJ} into eq.6, then solve for Q_{AJ}.

$$Q_{AJ} = 0.0781\,[m^3/s] + 0.1057\,[m^3/s]$$

$$Q_{AJ} = 0.1838\,[m^3/s]$$

$f_{AJ} = 0.018$ $\quad$ $L_{AJ} = 500\,[m]$ $\quad$ $Q_{AJ} = 0.1838\,[m^3/s]$

$$D_{AJ} = \left(\frac{8 * f_{AJ} * L_{AJ} * Q_{AJ}^2}{(WSEL_A - W_{TJ}) * g * \pi^2} \right)^{0.2} \quad \leftarrow eq.4$$

$WSEL_A = 88\,[m]$ $\qquad$ $W_{TJ} = 62\,[m]$ $\qquad$ $g = 9.81\,[m/s^2]$

$$D_{AJ} = \left(\frac{8 * 0.018 * 500\,[m] * (0.1838\,[m^3/s])^2}{(88\,[m] - 62\,[m]) * 9.81\,[m/s^2] * \pi^2} \right)^{0.2}$$

$$D_{AJ} = 0.2495\,[m] * 1{,}000 \left[\frac{mm}{m} \right] \leftarrow eq.10$$

Eq.10 converts the diameter to millimeters.

conversion factor

$$D_{AJ} = 249.5\,[mm]$$

Answer: $\boxed{B}$

Water Resources Practice Problems

Network Flows #9

Find: $WSEL_C$ ← the water surface elevation of reservoir C

Given:

Q_{AJ}=414 [gal/min] ← the flow rate through pipe AJ

C=100 ← all roughness coefficient

L=120 [ft] ← all pipe length

D_{AJ}=4 [in] ⎫ pipe diameters

D_{BJ}=12 [in] $WSEL_A$=150 [ft] ⎫ water surface elevations

D_{CJ}=8 [in] ⎭ $WSEL_B$=135 [ft] ⎭

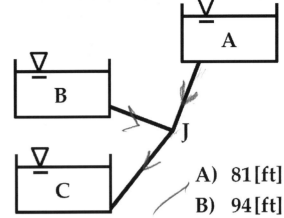

A) 81 [ft]

B) 94 [ft]

C) 98 [ft]

D) 102 [ft]

Analysis:

$$WSEL_C = h_{T,J} - h_{f,CJ} \quad ←eq.1$$

total head at the junction   headloss through pipe CJ

Eq. 1 computes the water surface elevation of reservoir C.

$$h_{T,J} = WSEL_A - h_{f,AJ} \quad ←eq.2$$

water surface elevation at reservoir A   headloss through pipe AJ

Eq. 2 computes the total head at the junction.

Eq. 3 computes the headloss through pipe AJ.

headloss [ft] L_{AJ}=120 [ft] Q_{AJ}=414 [gal/min]

$$h_{f,AJ} = \frac{10.44 * L_{AJ} * Q_{AJ}^{1.85}}{C_{AJ}^{1.85} * D_{AJ}^{4.87}} \quad ←eq.3$$

C_{AJ}=100 D_{AJ}=4 [in]

Plug in the known variables into eq.3, then solve for $h_{f,AJ}$

In eq.3, the units are specified to be:

headloss ⟶ feet
pipe length ⟶ feet
flow rate ⟶ gal/min
roughness ⟶ (none)
diameter ⟶ in

$$h_{f,AJ} = \frac{10.44 * 120 * (414)^{1.85}}{(100)^{1.85} * (4)^{4.87}}$$

$$h_{f,AJ} = 20.29 \,[ft]$$

Network Flows #9 (cont.)

$$h_{T,J}=WSEL_A-h_{f,AJ} \leftarrow eq.2$$

$WSEL_A=150\,[ft]$ $h_{f,AJ}=20.29\,[ft]$

Plug in variables $WSEL_A$ and $h_{f,AJ}$ into eq.2, then solve for $h_{T,J}$.

$$h_{T,J}=150\,[ft]-20.29\,[ft]$$

$$h_{T,J}=129.71\,[ft]$$

Since the total head at the junction is less than the water surface elevation at reservoir B, we know water flows from reservoir B towards the junction

headloss [ft]   pipe length [ft]   flow rate [gal/min]

$$h_{f,CJ}=\frac{10.44*L_{CJ}*Q_{CJ}^{1.85}}{C_{CJ}^{1.85}*D_{CJ}^{4.87}} \leftarrow eq.4$$

roughness coefficient   pipe diameter [in]

Eq.4 computes the headloss through pipe CJ.

$$0=Q_{AJ}+Q_{BJ}-Q_{CJ} \leftarrow eq.5$$

Eq.5 shows the total flow into the junction equals the total flow exiting the junction.

$$Q_{CJ}=Q_{AJ}+Q_{BJ} \leftarrow eq.6$$

Solve eq.5 for Q_{CJ}.

$$Q_{BJ}=\left(\frac{h_{f,BJ}*C_{BJ}^{1.85}*D_{BJ}^{4.87}}{10.44*L_{BJ}}\right)^{0.5405} \leftarrow eq.7$$

Eq.7 computes the flow rate through pipes BJ.

$$h_{f,BJ}=WSEL_B-h_{T,J} \leftarrow eq.8$$

$WSEL_B=135\,[ft]$ $h_{T,J}=129.71\,[ft]$

Eq.8 computes the headloss through pipe BJ.

Plug in variables $WSEL_B$ and $h_{T,J}$ into eq.8, then solve for $h_{f,BJ}$.

$$h_{f,BJ}=135\,[ft]-129.71\,[ft]$$

$$h_{f,BJ}=5.29\,[ft]$$

Water Resources Practice Problems

Network Flows #9 (cont.)

Plug in variables $h_{f,BJ}$, C_{BJ}, L_{BJ}, and D_{BJ} into eq.7, then solve for Q_{BJ}.

$C_{BJ}=100$ $D_{BJ}=12\,[in]$

$$Q_{BJ}=\left(\frac{h_{f,BJ}*C_{BJ}^{1.85}*D_{BJ}^{4.87}}{10.44*L_{BJ}}\right)^{0.5405} \leftarrow eq.7$$

$h_{f,BJ}=5.29\,[ft]$ $L_{BJ}=120\,[ft]$

$$Q_{BJ}=\left(\frac{5.29*(100)^{1.85}*(12)^{4.87}}{10.44*120}\right)^{0.5405}$$

Drop the units from eq.7, but remember the flow rate has units of gallons per minute.

$$Q_{BJ}=3,607\,[gal/min]$$

$Q_{AJ}=411\,[gal/min]$ $Q_{BJ}=3,607\,[gal/min]$

$$Q_{CJ}=Q_{AJ}+Q_{BJ} \leftarrow eq.6$$

Plug in variables Q_{AJ} and Q_{BJ} into eq.6, then solve for Q_{CJ}.

$$Q_{CJ}=411\,[gal/min]+3,607\,[gal/min]$$

$$Q_{CJ}=4,018\,[gal/min]$$

headloss [ft] $L_{CJ}=120\,[ft]$ $Q_{CJ}=4,108\,[gal/min]$

$$h_{f,CJ}=\frac{10.44*L_{CJ}*Q_{CJ}^{1.85}}{C_{CJ}^{1.85}*D_{CJ}^{4.87}} \leftarrow eq.4$$

$C_{CJ}=100$ $D_{CJ}=8\,[in]$

Plug in variables L_{CJ}, Q_{CJ}, C_{CJ} and D_{CJ} into eq.4, then solve for $h_{f,CJ}$.

$$h_{f,CJ}=\frac{10.44*120*(4,108)^{1.85}}{(100)^{1.85}*(8)^{4.87}}$$

$$h_{f,CJ}=48.42\,[ft]$$

Network Flows #9 (cont.)

$$WSEL_C = h_{T,J} - h_{f,CJ} \leftarrow eq.1$$

$h_{T,J} = 129.71 \, [ft] \qquad h_{f,CJ} = 48.42 \, [ft]$

Plug in variables $h_{T,J}$ and $h_{f,CJ}$ into eq.1, then solve for $WSEL_C$.

$$WSEL_C = 129.71 \, [ft] - 48.42 \, [ft]$$

$$WSEL_C = 81.29 \, [ft]$$

Answer: $\boxed{A}$

Water Resources Practice Problems

Pumps #1

Find: h_T ← the total head lift provided by the pump

Given:

$Q = 6.613 \, [\text{ft}^3/\text{s}]$ ← flow rate

$p_s = 42.1 \, [\text{lb}_f/\text{in}^2]$ ← suction pressure

$p_d = 118.4 \, [\text{lb}_f/\text{in}^2]$ ← discharge pressure

$d_s = 12 \, [\text{in}]$ ← diameter of the suction pipe

$d_d = 6 \, [\text{in}]$ ← diameter of the discharge pipe

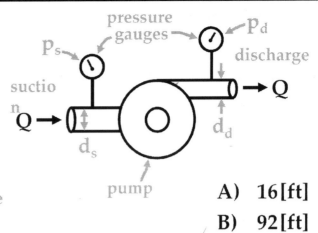

A) 16 [ft]

B) 92 [ft]

✓ C) 176 [ft]

D) 193 [ft]

Analysis:

total discharge head, total suction head

total head

$$h_T = h_d - h_s \leftarrow eq.1$$

$$h_d = h_{d,p} + h_{d,v} \qquad h_s = h_{s,p} + h_{s,v}$$

Eq.1 computes the total head lift generated by the pump.

The total head equals pressure head plus the velocity head plus the elevation head. The elevation head cancels out.

discharge   suction

$$h_T = (h_{d,p} + h_{d,v}) - (h_{s,p} + h_{s,v}) \leftarrow eq.2$$

pressure head   velocity head

Plug in the pressure head and velocity head terms into eq.1, for both discharge and suction total head terms.

$$h_{s,v} = \frac{v_s^2}{2*g} \leftarrow eq.3$$

Eq.3 computes the velocity head through the suction pipe.

$$v_s = Q / A_s \leftarrow eq.4$$

Eq.4 computes the velocity through the suction pipe.

$d_s = 12 \, [\text{in}]$

$$A_s = \frac{\pi * d_s^2}{4} \leftarrow eq.5$$

Eq.5 computes the area of the suction pipe. Plug in variable d_s, then solve for A_s.

Pumps #1 (cont.)

$$A_s = \frac{\pi*(12\,[in])^2}{4} * \left(\frac{1}{12}\left[\frac{ft}{in}\right]\right)^2$$

Convert the area to units of feet squared.

conversion factor

$$A_s = 0.7854\,[ft^2]$$

$A_s = 0.7854\,[ft^2]$

$$v_s = Q/A_s \leftarrow eq.4$$

$Q = 6.613\,[ft^3/s]$

Plug in variables Q and A_s into eq.4, then solve for v_s.

$$v_s = 6.613\,[ft^3/s]/0.7854\,[ft^2]$$

$$v_s = 8.420\,[ft/s]$$

$v_s = 8.420\,[ft/s]$

$$h_{s,v} = \frac{v_s^2}{2*g} \leftarrow eq.3$$

$g = 32.2\,[ft/s^2]$

Plug in variables v_s and g into eq.3, then solve for $h_{s,v}$.

$$h_{s,v} = \frac{(8.420\,[ft/s])^2}{2*32.2\,[ft/s^2]}$$

$$h_{s,v} = 1.101\,[ft]$$

$$h_{d,v} = \frac{v_d^2}{2*g} \leftarrow eq.6$$

Eq.6 computes the velocity head through the discharge pipe.

$$v_d = Q/A_d \leftarrow eq.7$$

Eq.7 computes the velocity through the discharge pipe.

Water Resources Practice Problems

$$d_d = 6 [in]$$

$$A_d = \frac{\pi * d_d^2}{4} \leftarrow eq.8$$

Eq. 8 computes the area of the suction pipe. Plug in variable d_s, then solve for A_s.

$$A_d = \frac{\pi * (6[in])^2}{4} * \left(\frac{1}{12} \left[\frac{ft}{in} \right] \right)^2$$

Convert the area to units of feet squared.

conversion factor

$$A_d = 0.1963 [ft^2]$$

$$A_d = 0.1963 [ft^2]$$

$$v_d = Q / A_s \leftarrow eq.7$$

Plug in variables Q and A_d into eq. 7, then solve for v_d.

$$Q = 6.613 [ft^3/s]$$

$$v_d = 6.613 [ft^3/s] / 0.1963 [ft^2]$$

$$v_d = 33.69 [ft/s]$$

$$v_d = 33.69 [ft/s]$$

$$h_{d,v} = \frac{v_d^2}{2*g} \leftarrow eq.6$$

Plug in variables v_d and g into eq. 6, then solve for $h_{d,v}$.

$$g = 32.2 [ft/s^2]$$

$$h_{d,v} = \frac{(33.69 [ft/s])^2}{2 * 32.2 [ft/s^2]}$$

$$h_{d,v} = 17.62 [ft]$$

$$p_s = 42.1 [lb_f/in^2]$$

$$h_{s,p} = \frac{p_s}{\varrho * g} \leftarrow eq.9$$

Eq. 9 computes the pressure head in the suction pipe. Plug in variables p_s, ϱ and g, then solve for $h_{s,p}$

$$\varrho = 62.4 [lb_m/ft^3] \qquad g = 32.2 [ft/s^2]$$

Pumps #1 (cont.)

$$h_{s,p} = \frac{42.1\,[lb_f/in^2]}{62.4\,[lb_m/ft^3]*32.2\,[ft/s^2]} * 32.2\left[\frac{lb_m*ft}{lb_f*s^2}\right] * \left(12\left[\frac{in}{ft}\right]\right)^2$$

conversion factors

$$h_{s,p} = 97.15\,[ft]$$

Convert the pressure head to units of feet.

$$p_d = 118.4\,[lb_f/in^2]$$

$$h_{d,p} = \frac{p_d}{\varrho*g} \leftarrow eq.\,10$$

$$\varrho = 62.4\,[lb_m/ft^3] \qquad g = 32.2\,[ft/s^2]$$

Eq. 10 computes the pressure head in the discharge pipe. Plug in variables p_d, ϱ and g, then solve for $h_{d,p}$.

$$h_{d,p} = \frac{118.4\,[lb_f/in^2]}{62.4\,[lb_m/ft^3]*32.2\,[ft/s^2]} * 32.2\left[\frac{lb_m*ft}{lb_f*s^2}\right] * \left(12\left[\frac{in}{ft}\right]\right)^2$$

conversion factors

$$h_{d,p} = 273.2\,[ft]$$

Convert the pressure head to units of feet.

$$h_{d,p} = 273.2\,[ft] \qquad h_{s,p} = 97.15\,[ft]$$

$$h_T = (h_{d,p} + h_{d,v}) - (h_{s,p} + h_{s,v}) \leftarrow eq.\,2$$

$$h_{d,v} = 17.62\,[ft] \qquad h_{s,v} = 1.101\,[ft]$$

Plug in variables $h_{d,p}$, $h_{d,v}$, $h_{s,p}$ and $h_{s,v}$ into eq. 2, then solve for h_T.

$$h_T = (273.2\,[ft] + 17.62\,[ft]) - (97.15\,[ft] + 1.101\,[ft])$$

$$h_T = 192.6\,[ft]$$

Answer: $\boxed{D}$

Water Resources Practice Problems

Pumps #2

<u>Find: Q</u> ←the flow rate

<u>Given:</u>

$p_s=100[kPa]$ ←suction pressure

$p_d=250[kPa]$ ←discharge pressure

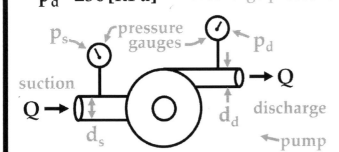

$d_s=300[mm]$ $d_d=165[mm]$
diameter of the   diameter of the
suction pipe   discharge pipe

$h_T=18.20[m]$
the total head
lift provided by
the pump

A) $0.100[m^3/s]$
B) $0.135[m^3/s]$
C) $0.170[m^3/s]$
D) $0.250[m^3/s]$

Analysis:

pressure head   velocity head

$h_T=(h_{d,p}+h_{d,v})-(h_{s,p}+h_{s,v})$ ←eq.1

discharge   suction

total head lift
by the pump

Eq.1 computes the total head lift by the pump in terms of the pressure head and velocity head immediately upstream (suction) and downstream (discharge) of the pump.

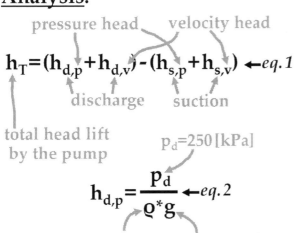

$p_d=250[kPa]$

$h_{d,p}=\dfrac{p_d}{\varrho*g}$ ←eq.2

$\varrho=1,000[kg/m^3]$ $g=9.81[m/s^2]$

Eq.2 computes the pressure head of the discharge pipe.

Plug in variables p_d, ϱ and g into eq.2, then solve for $h_{d,p}$.

$$h_{d,p}=250[kPa]*1,000\left[\frac{Pa}{kPa}\right]*1\left[\frac{kg}{Pa*m*s^2}\right]*\frac{1}{1,000}\left[\frac{m^3}{kg}\right]*\frac{1}{9.81}\left[\frac{s^2}{m}\right]$$

conversion factors

$h_{d,p}=25.48[m]$

$p_s=100[kPa]$

$h_{s,p}=\dfrac{p_s}{\varrho*g}$ ←eq.3

$\varrho=1,000[kg/m^3]$ $g=9.81[m/s^2]$

Eq.3 computes the pressure head of the suction pipe.

Plug in variables p_s, ϱ and g into eq.3, then solve for $h_{s,p}$.

Pumps #2 (cont.)

conversion factors

$$h_{s,p}=100\,[kPa]*1,000\left[\dfrac{Pa}{kPa}\right]*1\left[\dfrac{kg}{Pa*m*s^2}\right]*\dfrac{1}{1,000}\left[\dfrac{m^3}{kg}\right]*\dfrac{1}{9.81}\left[\dfrac{s^2}{m}\right]$$

$$h_{s,p}=10.19\,[m]$$

$$v_d=Q/A_d$$

$$h_{d,v}=\dfrac{v_d^2}{2*g}\quad\leftarrow eq.4$$

Eq. 4 computes the velocity head through the discharge pipe.

Plug in the flow rate divided by flow area of the discharge pipe in for velocity in eq. 4.

$$h_{d,v}=\dfrac{Q^2}{2*g*A_d^2}\quad\leftarrow eq.5$$

$$d_d=165\,[mm]$$

$$A_d=\dfrac{\pi*d_d^2}{4}\quad\leftarrow eq.6$$

Eq. 6 computes the area of the discharge pipe. Plug in variable d_d, then solve for A_d.

$$A_d=\dfrac{\pi*(165\,[mm])^2}{4}*\left(\dfrac{1}{1,000}\left[\dfrac{m}{mm}\right]\right)^2$$

Convert the area to units of meters squared.

conversion factor

$$A_d=2.138*10^{-2}\,[m^2]$$

$$h_{d,v}=\dfrac{Q^2}{2*g*A_d^2}\quad\leftarrow eq.5$$

Plug in variables g and A_d into eq. 5, then solve for $h_{d,v}$.

$$g=9.81\,[m/s^2]\qquad A_d=2.138*10^{-2}\,[m^2]$$

$$h_{d,v}=111.50\,[s^2/m^5]*Q^2$$

Eq. 7 computes the velocity head through the discharge pipe.

$$v_s=Q/A_s$$

$$h_{s,v}=\dfrac{v_s^2}{2*g}\quad\leftarrow eq.7$$

Plug in the flow rate divided by the flow area of the suction pipe in for velocity, in eq. 7.

Water Resources Practice Problems

$$h_{s,v} = \frac{Q^2}{2 \cdot g \cdot A_s^2} \leftarrow eq.\, 8$$

$d_s = 300\,[\text{mm}]$

$$A_s = \frac{\pi \cdot d_s^2}{4} \leftarrow eq.\, 9$$

Eq. 9 computes the area of the discharge pipe. Plug in variable d_s, then solve for A_s.

$$A_s = \frac{\pi \cdot (300\,[\text{mm}])^2}{4} \cdot \left(\frac{1}{1,000} \left[\frac{\text{m}}{\text{mm}} \right] \right)^2$$

conversion factor

Convert the area to units of meters squared.

$$A_s = 7.069 \cdot 10^{-2}\,[\text{m}^2]$$

$$h_{s,v} = \frac{Q^2}{2 \cdot g \cdot A_s^2} \leftarrow eq.\, 8$$

$g = 9.81\,[\text{m/s}^2]$ $A_s = 7.069 \cdot 10^{-2}\,[\text{m}^2]$

Plug in variables g and A_s into eq. 5, then solve for $h_{d,v}$

$$h_{s,v} = 10.20\,[\text{s}^2/\text{m}^5] \cdot Q^2$$

$h_T = 18.20\,[\text{m}]$ $h_{s,v} = 10.20\,[\text{s}^2/\text{m}^5] \cdot Q^2$

$$h_T = (h_{d,p} + h_{d,v}) - (h_{s,p} + h_{s,v}) \leftarrow eq.\, 1$$

$h_{d,p} = 25.48\,[\text{m}]$ $h_{s,p} = 10.19\,[\text{m}]$

$h_{d,v} = 111.50\,[\text{s}^2/\text{m}^5] \cdot Q^2$

Plug in variables h_T, $h_{d,p}$, $h_{d,v}$, $h_{s,p}$ and $h_{s,v}$ into eq. 1, then solve for Q.

$$18.20\,[\text{m}] = (25.48\,[\text{m}] + 111.50[\text{s}^2/\text{m}^5] \cdot Q^2) - (10.19\,[\text{m}] + 10.20\,[\text{s}^2/\text{m}^5] \cdot Q^2)$$

$$Q = 0.170\,[\text{m}^3/\text{s}]$$

Answer: $\boxed{C}$

Pumps #3

<u>Find:</u> Q ← flow rate

<u>Given:</u>

SG=1.00 ← specific gravity

P=25.0[hp] ← motor power

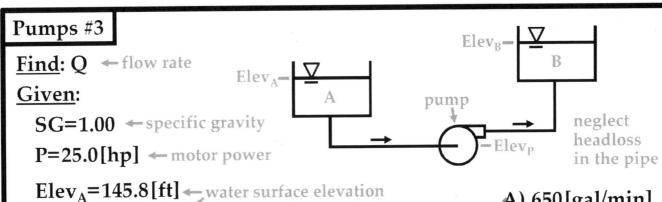

Elev$_A$=145.8[ft] ← water surface elevation in reservoirs A and B

Elev$_B$=260.1[ft]

Elev$_P$=85.4[ft] η_p=0.75

pump elevation   pump efficiency

neglect headloss in the pipe

A) 650[gal/min]

B) 720[gal/min]

C) 780[gal/min]

D) 865[gal/min]

Analysis:

head lift from the pump [ft]   flow rate [gal/min]   specific gravity

$$P = \frac{h_T * Q * SG}{3,956 * \eta_p} \leftarrow eq.1$$

hydraulic horsepower [hp]   pump efficiency

Eq.1 computes the hydraulic horsepower of the pump.

Solve eq.1 for the flow rate, Q.

$$Q = \frac{3,956 * P * \eta_p}{h_T * SG} \leftarrow eq.2$$

$$h_T = Elev_B - Elev_A \leftarrow eq.3$$

Elev$_B$=260.1[ft]   Elev$_A$=145.8[ft]

$$h_T = 260.1[ft] - 145.8[ft]$$

$$h_T = 114.3[ft]$$

Eq.3 computes the total head lift from the pump

Plug in variables Elev$_B$ and Elev$_A$, then solve for h_T.

P=25.0[hp] η_p=0.75

$$Q = \frac{3,956 * P * \eta_p}{h_T * SG} \leftarrow eq.2$$

h_T=114.3[ft]   SG=1.00

Plug in variables P, η_p, h_T and SG into eq.2, then solve for Q.

Pumps #3 (cont.)

$$Q = \frac{3{,}956 * 25.0\,[hp] * 0.75}{114.3\,[ft] * 1.00}$$

$$Q = 649.0\,[gal/min]$$

Answer: $\boxed{A}$

Detailed Solutions: Pumps

Pumps #4

Find: **d** ← the pipe diameter

Given: (all pipe has the same diameter)

$Q=1{,}253\,[\text{gal/min}]$ ← flow rate

$C=100$ ← roughness coefficient

$L=500\,[\text{ft}]$ ← total length of pipe

$P=50\,[\text{hp}]$ ← motor power

$\text{Elev}_A=52.11\,[\text{ft}]$ ← water surface elevation in reservoirs A and B

$\text{Elev}_B=145.97\,[\text{ft}]$

$\eta_p=0.737$ ← pump efficiency

water

neglect minor headloss

A) 6 [in]
B) 8 [in]
C) 12 [in]
D) 18 [in]

Analysis:

$$h_f=\frac{10.44*L*Q^{1.85}}{C^{1.85}*d^{4.87}} \leftarrow eq.1$$

pipe length [ft], flow rate [gal/min], headloss, roughness coefficient, pipe diameter [in]

Eq. 1 computes the headloss through the pipe.

Solve eq. 1 for the pipe diameter

$$d=\left(\frac{10.44*L*Q^{1.85}}{C^{1.85}*h_f}\right)^{0.2053} \leftarrow eq.2$$

total head added by the pump, headloss through the pipe

$$h_T=\text{Elev}_B-\text{Elev}_A+h_f \leftarrow eq.3$$

water surface elevation in reservoirs B and A

Eq. 3 computes the total head added to the water by the pump.

Solve eq. 3 for the headloss, h_f.

$$h_f=\text{Elev}_A-\text{Elev}_B+h_T \leftarrow eq.4$$

$\text{Elev}_A=52.11\,[\text{ft}]$ $\text{Elev}_B=145.97\,[\text{ft}]$

Plug in Elev_A and Elev_B into eq.4, then solve for h_f.

$$h_f=52.11\,[\text{ft}]-145.97\,[\text{ft}]+h_T$$

Water Resources Practice Problems

Pumps #4 (cont.)

$$h_f = -93.86 \, [ft] + h_T \leftarrow eq.5$$

$$P = \frac{h_T * Q * SG}{3,956 * \eta_p} \leftarrow eq.6$$

head lift from the pump [ft]
flow rate [gal/min]
specific gravity
hydraulic horsepower [hp]
pump efficiency

Eq. 6 computes the hydraulic horsepower of the pump.

Solve eq. 6 for the head lift from the pump, h_T.

$$h_T = \frac{3,956 * P * \eta_p}{Q * SG} \leftarrow eq.7$$

P=50 [hp] η_p=0.737
Q=1,253 [gal/min]   SG=1.00

Plug in variables P, η_p, Q and SG into eq. 7, then solve for h_T.

The specific gravity of water equals 1.00.

$$h_T = \frac{3,956 * 50 \, [hp] * 0.737}{1,253 \, [gal/min] * 1.00}$$

$$h_T = 116.3 \, [ft]$$

h_T=116.3 [ft]

$$h_f = -93.86 \, [ft] + h_T \leftarrow eq.5$$

Plug in variable h_T into eq. 5, then solve for the headloss through the pipe, h_f.

$$h_f = -93.86 \, [ft] + 116.3 \, [ft]$$

$$h_f = 22.44 \, [ft]$$

L=500 [ft]   Q=1,253 [gal/min]

$$d = \left(\frac{10.44 * L * Q^{1.85}}{C^{1.85} * h_f} \right)^{0.2053} \leftarrow eq.2$$

C=100 h_f=22.44 [ft]

Plug in variables L, Q, C and h_f into eq. 2, then solve for d.

Pumps #4 (cont.)

$$d = \left(\frac{10.44 * 500 * (1{,}253)^{1.85}}{(100)^{1.85} * 22.44} \right)^{0.2053}$$

Drop the units in the right hand side of eq. 2, and remember the diameter has units of inches.

$$d = 8.00\,[\text{in}]$$

Answer: **B**

Water Resources Practice Problems

Pumps #5

Find: t ← the total time the pump can run

Given:

$Q=0.0147\,[\text{m}^3/\text{s}]$ ← flow rate

$\Delta h=45\,[\text{m}]$ ← elevation change

$\eta_m=0.80$ ← motor efficiency

$\eta_p=0.65$ ← pump efficiency

$c=\$0.12/[\text{kW}*\text{hr}]$

unit cost of electricity

$C=\$3.00$

total funds to be spent on pumping

A) 1 [hr]

B) 2 [hr]

C) 3 [hr]

D) 4 [hr]

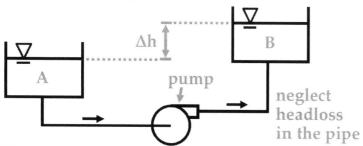

pump

neglect headloss in the pipe

Analysis:

$W = P*t$, work   unit cost of electricty

$$C=\frac{W*c}{\eta_m} \quad \leftarrow eq.1$$

total cost of pumping   motor efficiency

Eq.1 computes the total cost of pumping.

motor power   time

$$C=\frac{P*t*c}{\eta_m}$$

Substitute in power times time for work into eq.1, then solve for time.

$$t = \frac{C*\eta_m}{P*c} \quad \leftarrow eq.2$$

total head lift added by the pump [m]   mass flow rate [kg/s]

$$P=\frac{9.81*h_T*\dot{m}}{1000*\eta_p} \quad \leftarrow eq.3$$

hydraulic power [kW]   pump efficiency

$$h_T=\Delta h$$

$\Delta h=45\,[\text{m}]$

Eq.3 computes the hydraulic power of the pump.

Assuming no headloss through the pipe, the head lift added by the pump equals the change in water surface elevation between the two reservoirs.

Pumps #5 (cont.)

$$h_T = 45 \, [m]$$

mass flow rate → $\dot{m} = Q * \rho$ ←eq.4

$Q = 0.0147 \, [m^3/s]$

$\rho = 1,000 \, [kg/m^3]$

Eq.4 computes the mass flow rate as the volumetric flow rate times the fluid density.

Plug in variables Q and ρ into eq.4, then solve for $\dot{m}$.

$$\dot{m} = 0.0147 \left[\frac{m^3}{s}\right] * 1,000 \left[\frac{kg}{m^3}\right]$$

$$\dot{m} = 14.7 \, [kg/s]$$

$h_T = 45 \, [m]$ $\dot{m} = 14.7 \, [kg/s]$

$$P = \frac{9.81 * h_T * \dot{m}}{1000 * \eta_p} \leftarrow eq.3$$

$\eta_p = 0.65$

Plug in variables h_T, $\dot{m}$ and η_p into eq.3, then solve for P.

$$P = \frac{9.81 * 45 \, [m] * 14.7 \, [kg/s]}{1000 * 0.65}$$

$$P = 9.984 \, [kW]$$

$C = \$3.00$ $\eta_m = 0.80$

$$t = \frac{C * \eta_m}{P * c} \leftarrow eq.2$$

$P = 9.984 \, [kW]$ $c = \$0.12 / [kW*hr]$

Plug in variables C, η_m, P and c into eq.2, then solve for t.

$$t = \frac{\$3.00 * 0.80}{9.984 \, [kW] * \$0.12 / [kW*hr]}$$

$$t = 2.00 \, [hr]$$ <u>Answer:</u> $\boxed{B}$

Water Resources Practice Problems

Pumps #6

Find: Δz_{PB} ← the vertical rise between the pump and the water surface in reservoir B

Given:

$h_{T,s}=130\,[ft]$ ← total suction head

$SG=0.9$ ← specific gravity

$L=100\,[ft]$ ← pipe length

$f=0.018$ ← friction factor

$\eta_p=0.70$ ← pump efficiency

$Q=8.54\,[ft^3/s]$ ← flow rate

$P=50\,[hp]$ ← pump power

$D=12\,[in]$ ← pipe diameter

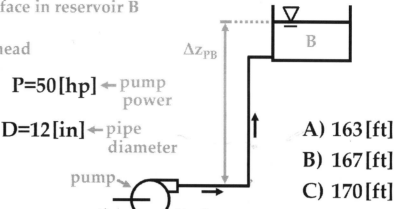

A) 163 [ft]

B) 167 [ft]

C) 170 [ft]

D) 184 [ft]

Analysis:

discharge   suction

$$h_T=h_{T,d}-h_{T,s} \leftarrow eq.1$$

total head at the discharge and suction ends of the pump

Eq. 1 computes the total head lift by the pump.

velocity head at Reservoir B

headloss through the pipe between the pump and Reservoir B

$$h_{T,d}=h_{B,p}^{\;0}+h_{B,v}^{\;0}+\Delta z_{PB}+h_{f,PB} \leftarrow eq.2$$

pressure head at Reservoir B

the vertical rise between the pump and the water surface in reservoir B

Eq. 2 computes the total head at the discharge end of the pump.

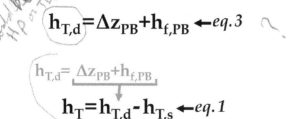

$$h_{T,d}=\Delta z_{PB}+h_{f,PB} \leftarrow eq.3$$

The pressure head and velocity head terms in eq.2 equal zero at the water surface of Reservoir B.

$$h_{T,d}=\Delta z_{PB}+h_{f,PB}$$

$$h_T=h_{T,d}-h_{T,s} \leftarrow eq.1$$

Plug in the total discharge head into eq. 1.

$$h_T=\Delta z_{PB}+h_{f,PB}-h_{T,s} \leftarrow eq.4$$

Solve eq. 4 for Δz_{PB}.

$$\Delta z_{PB}=h_T-h_{f,PB}+h_{T,s} \leftarrow eq.5$$

Pumps #6 (cont.)

friction
factor
headloss pipe length

$$h_{f,PB} = \frac{f*L*v^2}{2*g*D} \leftarrow eq.6$$

gravitational
acceleration   diameter

fluid velocity

Eq. 6 computes the headloss through the discharge pipe using the Darcy equation.

$$v = Q/A \leftarrow eq.7$$

flow rate   cross-sectional
area of the pipe

Eq. 7 computes the fluid velocity through the pipe.

$d = 12\,[in]$

$$A = \frac{\pi*d^2}{4} \leftarrow eq.8$$

Eq. 8 computes the area of the pipe. Plug in variable d, then solve for A.

$$A = \frac{\pi*(12\,[in])^2}{4} * \left(\frac{1}{12}\left[\frac{ft}{in}\right]\right)^2$$

conversion
factor

Convert the area to units of feet squared.

$$A = 0.7854\,[ft^2]$$

$Q = 8.54\,[ft^3/s]$ $A = 0.7854\,[ft^2]$

$$v = Q/A \leftarrow eq.7$$

Plug in variables Q and A into eq. 7, then solve for v.

$$v = \frac{8.54\,[ft^3/s]}{0.7854\,[ft^2]}$$

$$v = 10.87\,[ft/s]$$

$L = 100\,[ft]$

$f = 0.018$ $v = 10.87\,[ft/s]$

$$h_{f,PB} = \frac{f*L*v^2}{2*g*D} \leftarrow eq.6$$

$g = 32.2\,[ft/s^2]$ $D = 1.0\,[ft]$

Plug in variables f, L, v, g and D into eq. 6, then solve for $h_{f,PB}$.

Water Resources Practice Problems

Pumps #6 (cont.)

$$h_{f,PB} = \frac{0.018 * 100\,[\text{ft}] * (10.87\,[\text{ft/s}])^2}{2 * 32.2\,[\text{ft/s}^2] * 1.0\,[\text{ft}]}$$

$$h_{f,PB} = 3.30\,[\text{ft}]$$

head lift from the pump [ft]

flow rate [ft³/s]

specific gravity

$$P = \frac{h_T * Q * SG}{8.814 * \eta_P} \leftarrow eq.\,9$$

hydraulic horsepower [hp]

pump efficiency

Eq. 9 computes the hydraulic horsepower of the pump.

Solve eq. 9 for h_T.

$P = 50\,[\text{hp}]$ $\eta_p = 0.70$

$$h_T = \frac{8.814 * P * \eta_p}{Q * SG} \leftarrow eq.\,10$$

$Q = 8.54\,[\text{ft}^3/\text{s}]$ $SG = 0.9$

Plug in variables P, η_p, Q and SG into eq.10, then solve for h_T.

$$h_T = \frac{8.814 * 50 * 0.70}{8.54 * 0.9}$$

We removed the units from the right hand side of eq. 10 and remember h_T is in units of ft.

$$h_T = 40.14\,[\text{ft}]$$

$h_T = 40.14\,[\text{ft}]$ $h_{T,s} = 130\,[\text{ft}]$

$$\Delta z_{PB} = h_T - h_{f,PB} + h_{T,s} \leftarrow eq.\,5$$

$h_{f,PB} = 3.30\,[\text{ft}]$

Plug in variables h_T, $h_{f,PB}$ and $h_{T,s}$ into eq. 5, then solve for Δz_{PB}.

$$\Delta z_{PB} = 40.14\,[\text{ft}] - 3.30\,[\text{ft}] + 130\,[\text{ft}]$$

$$\Delta z_{PB} = 166.8\,[\text{ft}]$$

__Answer:__ | B |

Pumps #7

$\Delta h_{AB}=463.5\,[\text{ft}]$ ← change in total head
between reservoir A
and reservoir B

<u>Find:</u> η_p ← the pump efficiency

3 stage pump

<u>Given:</u>

$Q=5.75\,[\text{ft}^3/\text{s}]$
↑
flow rate

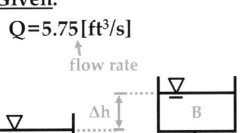

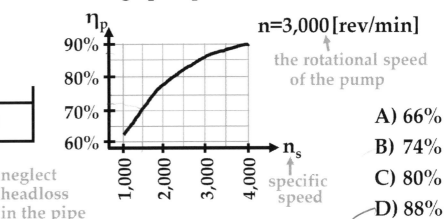

$n=3{,}000\,[\text{rev/min}]$
↑
the rotational speed
of the pump

A) 66%

B) 74%

C) 80%

D) 88%

neglect
headloss
in the pipe

specific
speed

Analysis:

$$\eta_p=f(n_s) \leftarrow eq.1$$

pump
efficiency

specific
speed

Eq. 1 shows the pump efficiency is a
function of the specific speed of the
pump.

rotation speed
[rev/min]

flow rate
[gal/min]

$$n_s=\frac{n*\sqrt{Q}}{h^{0.75}} \leftarrow eq.2$$

head added by a single
stage of the pump [ft]

Eq. 2 computes the specific speed.

$$h=h_T/\text{stages} \leftarrow eq.3$$

total head
added by pump

number of stages
in the pump

Eq. 3 computes the head added by
a single stage of the pump.

total head gain
between the
reservoirs

headloss
in the pipe

Eq. 4 computes the total head
added to the water by the pump.

$$h_T=\Delta h_{AB}+h_f \leftarrow eq.4$$

$\Delta h_{AB}=463.5\,[\text{ft}]$ $h_f=0\,[\text{ft}]$

If we neglect headloss in the
pipe, then h_f equals zero.

Plug in variables Δh_{AB} and h_f
into eq.4, then solve for h_T.

$$h_T=463.5\,[\text{ft}]+0\,[\text{ft}]$$

Pumps #7 (cont.)

$$h_T = 463.5 \, [\text{ft}]$$

$$h = h_T / \text{stages} \leftarrow eq.3$$

$h_T = 463.5 \, [\text{ft}]$ $\text{stages} = 3$

Plug in variables h_T and stages into eq. 3, then solve for h.

$$h = 463.5 \, [\text{ft}] / 3$$

$$h = 154.5 \, [\text{ft}]$$

Eq. 5 converts the flow rate to units of gallons per minute.

$$Q = 5.75 \, [\text{ft}^3/\text{s}] * 7.48 \left[\frac{\text{gal}}{\text{ft}^3}\right] * 60 \left[\frac{\text{s}}{\text{min}}\right] \leftarrow eq.5$$

conversion factors

$$Q = 2,581 \, [\text{gal/min}]$$

$n = 3,000 \, [\text{rev/min}]$ $Q = 2,581 \, [\text{gal/min}]$

$$n_s = \frac{n * \sqrt{Q}}{h^{0.75}} \leftarrow eq.2$$

$h = 154.3 \, [\text{ft}]$

Plug in variables n, Q and h into eq. 2, then solve for n_s.

Drop the units from the right hand side of eq. 2.

$$n_s = \frac{3,000 * \sqrt{2,581}}{(154.5)^{0.75}}$$

$$n_s = 3,478$$

Determine the pump efficiency based on Figure 1 and the specific speed.

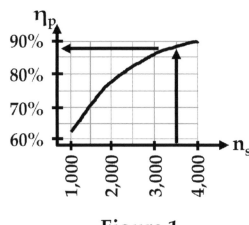

$$\eta_p = 88\%$$

Answer: $\boxed{\text{D}}$

Figure 1

Pumps #8

<u>Find:</u> C ← the pumping cost

<u>Given:</u> n_s=47.33 ← specific speed

t=18[hr] ← pumping duration

c=$0.13/[kW*hr] ← cost of energy

η_m=0.74 ← motor efficiency

η_p=0.82 ← pump efficiency

SG=1.05 ← specific gravity

Δh_{AB}=15.7[m] ← difference in total head between reservoir A and reservoir B

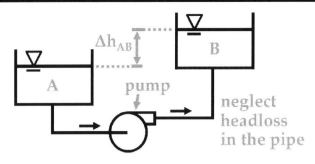

n=2500[rev/min]
↑
rotational speed
of the pump

A) $10.30

B) $11.40

C) $13.90

D) $15.70

Analysis:

energy cost   duration

$$C = c * P * t / \eta_m \quad \leftarrow eq.1$$

pumping cost   pump power   motor efficiency

Eq.1 computes the pumping cost.

head lift by the pump [m]   flow rate [m³/s]

$$P = \frac{9.81 * h * Q * SG}{\eta_p} \quad \leftarrow eq.2$$

power [kW]   pump efficiency   specific gravity

Eq.2 computes the pump power.

rotation speed [rev/min]   flow rate [m³/s]

$$n_s = \frac{n * \sqrt{Q}}{h^{0.75}} \quad \leftarrow eq.3$$

head added by the pump [m]

Eq.3 computes the specific speed.

the difference in total head between the two reservoirs   headloss in the pipe

Eq.4 computes the total head added to the water by the pump.

$$h = \Delta h_{AB} + h_f \quad \leftarrow eq.4$$

Δh_{AB}=15.7[m] h_f=0[m]

If we neglect headloss in the pipe, then h_f equals zero.

Water Resources Practice Problems

$$h = 15.7\,[m] + 0\,[m]$$

$$h = 15.7\,[m]$$

Solve eq. 3 for the flow rate.

$$n_s = 47.33 \qquad h = 15.7\,[m]$$

$$Q = \left(\frac{n_s * h^{0.75}}{n}\right)^2 \leftarrow eq.5$$

$$n = 2{,}500\,[rev/min]$$

Plug in variables n_s, h and n into eq. 5, then solve for Q.

$$Q = \left(\frac{47.33 * (15.7)^{0.75}}{2{,}500}\right)^2$$

Drop the units from the right hand side of eq. 5, and recall the flow rate, Q, has units of meters cubed per second.

$$Q = 0.0223\,[m^3/s]$$

$$h = 15.7\,[m] \qquad Q = 0.0223\,[m^3/s]$$

$$P = \frac{9.81 * h * Q * SG}{\eta_p} \leftarrow eq.2$$

$$\eta_p = 0.82 \qquad SG = 1.05$$

Plug in variables h, Q, SG and η_p into eq. 2, then solve for P.

$$P = \frac{9.81 * 15.7 * 0.0223 * 1.05}{0.82}$$

Drop the units for the right hand side of eq. 2, and use kilowatts for the units of power.

$$P = 4.40\,[kW]$$

$$c = \$0.13/[kW*hr] \qquad \eta_m = 0.74$$

$$C = c * P * t / \eta_m \leftarrow eq.1$$

$$P = 4.40\,[kW] \qquad t = 18\,[hr]$$

Plug in variables c, P, t and η_m into eq. 1, then solve for C.

$$C = \$0.13[kW*hr]^{-1} * 4.40[kW] * 18[hr] / 0.74$$

$$C = \$13.91 \qquad \underline{Answer:} \boxed{C}$$

Pumps #9

<u>Find:</u> **P** ← the power
of each pump

<u>Given:</u>

h_d=58.3[m] ← discharge head
just downstream
of each pump

h_s=14.8[m] ← suction head
just upstream
of each pump

η_p=0.82 ← pump efficiency

SG=1.05 ← specific gravity

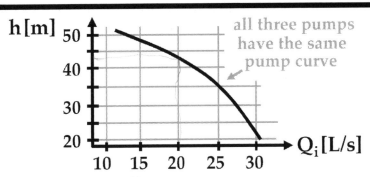

all three pumps
have the same
pump curve

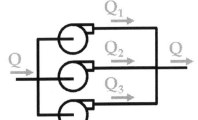

A) 3[kW]

B) 10[kW]

C) 20[kW]

D) 30[kW]

Analysis:

head lift by
one pump [m]   flow rate [L/s]

$$P = \frac{9.81 * h * Q * SG}{1,000 * \eta_p} \leftarrow eq.1$$

power
[kW]   pump   specific
efficiency   gravity

Eq.1 computes the pump power.

Eq.2 computes the total head
lift by each pump.

h_d=58.3[m] h_s=14.8[m]

$$h = h_T = h_d - h_s \leftarrow eq.2$$

total   discharge   suction
head   head   head

Plug in variables h_d and h_s
into eq.2, then solve for h.

$$h = 58.3[m] - 14.8[m]$$

$$h = 43.5[m]$$

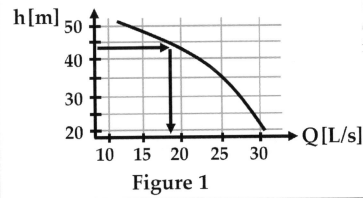

Determine the flow rate through
each pump using the pump curve
in Figure 1 and the head lift, h.

Figure 1

Water Resources Practice Problems

$$Q = 18.4 \, [\text{L/s}]$$

Although not an exact value, the flow rate is determined to be approximately 18.4 liters per second.

$h = 43.5 \, [\text{m}]$ $Q = 18.4 \, [\text{L/s}]$

$$P = \frac{9.81 * h * Q * SG}{1,000 * \eta_p} \leftarrow eq.1$$

$SG = 1.05$

$\eta_p = 0.82$

Plug in variables h, Q, SG and η_p into eq.1, then solve for P.

$$P = \frac{9.81 * 43.5 * 18.4 * 1.05}{1,000 * 0.82}$$

Drop the units from the right hand side of eq.1, and remember the power is in kilowatts.

$$P = 10.05 \, [\text{kW}]$$

Answer: $\boxed{\text{B}}$

Pumps #10

<u>Find</u>: v ← the fluid velocity

<u>Given</u>:

$$h = 40[ft] + 0.08 * Q^2 \left[\frac{ft*min^2}{gal^2}\right]$$

system curve

h

pump curve

Q

$P = 5[hp]$ ← pump power

$\eta_p = 0.73$ ← pump efficiency (assume constant)

$d = 6[in]$ ← pipe diameter

(assume only one pipe in the system)

A) 0.61 [ft/s]
B) 2.21 [ft/s]
C) 4.09 [ft/s]
D) 7.32 [ft/s]

Analysis:

$$v = Q/A \leftarrow eq.1$$

fluid velocity   flow rate   pipe area

Eq.1 computes the fluid velocity in the pipe.

$$A = \frac{\pi * d^2}{4} \leftarrow eq.2$$

d=6[in]

Eq.2 computes the cross-sectional area of the pipe. Plug in variable d, then solve for A.

$$A = \frac{\pi * (6[in])^2}{4} * \left(\frac{1}{12}\left[\frac{ft}{in}\right]\right)^2$$

conversion factor

Convert the area to units of feet squared.

$$A = 0.1963[ft^2]$$

head lift from the pump [ft]   flow rate [gal/min]   specific gravity

$$P = \frac{h * Q * SG}{3{,}956 * \eta_p} \leftarrow eq.3$$

power [hp]   pump efficiency

Eq.3 computes the hydraulic horsepower of the pump.

$P=5[hp]$ $\eta_p=0.73$

$$h = \frac{3{,}956 * P * \eta_p}{Q * SG} \leftarrow eq.4$$

SG=1.00

Solve eq.3 for the head lift, h.

Plug in variables P, η_p and SG into eq. 4, then solve for h.

Water Resources Practice Problems

$$h = \frac{3,956 * 5\,[hp] * 0.73}{Q * 1.00}$$

$$h = \frac{14,440}{Q} \left[\frac{ft*gal}{min}\right] \leftarrow eq.5$$

Replace the units in eq.5 to maintain dimensional consistency.

The operating flow rate of the pump occurs where the pump curve intersects the system curve.

$$h_{pump\ curve} = h_{system\ curve} \leftarrow eq.6$$

$$h = \frac{14,440}{Q}\left[\frac{ft*gal}{min}\right] \qquad h = 40\,[ft] + 0.08*Q^2\left[\frac{ft*min^2}{gal^2}\right]$$

Plug in the pump curve head and system curve head into eq.6, then solve for the flow rate, Q.

$$\frac{14,440}{Q}\left[\frac{ft*gal}{min}\right] = 40\,[ft] + 0.08*Q^2\left[\frac{ft*min^2}{gal^2}\right] \leftarrow eq.7$$

$$0 = 0.08*Q^3 + 40*Q - 14,440 \leftarrow eq.8$$

$v_B = 2.21\,[ft/s]$
$v_C = 4.09\,[ft/s]$
$v_D = 7.32\,[ft/s]$
$v_A = 0.61\,[ft/s]$
$A = 0.1963\,[ft^2]$

Solve eq.1 for the flow rate.

Plug in variables A, v_A, v_B, v_C and v_D into eq.9, then compute the four possible flow rates.

$$Q = v * A \leftarrow eq.9$$

Eq.10 converts the flow rates to gallons per minute.

$$\left.\begin{array}{l} Q_A = 0.120\,[ft^3/s] \\ Q_B = 0.434\,[ft^3/s] \\ Q_C = 0.803\,[ft^3/s] \\ Q_D = 1.437\,[ft^3/s] \end{array}\right\} * 7.48\left[\frac{gal}{ft^3}\right] * 60\left[\frac{s}{min}\right] \leftarrow eq.10$$

conversion factors

$Q_A = 53.9\,[gal/min]$
$Q_B = 194.8\,[gal/min]$
$Q_C = 360.4\,[gal/min]$
$Q_D = 645.0\,[gal/min]$

Next, plug in variables Q_A, Q_B, Q_C and Q_D into the right hand side (RHS) of eq.8. The value of Q which results in a RHS value closest to zero is the correct flow rate.

Pumps #10 (cont.)

Q_A=53.9[gal/min] Q_C=360.4[gal/min]

Q_B=194.8[gal/min] Q_D=645.0[gal/min]

$$0 = 0.08 * Q^3 + 40 * Q - 14{,}440 \leftarrow eq.\,8$$

RHS_{Q_A}=243 $\longrightarrow$ $Q = Q_A$=53.9[gal/min]

RHS_{Q_B}=5.8*10^5

RHS_{Q_C}=3.7*10^6 } values way too large

RHS_{Q_D}=2.1*10^7

Eq. 11 converts the flow rate back to cubic feet per second.

$$Q_A = 53.9 \left[\frac{gal}{min}\right] * \frac{1}{7.48}\left[\frac{ft^3}{gal}\right] * \frac{1}{60}\left[\frac{min}{s}\right] \leftarrow eq.\,11$$

conversion factors

$$Q_A = 0.120\,[ft^3/s]$$

$Q = Q_A = 0.120\,[ft^3/s]$ $A = 0.1963\,[ft^2]$

$$v = Q/A \leftarrow eq.\,1$$

Plug in variables Q and A into eq. 1, then solve for v.

$$v = 0.120\,[ft^3/s] / 0.1963\,[ft^2]$$

$$v = 0.61\,[ft/s]$$

Answer: $\boxed{A}$

Water Resources Practice Problems

Pumps #11

Find: Q_1 ← the flow rate through pump 1
(at the operating point)

assume all pumps are running

Given:

$P_1 = 10\,[kW]$ ← the power of

$P_2 = 20\,[kW]$ ← pumps 1, 2 and 3

$P_3 = 5\,[kW]$

$\eta_p = 0.82$ ← efficiency of all pumps

$f = 0.015$ ← friction factor

$L = 200\,[m]$ ← pipe length

$D = 0.1\,[m]$ ← pipe diameter

water

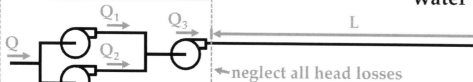

L

← neglect all head losses through the pump station

A) 16 [L/s]

B) 24 [L/s]

C) 49 [L/s]

D) 73 [L/s]

Analysis:

$$Q = Q_1 + Q_2 \leftarrow eq.1$$

total flow rate

flow rate through pumps 1 and 2

Eq. 1 computes the total flow rate through the system.

$$Q_1 = Q - Q_2 \leftarrow eq.2$$

Solve eq.1 for the flow rate through pump 1.

$$h_1 = h_2 \leftarrow eq.3$$

$$h_1 = \frac{P_1 * \eta_p}{9.81 * Q_1 * SG} \qquad h_2 = \frac{P_2 * \eta_p}{9.81 * Q_2 * SG}$$

The operating point occurs where the head and flow rate match for the system curve and the combined pump curve.

pump power   pump efficiency

$$\frac{P_1 * \eta_p}{9.81 * Q_1 * SG} = \frac{P_2 * \eta_p}{9.81 * Q_2 * SG} \leftarrow eq.4$$

flow rate [m³/s]   specific gravity

Eq. 3 sets the head lift across pump 1 equal to the head lift across pump 2.

Plug in the pump head equation into eq. 3, then cancel out equivalent values from both sides of eq. 4.

$P_1 = 10\,[kW]$

$$Q_1 = Q_2 * \frac{P_1}{P_2} \leftarrow eq.5$$

$P_2 = 20\,[kW]$

Solve eq. 4 for Q_1.

Plug in variables P_1 and P_2 into eq. 5, then solve for Q_1.

$$Q_1 = Q_2 * \frac{10\,[kW]}{20\,[kW]}$$

Pumps #11 (cont.)

$$Q_1 = 0.5 * Q_2$$

$$Q_2 = \boxed{\frac{P_2 * \eta_p}{9.81 * h_2 * SG}}$$

Eq.6 computes the total flow rate through the system.

$$Q_1 + Q_2 = Q_3 \quad \leftarrow eq.6$$

$$Q_1 = \boxed{\frac{P_1 * \eta_p}{9.81 * h_1 * SG}} \qquad Q_3 = \boxed{\frac{P_3 * \eta_p}{9.81 * h_3 * SG}}$$

Substitute in the equations for Q_1, Q_2 and Q_3 into eq.6.

$$\frac{P_1 * \eta_p}{9.81 * h_1 * SG} + \frac{P_2 * \eta_p}{9.81 * h_2 * SG} = \frac{P_3 * \eta_p}{9.81 * h_3 * SG} \quad \leftarrow eq.7$$

$$h_2 = h_1$$

Plug in h_2 into eq.7, then combine the terms on the left hand side of eq.7.

$$\frac{(P_1 + P_2) * \cancel{\eta_p}}{\cancel{9.81} * h_1 * \cancel{SG}} = \frac{P_3 * \cancel{\eta_p}}{\cancel{9.81} * h_3 * \cancel{SG}} \quad \leftarrow eq.8$$

Cancel out the 9.81, η_p and SG from both sides of eq.8, then solve for h_1.

$$P_1 = 10[kW] \qquad P_2 = 20[kW]$$

$$h_1 = h_3 * \frac{P_1 + P_2}{P_3} \quad \leftarrow eq.9$$

$$P_3 = 5[kW]$$

Plug in variables P_1, P_2 and P_3 into eq.9, then solve for h_1.

$$h_1 = h_3 * \frac{10[kW] + 20[kW]}{5[kW]} \quad \leftarrow eq.10$$

$$h_1 = 6 * h_3 \quad \checkmark$$

Pumps 1 and 2 increase the total head of the water 6 times as much as pump 3.

$$h_1 = 6 * h_3$$

$$h = h_1 + h_3 \leftarrow eq.11$$

Plug in h_1 into eq.11, then solve for the total head lift through the pump station, h.

$$h = 6 * h_3 + h_3$$

$$h = 7 * h_3$$

Water Resources Practice Problems

Pumps #11 (cont.)

$h_3 = h/7$

$$h_3 = \frac{P_3 * \eta_p}{9.81 * Q_3 * SG} \leftarrow eq.\,12$$

$Q_3 = Q$

Eq. 12 computes the head lift by pump 3.

Plug in variables h_3 and Q_3 into eq. 12, then solve for h.

$P_3 = 5\,[kW]$ $\eta_p = 0.82$

$$\frac{h}{7} = \frac{P_3 * \eta_p}{9.81 * Q * SG} \leftarrow eq.\,13$$

$SG = 1.00$

Plug in variables P_3, η_p and SG into eq. 13, then simplify to solve for the combined pump curve equation.

$$\frac{h}{7} = \frac{5 * 0.82}{9.81 * Q * 1.00}$$

Drop the units from the right hand side of eq. 13, and remember the head lift is in units of meters and flow rate is in units of meters cubed per second.

$$h = \frac{2.926}{Q} \leftarrow eq.\,14$$

head lift [m]   flow rate [m³/s]

Eq. 14 is the combined pump curve equation.

friction factor   pipe length

headloss

$$h_f = \frac{f * L * v^2}{2 * g * D} \leftarrow eq.\,15$$

$v = Q/A$

gravitational acceleration   diameter

Eq. 15 computes the headloss through the downstream pipe.

Plug in the fluid velocity into eq. 15.

$$h_f = \frac{f * L * Q^2}{2 * g * D * A^2} \leftarrow eq.\,16$$

$$v = Q/A \leftarrow eq.\,17$$

Eq. 17 computes the fluid velocity.

Eq. 18 computes the flow area of a circular pipe.

$D = 0.1\,[m]$

$$A = \frac{\pi * D^2}{4} \leftarrow eq.\,18$$

Plug in the pipe diameter, d, into eq. 18, then solve for the area.

Pumps #11 (cont.)

$$A = \frac{\pi * (0.1 \, [m])^2}{4}$$

$$A = 7.854 * 10^{-3} \, [m^2]$$

Plug in variables f, L, g, D and A into eq.16, then solve for h_f, the system curve.

$$h_f = \frac{f * L * Q^2}{2 * g * D * A^2} \leftarrow eq.\,16$$

$f = 0.015$ $L = 200 \, [m]$ $A = 7.854 * 10^{-3} \, [m^2]$ $g = 9.81 \, [m/s^2]$ $D = 0.1 \, [m]$

$$h_f = \frac{0.015 * 200 \, [m] * Q^2}{2 * 9.81 \, [m/s^2] * 0.1 \, [m] * (7.854 * 10^{-3} \, [m^2])^2}$$

only True if $\Delta z = 0$?

$$h_f = 24{,}788 * Q^2 \left[\frac{s^2}{m^5}\right] \leftarrow eq.\,19$$

$$h = \frac{2.926}{Q} = 24{,}778 * Q^2 \leftarrow eq.\,20$$

head [m]   flow rate [m³/s]

Set the combined pump curve equation (eq.14) equal to the system curve equation (eq.19), then solve for Q.

$$Q = (1.1809 * 10^{-4} \, [m^9/s^3])^{1/3}$$

$$Q = 0.0491 \, [m^3/s]$$

The total flow through the system equal 0.0491 meters cubed per second.

$$Q = Q_1 + Q_2 \leftarrow eq.\,1$$

$$Q_2 = 2 * Q_1$$

Determine what faction of the total flow goes through pump 1.

$$Q = Q_1 + 2 * Q_1$$

Water Resources Practice Problems

Pumps #11 (cont.)

$$Q_1 = Q/3 \leftarrow eq.\,21$$

$$Q = 0.0491\,[\text{m}^3/\text{s}]$$

Plug in the total flow rate into eq. 21, then solve for the flow through pump 1, Q_1.

$$Q_1 = 0.0491\,[\text{m}^3/\text{s}]/3$$

$$Q_1 = 0.0164 \left[\frac{\text{m}^3}{\text{s}}\right] * 1{,}000 \left[\frac{\text{L}}{\text{m}^3}\right]$$

Convert the flow rate to units of liters per second.

$$Q_1 = 16.4\,[\text{L/s}]$$

Answer: $\boxed{\text{A}}$

Pumps #12

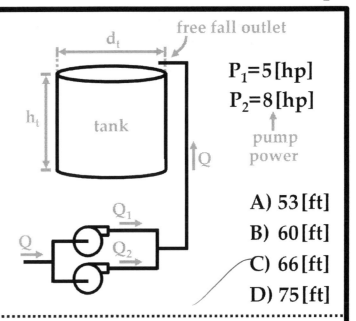

Find: h ← the head lift provided
by the pumps

Given:

$\eta_{p,1}=60\%$ ← efficiency of pump 1

$\eta_{p,2}=85\%$ ← efficiency of pump 2

$d_t=120\,[ft]$ ← tank diameter

$h_t=30\,[ft]$ ← tank height

$t=3\,[days]$ ← time required to fill
the tank completely
water (starting empty)

$P_1=5\,[hp]$
$P_2=8\,[hp]$
↑
pump
power

A) 53 [ft]

B) 60 [ft]

C) 66 [ft]

D) 75 [ft]

Analysis:

$$h=h_1=h_2 \leftarrow eq.1$$

$$h_1=\frac{8.814*P_1*\eta_{p,1}}{Q_1*SG} \qquad h_2=\frac{8.814*P_2*\eta_{p,2}}{Q_2*SG}$$

Eq. 1 shows that head difference across pumps in parallel is equal.

Plug in the equations for pump head in for variables h_1 and h_2 in eq. 1.

pump power   pump efficiency

$$h=\frac{\cancel{8.814}*P_1*\eta_{p,1}}{Q_1*\cancel{SG}}=\frac{\cancel{8.814}*P_2*\eta_{p,2}}{Q_2*\cancel{SG}} \leftarrow eq.2$$

flow rate   specific
$[ft^3/s]$ gravity

Cancel out common terms on both sides of eq. 2.

Solve eq. 2 for Q_1.

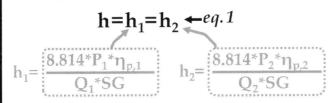

$P_1=5\,[hp]$ $\eta_{p,1}=60\%=0.60$

$$Q_1=Q_2*\frac{P_1*\eta_{p,1}}{P_2*\eta_{p,2}} \leftarrow eq.3$$

$P_2=8\,[hp]$ $\eta_{p,2}=85\%=0.85$

Plug in variables P_1, P_2, $\eta_{p,1}$ and $\eta_{p,2}$ into eq. 3, then solve for Q_1.

$$Q_1=Q_2*\frac{5\,[hp]*0.60}{8\,[hp]*0.85}$$

$$Q_1=0.4412*Q_2 \leftarrow eq.4$$

$$Q_2=2.2665*Q_1 \leftarrow eq.5$$

Water Resources Practice Problems

$$Q = Q_1 + Q_2 \leftarrow eq.6$$

$$Q_2 = 2.2665 * Q_1$$

Plug in variable Q_2 into eq.6, then solve for Q.

$$Q = Q_1 + 2.2665 * Q_1$$

$$Q = 3.2665 * Q_1 \leftarrow eq.7$$

flow rate $\rightarrow Q = V_t / t \leftarrow eq.8$

tank volume   time

Eq.8 computes the flow rate based on the tank volume and time to fill the tank.

$$V_t = \pi * d_t^2 * h_t / 4 \leftarrow eq.9$$

$$d_t = 120[ft] \quad h_t = 30[ft]$$

Eq.9 computes the volume of the tank.

Plug in variables d_t and h_t into eq.9, then solve for V_t.

$$V_t = \pi * (120[ft])^2 * 30[ft] / 4$$

$$V_t = 3.393 * 10^5 [ft^3]$$

$$Q = V_t / t \leftarrow eq.8$$

$$V_t = 3.393 * 10^5 [ft^3] \quad t = 3[days]$$

Plug in variables V_t and t into eq.7, then solve for Q.

$$Q = 1.131 * 10^5 \left[\frac{ft^3}{day}\right] * \frac{1}{24}\left[\frac{day}{hr}\right] * \frac{1}{60}\left[\frac{hr}{min}\right] * \frac{1}{60}\left[\frac{min}{s}\right] \leftarrow eq.10$$

conversion factors

$$Q = 1.309 [ft^3/s]$$

Eq.10 converts the flow rate to cubic feet per second.

$$Q = 1.309 [ft^3/s]$$

$$Q_1 = 0.3061 * Q \leftarrow eq.11$$

Solve eq.7 for Q_1.

$$Q_1 = 0.3061 * 1.309 [ft^3/s]$$

Plug in the flow rate Q into eq.11, then solve for Q_1.

Pumps #12 (cont.)

$$Q_1 = 0.401 \,[\text{ft}^3/\text{s}]$$

$$P_1 = 5 \,[\text{hp}] \qquad \eta_{p,1} = 0.60$$

$$h = \frac{8.814 * P_1 * \eta_{p,1}}{Q_1 * SG} \leftarrow eq.\,2$$

$$Q_1 = 0.401 \,[\text{ft}^3/\text{s}] \qquad SG = 1.00$$

Plug in variables P_1, $\eta_{p,1}$, Q_1 and SG into eq. 2, then solve for h.

$$h = \frac{8.814 * 5 * 0.6}{0.401 * 1.00}$$

Drop the units from the right hand side of eq. 2, and remember h has units of feet.

$$h = 65.94 \,[\text{ft}]$$

Answer: $\boxed{\text{C}}$

Water Resources Practice Problems

Find: $P_{3[hr]}$ ← total rainfall after 3 hours

Given:

C=0.65

runoff coefficient

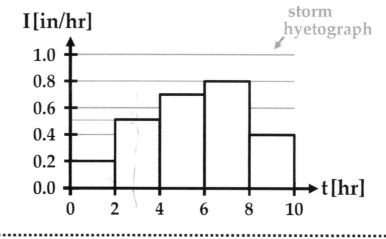

storm hyetograph

A) 0.5 [in]
B) 0.6 [in]
C) 0.7 [in]
D) 0.9 [in]

Analysis:

$$P = \sum_{i}^{j} i_t * t \leftarrow eq.1$$

total rainfall

rainfall intensity

duration

Eq. 1 computes the total rainfall of the storm from period i to period j.

Eq. 2 writes out the summation in eq. 1 for the first 3 hours.

$i_{0-1[hr]}=0.2 [in/hr]$ $i_{2-3[hr]}=0.5 [in/hr]$

$$P_{3[hr]} = i_{0-1[hr]} * t + i_{1-2[hr]} * t + i_{2-3[hr]} * t \leftarrow eq.2$$

$i_{1-2[hr]}=0.2 [in/hr]$ $t=1 [hr]$

Plug in the variables for duration and intensity into eq. 2, then solve for the rainfall after 3 hours, $P_{3[hr]}$.

$$P_{3[hr]}=0.2 [in/hr] * 1 [hr] + 0.2 [in/hr] * 1 [hr] + 0.5 [in/hr] * 1 [hr]$$

$$P_{3[hr]}=0.9 [in]$$

Answer: D

Hydrology #2

<u>Find:</u> $i_{2[hr]-5[hr]}$ ← average hourly rainfall rate (between hour 2 and hour 5)

<u>Given:</u>

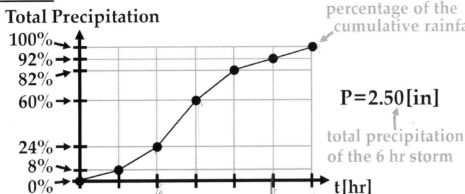

Total Precipitation

percentage of the cumulative rainfall

$P = 2.50 \, [in]$

total precipitation of the 6 hr storm

A) 0.43 [in/hr]

B) 0.57 [in/hr]

C) 0.83 [in/hr]

D) 0.90 [in/hr]

Analysis:

rainfall intensity

rainfall depth

Eq. 1 computes the average rainfall intensity during hours 2 through 5.

$$i_{2[hr]-5[hr]} = \frac{P_{2[hr]-3[hr]} + P_{3[hr]-4[hr]} + P_{4[hr]-5[hr]}}{t_{2[hr]-3[hr]} + t_{3[hr]-4[hr]} + t_{4[hr]-5[hr]}} \leftarrow eq.1$$

duration

$$t_{2[hr]-3[hr]} = 1 \, [hr]$$

$$t_{3[hr]-4[hr]} = 1 \, [hr]$$

$$t_{4[hr]-5[hr]} = 1 \, [hr]$$

The duration of each period equals 1 hour.

total rainfall

$$P_{i[hr]-j[hr]} = P * (\% P_{j[hr]} - \% P_{i[hr]}) \leftarrow eq.2$$

percentage of total rainfall after j hours and i hours

Eq. 2 computes the rainfall which occurs between hour i and hour j.

$P = 2.50 \, [in]$

$$P_{2[hr]-3[hr]} = P * (\% P_{3[hr]} - \% P_{2[hr]}) \leftarrow eq.3$$

$\% P_{3[hr]} = 0.60$ $\% P_{2[hr]} = 0.24$

Eq. 3 computes the rainfall between hour 2 and hour 3.

$$P_{2[hr]-3[hr]} = 2.50 \, [in] * (0.60 - 0.24)$$

Water Resources Practice Problems

Hydrology #2 (cont.)

$$P_{2[hr]-3[hr]}=0.90\,[in]$$

$$P=2.50\,[in]$$

$$P_{3[hr]-4[hr]}=P*(\%P_{4[hr]}-\%P_{3[hr]}) \leftarrow eq.4$$

$$\%P_{4[hr]}=0.82 \qquad \%P_{3[hr]}=0.60$$

Eq. 4 computes the rainfall between hour 3 and hour 4.

$$P_{3[hr]-4[hr]}=2.50\,[in]*(0.82-0.60)$$

$$P_{3[hr]-4[hr]}=0.55\,[in]$$

$$P=2.50\,[in]$$

$$P_{4[hr]-5[hr]}=P*(\%P_{5[hr]}-\%P_{4[hr]}) \leftarrow eq.5$$

$$\%P_{5[hr]}=0.92 \qquad \%P_{4[hr]}=0.82$$

Eq. 5 computes the rainfall between hour 4 and hour 5.

$$P_{4[hr]-5[hr]}=2.50\,[in]*(0.92-0.82)$$

$$P_{4[hr]-5[hr]}=0.25\,[in]$$

Plug in the known precipitation values and durations into eq.1, then solve for $i_{2[hr]-5[hr]}$.

$$P_{2[hr]-3[hr]}=0.90\,[in] \qquad P_{3[hr]-4[hr]}=0.55\,[in] \qquad P_{4[hr]-5[hr]}=0.25\,[in]$$

$$i_{2[hr]-5[hr]}=\frac{P_{2[hr]-3[hr]}+P_{3[hr]-4[hr]}+P_{4[hr]-5[hr]}}{t_{2[hr]-3[hr]}+t_{3[hr]-4[hr]}+t_{4[hr]-5[hr]}} \leftarrow eq.1$$

$$t_{2[hr]-3[hr]}=1\,[hr] \qquad t_{3[hr]-4[hr]}=1\,[hr] \qquad t_{4[hr]-5[hr]}=1\,[hr]$$

$$i_{2[hr]-5[hr]}=\frac{0.90\,[in]+0.55\,[in]+0.25\,[in]}{1\,[hr]+1\,[hr]+1\,[hr]}$$

$$i_{2[hr]-5[hr]}=0.566\,[in/hr] \qquad \underline{\text{Answer:}} \quad \boxed{B}$$

Hydrology #3

Find: $Q_{O,2}$ ← average outflow for month 2

Given: $E_A=0.12\,[\text{in/day}]$ ← evaporation rate

$Q_{I,1}=230\,[\text{ft}^3/\text{s}]$ ← average inflow for month 1

$Q_{I,2}=275\,[\text{ft}^3/\text{s}]$ ← average inflow for month 2

$Q_{O,1}=215\,[\text{ft}^3/\text{s}]$ ← average outflow for month 1

$A\,[\text{ft}^2]=12{,}150*V\,[\text{acre}*\text{ft}]^{0.37}$ ← reservoir geometry

$E_{F,2}=4{,}383\,[\text{ft}^3/\text{day}]$ ← evaporation rate at the end of the second month

$V_{I,1}=12{,}000\,[\text{acre}*\text{ft}]$ ← initial reservoir volume

reservoir $\downarrow Q_1$

$\downarrow Q_O$

A) $220\,[\text{ft}^3/\text{s}]$

B) $235\,[\text{ft}^3/\text{s}]$

C) $255\,[\text{ft}^3/\text{s}]$

D) $270\,[\text{ft}^3/\text{s}]$

Analysis:

Eq.1 computes the reservoir volume at the end of stage j.

No evaporation is taken

reservoir volume   average outflow

$$V_{F,j}=V_{I,i}+\sum_{i}^{j}Q_{I,m}*t-\sum_{i}^{j}Q_{O,m}*t \leftarrow eq.1$$

final   initial   average inflow   time

Write out the summation from eq.1 for flow rates from months 1 and 2

$$V_{F,j}=V_{I,i}+Q_{I,1}*t+Q_{I,2}*t-Q_{O,1}*t-Q_{O,2}*t \leftarrow eq.2$$

Solve eq.2 for $Q_{O,2}$.

$$Q_{O,2}=\frac{V_{I,i}-V_{F,j}}{t}+Q_{I,1}+Q_{I,2}-Q_{O,1} \leftarrow eq.3$$

Eq.4 computes the surface area of the reservoir after the end of the second month.

final area of the reservoir   evaporation rate (volumetric) $\frac{Vol}{t}$

$$A_{F,2}=\frac{E_{F,2}}{E_A} \leftarrow eq.4$$

evaporation rate (linear) $\frac{De}{t}$

Eq.5 converts the evaporation rate to units of feet per day.

$$E_A=0.12\left[\frac{\text{in}}{\text{day}}\right]*\frac{1}{12}\left[\frac{\text{ft}}{\text{in}}\right] \leftarrow eq.5$$

conversion factor

Water Resources Practice Problems

$$E_A = 0.01 \, [\text{ft/day}]$$

$E_{F,2} = 4{,}383 \, [\text{ft}^3/\text{day}]$

$$A_{F,2} = \frac{E_{F,2}}{E_A} \leftarrow eq.\,4$$

$E_A = 0.01 \, [\text{ft/day}]$

Plug in variables E_A and $E_{F,2}$ into eq. 4, then solve for the surface area of the reservoir after month 2, $A_{F,2}$.

$$A_{F,2} = \frac{4{,}383 \, [\text{ft}^3/\text{day}]}{0.01 \, [\text{ft/day}]}$$

$$A_{F,2} = 438{,}300 \, [\text{ft}^2]$$

Eq. 6 computes the surface area of the reservoir based on the volume.

area [ft²]   volume [acre*ft]

$$A = 12{,}150 * V^{0.37} \leftarrow eq.\,6$$

Solve eq. 6 for the volume, V, then add subscript "F,2" to indicate the end of the second month.

$$V_{F,2} = (8.2305 * 10^{-5} * A_{F,2})^{2.7027} \leftarrow eq.\,7$$

$A_{F,2} = 438{,}300 \, [\text{ft}^2]$

Plug in variable $A_{F,2}$ into eq. 7, then solve for $V_{F,2}$.

$$V_{F,2} = (8.2305 * 10^{-5} * 438{,}300)^{2.7027}$$

The units for $V_{F,2}$ in eq. 7 are acre*ft.

$$V_{F,2} = 16{,}167 \, [\text{acre*ft}]$$

Eq. 8 converts the final volume of the reservoir to cubic feet.

$$V_{F,2} = 16{,}167 \, [\text{acre*ft}] * 43{,}560 \left[\frac{\text{ft}^2}{\text{acre}}\right] \leftarrow eq.\,8$$

conversion factor

$$V_{F,2} = 7.0423 * 10^8 \, [\text{ft}^3]$$

Hydrology #3 (cont.)

Eq. 9 converts the initial volume of the reservoir to cubic feet.

$$A_{I,1}=12,000\ [acre*ft] * 43,560 \left[\frac{ft^2}{acre}\right] \leftarrow eq.\ 9$$

$$A_{I,1}=5.2272*10^8\ [ft^3]$$

conversion factors

$$t=1\ [months] * 30\left[\frac{day}{month}\right] * 24\left[\frac{hr}{day}\right] * 60\left[\frac{min}{hr}\right] * 60\left[\frac{s}{min}\right] \leftarrow eq.\ 10$$

$$t=2.592*10^6\ [s]$$

Eq. 10 converts the time to seconds, assuming 1 month equals 30 days.

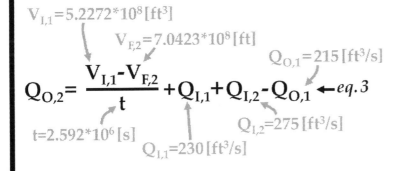

$$V_{I,1}=5.2272*10^8\ [ft^3]$$
$$V_{F,2}=7.0423*10^8\ [ft]$$
$$Q_{O,1}=215\ [ft^3/s]$$

$$Q_{O,2}= \frac{V_{I,1}-V_{F,2}}{t}+Q_{I,1}+Q_{I,2}-Q_{O,1} \leftarrow eq.\ 3$$

$$t=2.592*10^6\ [s]$$
$$Q_{I,2}=275\ [ft^3/s]$$
$$Q_{I,1}=230\ [ft^3/s]$$

Plug in variables $V_{I,1}$, $V_{F,2}$, t, $Q_{I,1}$, $Q_{I,2}$, and $Q_{O,1}$ into eq. 3, then solve for $Q_{O,2}$.

$$Q_{O,2}= \frac{5.2272*10^8\ [ft^3]-7.0423*10^8\ [ft^3]}{2.592*10^6\ [s]} +230\ [ft^3/s] +275\ [ft^3/s] -215\ [ft^3/s]$$

$$Q_{O,2}=220\ [ft^3/s]$$

Answer: ☐ A

Water Resources Practice Problems

Hydrology #4

Find: Q_{3-4} ← the average runoff flow rate between hours 3 and 4 of the storm

Given:

$P_{ave,excess}=0.893\,[cm]$

↑ average excess rainfall over the watershed (for the entire storm)

$A=25\,[km^2]$ ← area of the watershed

t [hr]	Q [m³/s]
0-1	7
1-2	18
2-3	20
3-4	Q_{3-4}
4-5	5

← runoff hydrograph

A) $10\,[m^3/s]$
B) $11\,[m^3/s]$
C) $12\,[m^3/s]$
D) $13\,[m^3/s]$

Analysis:

$$V_T = t * \Sigma Q_{i-j} \quad \leftarrow eq.\,1$$

total runoff volume — time period — average flow rate during time period

Eq. 1 computes the total runoff volume from the storm based on flow rates.

$$V_T = t * (Q_{0-1}+Q_{1-2}+Q_{2-3}+Q_{3-4}+Q_{4-5}) \quad \leftarrow eq.\,2$$

Write out the summation term in eq. 1.

$$Q_{3-4} = \frac{V_T}{t} - Q_{0-1} - Q_{1-2} - Q_{2-3} - Q_{4-5} \quad \leftarrow eq.\,3$$

Solve eq. 2 for Q_{3-4}.

$A=25\,[km^2]$ ↓

$$V_T = A * P_{ave,excess} \quad \leftarrow eq.\,4$$

$P_{ave,excess}=0.893\,[cm]$ ↑

Eq. 4 computes the total runoff volume of the storm based on the area and excess rainfall.

$$V_T = 25\,[km^2] * 0.893\,[cm]$$

Eq. 5 converts the total runoff volume to units of meters squared.

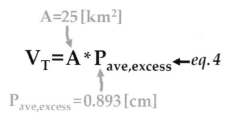

$$V_T = 22.325\,[cm*km^2] * \left(1{,}000\left[\frac{m}{km}\right]\right)^2 * \frac{1}{100}\left[\frac{m}{cm}\right] \quad \leftarrow eq.\,5$$

conversion factors

Hydrology #4 (cont.)

$$V_T = 2.2325 * 10^5 \, [m^3]$$

$$t = 1 \, [hr] * 60 \left[\frac{min}{hr} \right] * 60 \left[\frac{s}{min} \right] \leftarrow eq.\,6$$

conversion factors

Eq. 6 converts the time period to seconds.

$$t = 3,600 \, [s]$$

$V_T = 2.2325 * 10^5 \, [m^3]$ $Q_{1-2} = 18 \, [m^3/s]$ $Q_{4-5} = 5 \, [m^3/s]$

$$Q_{3-4} = \frac{V_T}{t} - Q_{0-1} - Q_{1-2} - Q_{2-3} - Q_{4-5} \leftarrow eq.\,3$$

$t = 3,600 \, [s]$ $Q_{0-1} = 7 \, [m^3/s]$ $Q_{2-3} = 20 \, [m^3/s]$

Plug in variables V_T, t, Q_{0-1}, Q_{1-2}, Q_{2-3}, and Q_{4-5} into eq. 3, then solve for Q_{3-4}.

$$Q_{3-4} = \frac{2.2325 * 10^5 \, [m^3]}{3,600 \, [s]} - 7 \, [m^3/s] - 18 \, [m^3/s] - 20 \, [m^3/s] - 5 \, [m^3/s]$$

$$Q_{3-4} = 12 \, [m^3/s]$$

Answer: $\boxed{C}$

Water Resources Practice Problems

Hydrology #5

<u>Find:</u> A ← the area of the watershed

<u>Given:</u>

$P_{ave,excess} = 1.5 \,[in]$

average excess rainfall depth of the storm contributing to runoff (for the entire storm)

$P = 2.0 \,[in]$

total rainfall depth

unit hydrograph of the watershed

t [hr]	Q [ft³/(s*in)]
0-1	150
1-2	620
2-3	700
3-4	400
4-5	80

A) 2 [mi²]

B) 3 [mi²]

C) 4 [mi²]

D) 5 [mi²]

1950

Analysis:

total runoff volume

$$A = V_T / P_{ave,excess} \quad \leftarrow eq.1$$

area of the watershed   excess depth of rainfall

Eq. 1 computes the area of the watershed.

actual rainfall depth

$$V_T = V_{T,u} * \frac{P}{P_u} \quad \leftarrow eq.2$$

unit rainfall depth

total runoff volume for a unit rainfall depth

Eq. 2 computes the total runoff volume from the storm.

$$V_{T,u} = \Sigma (Q_{i,u} * t) \quad \leftarrow eq.3$$

runoff from the unit hydrograph   duration of the period

Eq. 3 computes the total runoff volume for a unit rainfall depth.

Eq. 4 writes out the summation of unit flow rates, from eq. 3.

$$V_{T,u} = t * (Q_{0-10,u} + Q_{10-20,u} + Q_{20-30,u} + Q_{30-40,u} + Q_{40-50,u}) \quad \leftarrow eq.4$$

$$t = 1 \,[hr] * 60 \left[\frac{min}{hr}\right] * 60 \left[\frac{s}{min}\right] \quad \leftarrow eq.5$$

conversion factors

Eq. 5 converts the time period to seconds.

Hydrology #5 (cont.)

$$t = 3,600 \, [s]$$

Plug in the known variables into the right hand side of eq. 4, then solve for $V_{T,u}$.

$$t = 3,600 \, [s]$$

$$V_{T,u} = t * (Q_{0\text{-}10,u} + Q_{10\text{-}20,u} + Q_{20\text{-}30,u} + Q_{30\text{-}40,u} + Q_{40\text{-}50,u}) \leftarrow eq. 4$$

$$Q_{0\text{-}10,u} = 150 \, [ft^3/s] \qquad Q_{20\text{-}30,u} = 700 \, [ft^3/s] \qquad Q_{40\text{-}50,u} = 80 \, [ft^3/s]$$

$$Q_{10\text{-}20,u} = 620 \, [ft^3/s] \qquad Q_{30\text{-}40,u} = 400 \, [ft^3/s]$$

$$V_{T,u} = 3,600 \, [s] * (150 \, [ft^3/s] + 620 \, [ft^3/s] + 700 \, [ft^3/s] + 400 \, [ft^3/s] + 80 \, [ft^3/s])$$

$$V_{T,u} = 7.02 * 10^6 \, [ft^3]$$

$$V_{T,u} = 7.02 * 10^6 \, [ft^3] \qquad P = 2 \, [in]$$

Eq. 2 computes the total runoff volume from the storm.

$$V_T = V_{T,u} * \frac{P}{P_u} \leftarrow eq. 2$$

$$P_u = 1 \, [in]$$

Plug in variables $V_{T,u}$, P and P_u into eq. 2, then solve for V_T.

$$V_T = 7.02 * 10^6 \, [ft^3] * \frac{2 \, [in]}{1 \, [in]}$$

$$V_T = 1.404 * 10^7 \, [ft^3]$$

$$P_{ave,excess} = 1.5 \, [in] * \frac{1}{12} \left[\frac{ft}{in} \right] \leftarrow eq. 6$$

Eq. 6 converts the average excess rainfall to units of feet.

conversion factor

$$P_{ave,excess} = 0.125 \, [ft]$$

Water Resources Practice Problems

$$V_T = 1.404 * 10^7 \, [\text{ft}^3]$$

$$A = \frac{V_T}{P_{ave,excess}} \leftarrow eq.1$$

Plug in variables V_T and $P_{ave,excess}$ into eq.1, then solve for A.

$$P_{ave,excess} = 0.125 \, [\text{ft}]$$

$$A = \frac{1.404 * 10^7 \, [\text{ft}^3]}{0.125 \, [\text{ft}]}$$

Eq.7 converts the watershed area to units of miles squared.

$$A = 1.123 * 10^8 \, [\text{ft}^2] * \left(\frac{1}{5,280} \left[\frac{\text{mi}}{\text{ft}} \right] \right)^2 \leftarrow eq.7$$

conversion factor

$$A = 4.03 \, [\text{mi}^2]$$

4.53

Answer: $\boxed{C}$

224

Hydrology #6

Find: $Q_{p,u}$ ← the peak runoff of the NRCS synthetic unit hydrograph

Given:

$t_R = 5\,[hr]$ ← storm duration

$Elev_A = Elev_D = 271.41\,[ft]$

$Elev_B = 337.67\,[ft]$ ← ground elevations of the watershed

$Elev_C = 111.41\,[ft]$

$L_{AC} = 8,000\,[ft]$ ← the length between points A and C

$CN = 60$ ← curve number

the watershed has a uniform ground slope

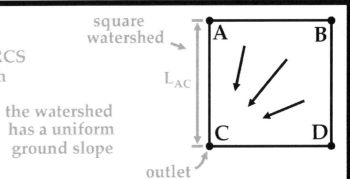
square watershed
L_{AC}
outlet

A) $68\,[ft^3/(s*in)]$

B) $121\,[ft^3/(s*in)]$

C) $213\,[ft^3/(s*in)]$

D) $576\,[ft^3/(s*in)]$

Analysis:

peak unit flow rate $[ft^3/(s*in)]$ drainage area [acre]

$$Q_p = \frac{0.756*A_d}{t_p} \leftarrow eq.1$$

time to peak flow [hr]

Eq.1 computes the peak unit flow rate from the watershed using the NRCS synthetic hydrograph.

$L_{CD} = L_{AC}$

$$A_d = L_{AC}*L_{CD} \leftarrow eq.2$$

side lengths of the square watershed

Eq.2 computes the drainage area, which is the total area of the watershed.

$L_{AC} = 8,000\,[ft]$

$$A_d = L_{AC}*L_{AC} \leftarrow eq.3$$

Plug in side length L_{AC} into eq.3, then solve for the drainage area.

$$A_d = 8,000\,[ft]*8,000\,[ft]$$

$$A_d = 6.4*10^7\,[ft^2]*\frac{1}{43,560}\left[\frac{acre}{ft^2}\right] \leftarrow eq.4$$

Eq.4 converts the drainage area to acres.

conversion factor

$$A_d = 1,469\,[acre]$$

Water Resources Practice Problems

$$t_p = 0.5 * t_R + t_1 \leftarrow eq.5$$

time to peak flow

storm duration

lag time

Eq.5 computes the time to the peak flow rate of the hydrograph.

longest distance to the outlet [ft]

soil water storage capacity [in]

$$t_1 = \frac{L_o^{0.8} * (S+1)^{0.7}}{1900 * \sqrt{S_o}} \leftarrow eq.6$$

lag time

average slope of the watershed [%]

Eq.6 computes the lag time.

$$L_o = L_{BC} = L_{AC} * \sqrt{2} \leftarrow eq.7$$

$L_{AC} = 8{,}000$ [ft]

Eq.7 computes longest distance from inside the watershed to the outlet point.

$$L_o = 8{,}000 \, [ft] * \sqrt{2}$$

$$L_o = 11{,}314 \, [ft]$$

$$S = 1{,}000 / CN - 10 \leftarrow eq.8$$

$CN = 60$

Eq.8 computes the soil water storage capacity.

$$S = 1{,}000 / 60 - 10$$

Plug in variable CN into eq.8, then solve for S.

$$S = 6.67$$

$Elev_B = 337.67$ [ft] $Elev_C = 111.41$ [ft]

$$S_o = \frac{Elev_B - Elev_C}{L_o} \leftarrow eq.9$$

$L_o = L_{BC} = 11{,}314$ [ft]

Eq.9 computes the average slope of the watershed.

Hydrology #6 (cont.)

$$S_o = \frac{337.67\,[\text{ft}] - 111.41\,[\text{ft}]}{11,314\,[\text{ft}]}$$

$$S_o = 0.020 * 100\% \leftarrow eq.\,10$$

Eq. 10 converts the average slope to a percentage.

$$S_o = 2.0\%$$

$L_o = 11,314\,[\text{ft}]$ $S = 6.67$

$$t_1 = \frac{L_o^{0.8} * (S+1)^{0.7}}{1900 * \sqrt{S_o}} \leftarrow eq.\,6$$

$S_o = 2.0\%$

Plug in variables L_o, S and S_o into eq. 6, then solve for t_1.

$$t_1 = \frac{(11,314)^{0.8} * (6.67+1)^{0.7}}{1900 * \sqrt{2.0}}$$

$$t_1 = 2.71\,[\text{hr}]$$

$t_R = 5\,[\text{hr}]$ $t_1 = 2.71\,[\text{hr}]$

$$t_p = 0.5 * t_R + t_1 \leftarrow eq.\,5$$

Eq. 5 computes the time to the peak flow rate of the hydrograph.

$$t_p = 0.5 * 5\,[\text{hr}] + 2.71\,[\text{hr}]$$

$$t_p = 5.21\,[\text{hr}]$$

$A_d = 1,469\,[\text{acre}]$ $t_p = 5.21\,[\text{hr}]$

$$Q_{p,u} = 0.756 * A_d / t_p \leftarrow eq.\,1$$

Plug in variables A_d and t_p into eq. 1, then solve for $Q_{p,u}$.

$$Q_{p,u} = 0.756 * \frac{1,469}{5.21}$$

$$Q_{p,u} = 213\,[\text{ft}^3/(\text{s}*\text{in})]$$

Answer: $\boxed{\text{C}}$

Water Resources Practice Problems

Hydrology #7

Find: $Q_{10[hr]}$ ← the runoff 10 hours into the storm

Given:

$A_d = 2.225 \, [mi^2]$ ← drainage area

$t_R = 8 \, [hr]$ ← storm duration

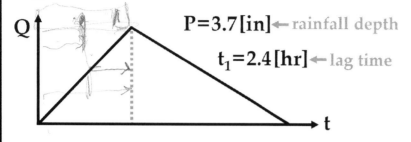

$P = 3.7 \, [in]$ ← rainfall depth

$t_1 = 2.4 \, [hr]$ ← lag time

use the NRCS synthetic unit triangular hydrograph

A) $70 \, [ft^3/s]$

B) $110 \, [ft^3/s]$

C) $170 \, [ft^3/s]$

D) $410 \, [ft^3/s]$

Analysis:

runoff at 10 hours

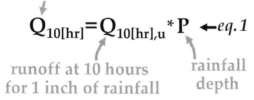

$$Q_{10[hr]} = Q_{10[hr],u} * P \quad ←eq.1$$

runoff at 10 hours for 1 inch of rainfall

rainfall depth

Eq. 1 computes the runoff at 10 hours.

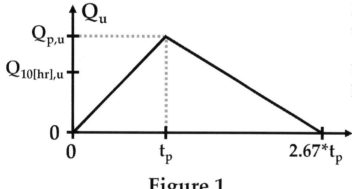

Figure 1

Figure 1 shows the NRCS synthetic unit triangular hydrograph.

Based on the value of t_p, we'll use linear interpolation to find $Q_{10[hr],u}$.

peak unit flow rate $[ft^3/s]$ drainage area $[mi^2]$

$$Q_{p,u} = \frac{484 * A_d}{t_p} \quad ←eq.2$$

time to peak flow rate [hr]

Eq. 2 computes the peak flow rate from the watershed using the NRCS synthetic hydrograph.

$$t_p = 0.5 * t_R + t_1 \quad ←eq.3$$

time to peak flow $t_R = 8 \, [hr]$ $t_1 = 2.4 \, [hr]$

Eq. 3 computes the time to the peak flow rate of the hydrograph.

Plug in variables t_R and t_1 into eq. 3, then solve for t_p.

Hydrology #7 (cont.)

$$t_p = 0.5 * 8 \, [hr] + 2.4 \, [hr]$$

$$t_p = 6.4 \, [hr]$$

$A_d = 2.225 \, [mi^2]$

$$Q_{p,u} = \frac{484 * A_d}{t_p} \leftarrow eq.\,2$$

$t_p = 6.4 \, [hr]$

Plug in variables t_p and A_d into eq. 2, then solve for $Q_{p,u}$.

$$Q_{p,u} = \frac{484 * 2.225}{6.4}$$

Drop the units for the right hand side of eq. 2, and remember the units of flow rate are in cubic feet per second.

$$Q_{p,u} = 168.3 \, [ft^3/(s*in)]$$

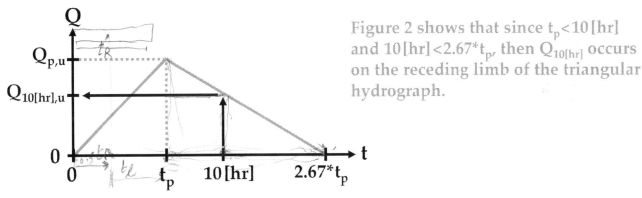

Figure 2

Figure 2 shows that since $t_p < 10 \, [hr]$ and $10 \, [hr] < 2.67 * t_p$, then $Q_{10[hr]}$ occurs on the receding limb of the triangular hydrograph.

Eq. 4 computes the flow rate of the unit hydrograph at 10 hours.

$t = 10 \, [hr]$ $t_p = 6.4 \, [hr]$

$$Q_{10[hr],u} = Q_{p,u} - Q_{p,u} * \frac{t - t_p}{2.67 * t_p - t_p} \leftarrow eq.\,4$$

$Q_{p,u} = 168.3 \, [ft^3/(s*in)]$

Plug in variables $Q_{p,u}$, t and t_p into eq. 4, then solve for $Q_{10[hr],u}$.

$$Q_{10[hr],u} = 168.3 \, [ft^3/(s*in)] - 168.3 \, [ft^3/(s*in)] * \frac{10 \, [hr] - 6.4 \, [hr]}{2.67 * 6.4 \, [hr] - 6.4 \, [hr]}$$

Hydrology #7 (cont.)

$$Q_{10[hr],u}=111.61\,[ft^3/(s*in)]$$

$$Q_{10[hr],u}=111.61\,[ft^3/(s*in)] \qquad P=3.7\,[in]$$

$$Q_{10[hr]}=Q_{10[hr],u}*P \quad \leftarrow eq.1$$

Plug in variables $Q_{10[hr],u}$ and P into eq.1, then solve for $Q_{10[hr]}$.

$$Q_{10[hr]}=111.61\,[ft^3/(s*in)]*3.7\,[in]$$

$$Q_{10[hr]}=413.0\,[ft^3/s]$$

Answer: $\boxed{D}$

Hydrology #8

Find: V_E ← the volume of water that evaporates from the reservoir

Given:

$T=24.5\,^{\circ}C$ ← air temperature

$u_2=3.5\,[m/s]$ ← wind velocity

$z_2=2\,[m]$ ← height of wind measurement

$z_0=0.03\,[cm]$ ← roughness height of the water surface

$V=12,000\,[m^3]$ ← reservoir volume

$V=3.7*A^{1.47}$ ← reservoir geometry relationship (where V in $[m^3]$ and A in $[m^2]$)

$t=7\,[days]$ ← duration of evaporation

$R_h=45\%$ ← relative humidity

reservoir

A) $2\,[m^3]$
B) $13\,[m^3]$
C) $25\,[m^3]$
D) $97\,[m^3]$

Analysis:

evaporation rate   surface area

$$V_E=E_A*t*A \leftarrow eq.1$$

volume evaporated   duration of evaporation

Eq. 1 computes the volume of water that evaporates from the reservoir

volume $[m^3]$ area $[m^2]$

$$V=3.7*A^{1.47} \leftarrow eq.2$$

Eq. 2 defines the volume-area relationship of the reservoir.

Solve eq. 2 for the surface area.

$V=12,000\,[m^3]$

$$A=(0.2703*V)^{0.6803} \leftarrow eq.3$$

Plug in variable V into eq.3, then compute the surface area, A.

$$A=(0.2703*12,000)^{0.6803}$$

$$A=244.7\,[m^2]$$

evaporation rate $[mm/day]$ vapor pressure at the water surface $[Pa]$

$$E_A=B*(e_{as}-e_a) \leftarrow eq.4$$

vapor transfer coefficient $[mm/(day*Pa)]$ vapor pressure at the height above the water where wind is measured $[Pa]$

Eq.4 computes the evaporation rate using the aerodynamic method

Water Resources Practice Problems

vapor transfer coefficient
[mm/(day*Pa)]

wind velocity [m/s]

$$B = \frac{0.102 * u_2}{\{\ln(z_2/z_0)\}^2} \leftarrow eq.5$$

Eq. 5 computes the vapor transfer coefficient.

height of wind measurement [cm]

roughness height of the water surface [cm]

$$z_2 = 2\,[m] * \boxed{100 \left[\frac{cm}{m}\right]} \leftarrow eq.6$$

Eq. 6 converts the height of wind measurement to centimeters.

conversion factor

$$z_2 = 200\,[cm]$$

$u_2 = 3.5\,[m/s]$

$$B = \frac{0.102 * u_2}{\{\ln(z_2/z_0)\}^2} \leftarrow eq.5$$

Plug in variables u_2, z_2 and z_0 into eq. 5, then solve for B.

$z_2 = 200\,[cm]$ $z_0 = 0.03\,[cm]$

$$B = \frac{0.102 * 3.5}{\{\ln(200/0.03)\}^2}$$

Drop the units from the right hand side of eq. 5 and remember the units of B is mm/day*Pa.

$$B = 4.604 * 10^{-3}\,[mm/(day*Pa)]$$

$$e_{as} = 611 * \exp\left(\frac{17.27 * T}{237.7 + T}\right) \leftarrow eq.7$$

Eq. 7 computes the vapor pressure at the water surface based on the air temperature in °C.

$T = 24.5°\,C$

$$e_{as} = 611 * \exp\left(\frac{17.27 * 24.5}{237.7 + 24.5}\right)$$

$$e_{as} = 3,068\,[Pa]$$

Hydrology #8 (cont.)

Eq. 8 computes the vapor pressure at the height above the water surface where the wind velocity is measured.

$$e_a = R_h * e_{as} \leftarrow eq.\,8$$

$R_h = 45\% = 0.45 \qquad e_{as} = 3{,}068\,[Pa]$

Plug in variables R_h and e_{as} into eq. 8, then solve for e_a.

$$e_a = 0.45 * 3{,}068\,[Pa]$$

$$e_a = 1{,}381\,[Pa]$$

$B = 4.604 * 10^{-3}\,[mm/(day*Pa)]$

$$E_A = B * (e_{as} - e_a) \leftarrow eq.\,4$$

$e_{as} = 3{,}068\,[Pa] \qquad e_a = 1{,}381\,[Pa]$

Plug in variables B, e_{as} and e_a into eq. 4, then solve for E_A.

$$E_A = 4.604 * 10^{-3} \left[\frac{mm}{day*Pa} \right] * (3{,}068\,[Pa] - 1{,}381\,[Pa]) \quad = 7.77$$

$$E_A = 7.77 \left[\frac{mm}{day} \right] * \frac{1}{1{,}000} \left[\frac{m}{mm} \right] \leftarrow eq.\,9$$

conversion factor

Eq. 9 converts the evaporation rate to units of meters per day

$$E_A = 7.77 * 10^{-3}\,[m/day]$$

$E_A = 7.77 * 10^{-3}\,[m/day]$

$$V_E = E_A * t * A \leftarrow eq.\,1$$

$t = 7\,[days] \qquad A = 244.7\,[m^2]$

Plug in variables V_A, t and A into eq. 1, then solve for V_E.

$$V_E = 7.77 * 10^{-3}\,[m/day] * 7\,[days] * 244.7\,[m^2]$$

$$V_E = 13.31\,[m^3]$$

Answer: $\boxed{B}$

Water Resources Practice Problems

Hydrology #9

Find: $f_{(t)}$ ← the infiltration rate

Given:

$K=0.15\,[cm/hr]$ ← hydraulic conductivity

$\Psi=21.85\,[cm]$ ← suction head

$\theta_e=0.330$ ← effective porosity

$\eta=0.398$ ← porosity

$\theta_i=0.180$ ← initial saturation

$t=2\,[hr]$ ← elapsed time

negligible ponding depth

soil profile

continuous ponding

use Green-Ampt infiltration method

A) 0.15 [cm/hr]

B) 0.57 [cm/hr]

C) 1.05 [cm/hr]

D) 3.28 [cm/hr]

Analysis:

infiltration rate
suction head
change in moisture content

$$f_{(t)}=K*\left[\frac{\Psi*\Delta\theta}{F_{(t)}}+1\right]\quad\leftarrow eq.1$$

hydraulic conductivity

$t=2\,[hr]$

cumulative infiltration

Eq. 1 computes the infiltration rate.

Plug in variable t into eq.1.

$$f_{(2[hr])}=K*\left[\frac{\Psi*\Delta\theta}{F_{(2[hr])}}+1\right]\quad\leftarrow eq.2$$

$$\Delta\theta=(1-\theta_i)*\theta_e\quad\leftarrow eq.3$$

$\theta_i=0.180 \qquad \theta_e=0.330$

Eq. 3 computes the change in moisture content

$$\Delta\theta=(1-0.180)*0.330$$

$$\Delta\theta=0.271$$

Eq. 4 computes the cumulative infiltration at time t.

$K=0.15\,[cm/hr]$ $\quad \Delta\theta=0.271$ $\quad t=2\,[hr]$

$$F_{(t)}=K*t+\Psi*\Delta\theta*\ln\left(1+\frac{F_{(t)}}{\Psi*\Delta\theta}\right)\quad\leftarrow eq.4$$

$t=2\,[hr]$ $\quad \Psi=21.85\,[cm]$

Plug in variables K, $\Delta\theta$, Ψ and t into eq. 4, then simplify.

Hydrology #9 (cont.)

$$F_{(2[hr])}=0.15\,[cm/hr]*2\,[hr]+21.85\,[cm]*0.271*\ln\left(1+\frac{F_{(2[hr])}}{21.85\,[cm]*0.271}\right)$$

$$F_{(2[hr])}=0.3\,[cm]+5.921\,[cm]*\ln\left(1+\frac{F_{(2[hr])}}{5.921\,[cm]}\right)\;\leftarrow eq.5$$

first guess: $F_{(2[hr])}=4\,[cm]$

$$F_{(2[hr])}\underset{?}{=}0.3\,[cm]+5.921\,[cm]*\ln\left(1+\frac{F_{(2[hr])}}{5.921\,[cm]}\right)\;\leftarrow eq.5$$

Solve eq.5 for $F_{(2[hr])}$ by success approximations.

$$4\,[cm]\underset{?}{=}0.3\,[cm]+5.921\,[cm]*\ln\left(1+\frac{4\,[cm]}{5.921\,[cm]}\right)$$

$$4\,[cm]>3.36\,[cm]$$

Since the LHS > RHS, we'll try a smaller value for $F_{(2[hr])}$.

second guess: $F_{(2[hr])}=2\,[cm]$

$$F_{(2[hr])}\underset{?}{=}0.3\,[cm]+5.921\,[cm]*\ln\left(1+\frac{F_{(2[hr])}}{5.921\,[cm]}\right)\;\leftarrow eq.5$$

$$2\,[cm]\underset{?}{=}0.3\,[cm]+5.921\,[cm]*\ln\left(1+\frac{2\,[cm]}{5.921\,[cm]}\right)$$

$$2\,[cm]<2.02\,[cm]$$

Since the LHS < RHS, we'll try a slightly larger value for $F_{(2[hr])}$.

third guess: $F_{(2[hr])}=2.10\,[cm]$

$$F_{(2[hr])}\underset{?}{=}0.3\,[cm]+5.921\,[cm]*\ln\left(1+\frac{F_{(2[hr])}}{5.921\,[cm]}\right)\;\leftarrow eq.5$$

Hydrology #9 (cont.)

$$2.10[cm] \underset{?}{\overset{\uparrow}{=}} 0.3[cm] + 5.921[cm] * \ln\left(1 + \frac{2.10[cm]}{5.921[cm]}\right)$$

$$2.10[cm] = 2.10[cm]$$

Since the LHS = RHS, then the selected value for $F_{(2[hr])}$ is correct.

$$F_{(2[hr])} = 2.10[cm]$$

$K = 0.15[cm/hr]$

$\Psi = 21.85[cm]$

$\Delta\theta = 0.271$

$$f_{(2[hr])} = K * \left[\frac{\Psi * \Delta\theta}{F_{(2[hr])}} + 1\right] \leftarrow eq.2$$

$F_{(2[hr])} = 2.10[cm]$

Plug in variables K, Ψ, $\Delta\theta$ and $F_{(2[hr])}$ into eq.2, then solve for $f_{(2[hr])}$.

$$f_{(2[hr])} = 0.15[cm/hr] * \left[\frac{21.85[cm] * 0.271}{2.10[cm]} + 1\right]$$

$$f_{(2[hr])} = 0.573[cm/hr]$$

Answer: $\boxed{B}$

Hydrology #10

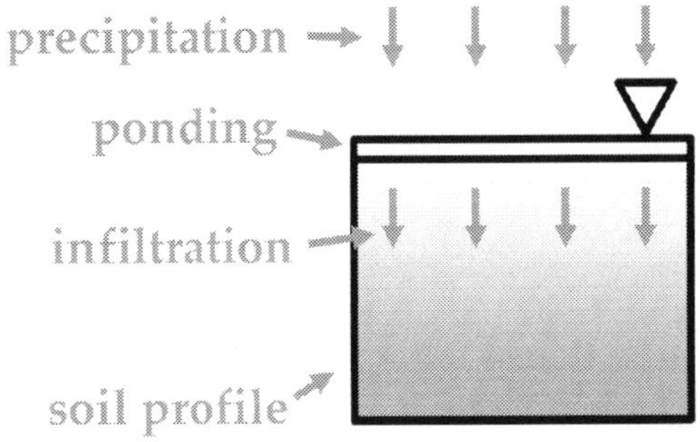

Find: t_p ← the time it takes for ponding to begin

Given:

$i = 0.60\,[\text{in/hr}]$ ← rainfall intensity for the entire storm

$f_o = 1.5\,[\text{in/hr}]$ ← initial infiltration rate

$f_c = 0.2\,[\text{in/hr}]$ ← final infiltration rate

$k = 0.5\,[\text{hr}^{-1}]$ ← decay constant

use the Horton infiltration method

the storm lasts long enough for the ponding to begin

precipitation → ↓ ↓ ↓ ↓
ponding
infiltration
soil profile

A) 1.85 [hr]

B) 2.35 [hr]

C) 3.00 [hr]

D) 3.55 [hr]

Analysis:

$$i > f_t \quad \leftarrow ieq.\,1$$

condition for ponding

Ponding begins when the rainfall rate exceeds the infiltration rate.

rate [in/hr]

potential infiltrate rate

← rainfall rate (constant)
← actual infiltration rate

→ t [hr]

t_p

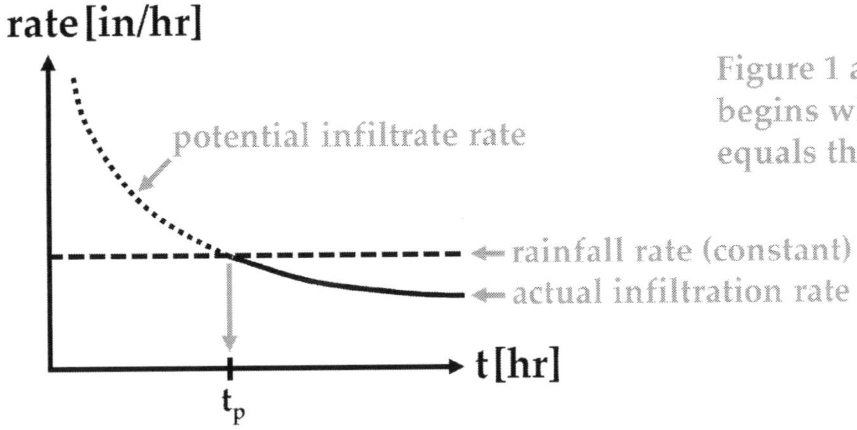

Figure 1

Figure 1 and eq. 2 show that ponding begins when the infiltrate rate equals the rainfall rate.

Plug in Horton's infiltrate rate equation into eq. 1.

condition for the start of ponding

$$i = f_t \quad \leftarrow eq.\,1$$

$$f_t = f_c + (f_o - f_c) * e^{-k*t}$$

Variable f_t represents the infiltration rate of the soil at time t, using Horton's method

$$i = f_c + (f_o - f_c) * e^{-k*t_P} \quad \leftarrow eq.\,2$$

Add a subscript "p" to the time variable in eq. 2, to represent the time when ponding begins.

Water Resources Practice Problems

Hydrology #10 (cont.)

Solve eq. 2 for variable t_p.

$i = 0.60\,[in/hr]$ $f_c = 0.2\,[in/hr]$

$$t_p = -\frac{1}{k} * \ln\left(\frac{i - f_c}{f_o - f_c}\right) \leftarrow eq.3$$

$k = 0.5\,[hr^{-1}]$ $f_o = 1.5\,[in/hr]$

Plug in variables k, i, f_o and f_c into eq. 3, then solve for t_p.

$$t_p = -\frac{1}{0.5[hr^{-1}]} * \ln\left(\frac{0.60\,[in/hr] - 0.2\,[in/hr]}{1.5\,[in/hr] - 0.2\,[in/hr]}\right)$$

$$t_p = 2.36\,[hr]$$

Answer: $\boxed{B}$

Hydrology #11

Find: $Q_{5[hr]-6[hr]}$ ← total direct runoff from the storm, between hours 5 and 6

Given:

t[hr]	$Q_u [m^3/(s*in)]$
0-1	50
1-2	200
2-3	250
3-4	70
4-5	20

← unit hydrograph

$i=1.00 [in/hr]$ ← rainfall intensity, and

$f=0.20 [in/hr]$ ← infiltration rate for the entire storm

$d=4 [hr]$
↑
storm duration

A) $0 [ft^3/s]$

B) $118 [ft^3/s]$

C) $272 [ft^3/s]$

D) $472 [ft^3/s]$

Analysis:

$$Q_1=Q_{0[hr]-1[hr]}$$
$$Q_2=Q_{1[hr]-2[hr]}$$
$$\vdots$$
$$Q_t=Q_{t-1[hr]-t[hr]}$$

We'll define Q_1 as the total direct runoff for the first hour of the storm. Therefore we want to solve for Q_6.

direct runoff in hour t   t=6

$$Q_t=\sum_{m=1}^{t} Q_{u,m}*P_{t-m+1} \leftarrow eq.1$$

unit hydrograph value in hour m   excess rainfall in hour t-m+1

Eq. 1 is the discrete convolution equation which computes the total direct runoff during hour t.

Plug in t=6 into eq. 1, and write out the summation.

$$Q_{5[hr]-6[hr]}=Q_6=Q_{u,1}*P_6+Q_{u,2}*P_5+Q_{u,3}*P_4$$
$$+Q_{u,4}*P_3+Q_{u,5}*P_1+Q_{u,6}*P_1 \leftarrow eq.2$$

t=1[hr]

$$P_t=t*(i-f) \leftarrow eq.3 \quad \text{(for all t)}$$

i=1.00[in/hr]   f=0.20 [in/hr]

Eq. 3 computes the excess rainfall depth by multiplying the time period by the difference between the infiltration rate and rainfall rate.

$$P_t=1[hr]*(1.00[in/hr]-0.20[in/hr])$$

Plug in variables t, i and f into eq. 3, then solve for P.

Water Resources Practice Problems

Hydrology #11 (cont.)

$$P_t = 0.80 \,[\text{in}] \qquad \text{for } 1 \le t \le 4$$

$$P_t = 0 \,[\text{in}] \qquad \text{for } t \ge 5$$

Since the infiltration rate and rain-fall rate are constant, the excess rainfall depth, P_t, is constant for all time periods of the storm.

$P_{t \ge 5} = 0 \,[\text{in}]$

$Q_{U,1} = 50 \,[\text{ft}^3/(s*\text{in})]$ $Q_{U,2} = 200 \,[\text{ft}^3/(s*\text{in})]$ $Q_{U,3} = 250 \,[\text{ft}^3/(s*\text{in})]$

$$Q_{5[\text{hr}]-6[\text{hr}]} = Q_6 = Q_{u,1} * P_6 + Q_{u,2} * P_5 + Q_{u,3} * P_4 \qquad P_{1 \le t \le 4} = 0.80 \,[\text{in}]$$

$$+ Q_{u,4} * P_3 + Q_{u,5} * P_2 + Q_{u,6} * P_1 \leftarrow eq.\,2$$

$Q_{U,4} = 70 \,[\text{ft}^3/(s*\text{in})]$ $Q_{U,5} = 20 \,[\text{ft}^3/(s*\text{in})]$ $Q_{U,6} = 0 \,[\text{ft}^3/(s*\text{in})]$

$$Q_{5[\text{hr}]-6[\text{hr}]} = 50 \,[\text{ft}^3/(s*\text{in})] * 0 \,[\text{in}] + 200 \,[\text{ft}^3/(s*\text{in})] * 0 \,[\text{in}]$$

$$+ 250 \,[\text{ft}^3/(s*\text{in})] * 0.80 \,[\text{in}] + 70 \,[\text{ft}^3/(s*\text{in})] * 0.80 \,[\text{in}]$$

$$+ 20 \,[\text{ft}^3/(s*\text{in})] * 0.80 \,[\text{in}] + 0 \,[\text{ft}^3/(s*\text{in})] * 0.80 \,[\text{in}]$$

$$Q_{5[\text{hr}]-6[\text{hr}]} = 272 \,[\text{ft}^3/s]$$

Plug in the known values into the right hand side of eq. 2, then solve for $Q_{5[\text{hr}]-6[\text{hr}]}$.

<u>Answer:</u> $\boxed{\text{C}}$

Hydrology #12

the unit hydrograph value during the third hour of the storm

Find: $Q_{u,2[hr]-3[hr]}$

Given: $f = 0.31 \, [cm/hr]$ ← infiltration rate for the entire storm

t[hr]	i[cm/hr]
0-1	0.78
1-2	2.31
2-3	1.76

t[hr]	Q[m³/s]
0-1	8.46
1-2	58.09
2-3	132.32
3-4	120.15

← direct hydrograph runoff flow rates

t[hr]	Q[m³/s]
4-5	37.7
5-6	0

rainfall intensities

A) $18 \, [m^3/(s \cdot cm)]$

B) $26 \, [m^3/(s \cdot cm)]$

C) $47 \, [m^3/(s \cdot cm)]$

D) $75 \, [m^3/(s \cdot cm)]$

Analysis:

direct runoff in hour t

$t=3$

$t=3$

$$Q_{t-1[hr]-t[hr]} = \sum_{m=1}^{t} Q_{u,m-1[hr]-m[hr]} * P_{t-m+1} \quad \leftarrow eq.1$$

unit hydrograph value in hour m

excess rainfall in hour t-m+1

Eq.1 computes the direct runoff flow rates for a given hour t.

Plug in t=3 into eq.1 to solve for the direct runoff during the third hour.

$$Q_{2[hr]-3[hr]} = \sum_{m=1}^{3} Q_{u,m-1[hr]-m[hr]} * P_{4-m} \quad \leftarrow eq.2$$

Expand the summation in eq.2.

$$Q_{2[hr]-3[hr]} = Q_{u,0[hr]-1[hr]} * P_3 + Q_{u,1[hr]-2[hr]} * P_2 + Q_{u,2[hr]-3[hr]} * P_1 \quad \leftarrow eq.3$$

Solve eq.3 for $Q_{u,2[hr]-3[hr]}$.

$$Q_{u,2[hr]-3[hr]} = \frac{Q_{2[hr]-3[hr]} - Q_{u,0[hr]-1[hr]} * P_3 - Q_{u,1[hr]-2[hr]} * P_2}{P_1} \quad \leftarrow eq.4$$

$i_1 = 0.78 \, [cm/hr]$ $f = 0.31 \, [cm/hr]$

Eq.5 computes the excess rainfall during the first hour.

$$P_1 = t * (i_1 - f) \quad \leftarrow eq.5$$

$t = 1 \, [hr]$

Plug in variables t, i_1 and f into eq.5, then solve for P_1.

$$P_1 = 1 \, [hr] * (0.78 \, [cm/hr] - 0.31 \, [cm/hr])$$

Hydrology #12 (cont.)

$$P_1 = 0.47 \, [cm]$$

$i_2 = 2.31 \, [cm/hr] \qquad f = 0.31 \, [cm/hr]$

$$P_2 = t*(i_2 - f) \leftarrow eq.6$$

$t = 1 \, [hr]$

Eq. 6 computes the excess rainfall during the second hour.

Plug in variables t, i_2 and f into eq. 6, then solve for P_2.

$$P_2 = 1 \, [hr] * (2.31 \, [cm/hr] - 0.31 \, [cm/hr])$$

$$P_2 = 2.00 \, [cm]$$

$i_3 = 1.76 \, [cm/hr] \qquad f = 0.31 \, [cm/hr]$

$$P_3 = t*(i_3 - f) \leftarrow eq.7$$

$t = 1 \, [hr]$

Eq. 7 computes the excess rainfall during the third hour.

Plug in variables t, i_3 and f into eq. 7, then solve for P_3.

$$P_3 = 1 \, [hr] * (1.76 \, [cm/hr] - 0.31 \, [cm/hr])$$

$$P_3 = 1.45 \, [cm]$$

$t = 1 \qquad\qquad t = 1$

$$Q_{t-1[hr]-t[hr]} = \sum_{m=1}^{t} Q_{u,m-1[hr]-m[hr]} * P_{t-m+1} \leftarrow eq.1$$

Plug in $t=1$ into eq. 1 to solve for the direct runoff during the first hour.

$$Q_{0[hr]-1[hr]} = \sum_{m=1}^{1} Q_{u,m-1[hr]-m[hr]} * P_{2-m} \leftarrow eq.8$$

Write out the summation in eq. 8.

$$Q_{0[hr]-1[hr]} = Q_{u,0[hr]-1[hr]} * P_1 \leftarrow eq.9$$

Solve eq. 9 for $Q_{u,0[hr]-1[hr]}$.

$$Q_{u,0[hr]-1[hr]} = Q_{0[hr]-1[hr]} / P_1 \leftarrow eq.10$$

$Q_{0[hr]-1[hr]} = 8.46 \, [m^3/s] \qquad P_1 = 0.47 \, [cm]$

Plug in $Q_{0[hr]-1[hr]}$ and P_1 into eq. 10, then solve for $Q_{u,0[hr]-1[hr]}$.

Hydrology #12 (cont.)

$$Q_{u,0[hr]-1[hr]}=8.46[m^3/s]/0.47[cm]$$

$$Q_{u,0[hr]-1[hr]}=18[m^3/(s*cm)]$$

$$Q_{t-1[hr]-t[hr]}=\sum_{m=1}^{t}Q_{u,m-1[hr]-m[hr]}*P_{t-m+1} \leftarrow eq.1$$

Plug in t=2 into eq.1 to solve for the direct runoff during the second hour.

$$Q_{1[hr]-2[hr]}=\sum_{m=1}^{2}Q_{u,m-1[hr]-m[hr]}*P_{3-m} \leftarrow eq.11$$

Write out the summation in eq.11.

$$Q_{1[hr]-2[hr]}=Q_{u,0[hr]-1[hr]}*P_2+Q_{u,1[hr]-2[hr]}*P_1 \leftarrow eq.12$$

Solve eq.12 for $Q_{u,1[hr]-2[hr]}$.

$$Q_{u,1[hr]-2[hr]}=\frac{Q_{1[hr]-2[hr]}-Q_{u,0[hr]-1[hr]}*P_2}{P_1} \leftarrow eq.13$$

$Q_{u,0[hr]-1[hr]}=18[m^3/(s*cm)]$

$Q_{1[hr]-2[hr]}=58.09[m^3/s]$

$P_1=0.47[cm]$

$P_2=2.00[cm]$

Plug in the known variables into eq.13, then solve for $Q_{u,1[hr]-2[hr]}$.

$$Q_{u,1[hr]-2[hr]}=\frac{58.09[m^3/s]-18[m^3/(s*cm)]*2.00[cm]}{0.47[cm]}$$

$$Q_{u,1[hr]-2[hr]}=47[m^3/(s*cm)]$$

Plug in the known variables into eq.4, then solve for $Q_{u,2[hr]-3[hr]}$.

$Q_{2[hr]-3[hr]}=132.32[m^3/s]$ $P_3=1.45[cm]$ $P_2=2.00[cm]$

$$Q_{u,2[hr]-3[hr]}=\frac{Q_{2[hr]-3[hr]}-Q_{u,0[hr]-1[hr]}*P_3-Q_{u,1[hr]-2[hr]}*P_2}{P_1} \leftarrow eq.4$$

$Q_{u,0[hr]-1[hr]}=18[m^3/(s*cm)]$ $P_1=0.47[cm]$ $Q_{u,1[hr]-2[hr]}=47[m^3/(s*cm)]$

Water Resources Practice Problems

Hydrology #12 (cont.)

$$Q_{u,2[hr]-3[hr]} = \frac{132.32\,[m^3/s] - 18\,[m^3/(s*cm)] * 1.45\,[cm] \atop -47\,[m^3/(s*cm)] * 2.00\,[cm]}{0.47\,[cm]}$$

$$Q_{u,2[hr]-3[hr]} = 26\,[m^3/(s*cm)]$$

Answer: $\boxed{B}$

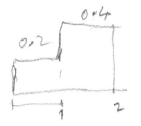

t	UH	Q_{Dr_1}	Q_{Dr_2}	Q_{DR}
0-1	1	0.2	0	0.2
1-2	3	0.6	0.4	1.0
2-3	2	0.4	1.2	1.6
3-4	0	0	0.8	0.8

Hydrology #13

$Q_u[ft^3/(s*in)]$

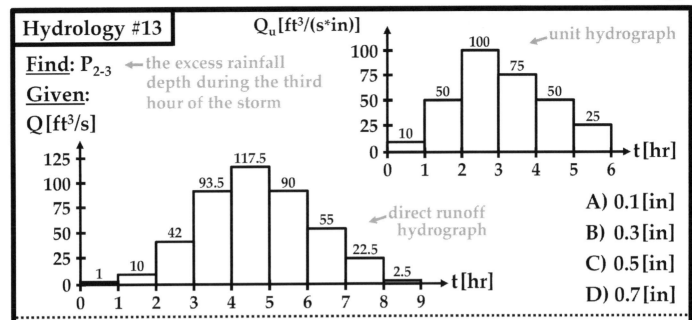

unit hydrograph

Find: P_{2-3} ← the excess rainfall depth during the third hour of the storm

Given:

$Q[ft^3/s]$

direct runoff hydrograph

A) 0.1 [in]

B) 0.3 [in]

C) 0.5 [in]

D) 0.7 [in]

Analysis:

Eq.1 computes the direct runoff flow rates for a given hour m.

direct runoff in hour t

$t=3$

$t=3$

$$Q_{t-1[hr]-t[hr]} = \sum_{m=1}^{t} Q_{u,m-1[hr]-m[hr]} * P_{t-m+1} \leftarrow eq.1$$

unit hydrograph value in hour m

excess rainfall in hour t-m+1

Plug in t=3 into eq.1 to solve for the direct runoff during the third hour.

$$Q_{2[hr]-3[hr]} = \sum_{m=1}^{3} Q_{u,m-1[hr]-m[hr]} * P_{4-m} \leftarrow eq.2$$

Expand the summation in eq. 2.

$$Q_{2[hr]-3[hr]} = Q_{u,0[hr]-1[hr]} * P_3 + Q_{u,1[hr]-2[hr]} * P_2 + Q_{u,2[hr]-3[hr]} * P_1 \leftarrow eq.3$$

Solve eq. 3 for P_3.

$$P_3 = \frac{Q_{2[hr]-3[hr]} - Q_{u,1[hr]-2[hr]} * P_2 - Q_{u,2[hr]-3[hr]} * P_1}{Q_{u,0[hr]-1[hr]}} \leftarrow eq.4$$

Plug in t=1 into eq.1 to solve for the excess rain-fall during the first hour.

$t=1$

$t=1$

$$Q_{t-1[hr]-t[hr]} = \sum_{m=1}^{t} Q_{u,m-1[hr]-m[hr]} * P_{t-m+1} \leftarrow eq.1$$

Write out the summation in eq. 5 by setting m=1.

$m=1$

$$Q_{0[hr]-1[hr]} = \sum_{m=1}^{1} Q_{u,m-1[hr]-m[hr]} * P_{2-m} \leftarrow eq.5$$

Hydrology #13 (cont.)

$$Q_{0[hr]-1[hr]} = Q_{u,0[hr]-1[hr]} * P_1 \leftarrow eq.6$$

Solve eq. 6 for P_1.

$$Q_{0[hr]-1[hr]} = 1\,[ft^3/s]$$

$$P_1 = \frac{Q_{0[hr]-1[hr]}}{Q_{u,0[hr]-1[hr]}} \leftarrow eq.7$$

Plug in $Q_{0[hr]-1[hr]}$ and $Q_{u,0[hr]-1[hr]}$ into eq. 7, then solve for P_1.

$$Q_{u,0[hr]-1[hr]} = 10\,[ft^3/(s*in)]$$

$$P_1 = \frac{1\,[ft^3/s]}{10\,[ft^3/(s*in)]}$$

$$P_1 = 0.10\,[in]$$

$$Q_{t-1[hr]-t[hr]} \overset{t=2}{=} \sum_{m=1}^{t} Q_{u,m-1[hr]-m[hr]} * P_{t-m+1}^{t=2} \leftarrow eq.8$$

Plug in t=2 into eq.1 to solve for the excess rain-fall during the second hour

$$Q_{1[hr]-2[hr]} = \sum_{m=1}^{2} Q_{u,m-1[hr]-m[hr]} * P_{3-m} \leftarrow eq.9$$

Write out the summation in eq. 9.

$$Q_{1[hr]-2[hr]} = Q_{u,0[hr]-1[hr]} * P_2 + Q_{u,1[hr]-2[hr]} * P_1 \leftarrow eq.10$$

Solve eq. 10 for P_2.

$$Q_{1[hr]-2[hr]} = 10\,[ft^3/s] \qquad Q_{u,1[hr]-2[hr]} = 50\,[ft^3/(s*in)]$$

$$P_2 = \frac{Q_{1[hr]-2[hr]} - Q_{u,1[hr]-2[hr]} * P_1}{Q_{u,0[hr]-1[hr]}} \leftarrow eq.11$$

Plug in the known variables into the right hand side of eq. 11, then solve for P_2.

$$P_1 = 0.10\,[in]$$

$$Q_{u,0[hr]-1[hr]} = 10\,[ft^3/(s*in)]$$

$$P_2 = \frac{10\,[ft^3/s] - 50\,[ft^3/(s*in)] * 0.10\,[in]}{10\,[ft^3/(s*in)]}$$

$$P_2 = 0.50\,[in]$$

Hydrology #13 (cont.)

Plug in the known variables into the right hand side of eq. 4, then solve for P_3.

$Q_{u,1[hr]-2[hr]}=50\,[ft^3/(s*in)]$

$Q_{u,2[hr]-3[hr]}=100\,[ft^3/(s*in)]$

$Q_{2[hr]-3[hr]}=42\,[ft^3/s]$

$P_2=0.50\,[in]$

$P_1=0.10\,[in]$

$$P_3=\frac{Q_{2[hr]-3[hr]}-Q_{u,1[hr]-2[hr]}*P_2-Q_{u,2[hr]-3[hr]}*P_1}{Q_{u,0[hr]-1[hr]}} \leftarrow eq.\,4$$

$Q_{u,0[hr]-1[hr]}=10\,[ft^3/(s*in)]$

$$P_3=\frac{42\,[ft^3/s]-50\,[ft^3/(s*in)]*0.50\,[in]-100\,[ft^3/(s*in)]*0.10\,[in]}{10\,[ft^3/(s*in)]}$$

$$P_3=0.7\,[in]$$

Answer: $\boxed{D}$

Water Resources Practice Problems

Hydrology #14

<u>Find:</u> Q_p ← peak runoff from the watersheds
　　　　　　　(measured at the outlet)

<u>Given:</u>

$A_A = 6$ [acre] ← area of watershed A

$A_B = 10$ [acre] ← area of watershed B

$t_{c,A} = 40$ [min] ← time of concentration
$t_{c,B} = 60$ [min] ← of watersheds A and B

storm intensity relationship

$C_A = 0.45$ ← runoff coefficient
$C_B = 0.70$ ← of watershed A
　　　　　　and watershed B

$$i = \frac{120\,[in*min/hr]}{t_c + 20\,[min]}$$

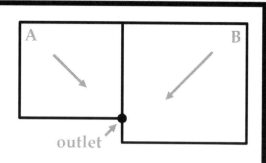

A) 9.7 [ft³/s]

B) 10.5 [ft³/s]

C) 14.5 [ft³/s]

D) 16.8 [ft³/s]

Analysis:

peak flow rate　　　area

$$Q_p = C * i * A \quad ←eq.1$$

runoff　　　rainfall
coefficient　intensity

Eq.1 computes the peak flow rate from the watershed using the Rational Formula.

$$A = \Sigma\, A_i = A_A + A_B \quad ←eq.2$$

$A_A = 6$ [acre]　　$A_B = 10$ [acre]

Eq.2 computes the total area contributing to runoff by adding the area of each watershed.

$$A = 6\,[acre] + 10\,[acre]$$

$$A = 16\,[acre]$$

Plug in A_A and A_B into eq.2, then solve for A.

runoff coefficient
of watershed i　　area of
　　　　　　　　watershed i

$$C = \frac{\Sigma\, C_i * A_i}{\Sigma\, A_i} \quad ←eq.3$$

Eq.3 computes the combined runoff coefficient of the two watershed.

$C_A = 0.45$　　　$C_B = 0.70$

$$C = \frac{C_A * A_A + C_B * A_B}{A_A + A_B} \quad ←eq.4$$

$A_A = 6$ [acre]　　$A_B = 10$ [acre]

Expand the summation terms in eq.3.

Plug in variables C_A, A_A, C_B and A_B into eq.4, then solve for C.

248

Hydrology #14 (cont.)

$$C = \frac{0.45 * 6 [acre] + 0.70 * 10 [acre]}{6 [acre] + 10 [acre]}$$

$$C = 0.606$$

$$t_c = \max(t_{c,i}) \leftarrow eq.5$$

Eq. 5 computes the time of concentration of the two watersheds as the maximum time of concentra-tion of each individual watershed.

$$t_c = \max(t_{c,A}, t_{c,B}) \leftarrow eq.6$$

$t_{c,A} = 40 [min]$ $t_{c,B} = 60 [min]$

Plug in $t_{c,A}$ and $t_{c,B}$ into eq. 6, then solve for t_c.

$$t_c = \max(40 [min], 60 [min])$$

$$t_c = 60 [min]$$

$$i = \frac{120 [in*min/hr]}{t_c + 20 [min]} \leftarrow eq.7$$

$t_c = 60 [min]$

Plug in t_c into eq. 7 (the given storm intensity relationship), then solve for i.

$$i = \frac{120 [in*min/hr]}{60 [min] + 20 [min]}$$

$$i = 1.5 [in/hr]$$

$i = 1.5 [in/hr]$

$$Q_p = C * i * A \leftarrow eq.1$$

$C = 0.606$ $A = 16 [acre]$

Plug in variables C, i and A into eq. 1, then solve for Q_p.

Assume the units of cubic feet per second equals inch acres per hour.

$$Q_p = 0.606 * 1.5 [in/hr] * 16 [acre]$$

$$Q_p = 14.54 [ft^3/s]$$

Answer: $\boxed{C}$

Water Resources Practice Problems

Find: $Q_p \leftarrow$ peak runoff (at the outlet)

Given:

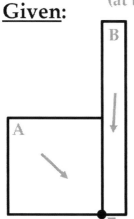

$C_A = 0.80$ $C_B = 0.50$

runoff coefficients of watersheds A and B

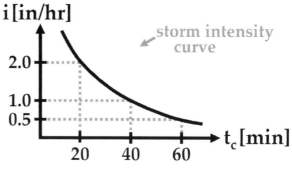

storm intensity curve

$A_A = 4.0\,[acre] \leftarrow$ area of watershed A

$A_B = 1.5\,[acre] \leftarrow$ area of watershed B

$t_{c,A} = 20\,[min] \leftarrow$ time of

$t_{c,B} = 40\,[min] \leftarrow$ concentrations

outlet

A) $2.0\,[ft^3/s]$

B) $3.2\,[ft^3/s]$

C) $4.0\,[ft^3/s]$

D) $6.4\,[ft^3/s]$

Analysis:

$$Q_p = max(Q_{p,A}, Q_{p,B}, Q_{p,A+B}) \leftarrow eq.1$$

peak flow rate   watershed A   watershed B

Eq.1 computes the peak flow rate when considering each watershed individually and the two watersheds combined.

peak flow rate $Q_{p,A} = C_A * i_A * A_A \leftarrow eq.2$

runoff coefficient   rainfall intensity   drainage area

Eq.2 computes the peak flow rate when considering only watershed A.

$$t_{c,A} = 20\,[min] \rightarrow i_A = 2.0\,[in/hr]$$

Determine the storm intensity for watershed A based on the time of concentration and the storm intensity curve.

$C_A = 0.80$ $A_A = 4.0\,[acre]$

$$Q_{p,A} = C_A * i_A * A_A \leftarrow eq.2$$

$i_A = 2.0\,[in/hr]$

Plug in variables C_A, i_A, and A_A into eq.2, then solve for $Q_{p,A}$.

$$Q_{p,A} = 0.80 * 2.0\,[in/hr] * 4.0\,[acre]$$

$$Q_{p,A} = 6.40\,[ft^3/s] \checkmark$$

Assume acre inch per hour equals cubic feet per second.

$$Q_{p,B} = C_B * i_B * A_B \leftarrow eq.3$$

Eq.3 computes the peak flow rate when considering only watershed B.

Hydrology #15 (cont.)

$$t_{c,B}=40\,[\text{min}] \longrightarrow i_B=1.0\,[\text{in/hr}]$$

Determine the storm intensity for watershed B based on the time of concentration and the storm intensity curve.

$$\overset{C_B=0.50}{\downarrow} \quad \overset{A_B=1.5\,[\text{acre}]}{\downarrow}$$
$$Q_{p,B}=C_B*i_B*A_B \quad \leftarrow eq.3$$
$$\underset{i_B=1.0\,[\text{in/hr}]}{\uparrow}$$

Plug in variables C_B, i_B, and A_B into eq.3, then solve for $Q_{p,B}$.

$$Q_{p,B}=0.50*1.0\,[\text{in/hr}]*1.5\,[\text{acre}]$$

$$Q_{p,B}=0.75\,[\text{ft}^3/\text{s}]$$

$$Q_{p,A+B}=C_{A+B}*i_{A+B}*A_{A+B} \quad \leftarrow eq.4$$

Eq.4 computes the peak flow rate when considering both watershed A and watershed B.

$$A_{A+B}=A_A+A_B \leftarrow eq.5$$
$$\underset{A_A=4.0\,[\text{acre}]}{\nearrow} \quad \underset{A_B=1.5\,[\text{acre}]}{\nwarrow}$$

Eq. 5 computes the total area of both watersheds.

$$A_{A+B}=4.0\,[\text{acre}]+1.5\,[\text{acre}]$$

Plug in variables A_A and A_B into eq.5, then solve for A_{A+B}.

$$A_{A+B}=5.5\,[\text{acre}]$$

$$\overset{C_A=0.80}{\downarrow} \quad \overset{C_B=0.50}{\downarrow}$$
$$C_{A+B}=\frac{C_A*A_A+C_B*A_B}{A_A+A_B} \quad \leftarrow eq.6$$
$$\underset{A_A=4\,[\text{acre}]}{} \quad \underset{A_B=1.5\,[\text{acre}]}{}$$

Eq.6 computes the composite runoff coefficient for both watersheds.

Plug in variables C_A, A_A, C_B and A_B into eq.6, then solve for C_{A+B}.

$$C_{A+B}=\frac{0.80*4\,[\text{acre}]+0.50*1.5\,[\text{acre}]}{4\,[\text{acre}]+1.5\,[\text{acre}]}$$

$$C_{A+B}=0.718$$

Water Resources Practice Problems

Hydrology #15 (cont.)

$$t_{c,A+B}=\max(t_{c,A}, t_{c,B}) \leftarrow eq.7$$

$$t_{c,A}=20\,[\text{min}] \qquad t_{c,B}=40\,[\text{min}]$$

Eq. 7 computes the time of con-centration of the two watersheds as the maximum time of concentra-tion of each individual watershed.

$$t_{c,A+B}=\max(20\,[\text{min}], 40\,[\text{min}])$$

Plug in $t_{c,A}$ and $t_{c,B}$ into eq. 7, then solve for $t_{c,A+B}$.

$$t_{c,A+B}=40\,[\text{min}] \rightarrow i_{A+B}=1.0\,[\text{in/hr}]$$

Determine the storm intensity for watershed B based on the time of concentration and the storm intensity curve.

$$C_{A+B}=0.718 \qquad A_{A+B}=5.5\,[\text{acre}]$$

$$Q_{p,A+B}=C_{A+B}*i_{A+B}*A_{A+B} \leftarrow eq.4$$

$$i_{A+B}=1.0\,[\text{in/hr}]$$

Plug in variables C_{A+B}, i_{A+B}, and A_{A+B}, then solve for $Q_{p,A+B}$.

$$Q_{p,A+B}=0.718*1.0\,[\text{in/hr}]*5.5\,[\text{acre}]$$

$$Q_{p,A+B}=3.95\,[\text{ft}^3\text{/s}]$$

$$Q_{p,B}=0.75\,[\text{ft}^3\text{/s}]$$

Plug in variables $Q_{p,A}$, $Q_{p,B}$ and $Q_{p,A+B}$ into eq. 1, then solve for Q_p.

$$Q_p=\max(Q_{p,A}, Q_{p,B}, Q_{p,A+B}) \leftarrow eq.1$$

$$Q_{p,A}=6.40\,[\text{ft}^3\text{/s}] \qquad Q_{p,A+B}=3.95\,[\text{ft}^3\text{/s}]$$

$$Q_p=\max(6.40\,[\text{ft}^3\text{/s}], 0.75\,[\text{ft}^3\text{/s}], 3.95\,[\text{ft}^3\text{/s}])$$

$$Q_p=6.40\,[\text{ft}^3\text{/s}]$$

Answer: D

Hydrology #16

Find: Q_p ← peak hourly runoff flow rate

Given:

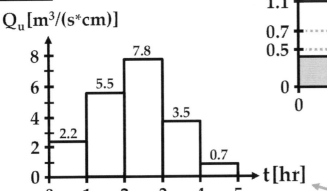

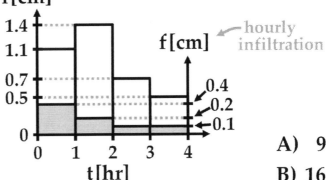

← unit hydrograph

A) 9 [m³/s]

B) 16 [m³/s]

C) 23 [m³/s]

D) 57 [m³/s]

Analysis:

$$Q_p = \max(Q_{t-1[hr]-t[hr]}) \leftarrow eq.1$$

Eq.1 shows the maximum runoff flow rate equals the largest runoff flow rate from all time periods.

direct runoff in hour t

$$Q_{t-1[hr]-t[hr]} = \sum_{m=1}^{t} Q_{u,m-1[hr]-m[hr]} * P_{t-m+1} \leftarrow eq.2$$

unit hydrograph value in hour m

excess rainfall in hour t-m+1

Eq.2 is the discrete convolution equation used to compute the direct runoff flow rate in a given hour.

$i_1 = 1.1\,[cm]$ $f_1 = 0.4\,[cm]$

$$P_1 = i_1 - f_1 \leftarrow eq.3$$

$$P_1 = 1.1\,[cm] - 0.4\,[cm]$$

$$P_1 = 0.7\,[cm]$$

$i_2 = 1.4\,[cm]$ $f_2 = 0.2\,[cm]$

$$P_2 = i_2 - f_2 \leftarrow eq.4$$

$$P_2 = 1.4\,[cm] - 0.2\,[cm]$$

$$P_2 = 1.2\,[cm]$$

Eq.3, 4, 5 and 6 compute the excess rainfall during each hour of the storm.

Plug in the rainfall and infiltration into eq.3, 4, 5 and 6, then solve for the excess rainfall depth contributing to runoff.

$i_3 = 0.7\,[cm]$ $f_3 = 0.1\,[cm]$

$$P_3 = i_3 - f_3 \leftarrow eq.5$$

$$P_3 = 0.7\,[cm] - 0.1\,[cm]$$

$$P_3 = 0.6\,[cm]$$

$i_4 = 0.5\,[cm]$ $f_4 = 0.1\,[cm]$

$$P_4 = i_4 - f_4 \leftarrow eq.6$$

$$P_4 = 0.5\,[cm] - 0.1\,[cm]$$

$$P_4 = 0.4\,[cm]$$

Water Resources Practice Problems

Hydrology #16 (cont.)

Solve for the direct runoff hydrograph values by setting up a table shown below. Variables A through I are computed in example calculations below, to show how to use the table.

time [hr]	Q_u [m³/(s*cm)]	$P_1^{0.7}$ [cm]	$P_2^{1.2}$ [cm]	$P_3^{0.6}$ [cm]	$P_4^{0.4}$ [cm]	Q [m³/s]
0-1	$Q_{u,0\text{-}1}$ 2.2	A	D	#	#	$Q_{0\text{-}1}$
1-2	$Q_{u,1\text{-}2}$ 5.5	B	E	H	I	$Q_{1\text{-}2}$
2-3	$Q_{u,2\text{-}3}$ 7.8	C	F	#	#	$Q_{2\text{-}3}$
3-4	$Q_{u,3\text{-}4}$ 3.5	#	#	#	#	$Q_{3\text{-}4}$
4-5	$Q_{u,4\text{-}5}$ 0.7	#	#	#	#	$Q_{4\text{-}5}$
5-6	$Q_{u,5\text{-}6}$ 0	G	#	#	#	$Q_{5\text{-}6}$
6-7	$Q_{u,6\text{-}7}$ 0	#	#	#	#	$Q_{6\text{-}7}$
7-8	$Q_{u,7\text{-}8}$ 0	#	#	#	#	$Q_{7\text{-}8}$

$P_1=0.7[cm]$

$$A=Q_{u,0\text{-}1}*P_1 \leftarrow eq.7$$

$Q_{u,0\text{-}1}=2.2[m^3/(s*cm)]$

Eq.7 computes the contribution to the first hour of runoff, from the first hour of rainfall.

$$A=2.2[m^3/(s*cm)]*0.7[cm]$$

Plug in $Q_{u,0\text{-}1}$ and P_1 into eq.7, then solve for A.

$$A=1.54[m^3/s]$$

$P_1=0.7[cm]$

$$B=Q_{u,1\text{-}2}*P_1 \leftarrow eq.8$$

$Q_{u,1\text{-}2}=5.5[m^3/(s*cm)]$

Eq.8 computes the contribution to the second hour of runoff, from the first hour of rainfall.

Plug in $Q_{u,1\text{-}2}$ and P_1 into eq.8, then solve for B.

$$B=5.5[m^3/(s*cm)]*0.7[cm]$$

254

Hydrology #16 (cont.)

$$B=3.85\,[m^3/s]$$

$$P_1=0.7\,[cm]$$

$$C=Q_{u,2\text{-}3}*P_1 \quad \leftarrow eq.9$$

$$Q_{u,2\text{-}3}=7.8\,[m^3/(s*cm)]$$

Eq. 9 computes the contribution to the third hour of runoff, from the first hour of rainfall.

Plug in $Q_{u,2\text{-}3}$ and P_1 into eq.9, then solve for C.

$$C=7.8\,[m^3/(s*cm)]*0.7\,[cm]$$

$$C=5.46\,[m^3/s]$$

$$D=0\,[m^3/s]$$

D equals zero because this cell computes the contribution to the first hour of runoff, from the second hour of rainfall.

$$P_2=1.2\,[cm]$$

$$E=Q_{u,0\text{-}1}*P_2 \quad \leftarrow eq.10$$

$$Q_{u,0\text{-}1}=2.2\,[m^3/(s*cm)]$$

Eq. 10 computes the contribution to the second hour of runoff, from the second hour of rainfall.

Plug in $Q_{u,0\text{-}1}$ and P_2 into eq.10, then solve for E.

$$E=2.2\,[m^3/(s*cm)]*1.2\,[cm]$$

$$E=2.64\,[m^3/s]$$

$$P_2=1.2\,[cm]$$

$$F=Q_{u,1\text{-}2}*P_2 \quad \leftarrow eq.11$$

$$Q_{u,1\text{-}2}=5.5\,[m^3/(s*cm)]$$

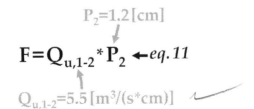

Eq. 11 computes the contribution to the third hour of runoff, from the second hour of rainfall.

Plug in $Q_{u,1\text{-}2}$ and P_2 into eq.11, then solve for F.

$$F=5.5\,[m^3/(s*cm)]*1.2\,[cm]$$

$$F=6.60\,[m^3/s]$$

Water Resources Practice Problems

$$P_1 = 0.7 \, [cm]$$

$$G = Q_{u,5\text{-}6} * P_1 \leftarrow eq.\ 12$$

$$Q_{u,5\text{-}6} = 0.0 \, [m^3/(s*cm)]$$

Eq. 12 computes the contribution to the sixth hour of runoff, from the first hour of rainfall.

$$G = 0.0 \, [m^3/(s*cm)] * 0.7 \, [cm]$$

Plug in $Q_{u,5\text{-}6}$ and P_1 into eq.12, then solve for C.

$$G = 0 \, [m^3/s]$$

$Q_{u,5\text{-}6}$ equals zero because the unit hydrograph shows that rainfall only contributes to the runoff in the current hour and the following 4 hours.

$$H = 0 \, [m^3/s]$$

$$I = 0 \, [m^3/s]$$

H and I equal zero because rainfall from the third and fourth hours cannot contribute to runoff in the second hour.

$$B = 3.85 \, [m^3/s] \quad I = 0 \, [m^3/s]$$

$$Q_{1\text{-}2} = B + E + H + I \quad \leftarrow eq.\ 13$$

$$E = 2.64 \, [m^3/s] \quad H = 0 \, [m^3/s]$$

Eq.13 computes the total direct runoff during the second hour.

Plug in variables B, E, H and I into eq. 13, then solve for $Q_{1\text{-}2}$.

$$Q_{1\text{-}2} = 3.85 \, [m^3/s] + 2.64 \, [m^3/s] + 0 \, [m^3/s] + 0 \, [m^3/s]$$

$$Q_{1\text{-}2} = 6.49 \, [m^3/s]$$

(see next page for completed table)

Hydrology #16 (cont.)

time [hr]	Q_u [m³/(s*cm)]	0.7 [cm]	1.2 [cm]	0.6 [cm]	0.4 [cm]	Q [m³/s]
0-1	2.2	1.54	0.0	0.0	0.0	1.54
1-2	5.5	3.85	2.64	0.0	0.0	6.49
2-3	7.8	5.46	6.60	1.32	0.0	13.38
3-4	3.5	2.54	9.36	3.30	0.88	15.99
4-5	0.7	0.49	4.20	4.68	2.20	11.57
5-6	0.0	0.0	0.84	2.10	3.12	6.06
6-7	0.0	0.0	0.0	0.42	1.40	1.82
7-8	0.0	0.0	0.0	0.0	0.28	0.28

Eq.14 writes out eq.1 for each time period

Plug in the known runoff flow rates into the right hand side of eq.14, then solve for Q_p.

$Q_{1[hr]-2[hr]} = 6.49 \,[m^3/s]$

$Q_{3[hr]-4[hr]} = 15.99 \,[m^3/s]$

$Q_{0[hr]-1[hr]} = 1.54 \,[m^3/s]$

$Q_{2[hr]-3[hr]} = 13.38 \,[m^3/s]$

$$Q_p = \max(Q_{0[hr]-1[hr]}, Q_{1[hr]-2[hr]}, Q_{2[hr]-3[hr]}, Q_{3[hr]-4[hr]},$$
$$Q_{4[hr]-5[hr]}, Q_{5[hr]-6[hr]}, Q_{6[hr]-7[hr]}, Q_{7[hr]-8[hr]}) \leftarrow eq.14$$

$Q_{4[hr]-5[hr]} = 11.57 \,[m^3/s]$

$Q_{6[hr]-7[hr]} = 1.82 \,[m^3/s]$

$Q_{5[hr]-6[hr]} = 6.06 \,[m^3/s]$

$Q_{7[hr]-8[hr]} = 0.28 \,[m^3/s]$

$$Q_p = \max(1.54\,[m^3/s], 6.49\,[m^3/s], 13.38\,[m^3/s], 15.99\,[m^3/s],$$
$$11.57\,[m^3/s], 6.06\,[m^3/s], 1.82\,[m^3/s], 0.28\,[m^3/s])$$

$Q_p = 15.99 \,[m^3/s]$ 　　 Answer: $\boxed{B}$

Water Resources Practice Problems

Hydrology #17

<u>Find:</u> P_e ← the excess rainfall depth
(which contributes to runoff)

<u>Given:</u>

P_g=2.50 [in] ← gross rainfall depth

ARC=I ← antecedent runoff condition

soil group=B

¼ acre residential lots ← land use

use NRCS method

A) 0.09 [in]
B) 0.65 [in]
C) 0.91 [in]
D) 1.34 [in]

Analysis:

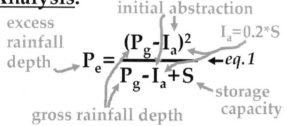

excess rainfall depth → $P_e = \dfrac{(P_g - I_a)^2}{P_g - I_a + S}$ ←eq.1

initial abstraction: $I_a = 0.2*S$

gross rainfall depth

storage capacity

Eq.1 computes the excess rainfall depth, which contributes to runoff.

The NRCS method assumes the initial abstraction equals 20% of the storage capacity.

$$P_e = \frac{(P_g - 0.2*S)^2}{P_g - 0.2*S + S}$$

Plug in I_a into eq.1, then simplify.

$$P_e = \frac{(P_g - 0.2*S)^2}{P_g + 0.8*S} \quad \text{←eq.2}$$

storage capacity → $S = \dfrac{1,000}{CN_I} - 10$ ←eq.3

curve number

Eq.3 computes the storage capacity based on the curve number for english units.

Add a subscript 'I' to the curve number in eq.3 because the antecedent runoff conditions is Type I.

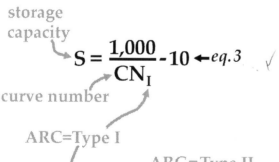

ARC=Type I

$CN_I = \dfrac{4.2*CN_{II}}{10 - 0.058*CN_{II}}$ ←eq.4

ARC=Type II

curve number

Eq.4 computes the ARC Type I curve number based on the ARC Type II curve number.

Hydrology #17 (cont.)

$$\left.\begin{array}{l} \text{soil group=B} \\ \text{¼ acre residential} \end{array}\right\} CN_{II}=75$$

Look up the CN_{II} for ¼ acre residential lots having with a soil group B.

$$CN_I = \frac{4.2 * \overset{CN_{II}=75}{CN_{II}}}{10 - 0.058 * CN_{II}} \leftarrow eq.4$$

Plug in variable CN_{II} into eq. 4, then solve for CN_I.

$$CN_I = \frac{4.2 * 75}{10 - 0.058 * 75}$$

$$CN_I = 55.75$$

$$S = \frac{1,000}{CN_I} - 10 \leftarrow eq.3$$
$$\underset{CN_I=55.75}{\uparrow}$$

Plug in variable CN_I into eq. 3, then solve for S.

$$S = \frac{1,000}{55.75} - 10$$

$$S = 7.937 \, [in]$$

$$P_e = \frac{\overset{P_g=2.50\,[in]}{(P_g - 0.2 * S)^2}}{P_g + 0.8 * S \, \overset{S=7.937\,[in]}{}} \leftarrow eq.2$$

Plug in variable P_g and S into eq. 2, then solve for P_e.

$$P_e = \frac{(2.50\,[in] - 0.2 * 7.937\,[in])^2}{2.50\,[in] + 0.8 * 7.937\,[in]}$$

$$P_e = 0.094 \, [in] \qquad \underline{\text{Answer:}} \boxed{A}$$

Water Resources Practice Problems

Hydrology #18

Find: T ← the recurrence interval of the storm

Given:

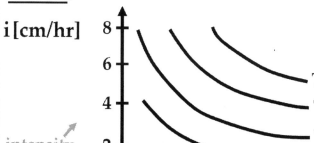

i[cm/hr]

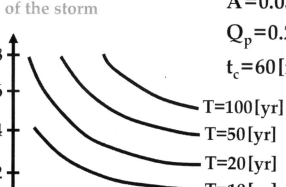

t_c [min]

intensity duration frequency plot

C=0.78 ← runoff coefficient

A=0.05 [km²] ← watershed area

Q_p=0.22 [m³/s] ← peak runoff rate

t_c=60 [min] ← time of concentration

A) T<10 [yr]

B) 10 [yr]<T<20 [yr]

C) 20 [yr]<T<50 [yr]

D) 50 [yr]<T<100 [yr]

Analysis:

$$T = f(i, t_c) \leftarrow eq.1$$

recurrence interval   rainfall intensity   time of concentration

Eq.1 shows that the recurrence interval of the storm is a based on the storm intensity and the time of concentration.

runoff coefficient

$$Q_p = C * i * A \leftarrow eq.2$$

peak flow rate   rainfall intensity   area of the watershed

Eq.2 computes the peak flow rate from the watershed.

$Q_p = 0.22$ [m³/s]

$$i = \frac{Q_p}{C * A} \leftarrow eq.3$$

C=0.78   A=0.05 [km²]

Solve eq.2 for the rainfall intensity

Plug in variables Q_p, C and A into eq.3, then solve for i.

$$i = \frac{0.22 \, [m^3/s]}{0.78 * 0.05 \, [km^2]}$$

Eq.4 converts the rainfall intensity to units of centimeters per hour.

$$i = 5.64 \left[\frac{m^3}{s*km^2}\right] * \left(\frac{1}{1,000}\left[\frac{km}{m}\right]\right)^2 * 3,600 \left[\frac{s}{hr}\right] * 100 \left[\frac{cm}{m}\right] \leftarrow eq.4$$

conversion factors

Hydrology #18 (cont.)

$$i = 2.03 \, [cm/hr]$$

i [cm/hr]

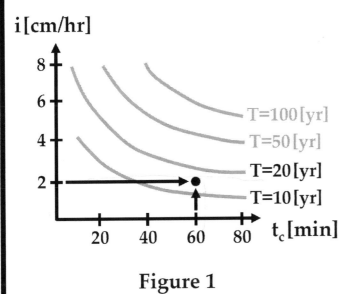

Figure 1

Determine the recurrence interval of the storm by plotting the time of concentration and rainfall inten-sity on the IDF curve in Figure 1

$$10 \, [yr] < T < 20 \, [yr]$$

Answer: B

Water Resources Practice Problems

Groundwater #1

b=200[m] ↑ aquifer width (into and out of the page)

Find: Q ← the flow rate

Given: $y_1=y_2=239.75$[m] ← aquifer thickness

$\Delta y_{1,2}=-4.61$[m] ← headloss between wells

$L_{1,2}=98.1$[m] ← horizontal length between observation wells 1 and 2.

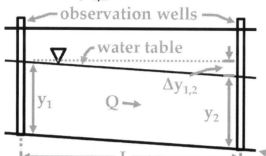

- observation wells
- water table
- ∇
- $\Delta y_{1,2}$
- y_1
- $Q\rightarrow$
- y_2
- L
- bedrock

$T=20^{\circ}C$ ← water temperature

$k=1*10^{-8}$[cm^2] ← intrinsic permeability

A) 0.02[m^3/s]

B) 0.07[m^3/s]

C) 0.18[m^3/s]

D) 0.47[m^3/s]

Analysis:

flow rate — gradient of the water table

$$Q=-K*i*A_{gross} \leftarrow eq.1$$

hydraulic conductivity — gross area

Eq. 1 computes the flow rate of a fluid through a porous media.

The negative sign on the right hand side of eq. 1 simply indicates the fluid moves in the direction of the negative gradient.

intrinsic permeability — specific weight

$$K=\frac{k*\gamma}{\mu} \leftarrow eq.2$$

absolute viscosity

Eq. 2 computes the hydraulic conductivity.

fluid density — gravitational acceleration

$$\gamma=\varrho*g \leftarrow eq.3$$

ϱ=998.23[kg/m^3]   g=9.81[m/s^2]

Eq. 3 computes the specific weight of the water based on a temperature of 20°C.

$$\gamma=998.23[kg/m^3]*9.81[m/s^2]$$

$$\gamma=9,793[N/m^3]$$

k=1*10^{-8}[cm^2] γ=9,793[N/m^3]

$$K=\frac{k*\gamma}{\mu} \leftarrow eq.2$$

μ=1.005*10^{-3}[Pa*s]

Plug in variables k, γ, and μ into eq. 2, then solve for K.

Groundwater #1 (cont.)

$$K = \frac{1*10^{-8}[cm^2]*9{,}793[N/m^3]}{1.005*10^{-3}[Pa*s]}$$

Eq.4 converts the hydraulic conductivity to units of meters per second.

$$K = 0.0975\left[\frac{cm^2*N}{Pa*s*m^3}\right] * 1\left[\frac{Pa*m^2}{N}\right] * \left(\frac{1}{100}\left[\frac{m}{cm}\right]\right)^2 \leftarrow eq.4$$

conversion factors

$$K = 9.74*10^{-6}[m/s]$$

$\Delta y_{1,2} = -4.61[m]$

$$i = \frac{\Delta y_{1,2}}{L_{1,2}} \leftarrow eq.5$$

$L_{1,2} = 98.1[m]$

Eq.5 computes the water table gradient between wells 1 and 2.

Plug in variables $\Delta y_{1,2}$ and $L_{1,2}$ into eq.5, then solve for i.

$$i = \frac{-4.61[m]}{98.1[m]}$$

$$i = -0.0470$$

$$A_{gross} = Y*b \leftarrow eq.6$$

$Y = y_1 = y_2 = 239.75[m]$ $b = 200[m]$

Eq.6 computes the gross area of the aquifer which contributes to the flow rate.

$$A_{gross} = 239.75[m]*200[m]$$

Plug in variables H and b into eq.6, then solve for A_{gross}.

$$A_{gross} = 47{,}950[m^2]$$

$K = 9.74*10^{-6}[m/s]$ $A_{gross} = 47{,}950[m^2]$

$$Q = -K*i*A_{gross} \leftarrow eq.1$$

$i = -0.0470$

Plug in variables K, i and A_{gross} into eq.1, then solve for Q.

Groundwater #1 (cont.)

$Q = -9.74 * 10^{-6} [m/s] * (-0.0470) * 47,950 [m^2]$

$Q = 0.022 [m^3/s]$

Answer: $\boxed{A}$

Groundwater #2

<u>Find:</u> v_{pore} ← the pore velocity

<u>Given:</u> $y_1 = y_2 = 250\,[ft]$ ← aquifer thickness

$e = 0.42$ ← void ratio

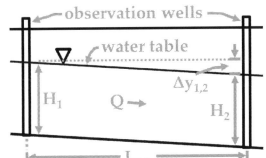

observation wells

water table

∇

$\Delta y_{1,2}$

H_1 $Q →$ H_2

$L_{1,2}$

$K = 10\,[ft/day]$ ↑ hydraulic conductivity

$L_{1,2} = 3.0\,[mi]$ ← horizontal length between observation wells 1 and 2.

$\Delta y_{1,2} = -317\,[ft]$ ← headloss between wells

$b = 1.2\,[mi]$ ← aquifer width

$\eta_e = 0.9 * \eta$ ↶ porosity
effective porosity

A) 0.20 [ft/day]

B) 0.40 [ft/day]

C) 0.55 [ft/day]

D) 0.75 [ft/day]

Analysis:

$$v_{pore} = \frac{Q}{A_{net}} \leftarrow eq.1$$

pore velocity   flow rate   net area

Eq. 1 computes the pore velocity of the groundwater.

$$A_{net} = A_{gross} * \eta_e \leftarrow eq.2$$

net area   gross area   effective porosity

Eq. 2 computes the net area of the aquifer through which the groundwater flows.

aquifer thickness   aquifer width

$$A_{gross} = Y * b \leftarrow eq.3$$

$Y = y_1 = y_2 = 250\,[ft]$ $b = 1.2\,[mi]$

Eq. 3 computes the gross area of the aquifer.

Plug in variables Y and b into eq. 3, then solve for A_{gross}.

$$A_{gross} = 300\,[ft*mi] * 5,280 \left[\frac{ft}{mi}\right] \leftarrow eq.4$$

conversion factor

Eq. 4 converts the gross area to square feet.

$$A_{gross} = 1.584 * 10^6\,[ft^2]$$

effective porosity

$$\eta_e = 0.9 * \eta \leftarrow eq.5$$

porosity

Eq. 5 computes the effective porosity of the soil.

Water Resources Practice Problems

Groundwater #2 (cont.)

void ratio → porosity

$$e = \frac{\eta}{1-\eta} \leftarrow eq.6$$

Eq. 6 computes the void ratio of the soil.

$e=0.42$

$$\eta = \frac{e}{1+e} \leftarrow eq.7$$

Solve eq. 6 for porosity.

Plug in variable e into eq. 7, then solve for η.

$$\eta = \frac{0.42}{1+0.42}$$

$$\eta = 0.296$$

$\eta=0.296$

$$\eta_e = 0.9*\eta \leftarrow eq.5$$

Plug in η into eq. 5, then solve for η_e.

$$\eta_e = 0.9*0.296 = 0.266$$

$$A_{net} = A_{gross}*\eta_e \leftarrow eq.2$$

$A_{gross} = 1.584*10^6\,[ft^2]$ $\eta_e = 0.266$

$$A_{net} = 1.584*10^6\,[ft^2]*0.266$$

$$A_{net} = 4.213*10^5\,[ft^2]$$

flow rate   gradient

$$Q = -K*i*A_{gross} \leftarrow eq.8$$

hydraulic conductivity   gross area

Eq. 8 computes the flow rate of a fluid through a porous media.

headloss

$$i = \frac{\Delta y_{1,2}}{L_{1,2}} \leftarrow eq.9$$

length

Eq. 9 computes the water table gradient between wells 1 and 2.

Groundwater #2 (cont.)

$$L_{1,2} = 3\,[\text{mi}] * \boxed{5,280\left[\frac{\text{ft}}{\text{mi}}\right]} \leftarrow eq.\,10$$

← conversion factor

Eq. 10 converts the length between wells 1 and 2 to units of feet.

$$L_{1,2} = 15,840\,[\text{ft}]$$

$$\Delta y_{1,2} = -317\,[\text{ft}]$$

$$i = \frac{\Delta y_{1,2}}{L_{1,2}} \leftarrow eq.\,9$$

$$L_{1,2} = 15,840\,[\text{ft}]$$

Plug in $\Delta y_{1,2}$ and $L_{1,2}$ into eq. 9, then solve for i.

$$i = \frac{-317\,[\text{ft}]}{15,840\,[\text{ft}]}$$

$$i = -0.020$$

$$i = -0.020$$

$$Q = -K * i * A_{\text{gross}} \leftarrow eq.\,8$$

$$K = 10\,[\text{ft/day}] \qquad A_{\text{gross}} = 1.584 * 10^6\,[\text{ft}^2]$$

Plug in variables K, i and A_{gross} into eq. 8, then solve for Q.

$$Q = -10\,[\text{ft/day}] * (-0.020) * 1.584 * 10^6\,[\text{ft}^2]$$

$$Q = 3.168 * 10^5\,[\text{ft}^3/\text{day}]$$

$$Q = 3.168 * 10^5\,[\text{ft}^3/\text{day}]$$

$$v_{\text{pore}} = \frac{Q}{A_{\text{net}}} \leftarrow eq.\,1$$

$$A_{\text{net}} = 4.213 * 10^5\,[\text{ft}^2]$$

Plug in variables Q and A_{net} into eq. 1, then solve for v_{pore}.

$$v_{\text{pore}} = \frac{3.168 * 10^5\,[\text{ft}^3/\text{day}]}{4.213 * 10^5\,[\text{ft}^2]}$$

$$v_{\text{pore}} = 0.752\,[\text{ft/day}]$$

Answer: $\boxed{\text{D}}$

Water Resources Practice Problems

Groundwater #3

Find: θ_Q ← the direction of the flow rate

Given:

$L_{AB} = L_{AC} = L_{BC} = 500\,[ft]$

  the distance between wells

$h_A = 243.5\,[ft]$

$h_B = 232.1\,[ft]$ ⟩ total head at all the wells

$h_C = 236.7\,[ft]$

$K = 8\,[ft/day]$ ← hydraulic conductivity

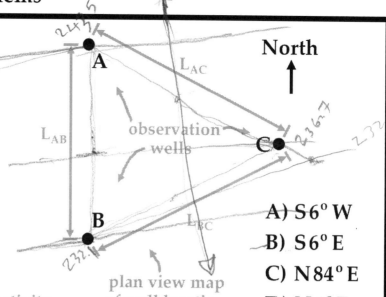

North

observation wells

plan view map of well locations

A) $S6°\,W$
B) $S6°\,E$
C) $N84°\,E$
D) $N6°\,E$

Analysis:

A) $S6°W$ ← 6 degrees west of south

B) $S6°E$ ← 6 degrees east of south

C) $N84°E$ ← 84 degrees east of north

D) $N6°E$ ← 6 degrees east of north

A description for each of the possible solutions is provided.

Figure 1 shows the directions of the four possible solutions.

Figure 2 divides the directions A, B, C and D into 4 quadrants.

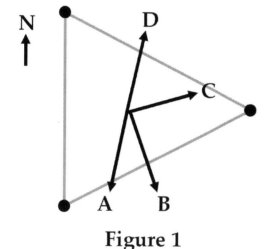

Figure 1

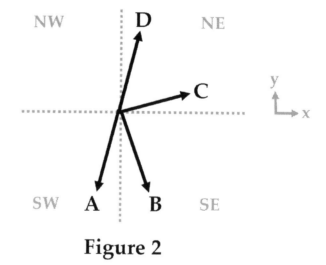

Figure 2

SW quadrant ⟶ A

SE quadrant ⟶ B

NE quadrant ⟶ C and D

We'll first determine the quadrant to help us determine the direction

Groundwater #3 (cont.)

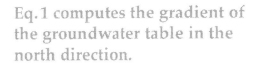

$$\frac{dh}{dy} = \frac{h_A - h_B}{L_{AB}} \leftarrow eq.1$$

$L_{AB} = 500\,[\text{ft}]$

Eq.1 computes the gradient of the groundwater table in the north direction.

Plug in variables h_A, h_B and L_{AB} into eq.1, then solve for dh/dy.

$$\frac{dh}{dy} = \frac{243.5\,[\text{ft}] - 232.1\,[\text{ft}]}{500\,[\text{ft}]}$$

$$\frac{dh}{dy} = 0.0228$$

Since the gradient of the water table increases in the northern direction, the gradient decreases in the southern direction, and the groundwater flows in the southern direction.

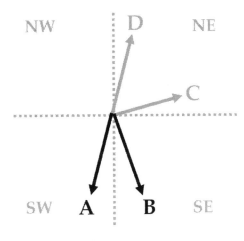

Figure 3

Figure 3 shows that only direction A and direction B flow in the southern direction.

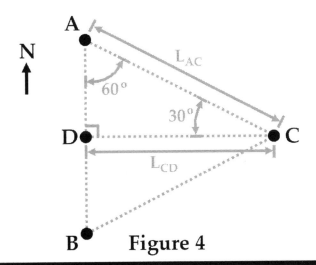

Figure 4

In Figure 4, we create a point D at the mid point between well A and well B.

Since triangle ABC is equilateral, triangle ADC is a 30°-60°-90°, right triangle

Water Resources Practice Problems

Groundwater #3 (cont.)

$$\frac{dh}{dx} = \frac{h_C - h_D}{L_{CD}} \leftarrow eq.2$$

total head at well C and point D

the length between well C and point D

Eq. 2 computes the gradient of the groundwater table in the east direction.

$h_A = 243.5\,[ft]$ $h_B = 232.1\,[ft]$

$$h_D = \frac{h_A + h_B}{2} \leftarrow eq.3$$

Eq. 3 computes the total head at point D as the average total head at wells A and B.

$$h_D = \frac{243.5\,[ft] + 232.1\,[ft]}{2}$$

Plug in variables h_A and h_B into eq. 3, then solve for h_D.

$$h_D = 237.8\,[ft]$$

$$L_{CD} = \frac{\sqrt{3}}{2} * L_{AC} \leftarrow eq.4$$

$L_{AC} = 500\,[ft]$

Since triangle ADC is a 30°-60°-90° triangle, we can compute L_{CD} using trigonometry.

$$L_{CD} = \frac{\sqrt{3}}{2} * 500\,[ft]$$

Plug in variable L_{AC} into eq. 4, then solve for L_{CD}.

$$L_{CD} = 433\,[ft]$$

$h_C = 236.7\,[ft]$ $h_D = 237.8\,[ft]$

$$\frac{dh}{dx} = \frac{h_C - h_D}{L_{CD}} \leftarrow eq.2$$

$L_{CD} = 433\,[ft]$

Plug in variables h_C, h_D and L_{CD} into eq. 2, then solve for dh/dx.

Groundwater #3 (cont.)

$$\frac{dh}{dx} = \frac{236.7\,[\text{ft}] - 237.8\,[\text{ft}]}{433\,[\text{ft}]}$$

$$\frac{dh}{dx} = -0.00254$$

Since the gradient is negative in the eastward direction, then groundwater flows eastward

$$\theta_Q = S6°E$$

Answer: $\boxed{B}$

Since the groundwater flows in the southeast quadrant, we know direction B is correct.

Water Resources Practice Problems

Groundwater #4

Find: h_B ← the head at well B

Given:

$L_{AB}=L_{BC}=300\,[m]$

$L_{AC}=600\,[m]$ ← horizontal length between the wells

$h_A=41.5\,[m]$ ← total head at well A

$h_C=34.5\,[m]$ ← total head at well C

$K_{AB}=5\,[m/day]$ ← permeability between wells A and B

$K_{BC}=20\,[m/day]$ ← permeability between wells B and C

profile view of the 3 observation wells

hypothetical water table

A) 36 [m]

B) 38 [m]

C) 39 [m]

D) 40 [m]

Analysis:

$$Q_{AC}=Q_{AB}=Q_{BC} \leftarrow eq.1$$

Eq.1 shows that the total flow rate within the aquifer is constant.

$$Q_{AB}=-K_{AB}*i_{AB}*A \qquad Q_{BC}=-K_{BC}*i_{BC}*A$$

Substitute in expressions for the groundwater flow rate into eq.1.

cancel area term

$$-K_{AB}*i_{AB}*A=-K_{BC}*i_{BC}*A \leftarrow eq.2$$

Cancel the area term from both sides of eq.2.

$$i_{AB}=\frac{h_B-h_A}{L_{AB}} \qquad i_{BC}=\frac{h_C-h_B}{L_{BC}}$$

Substitute in expressions for the water table gradient into eq.2.

$h_A=41.5\,[m]$ $\qquad$ $h_C=34.5\,[m]$

$K_{AB}=5\,[m/day]$ $\qquad$ $K_{BC}=20\,[m/day]$

$$-K_{AB}*\left(\frac{h_B-h_A}{L_{AB}}\right)=-K_{BC}*\left(\frac{h_C-h_B}{L_{BC}}\right) \leftarrow eq.3$$

$L_{AB}=300\,[m]$ $\qquad$ $L_{BC}=300\,[m]$

Plug in variables K_{AB}, K_{BC}, h_A, h_C, L_{AB} and L_{BC} into eq. 3, then solve for h_B.

$$-5[m/day]*\left(\frac{h_B-41.5\,[m]}{300\,[m]}\right)=-20[m/day]*\left(\frac{34.5\,[m]-h_B}{300\,[m]}\right)$$

$$h_B=35.9\,[m]$$

Answer: $\boxed{A}$

Groundwater #5

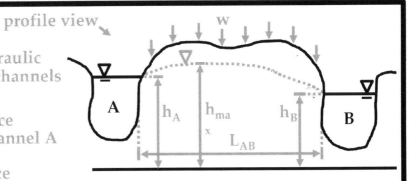

Find: h_{max} ← the maximum hydraulic
head between the channels

Given:

h_A=17.4 [m] ← the water surface
elevation in channel A

h_B=15.4 [m] ← the water surface
elevation in channel B

w=0.011 [m/day] ← recharge rate

L_{AB}=750 [m] ← horizontal distance
between the channels

K=32 [m/day]

hydraulic
conductivity

A) 17.4 [m]

B) 17.7 [m]

C) 18.0 [m]

D) 19.0 [m]

Analysis:

recharge rate

height of water table

distance from
channel A

Eq.1 computes the height (total
head) of the water table between
the two channels.

$$h_x = \sqrt{h_A{}^2 - \frac{(h_A{}^2 - h_B{}^2)*x}{L_{AB}} + \frac{w}{K}*(L_{AB}-x)*x} \quad \leftarrow eq.1$$

horizontal distance
between channels

hydraulic
conductivity

$$h_{max} = f_1(d) \quad \leftarrow eq.2$$

Eq.2 shows that the groundwater table
will be maximized at the groundwater
divide, where x=d.

$$h_{max} = \sqrt{h_A{}^2 - \frac{(h_A{}^2 - h_B{}^2)*d}{L_{AB}} + \frac{w}{K}*(L_{AB}-d)*d} \quad \leftarrow eq.3$$

Substitute in d for x, and h_{max} for h_x
in eq.1, then solve for h_{max}.

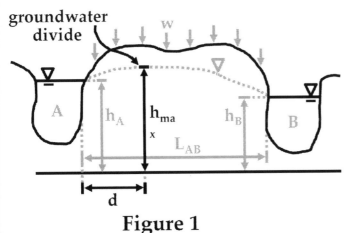

groundwater
divide

Figure 1 shows the distance d is the
horizontal distance from channel A to
the groundwater divide.

Figure 1

273

Water Resources Practice Problems

Groundwater #5 (cont.)

$h_A = 17.4\,[m]$
$K = 32\,[m/day]$
$h_B = 15.4\,[m]$

$$d = \frac{L_{AB}}{2} - \frac{K}{w} * \frac{(h_A^2 - h_B^2)}{2*L_{AB}} \quad \leftarrow eq.4$$

$w = 0.011\,[m/day]$
$L_{AB} = 750\,[m]$

Eq. 4 computes the horizontal distance from Channel A to the groundwater divide.

Plug in variables K, h_A, h_B, w and L_{AB} into eq. 4, then solve for d.

$$d = \frac{750\,[m]}{2} - \frac{32\,[m/day]}{0.011\,[m/day]} * \frac{((17.4\,[m])^2 - (15.4\,[m])^2)}{2*750\,[m]}$$

$$d = 247.8\,[m]$$

$h_A = 17.4\,[m]$ $h_B = 15.4\,[m]$ $d = 247.8\,[m]$

$$h_{max} = \sqrt{h_A^2 - \frac{(h_A^2 - h_B^2)*d}{L_{AB}} + \frac{w}{K} * (L_{AB} - d)*d} \quad \leftarrow eq.3$$

$L_{AB} = 750\,[m]$ $w = 0.011\,[m/day]$
$K = 32\,[m/day]$

Plug in variables K, h_A, h_B, d, w and L_{AB} into eq. 3, then solve for h_{max}.

$$h_{max} = \sqrt{(17.4\,[m])^2 - \frac{((17.4\,[m])^2 - (15.4\,[m])^2)*247.8\,[m]}{750\,[m]} + \frac{0.011\,[m/day]}{32\,[m/day]} * (750\,[m] - 247.8\,[m])*247.8\,[m]}$$

$$h_{max} = 18.0\,[m]$$

Answer: $\boxed{C}$

274

Groundwater #6

Find: x where h_x=159.0[ft]

the distance from channel A where the water table is at a height of 159.0 feet.

Given:

h_A=153.8[ft] ← the water surface elevation in channel A

h_B=157.4[ft] ← the water surface elevation in channel B

w=0.25[ft/day] ← recharge rate

L_{AB}=1,200[ft] ← distance between channels

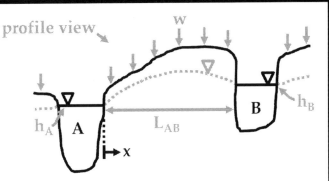
profile view

K=50[ft/day] ← hydraulic conductivity

A) 100[ft]
B) 200[ft]
C) 300[ft]
D) 400[ft]

Analysis:

recharge rate

height of water table

distance from channel A

$$h_x = \sqrt{h_A^2 - \frac{(h_A^2 - h_B^2)*x}{L_{AB}} + \frac{w}{K}*(L_{AB}-x)*x} \quad \leftarrow eq.1$$

horizontal distance between channels

hydraulic conductivity

Eq.1 computes the height of the water table at a distance x from channel A.

Since eq.1 is a quadratic equation, there may be 0, 1 or 2 real solutions, as shown in Figure 1.

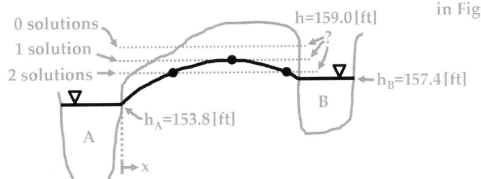

0 solutions
1 solution
2 solutions

h=159.0[ft]

h_B=157.4[ft]

h_A=153.8[ft]

Figure 1

Convert eq.1 to the general quadratic equation: $ax^2+bx+c=0$

$$0 = \underbrace{\frac{w}{K}}_{a}*x^2 + \underbrace{\left(\frac{(h_A^2-h_B^2)}{L_{AB}} - \frac{w*L_{AB}}{K}\right)}_{b}*x + \underbrace{h_x^2-h_A^2}_{c} \quad \leftarrow eq.2$$

Identify variables a, b and c from eq.2.

Water Resources Practice Problems

Groundwater #6 (cont.)

w=0.25 [ft/day]

$$a = \frac{w}{K} \leftarrow eq.3$$

K=50 [ft/day]

Eq. 3 computes variable a.

Plug in variables w and K into eq. 3, then solve for a.

$$a = \frac{0.25\,[\text{ft/day}]}{50\,[\text{ft/day}]}$$

$$a = 0.005$$

$h_B=157.4\,[\text{ft}]$

$h_A=153.8\,[\text{ft}]$ w=0.25 [ft/day]

$$b = \frac{(h_A{}^2 - h_B{}^2)}{L_{AB}} - \frac{w * L_{AB}}{K} \leftarrow eq.4$$

$L_{AB}=1{,}200\,[\text{ft}]$ K=50 [ft/day]

Eq. 4 computes variable b.

Plug in variables h_A, h_B, w, L_{AB} and K into eq. 4, then solve for b.

$$b = \frac{((153.8\,[\text{ft}])^2 - (157.4\,[\text{ft}])^2)}{1{,}200\,[\text{ft}]} - \frac{0.25\,[\text{ft/day}] * 1{,}200\,[\text{ft}]}{50\,[\text{ft/day}]}$$

$$b = -6.9336\,[\text{ft}]$$

Eq. 5 computes variable c.

$$c = h_x{}^2 - h_A{}^2 \leftarrow eq.5$$

$h_x=159.0\,[\text{ft}]$ $h_A=153.8\,[\text{ft}]$

Plug in variables h_x and h_A into eq. 5, then solve for c.

$$c = (159.0\,[\text{ft}])^2 - (153.8\,[\text{ft}])^2$$

$$c = 1{,}626.56\,[\text{ft}^2]$$

Groundwater #6 (cont.)

Eq. 6 solves the general form of the quadratic equation.

b=-6.9336 [ft]   c=1,626.56 [ft²]

$$x = \frac{-b \pm \sqrt{b^2 - 4*a*c}}{2*a} \leftarrow eq.6$$

a=0.005

Plug in variables a, b and c into eq. 6, then solve for x.

$$x = \frac{-6.9336\,[ft] \pm \sqrt{(-6.9336\,[ft])^2 - 4*0.005*1,625.56\,[ft^2]}}{2*0.005}$$

$$x = 299\,[ft],\ 1,088\,[ft]$$

Answer: $\boxed{C}$

Water Resources Practice Problems

Groundwater #7

constant head permeameter

Find: K ← the hydraulic conductivity

Given:

$h_A = 34\,[in]$ ← upstream head

$h_B = 20\,[in]$ ← downstream head

$L = 18\,[in]$ ← length of soil sample

$d = 2.111\,[in]$ ← diameter of the soil sample

$t = 3\,[min]$ ← time it takes to fill a known volume

$V = 13.41\,[in^3]$

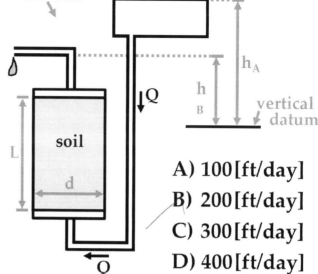

A) 100 [ft/day]

B) 200 [ft/day]

C) 300 [ft/day]

D) 400 [ft/day]

Analysis:

$$Q = K * A * \frac{\Delta h}{L} \leftarrow eq.1$$

flow rate — Q

area of the soil sample — A

headloss across the soil sample — Δh

hydraulic conductivity — K

length of the soil sample — L

Eq. 1 computes the flow rate through a constant head permeameter.

$$K = \frac{Q * L}{A * \Delta h} \leftarrow eq.2$$

Solve eq. 1 for the hydraulic conductivity.

$V = 13.41\,[in^3]$

$$Q = \frac{V}{t} \leftarrow eq.3$$

$t = 3\,[min]$

Eq. 3 computes the flow rate through the permeameter.

Plug in variables V and t into eq. 3, then solve for Q.

$$Q = \frac{13.41\,[in^3]}{3\,[min]} \checkmark$$

$$Q = 4.47\,[in^3/min] \checkmark$$

Eq.4 computes the head drop across the soil

$h_A = 34\,[in]$ $h_B = 20\,[in]$

$$\Delta h = h_A - h_B \leftarrow eq.4$$

Plug in variables h_A and h_B into eq. 4, then solve for Δh.

Groundwater #7 (cont.)

$$\Delta h = 34\,[in] - 20\,[in]$$

$$\Delta h = 14\,[in] \;\checkmark$$

$d = 2.111\,[in]$

$$A = \frac{\pi * d^2}{4} \leftarrow eq.5$$

Eq. 5 computes the cross sectional area of the soil sample in the permeameter.

Plug in variable d into eq. 5, then solve for A.

$$A = \frac{\pi * (2.111\,[in])^2}{4}$$

$$A = 3.50\,[in^2] \;\checkmark$$

$Q = 4.47\,[in^3/min]$ $\quad L = 18\,[in]$

$$K = \frac{Q * L}{A * \Delta h} \leftarrow eq.2$$

$A = 3.50\,[in^2]$ $\quad \Delta h = 14\,[in]$

Plug in variables Q, L, A and Δh into eq. 2, then solve for K.

$$K = \frac{4.47\,[in^3/min] * 18\,[in]}{3.50\,[in^2] * 14\,[in]}$$

Eq. 6 converts the units of hydraulic conductivity to feet per day.

$$K = 1.642 \left[\frac{in}{min}\right] * 1,440 \left[\frac{min}{day}\right] * \frac{1}{12}\left[\frac{ft}{in}\right] \leftarrow eq.6$$

conversion factors

$$K = 197\,[ft/day]$$

Answer: $\boxed{B}$

Water Resources Practice Problems

Groundwater #8

Find: t ← the time it takes the water level to drop from h_1 to h_2.

Given:

h_A=78[cm] ← initial headloss

Δh_{AB}=47[cm] ← change in headloss

L=14[cm] ← length of soil sample

d_s=8.5[cm] ← diameter of the soil sample

d_t=1.2[cm] ← diameter of the tube

K=0.13[cm/s] ← hydraulic conductivity

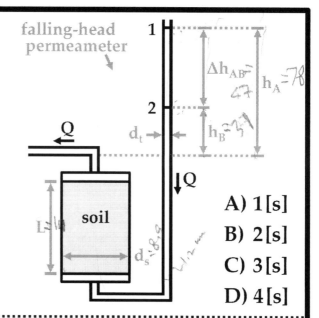

A) 1[s]

B) 2[s]

C) 3[s]

D) 4[s]

Analysis:

$$K = \frac{A_t * L}{A_s * \Delta t} * \ln\left(\frac{h_A}{h_B}\right) \leftarrow eq.1$$

area of the tube — A_t

length of the sample — L

initial headloss — h_A

hydraulic conductivity — K

area of the sample — A_s

duration of the test — Δt

final headloss — h_B

Eq.1 computes the hydraulic conductivity of the soil for the falling head permeability test.

$$\Delta t = t = \frac{A_t * L}{A_s * K} * \ln\left(\frac{h_A}{h_B}\right) \leftarrow eq.2$$

Solve eq.1 for the duration of the test.

$$h_B = h_A - \Delta h_{AB} \leftarrow eq.3$$

h_A=78[cm]

Δh_{AB}=47[cm]

Eq.3 computes the headloss across the soil sample at the end of the test.

$$h_B = 78[cm] - 47[cm]$$

Plug in variables h_A and Δh_{AB} into eq.3, then solve for h_B.

$$h_B = 31[cm]$$

d_s=8.5[cm]

$$A_s = \frac{\pi * d_s^2}{4} \leftarrow eq.4$$

Eq.4 computes the cross sectional area of the soil sample in the permeameter.

Groundwater #8 (cont.)

$$A_s = \frac{\pi * (8.5\,[cm])^2}{4}$$

Plug in variable d_s into eq. 4, then solve for A_s.

$$A_s = 56.75\,[cm^2]$$

$$A_t = \frac{\pi * d_t^2}{4} \leftarrow eq.5$$

$d_t = 1.2\,[cm]$

Eq. 5 computes the cross-sectional area of the tube of the permeameter.

$$A_t = \frac{\pi * (1.2\,[cm])^2}{4}$$

Plug in variable d_t into eq. 5, then solve for A_t.

$$A_t = 1.131\,[cm^2]$$

$$t = \frac{A_t * L}{A_s * K} * \ln\left(\frac{h_A}{h_B}\right) \leftarrow eq.2$$

$L = 14\,[cm]$
$A_t = 1.131\,[cm^2]$
$h_A = 78\,[cm]$
$A_s = 56.75\,[cm^2]$
$h_B = 31\,[cm]$
$K = 0.13\,[cm/s]$

Plug in variables A_t, L, A_s, K, h_A and h_B into eq. 2, then solve for t.

$$t = \frac{1.131\,[cm^2] * 14\,[cm]}{56.75\,[cm^2] * 0.13\,[cm/s]} * \ln\left(\frac{78\,[cm]}{31\,[cm]}\right)$$

$$t = 1.98\,[s]$$

Answer: $\boxed{B}$

Water Resources Practice Problems

Groundwater #9

Find: V ← the volume of water flowing beneath the embankment

Given:

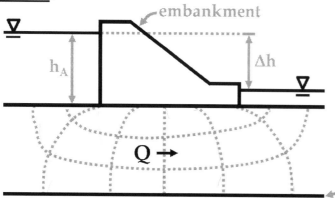

$h_A = 9.5\,[m]$ ← upstream depth

$\Delta h = 8\,[m]$ ← headloss across the embankment

$K = 0.001\,[cm/s]$ ← hydraulic conductivity

$t = 1\,[week]$ ← duration

$b = 20\,[m]$

width of the embankment

A) 7 [m³]

B) 28 [m³]

C) 480 [m³]

D) 1,940 [m³]

Analysis:

$$V = Q * t \leftarrow eq.1$$

volume   flow rate   duration

Eq.1 computes the volume of water flowing under the embankment.

Eq.2 computes the flow rate through the flow net.

headloss across the embankment

number of flow channels

flow rate

$$Q = K * \Delta h * b * \frac{N_F}{N_D} \leftarrow eq.2$$

number of drops

hydraulic conductivity

width of the embankment

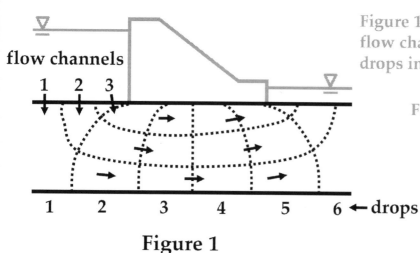

flow channels

1 2 3

1 2 3 4 5 6 ← drops

Figure 1

Figure 1 identifies the number of flow channels and the number of drops in the flow channel

From Figure 1 we learn

$$N_F = 3$$

$$N_D = 6$$

Groundwater #9 (cont.)

Eq. 3 converts the hydraulic conductivity to units of meters per day.

conversion factors

$$K = 0.001 \left[\frac{cm}{s}\right] * 86{,}400 \left[\frac{s}{day}\right] * \frac{1}{100} \left[\frac{m}{cm}\right] \leftarrow eq.\,3$$

$$K = 0.864 \left[\frac{m}{day}\right]$$

K = 0.864 [m/day]

$N_F = 3$

$$Q = K * \Delta h * b \quad * \frac{N_F}{N_D} \leftarrow eq.\,2$$

$\Delta h = 8\,[m]$ b = 20 [m] $N_D = 6$

Plug in variables K, Δh, b, N_F and N_D into eq. 2, then solve for Q.

$$Q = 0.864\,[m/day] * 8\,[m] * 20\,[m] * \frac{3}{6}$$

$$Q = 69.12\,[m^3/day]$$

conversion factor

$$t = 1\,[week] * 7 \left[\frac{day}{week}\right] \leftarrow eq.\,4$$

Eq. 4 converts the duration to days.

$$t = 7\,[days]$$

Q = 69.12 [m³/day]

$$V = Q * t \leftarrow eq.\,1$$

t = 7 [days]

Plug in variables Q and t into eq. 1, then solve for V.

$$V = 69.12\,[m^3/day] * 7\,[days]$$

$$V = 483.8\,[m^3] \qquad \underline{\text{Answer:}} \;\boxed{C}$$

Water Resources Practice Problems

Groundwater #10

__Find: r₂__ ←the radius from the well where the aquifer thickness equals y_2

__Given:__

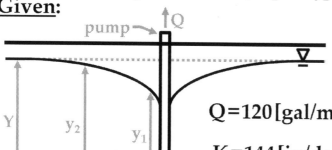

pump → ↑Q

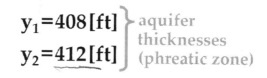

$y_1 = 408 \, [ft]$ ⎫ aquifer
$y_2 = 412 \, [ft]$ ⎬ thicknesses (phreatic zone)

$Q = 120 \, [gal/min]$ ←pumping rate

$K = 144 \, [in/day]$ ←hydraulic conductivity

$r_1 = 4 \, [ft]$ ←radius for y_1

A) 575 [ft]
B) 665 [ft]
C) 755 [ft]
D) 845 [ft]

Analysis:

hydraulic conductivity   aquifer thickness

$$Q = \frac{\pi * K * (y_1^2 - y_2^2)}{\ln(r_1/r_2)} \quad \leftarrow eq.1$$

pumping rate   radii from the well

Eq. 1 computes the pumping rate from an unconfined aquifer at equilibrium.

$$r_2 = \frac{r_1}{e^{\left(\frac{\pi * K * (y_1^2 - y_2^2)}{Q}\right)}} \quad \leftarrow eq.2$$

Solve eq. 1 for radius r_2.

Eq. 3 converts the pumping rate to units of cubic feet per day.

conversion factors

$$Q = 120 \left[\frac{gal}{min}\right] * \frac{1}{7.48}\left[\frac{ft^3}{gal}\right] * 1{,}440\left[\frac{min}{day}\right] \quad \leftarrow eq.3$$

$$Q = 23{,}102 \, [ft^3/day]$$

$$K = 144 \left[\frac{in}{day}\right] * \frac{1}{12}\left[\frac{ft}{in}\right] \quad \leftarrow eq.4$$

Eq. 4 converts the hydraulic conductivity of units of feet per day.

Groundwater #10 (cont.)

$$K = 12 \, [ft/day]$$

$$r_2 = \cfrac{r_1}{e^{\left(\cfrac{\pi * K * (y_1^2 - y_2^2)}{Q}\right)}} \leftarrow eq.2$$

K=12[ft/day] r_1=4[ft]   Plug in variables r_1, K, Q, y_1 and y_2 into eq. 2, then solve for r_2.

y_2=412[ft]

y_1=408[ft]

Q=23,102[ft³/day]

$$r_2 = \cfrac{4 \, [ft]}{e^{\left(\cfrac{\pi * 12 \, [ft/day] * ((408 \, [ft])^2 - (412 \, [ft])^2)}{23,102 \, [ft^3/day]}\right)}}$$

$$r_2 = 845 \, [ft]$$

Answer: $\boxed{D}$

Water Resources Practice Problems

Groundwater #11

Find: s ← the aquifer drawdown

Given:

Q=2,725 [m³/day] ← pumping rate

K=1 [cm/min] ← hydraulic conductivity

r=7 [m] ← radius from the well

t=1 [day] ← duration of pumping

Y=20.1 [m] ← aquifer thickness

S=0.0051 [m] ← aquifer storativity

non-steady state conditions

A) 0.34 [m]

B) 0.72 [m]

C) 1.72 [m]

D) 5.90 [m]

Analysis:

$$s = \left(\frac{Q}{4 * \pi * K * Y} \right) * W(u) \leftarrow eq.1$$

pumping rate → Q

hydraulic conductivity → K

drawdown → s

aquifer thickness → Y

well function → W(u)

Eq.1 is the Theis equation which computes the drawdown from an unconfined aquifer for non-steady state conditions.

$$u = \frac{r^2 * S}{4 * K * Y * t} \leftarrow eq.2$$

storativity → S

pumping duration → t

The value of the well function is based on the dimensionless value of variable u.

Eq.2 computes variable u.

$$K = 1 \left[\frac{cm}{min} \right] * \frac{1}{100} \left[\frac{m}{cm} \right] * 1{,}440 \left[\frac{min}{day} \right] \leftarrow eq.3$$

conversion factors

$$K = 14.4 \, [m/day]$$

Eq.3 converts the hydraulic conductivity to units of meters per day.

$$u = \frac{r^2 * S}{4 * K * Y * t} \leftarrow eq.2$$

r=7 [m]   S=0.0051 [m]   t=1 [day]

K=14.4 [m/day]   Y=20.1 [m]

Plug in variables r, S, K, Y and t into eq.2, then solve for u.

286

Groundwater #11 (cont.)

$$u = \frac{(7\,[m])^2 * 0.0051}{4 * 14.4\,[m/day] * 20.1\,[m] * 1\,[day]}$$

$$u = 2.158 * 10^{-4}$$

$$W(1*10^{-4}) = 8.63$$
$$W(2*10^{-4}) = 7.94$$
$$W(3*10^{-4}) = 7.53$$
$$W(4*10^{-4}) = 7.25$$

Figure 1

Figure 1 shows an excerpt of values from a table showing the well function, W(u), for different values of u.

Eq.4 computes the well function value for the computed value of u for values of u between $2*10^{-4}$ and $3*10^{-4}$, using linear interpolation.

$u = 2.158*10^{-4}$

$$W(u) = W(2*10^{-4}) + \left(\frac{u - 2*10^{-4}}{3*10^{-4} - 2*10^{-4}}\right) * (W(3*10^{-4}) - W(2*10^{-4})) \leftarrow eq.\,4$$

$W(2*10^{-4}) = 7.94$ $W(3*10^{-4}) = 7.53$

$$W(2.158*10^{-4}) = 7.94 + \left(\frac{2.158*10^{-4} - 2*10^{-4}}{3*10^{-4} - 2*10^{-4}}\right) * (7.53 - 7.94)$$

7.90

$$W(2.158*10^{-4}) = 7.88$$

Plug in variables u, $W(2*10^{-4})$ and $W(3*10^{-4})$ into eq.4, then solve for W(u).

$Q = 2,725\,[m^3/day]$ $W(2.158*10^{-4}) = 7.88$

$$s = \left(\frac{Q}{4 * \pi * K * Y}\right) * W(u) \leftarrow eq.\,1$$

$K = 14.4\,[m/day]$ $Y = 20.1\,[m]$

Plug in variables Q, K, Y and W(u) into eq.1, then solve for s.

$$s = \left(\frac{2,725\,[m^3/day]}{4 * \pi * 14.4\,[m/day] * 20.1\,[m]}\right) * 7.88$$

$$s = 5.90\,[m]$$ **Answer:** $\boxed{D}$

Water Resources Practice Problems

Groundwater #12

Find: t ← the duration of pumping

no cone of depression exists
at the time pumping begins

Given:

non-steady state conditions

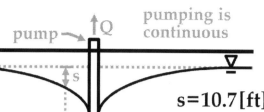

pump → ↑Q

pumping is continuous

$Q=100\,[\text{gal/min}]$ ← pumping rate

$s=10.7\,[\text{ft}]$ ← drawdown

$r=19\,[\text{ft}]$ ← radius

$S=0.002$ ← storativity

unconfined aquifer

r

A) 1[day]

B) 2[days]

C) 3[days]

D) 4[days]

$T=1{,}400\,[\text{ft}^2/\text{day}]$ ← transmissivity

Analysis:

radius   storativity

$$u = \frac{r^2 * S}{4 * T * t} \leftarrow eq.1$$

transmissivity   pumping duration

Eq.1 computes variable u, used to determine the value of the well function.

$$t = \frac{r^2 * S}{4 * T * u} \leftarrow eq.2$$

Solve eq.1 for the duration of pumping, t.

pumping rate   well function

$$s = \left(\frac{Q}{4 * \pi * T}\right) * W(u) \leftarrow eq.3$$

drawdown   transmissivity

Eq.3 computes the drawdown from an unconfined aquifer for non-steady state conditions.

Solve eq.3 for the well function.

$$W(u) = \left(\frac{4 * \pi * T * s}{Q}\right) \leftarrow eq.4$$

Eq.5 converts the pumping rate to units of cubic feet per second.

conversion factors

$$Q = 100 \left[\frac{\text{gal}}{\text{min}}\right] * \frac{1}{7.48}\left[\frac{\text{min}}{\text{day}}\right] * 1{,}440 \left[\frac{\text{min}}{\text{day}}\right] \leftarrow eq.5$$

$\frac{1}{7.48}\frac{ft^3}{gal}$

Groundwater #12 (cont.)

$$Q = 1.925*10^4 [ft^3/day]$$

T = 1,400 [ft²/day]   s = 10.7 [ft]

$$W(u) = \left(\frac{4*\pi*T*s}{Q}\right) \leftarrow eq.4$$

Q = 1.925*10⁴ [ft³/day]

Plug in variables T, Q and s into eq.4, then solve for W(u).

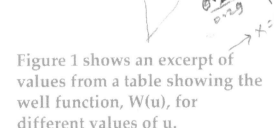

$$W(u) = \left(\frac{4*\pi*1,400[ft^2/day]*10.7[ft]}{1.925*10^4[ft^3/day]}\right)$$

$$W(u) = 9.78$$

$$W(2*10^{-5}) = 10.24$$
$$W(3*10^{-5}) = 9.84$$
$$W(4*10^{-5}) = 9.55$$
$$W(5*10^{-5}) = 9.33$$

Figure 1

Figure 1 shows an excerpt of values from a table showing the well function, W(u), for different values of u.

Eq.6 computes the well function using linear interpolation, based on the values in Figure 1.

$$W(u) = W(3*10^{-5}) + \left(\frac{u-3*10^{-5}}{4*10^{-5}-3*10^{-5}}\right)*(W(4*10^{-5})-W(3*10^{-5})) \leftarrow eq.6$$

W(u) = 9.78   W(3*10⁻⁵) = 9.84

Solve eq.6 for u.

$$u = \frac{W(u)-W(3*10^{-5})}{(W(4*10^{-5})-W(3*10^{-5}))}*(4*10^{-5}-3*10^{-5}) + 3*10^{-5} \leftarrow eq.7$$

W(4*10⁻⁵) = 9.55

Plug in variables W(u), W(3*10⁻⁵) and W(4*10⁻⁵) into eq.7, then solve for u.

$$u = \frac{9.78-9.84}{9.55-9.84}*(4*10^{-5}-3*10^{-5}) + 3*10^{-5}$$

Groundwater #12 (cont.)

3.4 × 10⁻⁵

$$u = 3.207 * 10^{-5}$$

r=19 [ft]   S=0.002

$$t = \frac{r^2 * S}{4 * T * u} \leftarrow eq.2$$

T=1,400 [ft²/day]   u=3.207*10⁻⁵

Plug in variables r, S, T and u into eq. 2, then solve for t.

$$t = \frac{(19 [ft])^2 * 0.002}{4 * 1,400 [ft^2/day] * 3.207*10^{-5}}$$

$$t = 4.02 [days]$$

Answer: D

Fluid Statics #1

Find: P_A ← the pressure at point A

Given: P_D=98.4[kPA] ← the pressure at point D

h_{AB}=30[cm]
h_{BC}=50[cm] } height between fluids in the monometer
h_{CD}=20[cm]

ϱ_b=879[kg/m³]
ϱ_w=998[kg/m³] } densities of the three fluids (at 20°C)
ϱ_k=804[kg/m³]

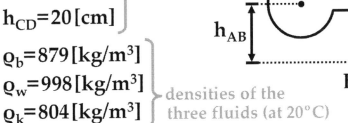

kerosene, ϱ_k
benzene, ϱ_b
water, ϱ_b
h_{BC}
h_C
h_{AB}
A
B
C
D

A) 94.5[kPa]
B) 101.3[kPa]
C) 102.3[kPa]
D) 107.1[kPa]

Analysis:

$$P_A=P_D+\Sigma \varrho_i * g * \Delta h_i \quad \leftarrow eq.1$$

density of fluid i   change in height across fluid i

Eq.1 computes the pressure at point A.

Expand the summation term in Eq.1, and add subscripts of 'b' for benzene, 'w' for water and 'k' for kerosene to the density term.

$$P_A=P_D+\varrho_b * g * (-h_{AB})+\varrho_w * g * h_{BC}+\varrho_k * g * h_{CD} \leftarrow eq.2$$

add a negative sign

In eq.2, we'll multiply by negative h_{AB}, not positive h_{AB}, because the pressure at point A is less than the pressure at point B.

unit conversion

h_{AB}=30[cm]
h_{BC}=50[cm] * $\frac{1}{100}\left[\frac{m}{cm}\right]$ →
h_{CD}=20[cm]

h_{AB}=0.30[m]
h_{BC}=0.50[m]
h_{CD}=0.20[m]

Convert the heights from centimeters to meters.

Simplify Eq.2, then plug in the known densities and heights.

ϱ_b=879[kg/m³] ϱ_w=998[kg/m³] ϱ_k=804[kg/m³]

$$P_A=P_D+g*\{(\varrho_b *(-h_{AB})+\varrho_w * h_{BC}+\varrho_k * h_{CD}\}$$

h_{AB}=0.30[m] h_{BC}=0.50[m] h_{CD}=0.20[m]

Water Resources Practice Problems

Fluid Statics #1 (cont.)

Plug in variables P_D and g, then solve for P_A.

$P_D=98.4[kPa]$

$$P_A=P_D+g*\{(879[kg/m^3]*(-0.30[m])$$
$$+998[kg/m^3]*0.50[m]$$
$$+804[kg/m^3]*0.20[m]\}$$

$g=9.81[m/s^2]$

convert the units of pressure to Pascals

$$P_A=98.4[kPa]+9.81[m/s^2]*396.1[kg/m^2]*\frac{1}{1}\left[\frac{Pa*m*s^2}{kg}\right]*\frac{1}{1,000}\left[\frac{kPa}{Pa}\right]$$

convert Pascals to kiloPascals.

$$P_A=98.4[kPa]+3.89[kPa]$$

$$P_A=102.29[kPa]$$

Answer: $\boxed{C}$

Fluid Statics #2

<u>Find:</u> h_{AB} ←the height between point A and point B

$h_{AC}=2.5\,[\text{ft}]$ ←the height between point A and point C

<u>Given:</u>

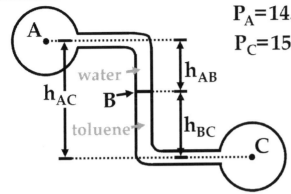

$P_A=14.70\,[\text{lb}_f/\text{in}^2]$ ⎫ pressure at point
$P_C=15.72\,[\text{lb}_f/\text{in}^2]$ ⎭ A and point C

$\varrho_w=62.3\,[\text{lb}_m/\text{ft}^3]$
$\varrho_t=54.0\,[\text{lb}_m/\text{ft}^3]$
the density of water and toluene at 20°C.

A) 0.44 [ft]

B) 0.88 [ft]

C) 1.44 [ft]

D) 1.88 [ft]

Analysis:

$$\Delta P = \Sigma\,\varrho_i * g * \Delta h_i \quad \leftarrow eq.1$$

change in pressure · · · density of fluid i · · · change in height across fluid i

Eq. 1 computes the change in pressure between two points.

Expand Eq. 1 to show the variables for pressure, density and height.

$$P_C-P_A = \varrho_w * g * h_{AB} + \varrho_t * g * h_{BC} \quad \leftarrow eq.2$$

From the problem statement, we notice the sum of h_{AB} and h_{BC} equals h_{AC}.

$$h_{AB} + h_{BC} = h_{AC} \quad \leftarrow eq.3$$

$h_{AC}=2.5\,[\text{ft}]$

In this problem, we have 2 equations (Eq. 2 & Eq. 4), and 2 unknown variables (h_{AB} & h_{BC}).

$$h_{AB} + h_{BC} = 2.5\,[\text{ft}] \quad \leftarrow eq.4$$

$$h_{BC} = 2.5\,[\text{ft}] - h_{AB}$$

Solve Eq. 4 for h_{BC}, then plug in value into h_{BC} in Eq. 2.

$h_{BC} = 2.5\,[\text{ft}] - h_{AB}$

$$P_C-P_A = \varrho_w * g * h_{AB} + \varrho_t * g * h_{BC} \quad \leftarrow eq.2$$

Solve Eq. 2 for h_{AB}.

$$P_C-P_A = \varrho_w * g * h_{AB} + \varrho_t * g * (2.5\,[\text{ft}] - h_{AB})$$

Water Resources Practice Problems

Fluid Statics #2 (cont.)

$P_A = 14.70 \, [\text{lb}_f/\text{in}^2]$ $\varrho_t = 54.0 \, [\text{lb}_m/\text{ft}^3]$

$$h_{AB} = \frac{P_C - P_A - 2.5 \, [\text{ft}] * \varrho_t * g}{(\varrho_w - \varrho_t) * g} \leftarrow eq.5$$

Plug in the known values into Eq.5, then solve for h_{AB}.

$P_C = 15.72 \, [\text{lb}_f/\text{in}^2]$ $g = 32.2 \, [\text{ft/s}^2]$

$\varrho_w = 62.3 \, [\text{lb}_m/\text{ft}^3]$

$$h_{AB} = \frac{15.72 \, [\text{lb}_f/\text{in}^2] - 14.70 \, [\text{lb}_f/\text{in}^2] - 2.5 \, [\text{ft}] * 54.0 \, [\text{lb}_m/\text{ft}^3] * 32.2 \, [\text{ft/s}^2]}{(62.3 \, [\text{lb}_m/\text{ft}^3] - 54.0 \, [\text{lb}_m/\text{ft}^3]) * 32.2 \, [\text{ft/s}^2]}$$

$$h_{AB} = \frac{1.02 \, [\text{lb}_f/\text{in}^2] - 4{,}374 \, [\text{lb}_m/\text{ft}*\text{s}^2]}{267.3 \, [\text{lb}_m/\text{ft}^2*\text{s}^2]} \leftarrow eq.6$$

convert the units of these two terms to lb_f and inches.

$$4{,}347 \, [\text{lb}_m/\text{ft}*\text{s}^2] * \frac{1}{32.2} \left[\frac{\text{lb}_f*\text{s}^2}{\text{lb}_m*\text{ft}}\right] * \left(\frac{1}{12} \left[\frac{\text{ft}}{\text{in}}\right]\right)^2 = 0.9375 \, [\text{lb}_f/\text{in}^2]$$

unit conversions

$$267.3 \, [\text{lb}_m/\text{ft}^2*\text{s}^2] * \frac{1}{32.2} \left[\frac{\text{lb}_f*\text{s}^2}{\text{lb}_m*\text{ft}}\right] * \left(\frac{1}{12} \left[\frac{\text{ft}}{\text{in}}\right]\right)^2 = 0.0576 \, [\text{lb}_f/\text{in}^2*\text{ft}]$$

Replace the converted values back into Eq.6, then solve for h_{AB}.

$$h_{AB} = \frac{1.02 \, [\text{lb}_f/\text{in}^2] - 0.9375 \, [\text{lb}_f/\text{in}^2]}{0.0576 \, [\text{lb}_f/\text{in}^2*\text{ft}]} \leftarrow eq.6$$

$$h_{AB} = 1.43 \, [\text{ft}]$$

Answer: C

294

Fluid Statics #3

Find: d ← the depth the cylinder sinks into the fluid, at equilibrium

$W_{cyl,A}=21,730\,[lb_f]$
↑
the weight of the cylinder, in air

Given:

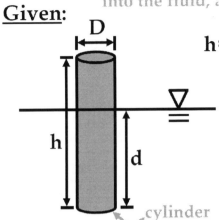

$h=22\,[ft]$ ← the height of the cylinder

$D=4\,[ft]$ ← the diameter of the cylinder

$SG=1.85$ ← specific gravity of the fluid

$T=70^\circ F$ ← temperature of the fluid

A) 15 [ft]

B) 16 [ft]

C) 17 [ft]

D) 18 [ft]

Analysis:

$$\Sigma F_y=0=F_b-W_{cyl,A} \leftarrow eq.1$$

Eq.1 computes the sum of the forces in the vertical direction at equilibrium.

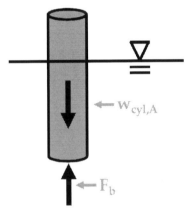

Figure 1

Figure 1 shows the buoyant force acts upward on the cylinder, to resist the weight of the cylinder.

$W_{cyl,A}=21,730\,[lb_f]$

$$F_b=W_{cyl,A} \leftarrow eq.2$$

Solve eq.1 for F_b.

$$F_b=21,730\,[lb_f]$$

density of water

$$F_b=SG*\varrho_w*g*V_{cyl,s} \leftarrow eq.3$$

specific gravity of the fluid

volume of the cylinder submerged

Eq.3 defines the buoyant force, F_b, is a function of the volume of the submerged cylinder, $V_{cyl,s}$.

Water Resources Practice Problems

Fluid Statics #3 (cont.)

$$V_{cyl,s} = 0.25 * \pi * D^2 * d \leftarrow eq.4$$

$D = 4\,[ft]$

submerged cylinder depth

Eq. 4 computes the volume of the cylinder.

Plug in variable D into eq.4 then solve $V_{cyl,s}$ as a function of d.

$$V_{cyl,s} = 0.25 * \pi * (4\,[ft])^2 * d$$

$$V_{cyl,s} = 12.566\,[ft^2] * d$$

$$T = 70^\circ\,F \longrightarrow \varrho_w = 62.3\,[lb_m/ft^3]$$

Determine the water density based on the water temperature

$$V_{cyl,s} = 12.566\,[ft^2] * d$$

$$F_b = SG * \varrho_w * g * V_{cyl,s} \leftarrow eq.3$$

Plug in $V_{cyl,s}$ into eq.3, then solve for d.

$$F_b = SG * \varrho_w * g * 12.566\,[ft^2] * d$$

$F_b = 21,730\,[lb_f]$ ＊＊＊ $SG = 1.85$

Plug in variables F_b, SG, ϱ_w, and g, into eq.5, then solve for the depth, d.

$$d = \frac{F_b}{12.566\,[ft^2] * SG * \varrho_w * g} \leftarrow eq.5$$

$\varrho_w = 62.3\,[lb_m/ft^3]$ $g = 32.2\,[ft/s^2]$

Multiply the depth, d, by a unit conversion factor.

$$d = \frac{21,730\,[lb_f]}{12.566\,[ft^2] * 1.85 * 62.3\,[lb_m/ft^3] * 32.2\,[ft/s^2]} * 32.2 \left[\frac{lb_m * ft}{lb_f * s^2}\right]$$

$d = 15.00\,[ft]$ Answer: ☐ A

Fluid Statics #4

<u>Find:</u> ϱ_{cube} ←the density
of the cube

<u>Given:</u>

$\varrho_o = 56.2\,[lb_m/ft^3]$ ←density of the oil

$\varrho_w = 62.4\,[lb_m/ft^3]$ ←density of the water

$h_{cube,o} = 8\,[in]$ ←height of the cube in the oil

$h_{cube,w} = 2\,[in]$ ←height of the cube in the water

$V_{cube} = 1,000\,[in]$ ←volume of the cube

equilibrium
condition→

air

oil $h_{cube,o}$ cube

$h_{cube,w}$

water

A) $57.4\,[lb_f/ft^3]$

B) $58.7\,[lb_f/ft^3]$

C) $60.0\,[lb_f/ft^3]$

D) $61.2\,[lb_f/ft^3]$

Analysis:

weight of the cube

$$\Sigma F_y = 0 = F_{b,w} + F_{b,o} - W_{cube} \quad ←eq.1$$

buoyant force
from the water

buoyant force
from the oil

Eq.1 computes the sum of the
vertical forces at equilibrium.

Solve Eq.1 for the
weight of the cube.

$$W_{cube} = F_{b,w} + F_{b,o} \quad ←eq.2$$

$W_{cube} = \varrho_{cube} * g * V_{cube}$

Substitute in $\varrho_{cube} * g * V_{cube}$ for the
weight of the cube, then solve for the
density of the cube, ϱ_{cube}.

$$\varrho_{cube} = \frac{F_{b,w} + F_{b,o}}{g * V_{cube}} \quad ←eq.3$$

volume of water
displaced by the cube

$$F_{b,w} = \varrho_w * g * V_{cube,w} \quad ←eq.4$$

Use Eq.4 to compute the
buoyant force from the water.

$$s_{cube} = \sqrt[3]{V_{cube}} \quad ←eq.5$$

$V_{cube} = 1,000\,[in^3]$

Eq.5 computes the side
length of the cube.

Fluid Statics #4 (cont.)

$$s_{cube}= \sqrt[3]{1,000\,[in^3]}$$

$$s_{cube}=10\,[in]$$

side length
of the cube

Each side of the
cube is 10 inches:

$$h_{cube}= 10\,[in]$$
$$w_{cube}=10\,[in]$$
$$d_{cube}= 10\,[in]$$

$$d_{cube}=10\,[in]$$

$$V_{cube,w}=w_{cube}*d_{cube}*h_{cube,w} \leftarrow eq.6$$

$$w_{cube}=10\,[in] \qquad h_{cube,w}=2\,[in]$$

Plug in the variables d_{cube}, w_{cube}
and $h_{cube,w}$ into eq.6, then solve
for $V_{cube,w}$.

$$V_{cube,w}=10\,[in]*10\,[in]*2\,[in]$$

$$V_{cube,w}=200\,[in^3]$$

$$V_{cube,w}=200\,[in^3]$$

$$F_{b,w}=\varrho_w*g*V_{cube,w} \leftarrow eq.4$$

$$\varrho_w=62.4\,[lb_m/ft^3] \qquad g=32.2\,[ft/s^2]$$

Plug in variables ϱ_w, g and $V_{cube,w}$
into eq.4, then solve for $F_{b,w}$.

$$F_{b,w}=62.4\,[lb_m/ft^3]*32.2\,[ft/s^2]*200\,[in^3]$$

$$F_{b,w}=4.0186*10^5 \left[\frac{lb_m*in^3}{ft^2*s^2}\right]*\left(\frac{1}{12}\left[\frac{ft}{in}\right]\right)^3*\frac{1}{32.2}\left[\frac{lb_f*s^2}{lb_m*ft}\right]$$

conversion
factors

$$F_{b,w}=7.22\,[lb_f]$$

$$F_{b,o}=\varrho_o*g*V_{cube,o} \leftarrow eq.7$$

Eq.7 computes the buoyant
force from the oil.

$$d_{cube}=10\,[in]$$

$$V_{cube,o}=w_{cube}*d_{cube}*h_{cube,o} \leftarrow eq.8$$

$$w_{cube}=10\,[in] \qquad h_{cube,o}=8\,[in]$$

Plug in variables d_{cube}, w_{cube}
and $h_{cube,o}$ into eq.8, then
solve for $V_{cube,o}$.

Fluid Statics #4 (cont.)

$$V_{cube,w} = 10\,[in]*10\,[in]*8\,[in]$$

$$V_{cube,w} = 800\,[in^3]$$

$V_{cube,o} = 800\,[in^3]$

$$F_{b,o} = \varrho_o * g * V_{cube,o} \leftarrow eq.7$$

$\varrho_w = 56.2\,[lb_m/ft^3]$ $g = 32.2\,[ft/s^2]$

Plug in variables ϱ_o, g and $V_{cube,o}$ into Eq.7, then solve for $F_{b,o}$.

$$F_{b,o} = 56.2\,[lb_m/ft^3] * 32.2\,[ft/s^2] * 800\,[in^3]$$

$$F_{b,o} = 1.4477*10^6 \left[\frac{lb_m*in^3}{ft^2*s^2}\right] * \left(\frac{1}{12}\left[\frac{ft}{in}\right]\right)^3 * \frac{1}{32.2}\left[\frac{lb_f*s^2}{lb_m*ft}\right]$$

conversion factors

$$F_{b,o} = 26.02\,[lb_f]$$

$F_{b,w} = 7.22\,[lb_f]$ $F_{b,o} = 26.02\,[lb_f]$

$$\varrho_{cube} = \frac{F_{b,w} + F_{b,o}}{g * V_{cube}} \leftarrow eq.3$$

$g = 32.2\,[ft/s^2]$ $V_{cube} = 1,000\,[in^3]$

Plug in variables $F_{b,w}$, $F_{b,o}$, g and V_{cube} into eq.3, then solve for W_{cube}.

$$\varrho_{cube} = \frac{7.22\,[lb_f] + 26.02\,[lb_f]}{32.2\,[ft/s^2] * 1,000\,[in^3]}$$

unit conversions

$$\varrho_{cube} = 1.0323*10^{-3} \left[\frac{lb_f*s^2}{ft*in^3}\right] * \left(12\left[\frac{in}{ft}\right]\right)^3 * 32.2\left[\frac{lb_m*ft}{lb_f*s^2}\right]$$

$$\varrho_{cube} = 57.44\,[lb_m/ft^3]$$ **Answer:** $\boxed{A}$

Water Resources Practice Problems

Fluid Statics #5

<u>Find:</u> $W_{sphere,A}$ ← weight of the entire sphere, in air

<u>Given:</u> $r=1.75\,[ft]$ ← sphere radius

$SG_o=0.89$ } the specific gravity of each fluid
$SG_w=1.00$

air
oil
d_o
water
d_w
r
sphere

$d_o=1.00\,[ft]$ } the depth of the sphere in each fluid
$d_w=2.00\,[ft]$

$T=70°F$
temperature of both fluids

A) $1,271\,[lb_f]$
B) $1,399\,[lb_f]$
C) $1,525\,[lb_f]$
D) $1,652\,[lb_f]$

Analysis:

$$\Sigma F_y=0=F_b-W_{sphere,A} \leftarrow eq.1$$

Eq.1 computes the sum the forces in the vertical direction.

$$W_{sphere,A}=F_b \leftarrow eq.2$$

Solve eq.1 for the weight of the sphere, $W_{sphere,A}$.

density   volume

$$F_b=\Sigma \varrho_i*g*V_i \leftarrow eq.3$$

gravitational acceleration constant

Eq.3 computes the buoyant force for the sphere in material i.

$$F_b=\varrho_o*g*V_o+\varrho_w*g*V_w \leftarrow eq.4$$

subscript o for oil   subscript w for water

Write out the summation from eq.3.

$$\varrho_o=\varrho_w*SG_o \leftarrow eq.5$$

Eq.5 computes the density of the oil.

$$\varrho_o=\varrho_w*SG_o$$

$$F_b=\varrho_o*g*V_o+\varrho_w*g*V_w \leftarrow eq.4$$

Substitute the density of oil into Eq.4, then simplify.

300

Fluid Statics #5 (cont.)

$$F_b = \varrho_w * SG_o * g * V_o + \varrho_w * g * V_w$$

$$F_b = \varrho_w * g * (SG_o * V_o + V_w) \leftarrow eq.6$$

$$T = 70\,^\circ F \longrightarrow \varrho_w = 62.3\,[lb_m/ft^3]$$

Determine the water density based on the temperature.

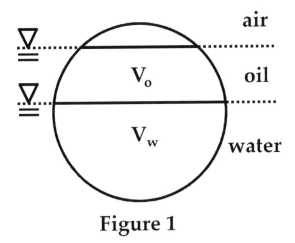

Figure 1

Figure 1 shows which parts of the sphere contribute to V_o and V_w.

It will be quicker and easier to approximate the volumes V_o and V_w, rather than compuate the exact values.

$$V_{sphere} = (4/3) * \pi * r^3 \leftarrow eq.7$$

$$r = 1.75\,[ft]$$

Eq.7 computes the volume of the entire sphere, V_{sphere}.

$$V_{sphere} = (4/3) * \pi * (1.75\,[ft])^3$$

$$V_{sphere} = 22.45\,[ft^3]$$

$$d_w = 2.00\,[ft]$$

$$d_a = 2 * r - d_w - d_o \leftarrow eq.8$$

$$r = 1.75\,[ft] \qquad d_o = 1.00\,[ft]$$

Eq.8 computes variable d_a, defined as the depth of the sphere exposed to air.

Fluid Statics #5 (cont.)

$$d_a = 2*1.75[ft] - 2.00[ft] - 1.00[ft]$$

$$d_a = 0.50[ft]$$

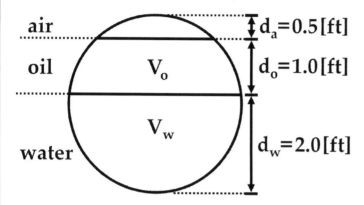

air $d_a = 0.5[ft]$

oil V_o $d_o = 1.0[ft]$

   V_w

water $d_w = 2.0[ft]$

Figure 2

We'll set approximate volumes $V_{w,1}$ and $V_{o,1}$ equal half the total volume of the sphere.

Substitute V_{sphere} into eq. 9, then compute $V_{w,1}$ and $V_{o,2}$.

$$V_{sphere} = 22.45[ft^3]$$

$$V_{w,1} = V_{o,1} = 0.5 * V_{sphere} \leftarrow eq.9$$

$$V_{w,1} = V_{o,1} = 0.5 * 22.45[ft^3]$$

$$V_{w,1} = V_{o,1} = 11.225[ft^3]$$

$$V_{w,1} = V_{o,1} = 11.225[ft^3]$$

$$g = 32.2[ft/s^2]$$

$$F_{b,1} = \varrho_w * g * (SG_o * V_{o,1} + V_{w,1}) \leftarrow eq.6$$

$$\varrho_w = 62.3[lb_m/ft^3]$$

$$SG_o = 0.89$$

Plug in variables $V_{w,1}$, $V_{o,1}$, g, ϱ_w and SG_o into eq. 6, then solve for $F_{b,1}$.

conversion factor

$$F_{b,1} = 62.3[lb_m/ft^3] * 32.2[ft/s^3]$$
$$* (0.89 * 11.225[ft^3] + 11.225[ft^3]) * \frac{1}{32.2}\left[\frac{lb_f * s^2}{lb_m * ft}\right]$$

Fluid Statics #5 (cont.)

$$F_{b,1}=1,322\,[lb_f]$$

Since $F_{b,1}=1,322\,[lb_f]$, the correct answer is most likely A or B.

A) 1,271 [lb$_f$]

B) 1,398 [lb$_f$]

~~C) 1,525 [lb$_f$]~~

~~D) 1,652 [lb$_f$]~~

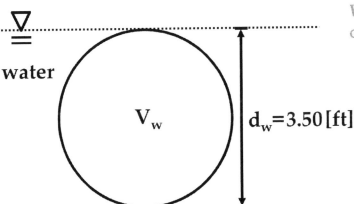

air

water

$$V_w$$

$$d_w=3.50\,[ft]$$

Compute a maximum value for $W_{sphere,A}$ by assuming the sphere is completely submerged in water.

Figure 3

$$V_{sphere}=22.45\,[ft^3]$$

$$V_{w,2}=V_{sphere} \leftarrow eq.11$$

Plug in V_{sphere} into eq.11, then solve for $V_{w,2}$.

$$V_{w,2}=22.45\,[ft^3]$$

Plug in the known variables into eq.6 and solve for the maximum buoyant force, F_b.

$$SG_o=0.89$$

$$g=32.2\,[ft/s^2]$$

$$V_{w,2}=22.45\,[ft^3]$$

$$F_{b,2}<\varrho_w*g*(SG_o*V_{o,2}+V_{w,2}) \leftarrow eq.6$$

$$\varrho_w=62.3\,[lb_m/ft^3]$$

$$V_{o,2}=0\,[ft^3]$$

$$F_b<62.3\,[lb_m/ft^3]*32.2\,[ft/s^3]*(0.89*0\,[ft^3]+22.45\,[ft^3])$$

Water Resources Practice Problems

Fluid Statics #5 (cont.)

$$F_b < 45,036 \left[\frac{lb_m * ft}{s^2} \right] * \frac{1}{32.2} \left[\frac{lb_f * s^2}{lb_m * ft} \right]$$

conversion factor

$$F_b < 1,399 \, [lb_f]$$

$$F_b = 1,271 \, [lb_f]$$

Since $F_b < 1,399 \, [lb_f]$, and our approximation $F_{b,1} = 1,322 \, [lb_f]$, then answer A is correct.

$$F_b = 1,271 \, [lb_f]$$

$$W_{sphere,A} = F_b \leftarrow eq.2$$

After plugging in F_b into eq.2, we can solve for $W_{sphere,A}$.

$$W_{sphere,A} = 1,271 \, [lb_f]$$

Answer: $\boxed{A}$

Fluid Statics #6

Find: ϱ_{cube} ← the density of the cube

Given:

$s=0.31\,[m]$ ← the side length of the cube

$m_{mass}=15\,[kg]$ ← the mass, m

$V_m=0.0070\,[m^3]$

volume of the mass, m

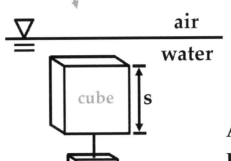

this system is in static equilibrium

air

water

cube | s

mass → m

temperature of the water

$T_w=25\,^{\circ}C$

A) $490\,[kg/m^3]$
B) $610\,[kg/m^3]$
C) $730\,[kg/m^3]$
D) $999\,[kg/m^3]$

Analysis:

cube mass

$$\varrho_{cube}=\frac{m_{cube}}{V_{cube}} \leftarrow eq.1$$

cube volume

Eq.1 computes the density of the cube.

$$V_{cube}=s^3 \leftarrow eq.2$$

$s=0.31\,[m]$

Eq.2 computes the volume of the cube.

Plug in variable s into eq.2, then solve for V_{cube}.

$$V_{cube}=0.0298\,[m^3]$$

$$\Sigma F_y=0=F_b-W_{cube}-W_m \leftarrow eq.3$$

Eq.3 sets the sum the forces in the vertical direction equal to 0.

$$W_{cube}=F_b-W_m \leftarrow eq.4$$

weight of the cube | buoyant force | weight of the mass

Solve Eq.3 for W_{cube}.

$g=9.81\,[m/s^2]$

$$W_m=m_{mass}*g \leftarrow eq.5$$

$m_{mass}=15\,[kg]$

Eq.5 computes the weight of the mass, which equals the mass, times the gravitational acceleration, g.

Plug in variables m_{mass} and g into eq.5, then solve for W_m.

Fluid Statics #6 (cont.)

$$W_m = 15\,[kg] * 9.81\,[m/s^2]$$

$$W_m = 147.2\,[N]$$

$$F_b = \varrho_w * g * V \leftarrow eq.6$$

Eq. 6 computes the buoyant force, F_b.

$$V_m = 0.0070\,[m^3]$$

$$V = V_{cube} + V_m \leftarrow eq.7$$

$$V_{cube} = 0.0298\,[m^3]$$

Eq. 7 computes the total volume.

Plug in variables V_{cube} and V_m into eq.7, then solve for V.

$$V = 0.0298\,[m^3] + 0.0070\,[m^3]$$

$$V = 0.0368\,[m^3]$$

$$T = 25\,^{\circ}C \longrightarrow \varrho_w = 997.1\,[kg/m^3]$$

Determine the water density based on the water temperature.

$$\varrho_w = 997.1\,[kg/m^3]$$

$$F_b = \varrho_w * g * V \leftarrow eq.6$$

$$g = 9.81\,[m/s^2] \qquad V = 0.0368\,[m^3]$$

Plug in variables ϱ_w, g, and V into eq.6, then solve for F_b.

$$F_b = 997.1\,[kg/m^3] * 9.81\,[m/s^2] * 0.0368[m^3]$$

$$F_b = 360.0\,[N]$$

$$F_b = 360.0\,[N] \qquad W_m = 147.2\,[N]$$

$$W_{cube} = F_b - W_m \leftarrow eq.4$$

Plug in variables F_b and W_m into eq.4, then solve for W_{cube}.

Fluid Statics #6 (cont.)

$$W_{cube}=360.0[N]-147.2[N]$$

$$W_{cube}=212.8[N]$$

$$W_{cube}=212.8[N]$$

$$m_{cube}=\frac{W_{cube}}{g} \leftarrow eq.8$$

$$g=9.81[m/s^2]$$

Eq.8 computes the mass of the cube.

Plug in variables W_{cube} and g into eq.8, then solve for m_{cube}.

$$m_{cube}=\frac{212.8[N]}{9.81[m/s^2]}$$

$$m_{cube}=21.69[kg]$$

$$m_{cube}=21.69[kg]$$

$$\varrho_{cube}=\frac{m_{cube}}{V_{cube}} \leftarrow eq.1$$

$$V_{cube}=0.0298[m^3]$$

Plug in variables m_{cube} and V_{cube} into eq.1, then solve for ϱ_{cube}.

$$\varrho_{cube}=\frac{21.69[kg]}{0.0298[m^3]}$$

$$\varrho_{cube}=727.9[kg/m^3]$$

Answer: $\boxed{C}$

Water Resources Practice Problems

Fluid Statics #7

Find: SG ←the specific gravity of the fluid

$\varrho_{cone}=850\,[kg/m^3]$ ← the density of the cone

Given:

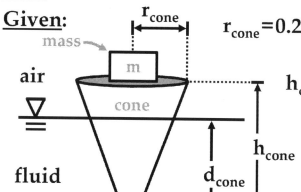

$r_{cone}=0.28\,[m]$ ← the radius of the cone

$h_{cone}=1.12\,[m]$ ← the height of the cone

$m_{mass}=20\,[kg]$

$d_{cone}=0.93\,[m]$ ← the depth of the cone submerged in the fluid

A) 1.05

B) 1.31

C) 1.58

D) 1.86

Analysis:

$F_b=SG*\varrho_w*g*V_{cone,s}$ ←eq.1

specific gravity

Eq.1 computes the buoyant force.

$SG=\dfrac{F_b}{\varrho_w*g*V_{cone,s}}$ ←eq.1

buoyant force

density of water

volume of the cone which is submerged

Solve eq.1 for SG.

When no temperature is given, assume standard temperature (20°C), therefore $\varrho_w=998.2\,[kg/m^3]$

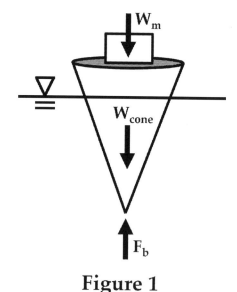

Figure 1 identifies the vertical forces acting on the system.

The downward force from the mass and cone is resisted by the buoyant force, F_b.

Figure 1

$\Sigma F_y=0=F_b-W_m-W_{cone}$ ←eq.3

Eq.3 computes the sum of the forces in the vertical direction.

Fluid Statics #7 (cont.)

$$F_b = W_m + W_{cone} \leftarrow eq.4$$

Solve eq. 3 for the buoyant force.

$$g=9.81\,[m/s^2]$$

Eq. 5 computes the weight of the mass.

$$W_m = m_m * g \leftarrow eq.5$$

$$m=20\,[kg]$$

Plug in variables g and m_m into eq. 5, then solve for W_m.

$$W_m = 20\,[kg] * 9.81\,[m/s^2]$$

$$W_m = 196.2\,[N]$$

$$W_{cone} = \varrho_{cone} * g * V_{cone} \leftarrow eq.6$$

Eq. 6 computes the weight of the cone.

$$V_{cone} = (1/3) * \pi * r_{cone}^2 * h_{cone} \leftarrow eq.7$$

$$r_{cone} = 0.28\,[m] \qquad h_{cone} = 1.12\,[m]$$

Eq. 7 computes the volume of the entire cone. Plug in variables r_{cone} and h_{cone} into eq. 7, then solve for V_{cone}.

$$V_{cone} = (1/3) * \pi * (0.28\,[m])^2 * 1.12\,[m]$$

$$V_{cone} = 0.0920\,[m^3]$$

$$V_{cone} = 0.0920\,[m^3]$$

$$W_{cone} = \varrho_{cone} * g * V_{cone} \leftarrow eq.6$$

$$\varrho_{cone} = 850\,[kg/m^3] \qquad g = 9.81\,[m/s^2]$$

Plug in variables ϱ_{cone}, g, and V_{cone} into eq. 6, then solve for W_{cone}.

$$W_{cone} = 850\,[kg/m^3] * 9.81\,[m/s^2] * 0.0920\,[m^3]$$

$$W_{cone} = 767.1\,[N]$$

Water Resources Practice Problems

Fluid Statics #7 (cont.)

$W_{cone} = 767.1\,[N]$

$$F_b = W_m + W_{cone} \leftarrow eq.4$$

$W_m = 196.2\,[N]$

Plug in variables W_m and W_{cone} into Eq. 4, and solve for variable F_b.

$$F_b = 196.2\,[N] + 767.1\,[N]$$

$$F_b = 963.3\,[N]$$

$$V_{cone,s} = (1/3) * \pi * r_{cone,s}^2 * d_{cone} \leftarrow eq.8$$

radius of the cone at the water level

submerged depth of the cone

Eq. 8 computes the submerged volume of the cone.

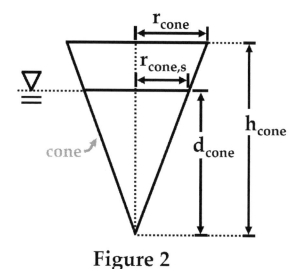

Figure 2

Figure 2 shows the similar triangles involving lengths d_{cone}, $r_{cone,s}$, h_{cone} and r_{cone}.

$$\frac{r_{cone,s}}{r_{cone}} = \frac{d_{cone}}{h_{cone}} \leftarrow eq.9$$

Eq. 9 relates $r_{cone,s}$ to the other three lengths shown in Figure 2.

$d_{cone} = 0.93\,[m]$

$$r_{cone,s} = r_{cone} * \frac{d_{cone}}{h_{cone}}$$

$r_{cone} = 0.28\,[m]$ $h_{cone} = 1.12\,[m]$

Solve Eq. 9 for $r_{cone,s}$, plug in r_{cone}, d_{cone} and h_{cone}, and solve for $r_{cone,s}$.

310

Fluid Statics #7 (cont.)

$$r_{cone,s} = 0.28[m] * \frac{0.93[m]}{1.12[m]}$$

$$r_{cone,s} = 0.233[m]$$

Plug in $r_{cone,s}$ and d_{cone} into eq.8, then solve for $V_{cone,s}$.

$$r_{cone,s} = 0.233[m]$$

$$V_{cone,s} = (1/3) * \pi * r_{cone,s}^2 * d_{cone} \leftarrow eq.8$$

$$d_{cone} = 0.93[m]$$

$$V_{cone,s} = (1/3) * \pi * (0.233[m])^2 * 0.93[m]$$

$$V_{cone,s} = 0.0529[m^3]$$

$$g = 9.81[m/s^2] \qquad F_b = 963.3[N]$$

$$SG = \frac{F_b}{\varrho_w * g * V_{cone,s}} \leftarrow eq.2$$

Plug in variables F_b, ϱ_w, g and $V_{cone,s}$, then solve for SG.

$$\varrho_w = 998.2[kg/m^3] \qquad V_{cone,s} = 0.0529[m^3]$$

$$SG = \frac{963.3[N]}{998.2[kg/m^3] * 9.81[m/s^2] * 0.0529[m^3]}$$

$$SG = 1.86$$

Answer: $\boxed{D}$

Water Resources Practice Problems

Fluid Statics #8

Find: F_R ← the hydrostatic force acting on the gate

Given:

$d_{top}=1[ft]$ ← vertical distance from the water surface to the top of the gate.

$w_{gate}=5[ft]$ ← width of the gate

$h_{gate}=4[ft]$ ← height of the gate

$T=50°F$
water temperature

cross section of the gate

$\theta=30°$
angle

A) $125[lb_f]$

B) $2,500[lb_f]$

C) $3,750[lb_f]$

D) $5,000[lb_f]$

Analysis:

$$F_R=P_c*A \leftarrow eq.1$$

centroidal pressure   area

Eq.1 computes the hydrostatic force at the centroid of the gate times the gate area.

$$A=w_{gate}*h_{gate} \leftarrow eq.2$$

$w_{gate}=5[ft]$ $h_{gate}=4[ft]$

Eq.2 computes the area of the gate. Plug in variables w_{gate} and h_{gate}, then solve for A.

$$A=5[ft]*4[ft]$$

$$A=20[ft^2]$$

$$P_c=\varrho*g*d_c \leftarrow eq.3$$

fluid density   depth to the centroid of the gate

Eq.3 computes the pressure at the centroid of the gate.

$h_{gate}=4[ft]$

Eq.4 computes the depth to the centroid of the gate.

$$d_c=d_{top}+0.5*h_{gate}*\sin(\theta) \leftarrow eq.4$$

$d_{top}=1[ft]$ $\theta=30°$

Plug in variables d_{top}, h_{gate} and θ into eq.4, then solve for d_c.

$$d_c=1[ft]+0.5*4[ft]*\sin(30°)$$

Fluid Statics #8 (cont.)

$$d_c = 2 \, [\text{ft}]$$

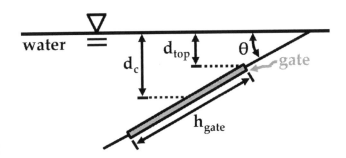

Figure 1

Figure 1 shows the depth to the centroid of the gate, d_c.

$$T = 50°F \longrightarrow \varrho_w = 62.4 \, [\text{lb}_m/\text{ft}^3]$$

Determine the water density based on the water temperature.

$\varrho = 62.4 \, [\text{lb}_m/\text{ft}^3]$

$$P_c = \varrho * g * d_c \longleftarrow eq.3$$

$g = 32.2 \, [\text{ft/s}^2] \qquad d_c = 2 \, [\text{ft}]$

Plug in variables ϱ_w, g, and d_c into Eq. 3, then solve for P_c.

$$P_c = 62.4 \, [\text{lb}_m/\text{ft}^3] * 32.2 \, [\text{ft/s}^2] * 2 \, [\text{ft}] * \frac{1}{32.2} \left[\frac{\text{lb}_f * \text{s}^2}{\text{lb}_m * \text{ft}} \right]$$

$$P_c = 124.8 \, [\text{lb}_f/\text{ft}^2]$$

conversion factor.

$P_c = 124.8 \, [\text{lb}_f/\text{ft}^2]$

$$F_R = P_c * A \longleftarrow eq.1$$

$A = 20 \, [\text{ft}^2]$

Return to eq. 1, plug in variables P_c and A, then solve for F_R.

$$F_R = 124.8 \, [\text{lb}_f/\text{ft}^2] * 20 \, [\text{ft}^2]$$

$$F_R = 2{,}496 \, [\text{lb}_f]$$

Answer: $\boxed{\text{B}}$

Water Resources Practice Problems

Fluid Statics #9

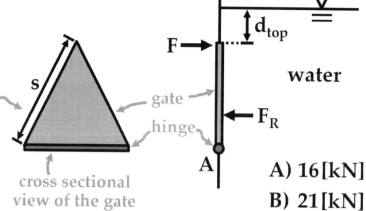

Find: F ← the force required to hold the gate shut

Given:

the gate is in the shape of an equilateral triangle

$s=3\,[m]$ ← the length of one side of the gate

$d_{top}=1\,[m]$ ← the depth to the top of the gate

cross sectional view of the gate

water

A) 16 [kN]

B) 21 [kN]

C) 26 [kN]

D) 31 [kN]

Analysis:

$$\Sigma M_A = 0 = F_R * x - F * h_{gate} \quad \leftarrow eq.1$$

Eq.1 computes sums the moments about the hinge of the gate at point A.

$$F = \frac{F_R * x}{h_{gate}} \quad \leftarrow eq.2$$

Solve eq.1 for force F.

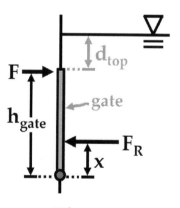

Figure 1

Figure 1 identifies the forces and distances used in Eq.2.

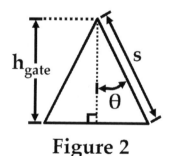

Figure 2

Figure 2 shows the trigonometric relationship between s, h_{gate}, and θ.

Fluid Statics #9 (cont.)

$$h_{gate}=s*\cos(\theta) \leftarrow eq.3$$

Eq.3 computes the height of the gate.

$$\theta=180°/6$$

$$\theta=30°$$

Compute angle theta, by knowing the gate is an equilateral triangle.

$$h_{gate}=s*\cos(\theta) \leftarrow eq.3$$
$$s=3[m] \quad \theta=30°$$

Plug in s and θ into eq.3, then solve for h_{gate}.

$$h_{gate}=3[m]*\cos(30°)$$

$$h_{gate}=2.598[m]$$

$$x=d_{top}+h_{gate}-d_{cp} \leftarrow eq.4$$

depth to the top of the gate

depth to the center of pressure of the gate

Eq.4 computes the distance x.

centroidal moment area of inertia

$$d_{cp}=d_{top}+y_c+\frac{I_c}{y_c*A} \leftarrow eq.5$$

area of the gate

vertical distance from the top of the gate to the centroid of the gate

Eq.5 computes the depth to the center of pressure of the gate.

$$s=b=3[m] \quad h_{gate}=2.598[m]$$

$$I_c=\frac{b*h_{gate}^3}{36} \leftarrow eq.6$$

Plug in b and h_{gate} into eq.6, then compute I_c.

$$I_c=\frac{3[m]*(2.598[m])^3}{36}$$

Water Resources Practice Problems

Fluid Statics #9 (cont.)

$$I_c = 1.461 \, [m^4]$$

$$A = 0.5 * b * h_{gate} \leftarrow eq.7$$

$$b = 3 \, [m] \quad h_{gate} = 2.598 \, [m]$$

Eq.7 computes the area of the gate.

Plug in variables b and h_{gate} into eq.7, then solve for A.

$$A = 0.5 * 3 \, [m] * 2.598 \, [m]$$

$$A = 3.897 \, [m^2]$$

$$y_c = (2/3) * h_{gate} \leftarrow eq.8$$

$$h_{gate} = 2.598 \, [m]$$

Eq.8 computes y_c, the distance from the top of the gate to the centroid of the gate.

Plug in variable h_{gate} into eq.8, then solve for y_c.

$$y_c = (2/3) * 2.598 \, [m]$$

$$y_c = 1.732 \, [m]$$

$$d_{cp} = d_{top} + y_c + \frac{I_c}{y_c * A} \leftarrow eq.5$$

$$d_{top} = 1 \, [m] \quad I_c = 1.461 \, [m^4]$$

$$y_c = 1.732 \, [m] \quad A = 3.897 \, [m^2]$$

Plug in variables d_{top}, y_c, I_c, and A into eq.5, then compute d_{cp}.

Should be $y_c + d_{top} = 2.732$

$$d_{cp} = 1 \, [m] + 1.732 \, [m] + \frac{1.461 \, [m^4]}{1.732 \, [m] * 3.897 \, [m^2]}$$

2.732 ?

$$d_{cp} = 2.948 \, [m]$$

$$x = d_{top} + h_{gate} - d_{cp} \leftarrow eq.4$$

$$h_{gate} = 2.598 \, [m]$$

$$d_{top} = 1 \, [m] \quad d_{cp} = 2.948 \, [m]$$

Plug in variables d_{top}, h_{gate}, and d_{cp} into eq.4, then compute x.

316

Fluid Statics #9 (cont.)

$$x=1[m]+2.598[m]-2.948[m]$$

$$x=0.65[m]$$

hydraulic force   gate area

$$F_R=\varrho*g*d_c*A \leftarrow eq.9$$

fluid density   depth to the centroid

Eq.9 computes the hydraulic force, F_R.

$$d_c=d_{top}+y_c \leftarrow eq.10$$

$d_{top}=1[m]$ $y_c=1.732[m]$

Compute the depth to the centroid using d_{top} and y_c, in eq.10.

$$d_c=1[m]+1.732[m]$$

$$d_c=2.732[m]$$

$\varrho=999[kg/m^3]$ $d_c=2.732[m]$

$$F_R=\varrho*g*d_c*A \leftarrow eq.9$$

$g=9.81[m/s^2]$ $A=3.897[m^2]$

Plug in variables ϱ, g, d_c and A into Eq.9, then solve for F_R.

$$F_R=999[kg/m^3]*9.81[m/s^2]*2.732[m]*3.897[m^2]$$

$$F_R=1.043*10^5[N]$$

$F_R=1.043*10^5[N]$

$$F=\frac{F_R*x}{h_{gate}} \leftarrow eq.2$$

$h_{gate}=2.598[m]$ $x=0.65[m]$

Plug in variables F_R, x and h_{gate} into eq.2, then solve for F.

$$F=\frac{1.043*10^5[N]*0.65[m]}{2.598[m]}$$

29,300 N

$$F=26,095[N]$$ Answer: $\boxed{C}$

X

Water Resources Practice Problems

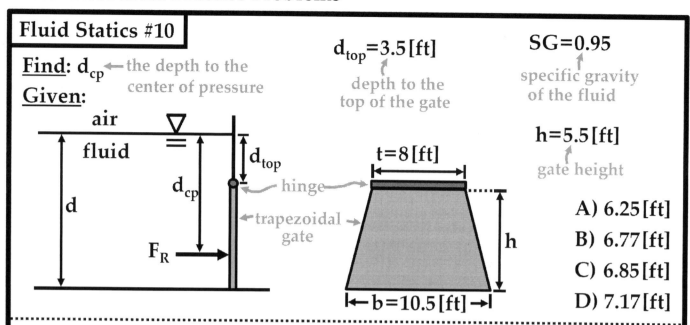

Fluid Statics #10

Find: d_{cp} ← the depth to the center of pressure

Given:

$d_{top}=3.5\,[ft]$ — depth to the top of the gate

$SG=0.95$ — specific gravity of the fluid

air

fluid

d

d_{top}

d_{cp}

F_R

hinge

trapezoidal gate

$t=8\,[ft]$

h

$b=10.5\,[ft]$

$h=5.5\,[ft]$ — gate height

A) 6.25 [ft]

B) 6.77 [ft]

C) 6.85 [ft]

D) 7.17 [ft]

Analysis:

$$d_{cp}=d_c+\frac{I_c}{d_c*A} \leftarrow eq.1$$

centroidal area moment of inertia of the gate

depth to the centroid of the gate

area of the gate

Eq.1 computes the depth to the center of pressure on the gate.

$$d_c=d-h*\left(\frac{b+2*t}{3*b+3*t}\right) \leftarrow eq.2$$

gate height

base width of the gate

depth of the fluid

top width of the gate

Eq.2 computes the depth to the centroid.

$$d=d_{top}+h \leftarrow eq.3$$

$d_{top}=3.5\,[ft]$ $h=5.5\,[ft]$

Plug in variables d_{top} and h into eq.3, then compute the depth of the fluid, d.

$$d=3.5\,[ft]+5.5\,[ft]$$

$$d=9.0\,[ft]$$

Fluid Statics #10 (cont.)

h=5.5 [ft]　　b=10.5 [ft]

$$d_c = d - h * \left(\frac{b + 2*t}{3*b + 3*t} \right) \leftarrow eq.2$$

d=9.0 [ft]　　t=8 [ft]

Plug in variables d, h, b and t into eq. 2, then solve for d_c.

$$d_c = 9[ft] - 5.5[ft] * \left(\frac{10.5[ft] + 2*8[ft]}{3*10.5[ft] + 3*8[ft]} \right)$$

$$d_c = 6.374 [ft]$$

t=8 [ft]　　h=5.5 [ft]

$$I_c = \frac{(b^2 + 4*t*b + t^2) * h^3}{36*(b+t)} \leftarrow eq.4$$

b=10.5 [ft]

Eq. 4 computes the area moment of inertia for a trapezoid.

Plug in variables b, t and h into eq. 4, then solve for I_c.

$$I_c = \frac{(10.5[ft]^2 + 4*8[ft]*10.5[ft] + 8[ft]^2) * 5.5[ft]^3}{36*(10.5[ft] + 8[ft])}$$

$$I_c = 127.5 [ft^4]$$

Eq. 5 computes the area of the trapezoidal gate.

t=8 [ft]　　h=5.5 [ft]

$$A = 0.5 * (t + b) * h \leftarrow eq.5$$

b=10.5 [ft]

Plug in variables t, b and h into eq. 5, then solve for A.

$$A = 0.5 * (8[ft] + 10.5[ft]) * 5.5[ft]$$

$$A = 50.88 [ft^2]$$

Water Resources Practice Problems

Fluid Statics #10 (cont.)

$$I_c = 127.5 \, [ft^4]$$

$$d_{cp} = d_c + \frac{I_c}{d_c * A} \quad \leftarrow eq.1$$

$$d_c = 6.374 \, [ft] \qquad A = 50.88 \, [ft^2]$$

Plug in variables d_c, I_c and A into eq.1, then solve for the depth to the center of pressure, d_{cp}.

$$d_{cp} = 6.374 \, [ft] + \frac{127.5 \, [ft^4]}{6.374 \, [ft] * 50.88 \, [ft^2]}$$

$$d_{cp} = 6.767 \, [ft]$$

Answer: B

Fluid Statics #11

Find: ϱ_A ← the density of the fluid A

Given:

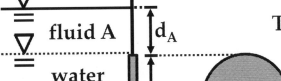

$D_{gate}=2\,[m]$
↑
diameter of the gate

$F_R=5.912*10^4\,[N]$
↑
reaction force acting on the gate caused by the fluids

$T=20\,^{\circ}C$ ← the temperature of both fluids

$d_A=1\,[m]$ ← depth of fluid A

A) $900\,[kg/m^3]$
B) $920\,[kg/m^3]$
C) $940\,[kg/m^3]$
D) $960\,[kg/m^3]$

gate   cross-section view of the gate

Analysis:

$$F_R=P_c*A \leftarrow eq.1$$

centroidal pressure   area

Eq.1 computes the hydraulic force on the gate, F_R.

density of the fluid A

$$P_c=\varrho_A*g*d_A+\varrho_w*g*(d_c-d_A) \leftarrow eq.2$$

Eq.2 computes the centroidal pressure.

Solve eq.2 for the density of fluid A.

$$\varrho_A=\frac{P_c-\varrho_w*g*(d_c-d_A)}{g*d_A} \leftarrow eq.3$$

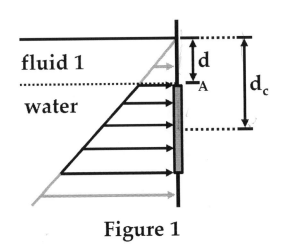

Figure 1 shows the pressure distribution, the depth of fluid A, d_A, and the depth to the centroid of the gate, d_c.

Figure 1

Water Resources Practice Problems

Fluid Statics #11 (cont.)

$$P_c = \frac{F_R}{A} \leftarrow eq.4$$

the resultant hydraulic force

the area of the gate

Solve eq. 1 for P_c.

$$A = \frac{\pi}{4} * D_{gate}^2 \leftarrow eq.5$$

$D_{gate} = 2 \, [m]$

Eq. 5 computes the area of the gate.

Plug in variable D_{gate} into eq. 5, then solve for A.

$$A = \frac{\pi}{4} * (2 \, [m])^2$$

$$A = 3.142 \, [m^2]$$

$F_R = 5.912 * 10^4 \, [N]$

$$P_c = \frac{F_R}{A} \leftarrow eq.4$$

$A = 3.142 \, [m^2]$

Plug in variables F_R and A into eq. 4, then solve for P_c.

$$P_c = \frac{5.912 * 10^4 \, [N]}{3.142 \, [m^2]}$$

$$P_c = 1.882 * 10^4 \, [N/m^2]$$

$$T = 20°C \rightarrow \varrho_w = 998.2 \, [kg/m^3]$$

Determine the density of water based on the water temperature.

$d_A = 1 \, [m]$

$$d_c = d_A + 0.5 * D_{gate} \leftarrow eq.6$$

$D_{gate} = 2 \, [m]$

Eq. 6 computes the depth to the centroid of the circular gate.

Plug in variables d_A and D_{gate} into eq. 6, then solve for d_c.

Fluid Statics #11 (cont.)

$$d_c = 1[m] + 0.5 * 2[m]$$

$$d_c = 2[m]$$

$$P_c = 1.882 * 10^4 [N/m^2] \qquad d_c = 2[m]$$

$$\varrho_A = \frac{P_c - \varrho_w * g * (d_c - d_A)}{g * d_A} \leftarrow eq.3$$

$$\varrho_w = 998.2 [kg/m^3] \qquad g = 9.81 [m/s^3] \qquad d_A = 1[m]$$

Plug in variables P_c, d_c, ϱ_w, g and d_A into eq.3, then solve for ϱ_A.

$$\varrho_A = \frac{1.882 * 10^4 [N/m^2] - \{998.2 [kg/m^3] * 9.81 [m/s^2] * (2[m] - 1[m])\}}{9.81 [m/s^2] * 1[m]}$$

$$\varrho_A = 920.3 [kg/m^3]$$

Answer: $\boxed{B}$

Water Resources Practice Problems

Fluid Statics #12

Find: F ← the force required to hold the gate shut

Given:

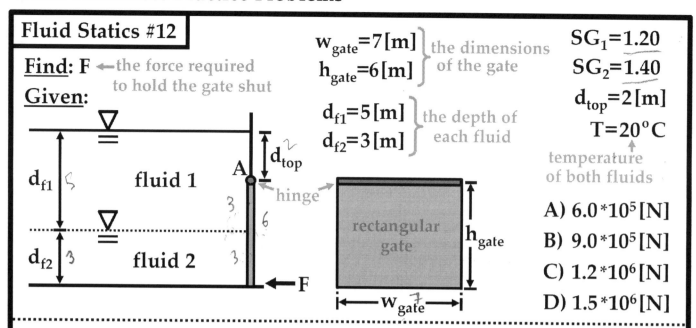

$w_{gate}=7\,[m]$ } the dimensions
$h_{gate}=6\,[m]$ } of the gate

$SG_1=1.20$
$SG_2=1.40$

$d_{f1}=5\,[m]$ } the depth of
$d_{f2}=3\,[m]$ } each fluid

$d_{top}=2\,[m]$
$T=20°C$

temperature of both fluids

A) $6.0*10^5\,[N]$
B) $9.0*10^5\,[N]$
C) $1.2*10^6\,[N]$
D) $1.5*10^6\,[N]$

Analysis:

We'll analyze the force from the fluids as two separate forces acting on two separate gates.

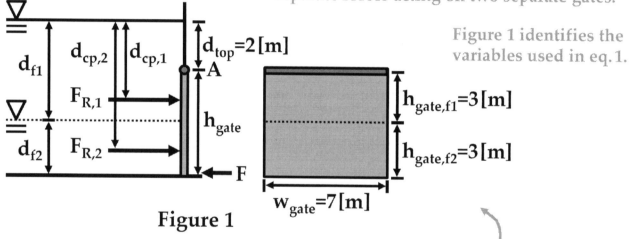

Figure 1 identifies the variables used in eq. 1.

$h_{gate,f1}=3\,[m]$
$h_{gate,f2}=3\,[m]$

Figure 1

$h_{gate,f1}$ is in contact with fluid 1.
$h_{gate,f2}$ is in contact with fluid 2.

Set the sum of the moments about the hinge at point A equal to zero.

$$\Sigma M_A=0=F_{R,1}*(d_{cp,1}-d_{top})+F_{R,2}*(d_{cp,2}-d_{top})-F*h_{gate} \leftarrow eq.1$$

depth to the center of pressure for fluid 1 and fluid 2

Solve eq. 1 for the force F.

$$F=\frac{F_{R,1}*(d_{cp,1}-d_{top})+F_{R,2}*(d_{cp,2}-d_{top})}{h_{gate}} \leftarrow eq.2 \;\checkmark$$

$F_{R,1}$ and $F_{R,2}$ is the static force caused by fluids 1 and 2 respectively. Variables $d_{cp,1}$ and $d_{cp,2}$ are the depth to the center of pressure for these two forces, and is slightly lower than $d_{c,1}$ and $d_{c,2}$, the centroidal depths.

Fluid Statics #12 (cont.)

$$F_{R,1}=SG_1*\varrho_w*g*d_{c,1}*A_1 \leftarrow eq.3$$

Eq.3 computes variable $F_{R,1}$.

$$A_1=w_{gate}*h_{gate,f1} \leftarrow eq.4$$

$w_{gate}=7\,[m] \qquad h_{gate,f1}=3\,[m]$

Plug in variables w_{gate} and $h_{gate,f1}$ into eq.4, then solve for A_1.

$$A_1=7\,[m]*3\,[m]$$

$$A_1=21\,[m^2]$$

$$d_{c,1}=d_{top}+0.5*h_{gate,f1} \leftarrow eq.5$$

Eq.5 computes variable $d_{c,1}$.

$d_{top}=2\,[m] \qquad h_{gate,f1}=3\,[m]$

Plug in variables d_{top} and $h_{gate,f1}$ into eq.5, then solve for $d_{c,1}$.

$$d_{c,1}=2\,[m]+0.5*3\,[m]$$

$$d_{c,1}=3.5\,[m]$$

$$T=20\,°C \rightarrow \varrho_w=998.2\,[kg/m^3]$$

Determine the density of water based on the given temperature.

$\varrho_w=998.2\,[kg/m^3] \qquad d_{c,1}=3.5\,[m]$

$$F_{R,1}=SG_1*\varrho_w*g*d_{c,1}*A_1 \leftarrow eq.3$$

$SG_1=1.20 \qquad g=9.81\,[m/s^2] \qquad A_1=21\,[m^2]$

Plug in variables SG_1, ϱ_w, g, $d_{c,1}$, and A_1 into eq.3, then solve for $F_{R,1}$.

$$F_{R,1}=1.20*998.2\,[kg/m^3]*9.81\,[m^3]*3.5\,[m]*21\,[m^2]$$

$$F_{R,1}=8.637*10^5\,[N]$$

Eq.6 computes variable $F_{R,2}$.

$$F_{R,2}=(SG_1*\varrho_w*g*(d_{top}+h_{gate,f1})+SG_2*\varrho_w*g*0.5*h_{gate,f2}))*A_2 \leftarrow eq.6$$

Water Resources Practice Problems

Fluid Statics #12 (cont.)

$$A_2 = w_{gate} * h_{gate,f2} \leftarrow eq.7$$

$$w_{gate} = 7\,[m] \qquad h_{gate,f2} = 3\,[m]$$

Eq.7 computes variable A_2. Plug in variables w_{gate} and $h_{gate,f2}$ into eq.7, then solve for A_2.

$$A_2 = 7\,[m] * 3\,[m]$$

$$A_2 = 21\,[m^2]$$

Simplify eq.6, then plug in the known variables and solve for $F_{R,2}$.

$$g = 9.81\,[m/s^2] \qquad SG_1 = 1.20 \qquad h_{gate,f1} = 3\,[m] \qquad A_2 = 21\,[m^2]$$

$$F_{R,2} = (\varrho_w * g * \{SG_1 * (d_{top} + h_{gate,f1}) + 0.5 * SG_2 * h_{gate,f2}\}) * A_2 \leftarrow eq.6$$

$$\varrho_w = 998.2\,[kg/m^3] \qquad d_{top} = 2\,[m] \qquad SG_2 = 1.40 \qquad h_{gate,f2} = 3\,[m]$$

$$F_{R,2} = (998.2\,[kg/m^3] * 9.81\,[m/s^2] * \{1.20 * (2\,[m] + 3\,[m])$$
$$+ 0.5 * 1.40 * 3\,[m]\}) * 21\,[m^2]$$

$$F_{R,2} = 1.666 * 10^6\,[N]$$

$$d_{cp,1} = d_{c,1} + \frac{I_{c,1}}{d_{c,1} * A_1} \leftarrow eq.8$$

Eq.8 computes the depth to the center of pressure on the gate for fluid 1.

$$w_{gate} = 7\,[m] \qquad h_{gate,f1} = 3\,[m]$$

$$I_{c,1} = \frac{w_{gate} * h_{gate,f1}^3}{12} \leftarrow eq.9$$

Eq.9 computes $I_{C,1}$ for a rectangle. Plug in variables w_{gate} and $h_{gate,f1}$ into eq.9, then solve for $I_{C,1}$.

$$I_{c,1} = \frac{7\,[m] * (3\,[m])^3}{12}$$

$$I_{c,1} = 15.75\,[m^4]$$

Fluid Statics #12 (cont.)

$I_{c,1}=15.75\,[\text{m}^4]$

$$d_{cp,1}=d_{c,1}+\frac{I_{c,1}}{d_{c,1}*A_1} \leftarrow eq.\,8$$

$d_{c,1}=3.5\,[\text{m}]$ $A_1=21\,[\text{m}^2]$

Plug in variables $d_{c,1}$, $I_{c,1}$ and A_1 into eq.8, then solve for $d_{cp,1}$.

$$d_{cp,1}=3.5\,[\text{m}]+\frac{15.75\,[\text{m}^4]}{3.5\,[\text{m}]*21\,[\text{m}^2]}$$

$$d_{cp,1}=3.714\,[\text{m}]$$

$$d_{cp,2}=d_{c,2}+\frac{I_{c,2}}{d_{c,2}*A_2} \leftarrow eq.\,10$$

Eq. 10 computes the depth to the center of pressure on the gate for fluid 1.

$w_{gate}=7\,[\text{m}]$ $h_{gate,f2}=3\,[\text{m}]$

$$I_{c,2}=\frac{w_{gate}*h_{gate,f2}^{3}}{12} \leftarrow eq.\,11$$

Eq.11 computes $I_{C,2}$ for a rectangle. Plug in variables w_{gate} and $h_{gate,f2}$ into eq.11, then solve for $I_{C,2}$.

$$I_{c,2}=\frac{7\,[\text{m}]*(3\,[\text{m}])^{3}}{12}$$

$$I_{c,2}=15.75\,[\text{m}^4]$$

$I_{c,2}=15.75\,[\text{m}^4]$

$$d_{cp,2}=d_{c,2}+\frac{I_{c,2}}{d_{c,2}*A_2} \leftarrow eq.\,10$$

$d_{c,2}=6.5\,[\text{m}]$ $A_2=21\,[\text{m}^2]$

Plug in variables $d_{c,2}$, $I_{c,2}$ and A_2 into eq.10, then solve for $d_{cp,2}$.

$$d_{cp,2}=6.5\,[\text{m}]+\frac{15.75\,[\text{m}^4]}{6.5\,[\text{m}]*21\,[\text{m}^2]}$$

Fluid Statics #12 (cont.)

$$d_{cp,2} = 6.615 \, [m]$$

Plug in the known variables into eq. 2, then solve for the force, F.

$d_{cp,1} = 3.714 \, [m]$ $d_{top} = 2 \, [m]$ $d_{cp,2} = 6.615 \, [m]$

$$F = \frac{F_{R,1} * (d_{cp,1} - d_{top}) + F_{R,2} * (d_{cp,2} - d_{top})}{h_{gate}} \leftarrow eq. \, 2$$

$F_{R,1} = 8.637 * 10^5 \, [N]$ $h_{gate} = 6 \, [m]$ $F_{R,2} = 1.666 * 10^6 \, [N]$

$$F = \frac{8.637 * 10^5 \, [N] * (3.714 \, [m] - 2 \, [m]) + 1.666 * 10^6 \, [N] * (6.615 \, [m] - 2 \, [m])}{6 \, [m]}$$

$$F = 1.528 * 10^6 \, [N]$$

Answer: $\boxed{D}$

Fluid Dynamics #1

<u>Find:</u> F_R ← the reaction force required to hold the vane stationary

<u>Given:</u>

$Q=0.10\,[m^3/s]$
    flow rate

$v_o=28\,[m/s]$ ← velocity of flow

$\varrho=900\,[kg/m^3]$ ← density of the fluid

    neglect forces due to gravity and pressure

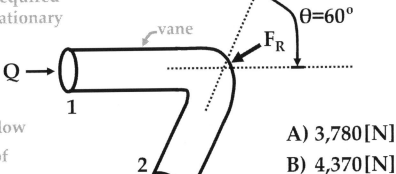

A) 3,780 [N]

B) 4,370 [N]

C) 5,180 [N]

D) 5,960 [N]

Analysis:

$$F_R=\sqrt{F_{R,x}^2+F_{R,y}^2} \quad \leftarrow eq.1$$

Eq.1 computes the reaction force F_R.

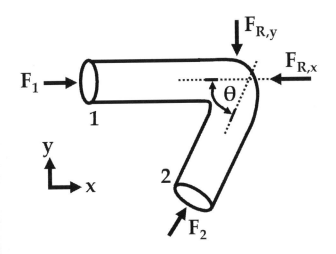

Figure 1

Figure 1 includes the x-y coordinate reference, and identifies the forces acting on the vane.

$$\Sigma F_x=0=F_1+F_2*\cos(\theta)-F_{R,x} \quad \leftarrow eq.2$$

Eq.2 sets the sum of the forces in the horizontal direction equal to zero.

$$F_{R,x}=F_1+F_2*\cos(\theta) \quad \leftarrow eq.3$$

Solve eq.2 for $F_{R,x}$.

$\varrho=900\,[kg/m^3] \quad v_o=28\,[m/s]$

$$F_1=F_2=\varrho*Q*v_o \quad \leftarrow eq.4$$

$Q=0.10\,[m^3/s]$

Plug in variables ϱ, v_o and Q into eq.4, then solve for the magnitude of F_1 and F_2.

Water Resources Practice Problems

$$F_1 = 900 \, [\text{kg/m}^3] * 0.10 \, [\text{m}^3/\text{s}] * 28 \, [\text{m/s}]$$

$$F_1 = F_2 = 2{,}520 \, [\text{N}]$$

$F_1 = F_2 = 2{,}520 \, [\text{N}] \qquad \theta = 60°$

$$F_{R,x} = F_1 + F_2 * \cos(\theta) \leftarrow eq.3$$

Plug in variables F_1, F_2, and θ into eq. 3, then solve for $F_{R,x}$.

$$F_{R,x} = 2{,}520 \, [\text{N}] + 2{,}520 \, [\text{N}] * \cos(60°)$$

$$F_{R,x} = 3{,}780 \, [\text{N}]$$

$$\Sigma F_y = 0 = F_2 * \sin(\theta) - F_{R,y} \leftarrow eq.4$$

Eq. 4 sets the sum of the forces in the vertical direction equal to zero.

$F_2 = 2{,}520 \, [\text{N}] \qquad \theta = 60°$

$$F_{R,y} = F_2 * \sin(\theta) \leftarrow eq.5$$

Solve eq. 4 for $F_{R,y}$. Plug in variables F_2 and θ, then solve for $F_{R,y}$.

$$F_{R,y} = 2{,}520 \, [\text{N}] * \sin(60°)$$

$$F_{R,y} = 2{,}182 \, [\text{N}]$$

$F_{R,x} = 3{,}780 \, [\text{N}] \qquad F_{R,y} = 2{,}182 \, [\text{N}]$

$$F_R = \sqrt{F_{R,x}^2 + F_{R,y}^2} \leftarrow eq.1$$

Plug in variables $F_{R,x}$ and $F_{R,y}$ into eq. 1, then solve for F_R.

$$F_R = \sqrt{(3{,}780 \, [\text{N}])^2 + (2{,}182 \, [\text{N}])^2}$$

$$F_R = 4{,}365 \, [\text{N}] \qquad \underline{\text{Answer:}} \quad \boxed{B}$$

Fluid Dynamics #2

Find: $F_{R,x}$ ← the reaction force in the x-direction to hold the nozzle stationary

Given:

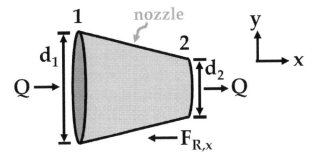

$\varrho = 62.3\,[lb_m/ft^3]$ ← the density of the fluid

$\left.\begin{array}{l} d_1 = 2\,[in] \\ d_2 = 1\,[in] \end{array}\right\}$ the diameter at the two ends of the nozzle

$P_1 = 45\,[lb_f/in^2]$ ← the pressure at end 1

$v_1 = 7\,[ft/s]$ ← the velocity at end 1

assume there is no headloss in the nozzle

A) $-6\,[lb_f]$

B) $6\,[lb_f]$

C) $99\,[lb_f]$

D) $104\,[lb_f]$

Analysis:

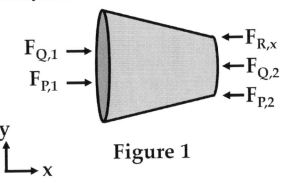

Figure 1

Figure 1 identifies the horizontal forces acting on the nozzle.

F_Q represents the force from fluid flow, and F_P represents force from the pressure.

Eq.1 sets the sum of all horizontal forces equal to zero.

forces due to fluid flow

$\Sigma F_x = 0 = F_{Q,1} + F_{P,1} - F_{Q,2} - F_{P,2} - F_{R,x}$ ←eq.1

forces due to pressure

$F_{R,x} = F_{Q,1} + F_{P,1} - F_{Q,2} - F_{P,2}$ ←eq.2

Eq.2 solves eq.1 for $F_{R,x}$.

$F_{Q,1} = \varrho * Q * v_1$ ←eq.3

fluid density   flow rate   fluid velocity

Eq.3 computes the dynamic hydraulic force, $F_{Q,1}$.

$Q = v_1 * A_1$ ←eq.4

Eq.4 computes the flow rate.

Water Resources Practice Problems

Fluid Dynamics #2 (cont.)

$$A_1 = \frac{\pi}{4} * d_1^2 \leftarrow eq.5$$

$$d_1 = 2\,[in]$$

Eq.5 computes the area at end 1. Plug in variable d_1 into eq.5, then solve for A_1.

$$A_1 = \frac{\pi}{4} * (2\,[in])^2$$

unit conversion

$$A_1 = 3.142\,[in^2] * \left(\frac{1}{12}\left[\frac{ft}{in}\right]\right)^2$$

Convert the area to feet squared.

$$A_1 = 0.0218\,[ft^2]$$

$$Q = v_1 * A_1 \leftarrow eq.4$$

$$v_1 = 7\,[ft/s] \qquad A_1 = 0.0218\,[ft^2]$$

Plug in variables v_1 and A_1 into eq.4, then solve for Q.

$$Q = 7\,[ft/s] * 0.0218\,[ft^2]$$

$$Q = 0.1526\,[ft^3/s]$$

$$Q = 0.1526\,[ft^3/s]$$

$$F_{Q,1} = \varrho * Q * v_1 \leftarrow eq.3$$

$$\varrho = 62.3\,[lb_m/ft^3] \qquad v_1 = 7\,[ft/s]$$

Plug in variables ϱ, Q, and v_1 into eq.3, then solve for $F_{Q,1}$.

unit conversion

$$F_{Q,1} = 62.3\,[lb_m/ft^3] * 0.1526\,[ft^3/s] * 7\,[ft/s] * \left(\frac{1}{32.2}\left[\frac{lb_f * s^2}{lb_m * ft}\right]\right)$$

$$F_{Q,1} = 2.067\,[lb_f]$$

$$F_{Q,2} = \varrho * Q * v_2 \leftarrow eq.6$$

Eq.6 computes force $F_{Q,2}$.

Fluid Dynamics #2 (cont.)

$$v_2 = \frac{Q}{A_2} \leftarrow eq.7$$

Eq. 7 compute variable v_2.

$$A_2 = \frac{\pi}{4} * d_2{}^2 \leftarrow eq.8$$

$$d_2 = 1 [in]$$

Plug in the variable d_2 into eq. 8, then solve for variable A_2.

$$A_2 = \frac{\pi}{4} * (1[in])^2$$

unit conversion

$$A_2 = 0.7854 [in^2] * \left(\frac{1}{12} \left[\frac{ft}{in} \right] \right)^2$$

Convert the area to feet squared.

$$A_2 = 0.00545 [ft^2]$$

$$Q = 0.1526 [ft^3/s]$$

$$v_2 = \frac{Q}{A_2} \leftarrow eq.7$$

$$A_2 = 0.00545 [ft^2]$$

Plug in variables Q and A_2 into eq. 7, then solve for v_2.

$$v_2 = \frac{0.1526 [ft^3/s]}{0.00545 [ft^2]}$$

$$v_2 = 28 [ft/s]$$

$$Q = 0.1526 [ft^3/s]$$

$$F_{Q,2} = \varrho * Q * v_2 \leftarrow eq.3$$

$$\varrho = 62.3 [lb_m/ft^3] \qquad v_2 = 28 [ft/s]$$

Plug in variables ϱ, Q, and v_2 into eq. 3, then solve for $F_{Q,2}$.

unit conversion

$$F_{Q,2} = 62.3 [lb_m/ft^3] * 0.1526 [ft^3/s] * 28 [ft/s] * \left(\frac{1}{32.2} \left[\frac{lb_f * s^2}{lb_m * ft} \right] \right)$$

Water Resources Practice Problems

Fluid Dynamics #2 (cont.)

$$F_{Q,2}=8.267\,[lb_f]$$

$$F_{P,1}=P_1 * A_1 \leftarrow eq.9$$

Eq.9 computes the force caused by the pressure at end 1.

$$P_1=45\,[lb_f/in^2] \qquad A_1=3.142\,[in^2]$$

Plug in variables P_1 and A_1 into eq.9, then solve for $F_{P,1}$.

$$F_{P,1}=45\,[lb_f/in^2] * 3.142\,[in^2]$$

$$F_{P,1}=141.4\,[lb_f]$$

$$F_{P,2}=P_2 * A_2 \leftarrow eq.10$$

Eq.10 computes the force caused by the pressure at end 2.

$$\frac{P_1}{\varrho}+\frac{v_1^2}{2}+z_1 * g=\frac{P_2}{\varrho}+\frac{v_2^2}{2}+z_2 * g+h_L \leftarrow eq.11$$

Eq.11 is Bernoulli's equation.

variables z_1 and z_2 cancel out because $z_1=z_2$.

$h_L=0$, because the problem states to assume there is zero headloss in the nozzle.

$$P_1=45\,[lb_f/in^2] \qquad \varrho=62.3\,[lb_m/ft^3]$$

Solve eq.11 for variable P_2.

$$P_2=P_1+ \frac{\varrho}{2} * (v_1^2-v_2^2) \leftarrow eq.12$$

Plug in variables P_1, ϱ, v_1 and v_2 into eq.12, then solve for P_2.

$$v_1=7\,[ft/s] \qquad v_2=28\,[ft/s]$$

$$P_2=45\,[lb_f/in^2]+ \frac{62.3\,[lb_m/ft^3]}{2} * ((7\,[ft/s])^2-(28\,[ft/s])^2)$$

$$P_2=45\,[lb_f/in^2]-22{,}895\,[lb_m/ft*s^2] * \left(\frac{1}{32.2}\left[\frac{lb_f*s^2}{lb_m*ft}\right]\right) * \left(\frac{1}{12}\left[\frac{ft}{in}\right]\right)^2$$

multiply by two unit conversion factors

$$P_2=45\,[lb_f/in^2]-4.94\,[lb_f/in^2]$$

334

Fluid Dynamics #2 (cont.)

$$P_2=40.06\,[lb_f/in^2]$$

$P_2=40.06\,[lb_f/in^2]$

$$F_{P,2}=P_2*A_2 \leftarrow eq.\,10$$

$A_2=0.7854\,[in^2]$

Plug in variables P_2 and A_2 into eq.10, then solve for $F_{P,2}$.

$$F_{P,2}=40.06\,[lb_f/in^2]*0.7854\,[in^2]$$

$$F_{P,2}=31.46\,[lb_f]$$

$F_{Q,1}=2.067\,[lb_f]$ $F_{Q,2}=8.267\,[lb_f]$

$$F_{R,x}=F_{Q,1}+F_{P,1}-F_{Q,2}-F_{P,2} \leftarrow eq.\,2$$

$F_{P,1}=141.4\,[lb_f]$ $F_{P,2}=31.46\,[lb_f]$

Plug in variables $F_{Q,1}$, $F_{P,1}$, $F_{Q,2}$, and $F_{P,2}$ into eq. 2, then solve for $F_{R,x}$.

$$F_{R,x}=2.067\,[lb_f]+141.4\,[lb_f]-8.267\,[lb_f]-31.46\,[lb_f]$$

$$F_{R,x}=103.74\,[lb_f]$$

Answer: D

Water Resources Practice Problems

Fluid Dynamics #3

Find: m_{block} ← the mass of the block

Given:

$h=3\,[m]$ ← the height difference between the tip of the nozzle and the block

$\varrho=998\,[kg/m^3]$ ← fluid density

$A_1=4.42*10^{-3}\,[m^2]$ ← flow area at the nozzle

$v_1=13.2\,[m/s]$ ← flow velocity at the nozzle

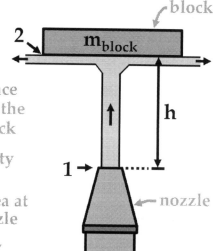

block

the block deflects all flow horizontally

the nozzle and block remain stationary

A) 63.7 [kg]
B) 78.3 [kg]
C) 127.4 [kg]
D) 156.6 [kg]

Analysis:

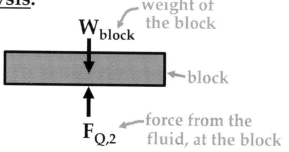

W_{block} ← weight of the block

← block

$F_{Q,2}$ ← force from the fluid, at the block

Figure 1

Figure 1 shows a free body diagram of the forces acting on the block.

$$\Sigma F_y = 0 = F_{Q,2} - W_{block} \leftarrow eq.1$$

$$W_{block} = m_{block}*g$$

Eq. 1 sets the sum of the forces in the vertical direction equal to zero.

$$0 = F_{Q,2} - m_{block}*g$$

Substitute in $m_{block}*g$ for the weight of the block in eq. 1, then solve for the mass of the block.

$$m_{block} = \frac{F_{Q,2}}{g} \leftarrow eq.2$$

$$F_{Q,2} = \varrho*Q*v_2 \leftarrow eq.3$$

Eq. 3 computes the force $F_{Q,2}$.

$$Q = v_1 * A_1 \leftarrow eq.4$$

$v_1=13.2\,[m/s] \quad A_1=4.42*10^{-3}\,[m^2]$

Plug in variables v_1 and A_1 into eq. 4, then solve for Q.

Fluid Dynamics #3 (cont.)

$$Q = 13.2 \, [m/s] * 4.42*10^{-3} \, [m^2]$$

$$Q = 0.0583 \, [m^3/s]$$

Eq. 5 is Bernoulli's Equation.

$$\cancel{\frac{P_1}{\rho}} + \frac{v_1^2}{2} + z_1 * g = \cancel{\frac{P_2}{\rho}} + \frac{v_2^2}{2} + z_2 * g + \cancel{h_L} \leftarrow eq. 5$$

the pressure head terms cancel out because $P_1 = P_2$

we'll assume there is no friction loss in the fluid between the nozzle and block

$$v_2 = \sqrt{v_1^2 + 2 * g * (z_1 - z_2)} \leftarrow eq. 6$$

$v_1 = 13.2 \, [m/s]$

$g = 9.81 \, [m/s^2]$

$z_1 - z_2 = -h = -3 \, [m]$

Solve eq. 5 for variable v_2.

Plug in the known variables into eq. 6, then solve for v_2.

$$v_2 = \sqrt{(13.2 \, [m/s])^2 + 2 * 9.81 \, [m/s^2] * -3 \, [m]}$$

$$v_2 = 10.74 \, [m/s]$$

$Q = 0.0583 \, [m^3/s]$

$$F_{Q,2} = \rho * Q * v_2 \leftarrow eq. 3$$

$\rho = 998 \, [kg/m^3]$

$v_2 = 10.74 \, [m/s]$

Plug in variables ρ, Q and v_2, into eq. 3, then solve for $F_{Q,2}$.

$$F_{Q,2} = 998 \, [kg/m^3] * 0.0583 \, [m^3/s] * 10.74 \, [m/s]$$

$$F_{Q,2} = 624.9 \, [N]$$

$F_{Q,2} = 624.9 \, [N]$

$$m_{block} = \frac{F_{Q,2}}{g} \leftarrow eq. 2$$

$g = 9.81 \, [m/s^2]$

Substitute in variables $F_{Q,2}$ and g into eq. 2, then solve for m_{block}.

Fluid Dynamics #3 (cont.)

$$m_{block} = \frac{624.9 \, [\text{N}]}{9.81 \, [\text{m/s}^2]}$$

$$m_{block} = 63.70 \, [\text{kg}]$$

Answer: $\boxed{\text{A}}$

Fluid Dynamics #4

Find: d ← the diameter of the vane

Given:

v=22[ft/s] ← velocity of the fluid

ϱ=75[lb$_m$/ft^3] ← density of the fluid

θ=65°

the vane has a circular cross-section and is held motionless by forces F$_{R,x}$ and F$_{R,y}$.

F$_{R,x}$=50[lb$_f$]
← reaction force in the x-direction

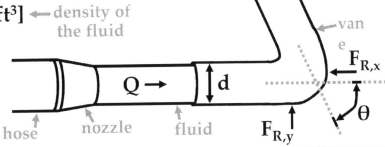

A) 2.4[in]

B) 2.5[in]

C) 2.6[in]

D) 2.7[in]

Analysis:

$$A = \frac{\pi}{4} * d^2 \quad \leftarrow eq.1$$

Eq.1 computes the area of the vane.

$$d = \sqrt{\frac{4*A}{\pi}} \quad \leftarrow eq.2$$

Solve eq.1 for the diameter, d.

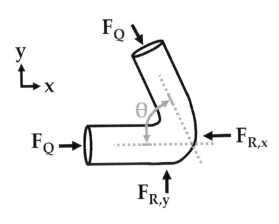

Figure 1

Figure 1 shows a free-body diagram of the vane.

$$\Sigma F_x = 0 = F_Q + F_Q*\cos(\theta) - F_{R,x} \leftarrow eq.3$$

Eq.3 sets the sum of the forces in the x-direction equal to zero.

$$F_{R,x} = F_Q*(1+\cos(\theta)) \leftarrow eq.4$$

$$F_Q = \varrho * v^2 * A$$

Simplify eq.3, then substitute in the hydraulic force of the fluid in for variable F$_Q$.

Water Resources Practice Problems

Fluid Dynamics #4 (cont.)

$$F_{R,x} = \varrho * v^2 * A * (1+\cos(\theta))$$

$\varrho = 75\,[\text{lb}_m/\text{ft}^3]$ $F_{R,x} = 50\,[\text{lb}_f]$

$$A = \frac{F_{R,x}}{\varrho * v^2 * (1+\cos(\theta))} \leftarrow eq.5$$

$v = 22\,[\text{ft/s}]$ $\theta = 65°$

Solve eq. 4 for the area, A.

Substitute in the variables $F_{R,x}$, ϱ, v and θ into eq. 5, then solve for the cross-sectional area, A.

$$A = \frac{50\,[\text{lb}_f]}{75\,[\text{lb}_m/\text{ft}^3] * (22\,[\text{ft/s}])^2 * (1+\cos(65°))}$$

$$A = 9.682*10^{-4}\left[\frac{\text{lb}_f * s^2 * \text{ft}}{\text{lb}_m}\right] * \left(32.2\left[\frac{\text{lb}_m * \text{ft}}{\text{lb}_f * s^2}\right]\right) * \left(12\left[\frac{\text{in}}{\text{ft}}\right]\right)^2$$

$$A = 4.489\,[\text{in}^2]$$

Convert the area to units of inches squared, by multiplying by two unit conversion factors.

$A = 4.489\,[\text{in}^2]$

$$d = \sqrt{\frac{4*A}{\pi}} \leftarrow eq.2$$

Plug in the computed area into eq. 2, then solve for d.

$$d = \sqrt{\frac{4*4.489\,[\text{in}^2]}{\pi}}$$

$$d = 2.39\,[\text{in}]$$

Answer: $\boxed{A}$

340

Fluid Dynamics #5

Find: $F_{R,y}$ ←the vertical reaction force, on the cart

Given:

$\rho = 999\,[kg/m^3]$ ←fluid density

$v_o = 30\,[m/s]$ ←fluid velocity

$v_{cart} = 15\,[m/s]$ ←cart velocity

$A = 600\,[mm^3]$ ←cross-sectional area of the fluid

θ

Q

$m_{cart} = 30\,[kg]$ ←the mass of the cart

Q → ← $F_{R,x}$

→ v_{cart}

$\theta = 60°$

frictionless surface

$F_{R,y}$ ↑

the cart maintains a constant velocity

A) 116 [N]

B) 411 [N]

C) 527 [N]

D) 741 [N]

Analysis:

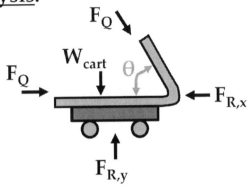

F_Q

W_{cart} θ

F_Q → ← $F_{R,x}$

$F_{R,y}$

Figure 1

Figure 1 shows a free body diagram of the cart and all forces involved.

Eq.1 sets the sum of the forces in the vertical direction equal to zero.

$$\Sigma F_y = 0 = F_{R,y} - F_Q * \sin(\theta) - W_{cart} \quad \leftarrow eq.1$$

vertical reaction force

dynamic force from the fluid

Solve Eq.1 for the vertical reaction force, $F_{R,y}$.

$$F_{R,y} = F_Q * \overset{cos}{\sin}(\theta) + W_{cart} \quad \leftarrow eq.2$$

$$W_{cart} = m_{cart} * g \quad \leftarrow eq.3$$

$m_{cart} = 30\,[kg]$ $g = 9.81\,[m/s^2]$

Eq.3 computes the weight of the cart. Plug in variables m_{cart} and g, then solve for W_{cart}.

$$W_{cart} = 30\,[kg] * 9.81\,[m/s^2]$$

Water Resources Practice Problems

Fluid Dynamics #5 (cont.)

$$W_{cart} = 294.3 \, [N]$$

$$F_Q = \dot{m} * v_r \; \leftarrow eq.4$$

mass flow rate — relative velocity of the fluid, from the cart

Eq.4 computes the hydraulic force.

$$\dot{m} = \varrho * Q \; \leftarrow eq.5$$

Eq. 5 computes the mass flow rate.

$$Q = v_r * A \; \leftarrow eq.6$$

relative velocity — area of the flow

Eq. 6 computes the flow rate.

$$v_r = v_o - v_{cart} \; \leftarrow eq.7$$

$v_o = 30 \, [m/s]$ $v_{cart} = 15 \, [m/s]$

Eq.7 computes the relative velocity.

Plug in variables v_o and v_{cart} into eq.7, then solve for v_r.

$$v_r = 30 \, [m/s] - 15 \, [m/s]$$

$$v_r = 15 \, [m/s]$$

$$Q = v_r * A \; \leftarrow eq.6$$

$v_r = 15 \, [m/s]$ $A = 600 \, [mm^2]$

Plug in variables v_r and A into eq.6, then solve for Q.

$$Q = 15 \, [m/s] * 600 \, [mm^2] * \left(\frac{1}{1,000} \left[\frac{m}{mm} \right] \right)^2$$

Convert the flow rate to units of cubic meters per second

$$Q = 9 * 10^{-3} \, [m^3/s]$$

unit conversion factor

$\varrho = 999 \, [kg/m^3]$ $Q = 9 * 10^{-3} \, [m^3/s]$

$$\dot{m} = \varrho * Q \; \leftarrow eq.5$$

Plug in variables ϱ and Q into eq.5, then solve for $\dot{m}$.

342

Fluid Dynamics #5 (cont.)

$$\dot{m} = 999\,[kg/m^3] * 9 * 10^{-3}\,[m^3/s]$$

$$\dot{m} = 8.991\,[kg/s]$$

$$F_Q = \dot{m} * v_r \leftarrow eq.\,4$$

$\dot{m} = 8.991\,[kg/s]$ $v_r = 15\,[m/s]$

Plug in variables $\dot{m}$ and v_r into eq. 4, then solve for F_Q.

$$F_Q = 8.991\,[kg/s] * 15\,[m/s]$$

$$F_Q = 134.9\,[N]$$

$\theta = 60°$

$$F_{R,y} = F_Q * \sin(\theta) + W_{cart} \leftarrow eq.\,2$$

$F_Q = 134.9\,[N]$ $W_{cart} = 294.3\,[N]$

Plug in variables F_Q, θ, and W_{cart} into eq. 2, then solve for $F_{R,y}$.

$$F_{R,y} = 134.9\,[N] * \sin(60°) + 294.3\,[N]$$

$$F_{R,y} = 411.1\,[N]$$

Answer: $\boxed{B}$

Water Resources Practice Problems

Fluid Dynamics #6

<u>Find:</u> P_2 ←the pressure at end 2

<u>Given:</u> $\varrho = 62.4 \, [lb_m/in^3]$ ←fluid density

$F_{R,x} = 1{,}022 \, [lb_f]$ ←horizontal reaction force

$P_2 = P_3$

$P_1 = 22 \, [lb_f/in^2]$ ←pressure at end 1

$d_1 = 6 \, [in]$ ←diameter at end 1

$d_2 = d_3 = 4 \, [in]$ ←diameter at ends 2 and 3

$Q_1 = 2*Q_2 = 2*Q_3 = 0.64 \, [ft^3/s]$ ←flow rates

the reaction forces $F_{R,x}$ and $F_{R,y}$ hold the vane stationary

$\theta = 30°$

A) $18 \, [lb_f/in^2]$

B) $19 \, [lb_f/in^2]$

C) $21 \, [lb_f/in^2]$

D) $22 \, [lb_f/in^2]$

Analysis:

$$P_2 = \frac{F_{P,2}}{A_2} \quad \leftarrow eq.1$$

pressure force at end 2

area at end 2

Eq. 1 computes the pressure at end 2.

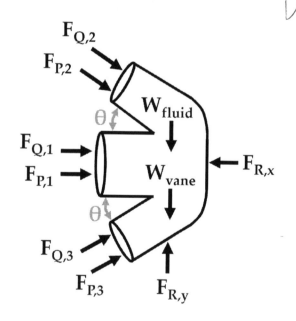

Figure 1

Figure 1 is a free body diagram showing all the forces acting on the vane.

In Figure 1, force F_Q refers to the dynamic force of the fluid, and force F_P refers to the force caused by the pressure

Eq.2 sets the sum of the horizontal forces equal to zero.

$$\Sigma F_x = 0 = -F_{R,x} + F_{Q,1} + F_{P,1} + F_{Q,2}*\cos(\theta)$$
$$+ F_{P,2}*\cos(\theta) + F_{Q,3}*\cos(\theta) + F_{P,3}*\cos(\theta) \leftarrow eq.2$$

Fluid Dynamics #6 (cont.)

Solve eq.2 for $F_{R,x}$ and simplify

$$F_{R,x} = F_{Q,1} + F_{P,1} + \cos(\theta) * (F_{Q,2} + F_{Q,3} + F_{P,2} + F_{P,3}) \leftarrow eq.2$$

$$F_{Q,3} = F_{Q,2} \qquad F_{P,3} = F_{P,2}$$

Since ends 2 and 3 have the same pressure, diameter, flow rate and fluid density, $F_{Q,2} = F_{Q,3}$ and $F_{P,2} = F_{P,2}$, and eq.3 simplifies.

$$F_{R,x} = F_{Q,1} + F_{P,1} + 2 * \cos(\theta) * (F_{Q,2} + F_{P,2}) \leftarrow eq.3$$

Solve eq.3 for $F_{P,2}$.

$$F_{P,2} = \frac{F_{R,x} - F_{Q,1} - F_{P,1} - 2 * \cos(\theta) * F_{Q,2}}{2 * \cos(\theta)} \leftarrow eq.4$$

$$F_{Q,1} = \varrho * Q_1 * v_1 \leftarrow eq.5$$

Eq.5 computes $F_{Q,1}$.

$$v_1 = \frac{Q_1}{A_1} \leftarrow eq.6$$

Eq.6 computes the fluid velocity entering the vane at end 1.

$$A_1 = \frac{\pi}{4} * d_1^2 \leftarrow eq.7$$

$$d_1 = 6 \, [in]$$

Eq.7 computes the cross-sectional area of the flow at end 1.

Plug in d_1 into eq.7, then solve for A_1.

$$A_1 = \frac{\pi}{4} * (6 \, [in])^2$$

$$A_1 = 28.27 \, [in^2] * \left(\frac{1}{12} \left[\frac{ft}{in} \right] \right)^2$$

conversion factor

$$A_1 = 0.196 \, [ft^2]$$

$$Q_1 = 0.64 \, [ft^3/s]$$

$$v_1 = \frac{Q_1}{A_1} \leftarrow eq.6$$

$$A_1 = 0.196 \, [ft^2]$$

Plug in the variables Q_1 and A_1 into eq.6, then solve for v_1.

Water Resources Practice Problems

Fluid Dynamics #6 (cont.)

$$v_1 = \frac{0.64\,[\text{ft}^3/\text{s}]}{0.196\,[\text{ft}^2]}$$

$$v_1 = 3.265\,[\text{ft/s}]$$

$Q_1 = 0.64\,[\text{ft}^3/\text{s}]$

$$F_{Q,1} = \varrho * Q_1 * v_1 \leftarrow eq.5$$

$\varrho = 62.4\,[\text{lb}_m/\text{in}^3]$ $v_1 = 3.265\,[\text{ft/s}]$

Plug in ϱ, Q_1, and v_1 into eq.5, then solve for $F_{Q,1}$.

$$F_{Q,1} = 62.4\,[\text{lb}_m/\text{in}^3] * 0.64\,[\text{ft}^3/\text{s}] * 3.265\,[\text{ft/s}] * \left(\frac{1}{32.2} \left[\frac{\text{lb}_f * \text{s}^2}{\text{lb}_m * \text{ft}} \right] \right)$$

$$F_{Q,1} = 4.05\,[\text{lb}_f]$$

Convert the force to lb_f.

$A_1 = 28.27\,[\text{in}^2]$

$$F_{P,1} = P_1 * A_1 \leftarrow eq.8$$

$P_1 = 22\,[\text{lb}_f/\text{in}^2]$

Eq.8 computes the pressure force at end 1.

Plug in variables P_1 and A_1 into eq.8, then solve for $F_{P,1}$.

$$F_{P,1} = 22\,[\text{lb}_f/\text{in}^2] * 28.27\,[\text{in}^2]$$

$$F_{P,1} = 621.9\,[\text{lb}_f]$$

$$F_{Q,2} = \varrho * Q_2 * v_2 \leftarrow eq.9$$

Eq.9 computes the force due to the fluid exiting the vane at end 2

$$v_2 = \frac{Q_2}{A_2} \leftarrow eq.10$$

Eq.10 computes the velocity at end 2, v_2.

$$A_2 = \frac{\pi}{4} * d_2^2 \leftarrow eq.11$$

$d_2 = 4\,[\text{in}]$

Plug in variable d_2 into eq.11, then solve for A_2.

Fluid Dynamics #6 (cont.)

$$A_2 = \frac{\pi}{4} * (4\,[in])^2$$

$$A_2 = 12.566\,[in^2] * \left(\frac{1}{12}\left[\frac{ft}{in}\right]\right)^2$$

conversion factor

$$A_2 = 0.0873\,[ft^2]$$

$Q_2 = 0.32\,[ft^3/s]$

$$v_2 = \frac{Q_2}{A_2} \leftarrow eq.10$$

$A_1 = 0.0873\,[ft^2]$

The problem states Q_2 is half of $0.64\,[ft^3/s]$, which is $0.32\,[ft^3/s]$.

Plug in the variables Q_2 and A_2 into eq.10, then solve v_2.

$$v_2 = \frac{0.32\,[ft^3/s]}{0.0873\,[ft^2]}$$

$$v_2 = 3.666\,[ft/s]$$

$Q_2 = 0.32\,[ft^3/s]$

$$F_{Q,2} = \varrho * Q_2 * v_2 \leftarrow eq.9$$

$\varrho = 62.4\,[lb_m/in^3]$ $v_2 = 3.666\,[ft/s]$

Plug in variables ϱ, Q_2, and v_2 into eq.9, then solve for $F_{Q,2}$.

$$F_{Q,2} = 62.4\,[lb_m/in^3] * 0.32\,[ft^3/s] * 3.666\,[ft/s] * \left(\frac{1}{32.2}\left[\frac{lb_f * s^2}{lb_m * ft}\right]\right)$$

unit conversion

$$F_{Q,2} = 2.273\,[lb_f]$$

$F_{R,x} = 1{,}022\,[lb_f]$ $F_{P,1} = 621.9\,[lb_f]$ $F_{Q,2} = 2.273\,[lb_f]$

$$F_{P,2} = \frac{F_{R,x} - F_{Q,1} - F_{P,1} - 2 * \cos(\theta) * F_{Q,2}}{2 * \cos(\theta)} \leftarrow eq.4$$

$F_{Q,1} = 4.05\,[lb_f]$ $\theta = 30°$

Plug in variables $F_{R,x}$, $F_{Q,1}$, $F_{P,1}$, $F_{Q,2}$, and θ into eq.4, then solve for $F_{P,2}$.

Water Resources Practice Problems

Fluid Dynamics #6 (cont.)

$$F_{P,2} = \frac{1{,}022\,[\text{lb}_f] - 4.05\,[\text{lb}_f] - 621.9\,[\text{lb}_f] - 2*\cos(30^\circ)*2.273\,[\text{lb}_f]}{2*\cos(30^\circ)}$$

$$F_{P,2} = 226.4\,[\text{lb}_f]$$

$$P_2 = \overset{F_{P,2}=226.4\,[\text{lb}_f]}{\underset{A_2=12.566\,[\text{in}^2]}{\frac{F_{P,2}}{A_2}}} \leftarrow eq.1$$

Plug in variables $F_{P,2}$ and A_2 into eq.1, then solve P_2.

$$P_2 = \frac{226.4\,[\text{lb}_f]}{12.566\,[\text{in}^2]}$$

$$P_2 = 18.02\ [\text{lb}_f/\text{in}^2]$$

Answer: $\boxed{A}$

Fluid Dynamics #7

<u>Find:</u> SG ←the specific gravity
of the fluid

<u>Given:</u>

$m_{cart}=20\,[kg]$ ←cart mass

$\theta=28°$ ←deflection angle

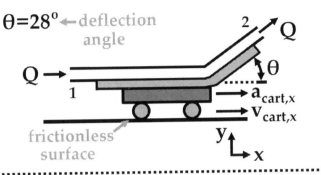

frictionless surface

$v_{cart,x}=0\,[m/s]$ ←the cart velocity in the x-direction

$v_1=v_2=30\,[m/s]$ ←the fluid velocity

$T=30°C$ ←the fluid temperature

$a_{cart,x}=4.62\,[m/s^2]$

the cart acceleration in the x-direction

$A_1=A_2=8\,[cm^2]$

the area of the fluid at ends 1 and 2

A) 1.0

B) 1.1

C) 1.2

D) 1.3

Analysis:

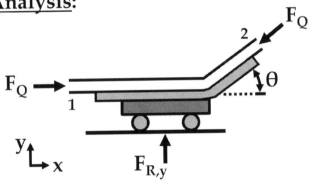

Figure 1

Figure 1 shows a free body diagram on the forces acting on the cart.

Eq.1 relates the sum of the forces acting on the cart in the x-direction.

$$\Sigma F_x=m_{cart}*a_{cart,x}=F_Q-F_Q*\cos(\theta) \leftarrow eq.1$$

$$F_Q=\frac{m_{cart}*a_{cart,x}}{(1-\cos(\theta))} \leftarrow eq.2$$

Solve eq.1 for the hydraulic force, F_Q.

$$F_Q=SG*\varrho_w*Q*v \leftarrow eq.3$$

specific gravity   density of water   fluid velocity

Eq.3 computes the hydraulic force based on the fluid properties.

$$T=30°C \rightarrow \varrho_w=995.7\,[kg/m^3]$$

Determine the density of water based on the temperature.

Water Resources Practice Problems

Fluid Dynamics #7 (cont.)

$$F_Q = \frac{m_{cart} * a_{cart,x}}{(1 - \cos(\theta))}$$

Solve eq. 3 for the specific gravity, SG, then substitute in the hydraulic force, F_Q.

$$SG = \frac{F_Q}{\varrho_w * Q * v} \leftarrow eq.4$$

$$SG = \frac{m_{cart} * a_{cart,x}}{\varrho_w * Q * v * (1 - \cos(\theta))} \leftarrow eq.5$$

Plug in variables v and A into eq. 6, then solve for Q.

$$A = 8 \,[cm^2]$$

$$Q = v * A \leftarrow eq.6$$

$$v = 30 \,[m/s]$$

The velocities and areas of the flow at both ends are equal.

$$v = v_1 = v_2$$
$$A = A_1 = A_2$$

$$Q = 30 \,[m/s] * 8 \,[cm^2] * \left(\frac{1}{100}\left[\frac{m}{cm}\right]\right)^2$$

conversion factor

$$Q = 0.024 \,[m^3/s]$$

$$m_{cart} = 20 \,[kg] \quad a_{cart,x} = 4.62 \,[m/s^2]$$

$$SG = \frac{m_{cart} * a_{cart,x}}{\varrho_w * Q * v * (1 - \cos(\theta))} \leftarrow eq.5$$

Plug in the known variables into eq. 5, then solve for SG.

$$v = 30 \,[m/s] \quad \theta = 28°$$

$$Q = 0.024 \,[m^3/s]$$

$$\varrho_w = 995.7 \,[kg/m^3]$$

$$SG = \frac{20 \,[kg] * 4.62 \,[m/s^2]}{995.7 \,[kg/m^3] * 0.024 \,[m^3/s] * 30 \,[m/s] * (1 - \cos(28°))}$$

$$SG = 1.10 \quad \sqrt{\qquad} \quad \underline{Answer:} \boxed{B}$$

Fluid Dynamics #8

Find: x ← the horizontal distance the fluid travels in the air

Given:

$C_v = 0.82$ ← coefficient of velocity

$C_c = 1.00$ ← coefficient of contraction

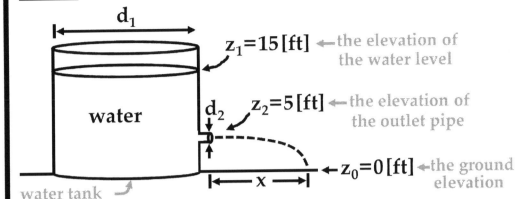

$z_1 = 15\,[\text{ft}]$ ← the elevation of the water level

$z_2 = 5\,[\text{ft}]$ ← the elevation of the outlet pipe

$z_0 = 0\,[\text{ft}]$ ← the ground elevation

$T = 70^\circ\,\text{F}$
↑
water temperature

A) 9.6 [ft]

B) 11.1 [ft]

C) 12.6 [ft]

D) 14.1 [ft]

Analysis:

$$x = v_{x,2} * t \quad \leftarrow eq.\,1$$

↑ horizontal velocity of the water as it exits the tank

duration of time the water is in the air

Eq.1 computes the horizontal distance the water travels in the air, x.

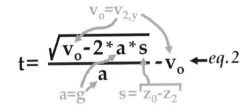

$v_o = v_{2,y}$

$$t = \frac{\sqrt{v_o - 2*a*s}}{a} - v_o \quad \leftarrow eq.\,2$$

$a = g \qquad s = z_0 - z_2$

Eq.2 computes the duration of time the water is in the air.

$g = 32.2\,[\text{ft/s}^2] \qquad z_0 = 0\,[\text{ft}]$

$$t = \frac{\sqrt{v_{2,y} - 2*g*(z_0 - z_2)}}{g} - v_{2,y} \quad \leftarrow eq.\,3$$

$v_{2,y} = 0\,[\text{ft/s}] \qquad z_2 = 5\,[\text{ft}] \qquad v_{2,y} = 0\,[\text{ft/s}]$

Plug in variables v_2, g, z_2 and z_0 into eq.3, then solve for t.

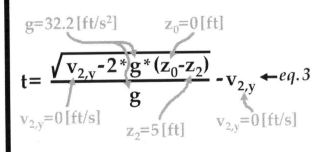

$$t = \frac{\sqrt{0\,[\text{ft/s}] - 2*32.2\,[\text{ft/s}^2]*(0\,[\text{ft}] - 5\,[\text{ft}])}}{32.2\,[\text{ft/s}^2]} - 0\,[\text{ft/s}]$$

$$t = 0.557\,[\text{s}]$$

The water is in the air for 0.557 seconds.

Water Resources Practice Problems

Fluid Dynamics #8 (cont.)

$$v_{x,2} = v_2 \quad \leftarrow eq.4$$

Since the water exits the tank in the horizontal direction, we know variable $v_{x,2}$ equals v_x.

$$v_2 = \overset{C_v=0.89}{C_v} * \sqrt{2 * \underset{g=32.2\,[ft/s^2]}{g} * (\overset{z_1=15\,[ft]}{z_1} - \underset{z_2=5\,[ft]}{z_2})} \quad \leftarrow eq.5$$

Plug in variables C_v, g, z_1 and z_2 into eq.5, then solve for v_2.

$$v_2 = \underset{0.82}{0.89} * \sqrt{2 * 32.2\,[ft/s^2] * (15\,[ft] - 5\,[ft])}$$

$$v_2 = 22.58\,[ft/s]$$

$$x = v_{x,2} * \overset{t=0.557\,[s]}{t} \quad \leftarrow eq.1$$

$$\underset{v_{x,2} = v_2 = 22.58\,[ft/s]}{}$$

Plug in variables $v_{x,2}$ and t into eq.1, then solve for x.

$$x = 22.58\,[ft/s] * 0.557\,[s]$$

$$x = 12.58\,[ft]$$

Answer: $\boxed{C}$

352

Fluid Dynamics #9

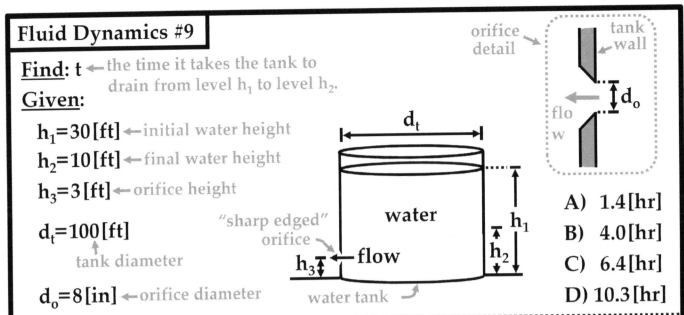

Find: t ← the time it takes the tank to drain from level h_1 to level h_2.

Given:

$h_1 = 30$ [ft] ← initial water height

$h_2 = 10$ [ft] ← final water height

$h_3 = 3$ [ft] ← orifice height

$d_t = 100$ [ft]

tank diameter

$d_o = 8$ [in] ← orifice diameter

"sharp edged" orifice

water tank

A) 1.4 [hr]

B) 4.0 [hr]

C) 6.4 [hr]

D) 10.3 [hr]

Analysis:

tank volume between heights h_1 and h_2

$$t = \frac{V}{Q} \leftarrow eq.1$$

discharge

Eq. 1 computes the time it takes the tank to drain.

$d_t = 100$ [ft] $h_2 = 10$ [ft]

$$V = \frac{\pi}{4} * d_t^2 * (h_1 - h_2) \leftarrow eq.2$$

$h_1 = 30$ [ft]

Eq. 2 computes the tank volume between heights h_1 and h_2.

Plug in variables d_t, h_1, and h_2 into eq. 2, then solve for the volume, V.

$$V = \frac{\pi}{4} * (100\,[ft])^2 * (30\,[ft] - 10\,[ft])$$

$$V = 1.571 * 10^5 \, [ft^3]$$

Eq. 3 to computes the instantaneous discharge from the tank.

coefficient of discharge   acceleration constant

$$Q = C_d * A_o * \sqrt{2 * g * \Delta h} \leftarrow eq.3$$

orifice area   height difference

In eq. 3, Δh refers to the height difference between the water level and the orifice.

From eq. 3, we notice that as the tank drains, Δh decreases, and the discharge decreases.

Water Resources Practice Problems

Fluid Dynamics #9 (cont.)

$$C_d = 0.62$$

Determine the coefficient of discharge for a 'sharp-edged' orifice.

$$A_o = \frac{\pi}{4} * d_o^2 \leftarrow eq.4$$

$d_o = 8\,[in]$

Plug in variable d_o into eq.4, then solve for A_o.

$$A_o = \frac{\pi}{4} * (8\,[in])^2$$

conversion factor

$$A_o = 50.27\,[in^2] * \left(\frac{1}{12}\left[\frac{ft}{in}\right]\right)^2$$

$$A_o = 0.3491\,[ft^2]$$

discharge while tank drains from h_1 to h_2

When draining from h_1 to h_2, the fastest discharge will occur when the water level is at h_1, and the slowest discharge will occur when the water level is at h_2.

$$Q_{h2} \leq Q \leq Q_{h1} \leftarrow ieq.1$$

discharge when $h=h_2$

discharge when $h=h_1$

$Q=Q_{h1}$

$\Delta h = \Delta h_{1,3} = h_1 - h_3$

Plug in Q_{h1} and $h_1 - h_3$ into eq.3.

$$Q = C_d * A_o * \sqrt{2*g*\Delta h} \leftarrow eq.3$$

$C_d = 0.62$

$g = 32.2\,[ft/s^2]$

$$Q_{h1} = C_d * A_o * \sqrt{2*g*(h_1-h_3)} \leftarrow eq.5$$

$A_o = 0.3491\,[ft^2]$

$h_1 = 30\,[ft]$

$h_3 = 3\,[ft]$

Plug in the known variables into eq.5, then solve for Q_{h1}.

$$Q_{h1} = 0.62 * 0.3491\,[ft^2] * \sqrt{2*32.2[ft/s^2]*(30[ft]-3[ft])}$$

$$Q_{h1} = 9.025\,[ft^3/s]$$

Fluid Dynamics #9 (cont.)

$Q = Q_{h2}$

$\Delta h = \Delta h_{2,3} = h_2 - h_3$

$$Q = C_d * A_o * \sqrt{2 * g * \Delta h} \leftarrow eq.3$$

Plug in Q_{h2} and $h_2 - h_3$ into eq. 3.

$C_d = 0.62$ $g = 32.2 \, [ft/s^2]$

$$Q_{h2} = C_d * A_o * \sqrt{2 * g * (h_2 - h_3)} \leftarrow eq.6$$

$A_o = 0.3491 \, [ft^2]$ $h_2 = 10 \, [ft]$ $h_3 = 3 \, [ft]$

Plug in the known variables into eq. 6, then solve for Q_{h2}.

$$Q_{h2} = 0.62 * 0.3491 \, [ft^2] * \sqrt{2 * 32.2 \, [ft/s^2] * (10 \, [ft] - 3 \, [ft])}$$

$$Q_{h2} = 4.596 \, [ft^3/s]$$

$Q_{h2} = 4.596 \, [ft^3/s]$

$$Q_{h2} \leq Q \leq Q_{h1} \leftarrow ieq.1$$

$Q_{h1} = 9.025 \, [ft^3/s]$

Substitute in Q_{h1} and Q_{h2} into ieq. 1, to define the minimum and maximum discharges from the tank.

$$4.596 \, [ft^3/s] \leq Q \leq 9.025 \, [ft^3/s]$$

$V = 1.571 * 10^5 \, [ft^3]$

$$\frac{V}{Q_{h1}} \leq t \leq \frac{V}{Q_{h2}} \leftarrow ieq.2$$

$Q_{h1} = 9.025 \, [ft^3/s]$ $Q_{h2} = 4.596 \, [ft^3/s]$

Compute an upper and lower bound on the duration of time it takes the tank to drain from h_1 to h_2, by plugging in variables V, Q_{h1} and Q_{h2} into ieq. 2.

$$\frac{1.571 * 10^5 \, [ft^3]}{9.025 \, [ft^3/s]} \leq t \leq \frac{1.571 * 10^5 \, [ft^3]}{4.596 \, [ft^3/s]}$$

$$17,407 \, [s] \leq t \leq 34,182 \, [s]$$

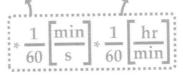

$$* \frac{1}{60} \left[\frac{min}{s}\right] * \frac{1}{60} \left[\frac{hr}{min}\right]$$

Convert the time from seconds to hours.

Fluid Dynamics #9 (cont.)

$$4.835\,[hr] \leq t \leq 9.495\,[hr]$$

A) 1.4 [hr]

B) 4.0 [hr]

C) 6.4 [hr]

D) 10.3 [hr]

Looking back at our possible solutions, answer C is the only possible solution that falls within the possible calculated duration.

Answer: $\boxed{C}$

Since the water tank has a constant cross-section, we could also use eq.7, to solve for t directly.

$A_t = 7,854\,[ft^2]$ $h_1 = 30\,[ft]$ $h_2 = 10\,[ft]$

$$t = \frac{2 * A_t * (\sqrt{(h_1 - h_3)} - \sqrt{(h_2 - h_3)})}{C_d * A_o * \sqrt{2 * g}} \leftarrow eq.7$$

$C_d = 0.62$ $h_3 = 3\,[ft]$

$A_o = 0.3491\,[ft^2]$ $g = 32.2\,[ft/s^2]$

For a tank diameter of 100 feet, the cross-sectional area equals 7,854 feet squared.

Eq. 17.83

$$t = \frac{2 * 7,854\,[ft^2] * (\sqrt{(30\,[ft] - 3\,[ft])} - \sqrt{(10\,[ft] - 3\,[ft])})}{0.62 * 0.3491\,[ft^2] * \sqrt{2 * 32.2\,[ft/s^2]}}$$

$$t = 23,065\,[s] * \frac{1}{60}\left[\frac{min}{s}\right] * \frac{1}{60}\left[\frac{hr}{min}\right]$$

conversion factors

convert the units of seconds to hours.

$$t = 6.41\,[hr]$$

Answer: $\boxed{C}$

Fluid Dynamics #10

Find: P ← the power generated by the dynamic fluid force

Given:

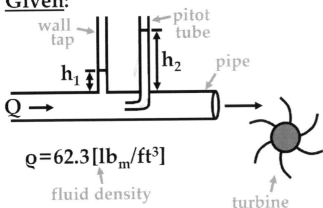

$\varrho = 62.3\,[lb_m/ft^3]$ ← fluid density

$h_1 = 2.4\,[in]$ ← height of the fluid in the wall tap

$h_2 = 13.7\,[in]$ ← height of the fluid in the pitot tube

$A = 5\,[in^2]$ ← area of the pipe

A) $2\,[lb_f * ft/s]$

B) $16\,[lb_f * ft/s]$

C) $510\,[lb_f * ft/s]$

D) $960\,[lb_f * ft/s]$

Analysis:

$$P = 0.5 * \overset{\bullet}{m} * v^2 \quad \leftarrow eq.1$$

power   mass flow rate   fluid velocity

Eq.1 computes the power generated by the fluid.

$$v = \sqrt{2 * g * \Delta h} \quad \leftarrow eq.2$$

$$\Delta h = h_2 - h_1$$

Eq.2 computes the fluid velocity.

The fluid height in the wall tap measures the pressure head only. The fluid height in pitot tube measures the pressure head and the velocity head.

$$h_2 = 13.7\,[in]$$

$$v = \sqrt{2 * g * (h_2 - h_1)} \quad \leftarrow eq.3$$

$$g = 386\,[in/s^2] \qquad h_1 = 2.4\,[in]$$

$$h_1 = \frac{P}{\varrho * g} \qquad h_2 = \frac{P}{\varrho * g} + \frac{v^2}{2 * g}$$

$$v = \sqrt{2 * 386\,[in/s^2] * (13.7\,[in] - 2.4\,[in]) * \left(\frac{1}{12}\left[\frac{ft}{in}\right]\right)^2}$$

← conversion factor

$$v = 7.783\,[ft/s]$$

Plug in variables g, h_1 and h_2 into eq.3, then solve for the velocity, v.

$$\overset{\bullet}{m} = \varrho * Q \quad \leftarrow eq.4$$

Eq.4 computes the mass flow rate.

Water Resources Practice Problems

Fluid Dynamics #10 (cont.)

Eq. 5 computes the flow rate through the pipe.

$A = 5 [in^2]$

$Q = v * A \leftarrow eq.5$

$v = 7.789 [ft/s]$

Plug in variables v and A into eq. 5, then solve for Q.

$Q = 7.789 [ft/s] * 5 [in] * \left(\frac{1}{12} \left[\frac{ft}{in} \right] \right)^2 \leftarrow$ conversion factor

$Q = 0.270 [ft^3/s]$

$Q = 0.270 [ft^3/s]$

$\dot{m} = \varrho * Q \leftarrow eq.4$

$\varrho = 62.3 [lb_m/ft^3]$

Plug in variables ϱ and Q into eq. 4, then solve for $\dot{m}$.

$\dot{m} = 62.3 [lb_m/ft^3] * 0.270 [ft^3/s]$

$\dot{m} = 16.82 [lb_m/s]$

$v = 7.783 [ft/s]$

$P = 0.5 * \dot{m} * v^2 \leftarrow eq.1$

$\dot{m} = 16.82 [lb_m/s]$

Plug in variables $\dot{m}$ and v into eq. 1, then solve for the power, P.

$P = 0.5 * 16.82 [lb_m/s] * (7.783 [ft/s])^2 * \left(\frac{1}{32.2} \left[\frac{lb_f * s^2}{lb_m * ft} \right] \right)$

conversion factor

$P = 15.82 [lb_f * ft/s]$

__Answer:__ $\boxed{B}$

Fluid Dynamics #11

Find: μ ← the absolute viscosity of the fluid

Given:

h = 150 [mm] ← viscometer height

D = 75 [mm] ← viscometer diameter

$\dot{\theta}$ = 100 [rev/min] ← angular velocity

T = 0.021 [N*m] ← torque

y = 0.02 [mm]
plate clearance

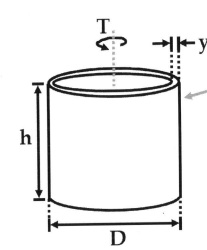

cylindrical viscometer

A) $3*10^{-3}$ [N*s/m²]

B) $8*10^{-3}$ [N*s/m²]

C) $3*10^{-4}$ [N*s/m²]

D) $8*10^{-4}$ [N*s/m²]

Analysis:

shear stress

$$\tau = \mu * \frac{dv}{dy} \leftarrow eq.1$$

absolute viscosity   velocity gradient

Eq.1 computes the shear stress in a sliding plate viscometer test.

Solve eq.1 for the absolute viscosity.

$$\mu = \tau * \frac{dy}{dv} \leftarrow eq.2$$

$\tau = F/A$

Substitute in the force divided by the area for the shear stress in eq.2.

force

$$\mu = \frac{F}{A} * \frac{dy}{dv} \leftarrow eq.3$$

area

conversion factor

$$y = 0.02 \,[mm] * \frac{1}{1,000}\left[\frac{m}{mm}\right] \leftarrow eq.4$$

Eq.4 converts the plate clearance to meters.

$$y = 2*10^{-5} \,[m]$$

Eq.5 computes the area between the plates of the viscometer.

$$A = \pi * D * h \leftarrow eq.5$$

D = 75 [mm]   h = 150 [mm]

Plug in variables D and h into eq.5, then solve for A.

Fluid Dynamics #11 (cont.)

$$A = \pi * 75\,[mm] * 150\,[mm]$$

$$A = 3.534 * 10^4\,[mm^2] * \left(\frac{1}{1{,}000}\left[\frac{m}{mm}\right]\right)^2 \leftarrow eq.6$$

Eq. 6 converts the area to meters squared.

$$A = 3.534 * 10^{-2}\,[m^2]$$

torque   force   distance

$$T = F * d \leftarrow eq.7$$

Eq. 7 computes the torque as a force times a distance. Solve eq. 7 for the force.

$$F = T/d \leftarrow eq.8$$

radius   diameter

$$d = r = D/2 \leftarrow eq.9$$

distance

$$D = 75\,[mm]$$

Eq. 9 computes the distance used to compute the torque in eq. 7. This distance equals the radius of the cylindrical viscometer.

$$d = 75\,[mm]/2$$

converstion factor

$$d = 37.5\,[mm] * \frac{1}{1{,}000}\left[\frac{m}{mm}\right] \leftarrow eq.10$$

Eq. 10 converts the distance to meters.

$$d = 0.0375\,[m]$$

$$T = 0.021\,[N*m] \qquad d = 0.0375\,[m]$$

$$F = T/d \leftarrow eq.8$$

Plug in variables T and d into eq. 8, then solve for the force, F.

$$F = \frac{0.021\,[N*m]}{0.0375\,[m]}$$

$$F = 0.56\,[N]$$

Fluid Dynamics #11 (cont.)

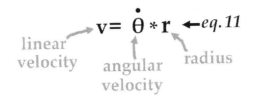

$$v = \dot{\theta} * r \leftarrow eq.\,11$$

linear velocity, angular velocity, radius

Eq.11 computes the linear velocity of the viscometer.

Eq.12 converts the angular velocity to radians per second.

$$\dot{\theta} = 100 \left[\frac{rev}{min}\right] * \frac{1}{60}\left[\frac{min}{s}\right] * 360\left[\frac{deg}{rev}\right] * \frac{\pi}{180}\left[\frac{rad}{deg}\right] \leftarrow eq.\,12$$

conversion factors

$$\dot{\theta} = 10.47 \left[\frac{rad}{s}\right]$$

$$\dot{\theta} = 10.47 \left[\frac{rad}{s}\right] \qquad r = 0.0375\,[m]$$

$$v = \dot{\theta} * r \leftarrow eq.\,11$$

Plug in variables $\dot{\theta}$ and r into eq. 11, then solve for v.

$$v = 10.47 \left[\frac{rad}{s}\right] * 0.0375\,[m]$$

$$v = 0.393\,[m/s]$$

Viscometer problems assume a constant change in fluid velocity between the two plates. Therefore we assume a constant velocity gradient between the plates.

$$F = 0.56\,[N] \qquad y = 2*10^{-5}\,[m]$$

$$\mu = \frac{F}{A} * \frac{dy}{dv} \leftarrow eq.\,3$$

$$A = 3.534*10^{-2}\,[m^2] \qquad v = 0.393\,[m/s]$$

Plug in variables F, A, y and v into eq.3, then solve for μ.

$$\mu = \frac{0.56\,[N]}{3.534*10^{-2}\,[m^2]} * \frac{2*10^{-5}\,[m]}{0.393\,[m/s]}$$

$$\mu = 8.06*10^{-4}\,[N*s/m^2]$$

Answer: $\boxed{D}$

Water Resources Practice Problems

Fluid Dynamics #12

Find: l ← the length of the plates

Given:

v_{top} = 8 [ft/s] ← plate velocities

v_{bottom} = 0 [ft/s]

w = 6 [in] ← width of the plates

y = 1*10⁻³ [in] ← plate clearance

F = 0.875 [lb_f] ← shear force on the plates

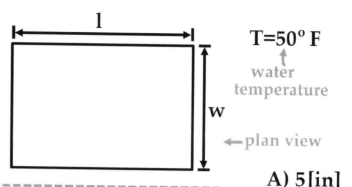

T = 50° F ← water temperature

← plan view

v_{top}

water ← profile view

y

A) 5 [in]

B) 6 [in]

C) 7 [in]

D) 8 [in]

Analysis:

shear stress

$$\tau = \mu * \frac{dv}{dy} \leftarrow eq.1$$

$\tau = F/A$

absolute viscosity

velocity gradient

Eq.1 computes the shear stress acting on the plates.

Substitute in the shear force divided by the area of the plate for the shear stress in eq.1.

force →

$$\frac{F}{A} = \mu * \frac{dv}{dy} \leftarrow eq.2$$

area   A = l*w

Substitute in the length times width for the area of the plates, in eq.2.

$$\frac{F}{l*w} = \mu * \frac{dv}{dy} \leftarrow eq.3$$

plate length   plate width

$$l = \frac{F}{w*\mu} * \frac{dy}{dv} \leftarrow eq.4$$

Solve eq.3 for the length of the plates.

T = 50° F water } μ = 2.735*10⁻⁵ [lb_f*s/ft²]

Look up the absolute viscosity of water at 50° F.

362

Fluid Dynamics #12 (cont.)

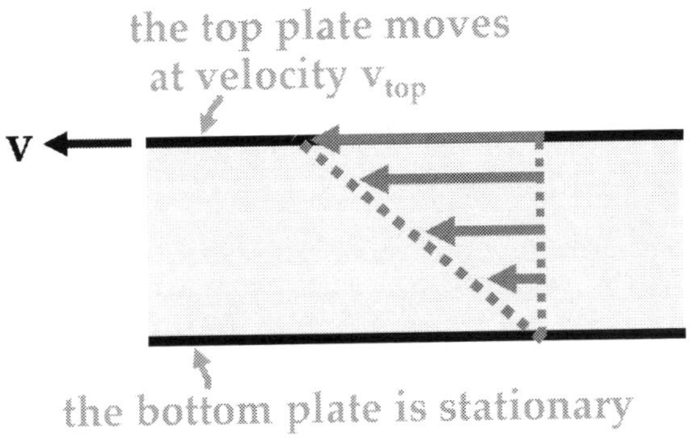

the top plate moves
at velocity v_{top}

$v \leftarrow$

the bottom plate is stationary

Figure 1

Figure 1 shows the velocity profile of the fluid between the plates. We assume a constant increase in fluid velocity as we move from the bottom plate to the top plate, hence:

$$\frac{dv}{dy} = constant$$

conversion factor

$$y = 1*10^{-3}[in] * \frac{1}{12}\left[\frac{ft}{in}\right] \leftarrow eq.5$$

Eq.5 converts the plate clearance to feet.

$$y = 8.333*10^{-5}[ft]$$

$$y = 8.333*10^{-5}[ft]$$

$$dy = y_{top} - y_{bottom} = y \leftarrow eq.6$$

Eq.6 shows variable dy equals the plate separation.

$$dy = 8.333*10^{-5}[ft]$$

$v_{top} = 8[ft/s]$ $v_{bottom} = 0[ft/s]$

$$dv = v_{top} - v_{bottom} \leftarrow eq.7$$

Eq.7 computes the change in fluid velocity from the top plate to the bottom plate.

$$dv = 8[ft/s] - 0[ft/s]$$

$$dv = 8[ft/s]$$

Plug in v_{top} and v_{bottom} into eq.7, then solve for dv.

conversion factor

$$w = 6[in] * \frac{1}{12}\left[\frac{ft}{in}\right] \leftarrow eq.8$$

Eq.8 converts the plate width to feet.

$$w = 0.5[ft]$$

Fluid Dynamics #12 (cont.)

$F=0.875\,[lb_f]$ $dy=8.333*10^{-5}\,[ft]$

$$l=\frac{F}{w*\mu}*\frac{dy}{dv} \leftarrow eq.4$$

$w=0.5\,[ft]$

$\mu=2.735*10^{-5}\,[lb_f*s/ft^2]$

$dv=8\,[ft/s]$

Plug in variables F, w, μ, dy and dv into eq. 4, then solve for l.

$$l=\frac{0.875\,[lb_f]}{0.5\,[ft]*2.735*10^{-5}\,[lb_f*s/ft^2]}*\frac{8.333*10^{-5}\,[ft]}{8\,[ft/s]}$$

$$l=0.666\,[ft] * \boxed{12\left[\frac{in}{ft}\right]} \leftarrow eq.9$$

conversion factor

Eq. 9 converts the length of the plates to inches.

$$l=8\,[in]$$

<u>Answer:</u> $\boxed{D}$

Section 3: Quick Solutions

(page intentionally left blank)

Open Channel Flow

1. D

2. D

3. A

4. C

5. B

6. D

7. C

8. B

9. B

10. D

11. B

12. B

13. A

14. C

15. C

16. C

17. A

18. C

19. B

20. A

21. B

Pressure Flow

1. B

2. D

3. C

4. A

5. B

6. C

7. A

8. B

9. D

10. C

11. D

12. A

13. B

14. D

15. D